THE WAR AT SEA IN THE MEDITERRANEAN 1940–1944

THE WAR DESPATCHES

The Commanding Officers' Reports From the Field and At Sea.

THE WAR AT SEA IN THE MEDITERRANEAN 1940–1944

Introduced and compiled by
Martin Mace and John Grehan
With additional research by
Sara Mitchell

Pen & Sword
MARITIME

First published in Great Britain in 2014 by
Pen & Sword Maritime
an imprint of
Pen & Sword Books Ltd
47 Church Street
Barnsley
South Yorkshire
S70 2AS

Copyright © Martin Mace and John Grehan, 2014

ISBN 978 1 78346 222 3

Printed and bound in England
By CPI Group (UK) Ltd, Croydon, CR0 4YY

Pen & Sword Books Ltd incorporates the Imprints of
Pen & Sword Aviation, Pen & Sword Family History,
Pen & Sword Maritime, Pen & Sword Military, Pen & Sword Discovery,
Pen & Sword Politics, Pen & Sword Atlas, Pen & Sword Archaeology,
Wharncliffe Local History, Wharncliffe True Crime, Wharncliffe Transport,
Pen & Sword Select, Pen & Sword Military Classics, Leo Cooper,
The Praetorian Press, Claymore Press, Remember When,
Seaforth Publishing and Frontline Publishing

For a complete list of Pen & Sword titles please contact:
PEN & SWORD BOOKS LIMITED
47 Church Street, Barnsley, South Yorkshire, S70 2AS, England
E-mail: enquiries@pen-and-sword.co.uk
Website: www.pen-and-sword.co.uk

CONTENTS

INTRODUCTION

For more than 150 years the Royal Navy had been the mightiest naval power on the planet. It expected to dominate every theatre of war in which it was deployed. Uniquely, this was not the case for considerable periods of time during the Second World War in the Mediterranean. The reason for this was not the Italian Navy, which, whilst far from being an insignificant force, proved to be no match for the British Mediterranean Fleet, but because of the advent of air power.

The entire Mediterranean was within reach of Axis aircraft operating from bases across southern Europe. This situation made every excursion beyond the Strait of Gibraltar a hazardous undertaking.

That having been stated, the first major aerial strike against warships in the Mediterranean was conducted by the Royal Navy. This was by aircraft of the Fleet Air Arm against the main Italian fleet base at Taranto on 11 November 1940. It is this attack that forms the first of the Mediterranean despatches from Admiral Andrew Cunningham.

As Cunningham explains, an attack on Taranto had been considered for many months before the outbreak of war. The long delay between the planning and the execution, Cunningham relates, was because conditions and circumstances had to be absolutely ideal before the attack could be risked. There could only be one strike of the nature that was planned, as the Italians would thereafter be on their guard. Cunningham had one chance and one chance only.

Cunningham arrived in Alexandria on 5 June 1939, to take command of the Mediterranean Fleet, hoisting his flag in the battleship HMS *Warspite* the following day. He described his new posting as "The finest command the Royal Navy has to offer" and he remarked in his memoirs that he probably knew the Mediterranean as well as any naval officer of his generation.

For an attack upon Taranto to be successful, detailed and accurate reconnaissance was vital in order to determine that the principal capital ships of the Italian navy, the *Regia Marina*, were in the port and to pinpoint their exact berthing positions. Until the arrival of Martin Maryland light reconnaissance aircraft at Malta, no suitable 'planes were available to Cunningham. Seaplanes and the Fairey Swordfish were too slow, too vulnerable and too obvious to carry out such a task. They would be easily spotted by the Italians (and easily shot out of the sky) who would then be alerted to the danger of a possible air attack.

The other reason for the delay in carrying out the raid was that the strike aircraft,

Fairey Swordfish, would need long range fuel tanks. These were not available to Cunningham until HMS *Illustrious* joined the Mediterranean Fleet in September 1940.

The raid, code-named Operation *Judgement*, was a remarkable success, resulting in the sinking of one Italian battleship, *Conte di Cavour*, with two other battleships being severely damaged. In a single night the Italians had lost half of their battleships and following the attack the remaining battleships sailed north for safety of Naples.

The immediate result of *Judgement* was that the balance of power had swung in favour of the Royal Navy; the Mediterranean Fleet then enjoyed more operational freedom.

Previously Cunningham had been forced to keep his fleet together to ensure that he had enough firepower to combat the main strength of the *Regia Marina*, but with only three battleships to oppose him, Cunningham could divide his force into two, knowing that each part was a match for the Italians.

The Taranto raid, the first major victory for naval air power in the world, is generally regarded as marking the beginning of the ascendancy of naval aviation. Indeed, According to Admiral Cunningham, "Taranto, and the night of November 11–12, 1940, should be remembered for ever as having shown once and for all that in the Fleet Air Arm the Navy has its most devastating weapon."

At the start of the naval war in the Mediterranean, the *Regia Marina* could count approximately 245 vessels of all descriptions in its fleet. Apart from the six battleships (with two other battleships nearing completion), the Italians had twenty-one cruisers, fifty-two destroyers, at least sixty large torpedo boats, and 106 submarines. This was a huge force concentrated within the confines of the Mediterranean. However, this was offset by the French Navy which had five battleships, fourteen cruisers, forty destroyers and thirty-six submarines in the region. It was only when the French surrendered in June 1940 that the Italian Navy became the dominant force in the Mediterranean.

The French withdrawal from the war left Cunningham in a difficult situation. He had under him the 1st Battle Squadron consisting of the battleships HMS *Warspite*, HMS *Barham*, and HMS *Malaya*, the 1st Cruiser Squadron which comprised the County-class heavy cruisers HMS *Devonshire*, HMS *Shropshire,* and HMS *Sussex*, the 3rd Cruiser Squadron with the light cruisers HMS *Arethusa*, HMS *Penelope* and HMS *Galatea*, and the 1st, 2nd, 3rd and 4th Destroyer Flotillas. In addition Cunningham had the aircraft carrier HMS *Glorious*, the only aircraft carrier in the Mediterranean. His entire force amounted to just fifty-nine ships.

With such a large disparity in numbers Cunningham had to do something to even up the score and the Taranto attack did exactly that. After Operation *Judgement* he formed two battle groups, each centred around one of his two aircraft carriers (*Glorious* and *Illustrious*) and two battleships. This allowed him to deploy two forces rather than the single one he had to maintain previously.

After the events at Taranto, the *Regia Marina* was never able to re-establish its dominance in the Mediterranean, though the aircraft of the *Regia Aeronautica Italiana* and the *Luftwaffe* presented Cunningham with an entirely different problem. This was especially evident in the evacuation of British and Commonwealth troops from

Crete in May 1941. Though some 15,000 troops were rescued, the German and Italian aircraft sunk three cruisers and six destroyers, with one aircraft carrier (the recently arrived HMS *Formidable*), five cruisers, five destroyers and the battleships HMS *Barham* and HMS *Warspite* being damaged.

Cunningham's main priority was to keep the sea lanes open to allow British forces in Malta and North Africa to be reinforced and resupplied. With the strength of the air forces against him, particularly the *Luftwaffe*, this proved a highly dangerous and costly business.

Five major convoy operations to the beleaguered island of Malta took place in 1941, with six being conducted in 1942.

The most famous of these was Operation *Pedestal* in August 1942 at the height of the siege of Malta. The island was so desperately short of food and material, particularly aviation fuel, if it was not rapidly resupplied, the authorities would be forced to surrender. Consequently, every warship that could be spared was employed to ensure that the ships got through.

The convoy of fourteen merchant ships, including the large oil tanker SS *Ohio*, was escorted by thirty-nine warships, including four aircraft carriers – the most ever assembled to protect a convoy. Suffering near-constant attacks from German aircraft and Italian submarines, the convoy fought its way through to Malta. Of the fourteen merchant ships, only five made it to the island. Four warships were also sunk, including the aircraft carrier HMS *Eagle*. Just 32,000 tons of supplies made it to Valetta, but it was enough to keep the island, and the RAF aircraft based there, fighting.

*

The naval war in the Mediterranean had been described as the war that Britain could never win. The Royal Navy's victories, the historian Vincent O'Hara has written, were mostly in sea denial, not the sea-control victories it required. Yet the Mediterranean Fleet fought right until the end of the war, with the *Kriegsmarine* taking over from the *Regia Marina* as the maritime enemy from September 1943 until its last action on 2 May 1945.

The despatches reproduced here include all those from Cunningham that were written for public consumption and cover most of the major actions of the Mediterranean war in which he was involved. The Mediterranean Fleet, however, was not the only Royal Navy force that operated in the Mediterranean. Force H, which was stationed at Gibraltar played a key role in the western Mediterranean, including the Battle of Cape Spartivento which was fought on 27 November 1940. Admiral James Somerville's report on the battle forms part of this collection of despatches.

In the first half of 1943 the Mediterranean Fleet Command was split into a command of ships and a command of ports and naval bases. As a result Cunningham maintained his position as Commander-in-Chief Mediterranean Fleet, but an additional position of Commander-in-Chief Levant was created which controlled the bases of Alexandria, Malta, Port Said, Haifa, Bizerta, Tripoli, Mersa Matruh,

Benghazi, Aden, Bone, Bougie, and Philippeville. The first man to hold this position was Admiral Sir John H.D. Cunningham from June to August 1943.

In October 1943, Andrew Cunningham was promoted to the position of First Sea Lord and this meant handing over command of the Mediterranean Fleet to his namesake John Cunningham. The latter relinquished his job as C-in-C Levant to Vice Admiral Sir Algernon U. Willis. The Levant Command was renamed Eastern Mediterranean Command in late December 1943. As a consequence there are despatches here from both Willis and John Cunningham.

*

The objective of this book is to reproduce those despatches as they first appeared to the general public some seventy years ago. They have not been modified, edited or interpreted in any way and are therefore the original and unique words of the commanding officers as they saw things at the time. Any grammatical or spelling errors have been left uncorrected to retain the authenticity of the documents. The authors of the despatches also made frequent use of abbreviations, some of which may not be immediately obvious to the reader; consequently we have included in the book an explanation of these.

LIST OF IMAGES

1   An early engagement in the sea war in the Mediterranean was the Battle of Cape Spada. On 19 July 1940, a combined Australian and British Naval Squadron, patrolling the Aegean and commanded by Captain John Collins in the light cruiser HMAS *Sydney*, encountered two Italian cruisers. The action that followed has since been called the Battle of Cape Spada, the north-western extremity of Crete. Having sighted the Italian cruisers, *Giovanni delle Banda Nere* and *Bartolomeo Colleoni*, the Allied destroyers headed north, hoping to draw the Italians behind them towards *Sydney*. The enemy took the bait. Roughly an hour after the chase had begun, at 08.26 hours, *Sydney* sighted the Italian ships. Three minutes later her main armament opened fire. The destroyers, no longer the decoy, also set about the Italians and the hunters suddenly found themselves the hunted. Here *Bartolomeo Colleoni*, viewed from one of the British destroyers, is surrounded by incoming shells. (HMP)

2   As the rearmost of the two Italian cruisers, *Bartolomeo Colleoni* was hit hardest of the Italian warships. So hard in fact that she was battered to a standstill. With her bows blown off, damage clearly visible in this image, *Bartolomeo Colleoni* quickly became a "raging furnace", a situation accentuated at 09.23 hours when a shell hit her rudder. It had been HMAS *Sydney* that, in the course of the running battle, had inflicted the most telling damage. (HMP)

3   Once *Bartolomeo Colleoni* fell still, Captain Collins ordered that the destroyers move in and administer the *coup de grâce*. HMS *Hyperion* and HMS *Ilex* duly obliged. Meanwhile, HMAS *Sydney* set of in pursuit of *Giovanni delle Banda Nere* but was forced to disengage due to a lack of ammunition. *Giovanni delle Banda Nere* escaped and reached Benghazi. This image is another view of *Bartolomeo Colleoni*, unable to manoeuvre, burning fiercely, her bows having fallen away into the water. The two Italian cruisers had been on route from Tripoli to Leros, at that time an Italian colony in the Dodecanese Islands. (HMP)

4   The original caption to this photograph, another from a series detailing the events of the Battle of Cape Spada, simply states: "The torpedo that finished her off." Taken from HMS *Hyperion*, it is therefore likely to show the torpedo which, fired at close quarters, finally caused *Bartolomeo Colleoni* to sink at 09.59 hours. (HMP)

5   The *Regia Aeronautica Italiana* also made its presence felt in the Battle of Cape Spada. Ironically, the Italian bombers singled out the destroyer HMS *Havock* for particular attention – at the very moment it was trying to pull survivors from *Bartolomeo Colleoni* from the water. This photograph is believed to have been taken from HMS *Havock*. For the Italian Navy, the battle was a disaster for the Italian Navy. Whilst some 525 crewmen from *Bartolomeo Colleoni* were rescued, 121 died. (HMP)

6   In the early hours on 12 October 1940, the British light cruiser HMS *Ajax* fought an Italian force of torpedo boats and destroyers south-east of Sicily in what is known as the Battle of Cape Passero. The engagement occurred during a Royal Navy supply operation to Malta. Having beaten off the torpedo boats, *Ajax* then battled the destroyers. One of the pair, *Aviere*, was battered by a sudden broadside from the British cruiser, forestalling a torpedo attack, and was forced to withdraw southwards, heavily damaged. The other, *Artigliere*, managed to fire a torpedo and four full 4.7-inch gun salvos at 2,800 yards before being hit and crippled. This image shows *Ajax*'s shells hitting *Artigliere*. (HMP)

7   The torpedo fired by *Artigliere* at *Ajax* during the Battle of Cape Passero missed, but four rounds struck two of *Ajax*'s secondary gun turrets and disabled her radar. *Ajax* then broke off the action; she had fired 490 rounds of different calibres and four torpedoes. Thirteen of her ship's company had been killed and more than twenty wounded. The cruiser required a month of repairs before she returned to active service. This shot shows the crippled *Artigliere* lying still in the water prior to *Ajax* breaking off the engagement. (HMP)

8   The disabled *Artigliere* – her commander and most staff officers killed – was taken in tow by *Camicia Nera*. However, they were surprised at first light by the cruiser HMS *York*, which drove off *Camicia Nera* before sinking *Artigliere*. This is the moment when, at 09.05 hours on the morning of 12 October 1940, *Artigliere*'s stern ammunition magazines exploded after the torpedo fired by HMS *York* hit. The battle of Cape Passero had been the *Regia Marina*'s first experience of the Royal Navy's superior skills and equipment in night actions. (HMP)

picked up by the three Royal Navy destroyers. In this photograph, some of these survivors can be seen on board HMS *Eridge*. (HMP)

14   Only a few months after the sinking of *U-568*, on 29 August 1942, HMS *Eridge* would find herself in trouble. Whilst carrying out a bombardment in support of the Eighth Army she was attacked and torpedoed by German E-boats. The damage was extensive, and in this picture *Eridge* can be seen taking water and listing. So bad was the damage that *Eridge* was deemed a Constructive Loss, and transferred to Alexandria where she became a base ship. HMS *Eridge* was finally scrapped in October 1946. (HMP)

15   As the month of July 1941 drew to close, a convoy consisting of six fast merchant ships and their escorts sailed from Gibraltar. Under the code-name Operation *Substance*, the ships' destination was the besieged island of Malta. In general terms the convoy was a success. All the merchantmen would reach their destination, successfully delivering some 65,000 tonnes of desperately needed supplies. One Royal Navy loss during *Substance* was the E-class destroyer HMS *Fearless*. On 23 July, whilst screening HMS *Ark Royal*, *Fearless* was torpedoed and heavily damaged by an Italian aircraft. Her crew was rescued by HMS *Forester*, which then sank the wrecked and burning warship with torpedoes about fifty nautical miles north-north-east of Bone, Algeria. The smoke rising in the background of this image is from the stricken *Fearless*. (HMP)

16   The aircraft carrier HMS *Illustrious* under attack sixty miles west of Malta, 10 January 1941. Those on ships around *Illustrious*, who had the time to do so, could only stand and stare in disbelief as the water around the carrier literally stared to boil. As *Illustrious* disappeared behind a wall of spray, everyone waited anxiously for her to reappear. She did reappear, but she was badly damaged. This image is one of a series believed to have been taken by a crewman onboard the escorting battleship HMS *Warspite*. Showing the *Luftwaffe* bombing at its peak, the "wall of water" so vividly recalled by many veterans of Convoy MC4, can clearly be seen. (HMP)

17   HMS *Eagle* was originally laid down in 1913 as a battleship for the Chilean Navy. But, on 28 February 1918, the hull was purchased by the Admiralty and converted for use as an aircraft carrier. During Operation *Pedestal*, on 11 August 1942, she was hit by four torpedoes fired by the German submarine *U-73*. On fire, and rolling over on to her port side (as evident in this image), she sank in just eight minutes south of the islands of Majorca. A total of 131 officers and men, mainly from the ship's machinery spaces, were lost in the sinking. Sixteen Sea Hurricanes were lost; four from 801 Naval Air Squadron were aloft

REPORT OF AN ACTION WITH THE ITALIAN FLEET OFF CALABRIA

9 JULY 1940

The following Despatch was submitted to the Lords Commissioners of the Admiralty on the 29th January, 1941, by Admiral Sir Andrew B. Cunningham, K.C.B., D.S.O., Commander-in-Chief, Mediterranean Station.

H.M.S. WARSPITE
29th January, 1941.

Be pleased to lay before Their Lordships the accompanying narrative of operations by the Mediterranean Fleet during the period 7th to 13th July, 1940 (Operation M.A.5) *, which included the brief engagement which took place with the Italian Fleet off the Calabrian Coast on the afternoon of 9th July.

2. It was during these operations that the Fleet first received serious attention from the Italian Air Force, and Calabria was the first time contact was made with Italian surface forces, other than destroyers.

3. It is still not clear what brought the enemy fleet to sea on this occasion, but it seems probable that it was engaged on an operation designed to cover the movement of a convoy to Libya. When our Fleet was reported South of Crete, it seems that the enemy retired close to his bases, fuelled his destroyers by relays, and then waited, hoping to draw us into an engagement in his own waters (under cover of his Air Force and possibly with a submarine concentration to the Southward of him) whence he could use his superior speed to withdraw at his own time.

4. If these were, in fact, the enemy's intentions, he was not altogether disappointed, but the submarines, if there were any in the vicinity of the action, did not materialise, and fortunately for us, his air attacks failed to synchronise with the gun action.

5. From an examination of enemy reports it appears that the enemy forces

consisted of two battleships, 16 (possibly 17 or 18) cruisers, of which 6 (and possibly 7) were 8-inch, and 25 to 30 destroyers.

6. It will be noted that the whole action took place at very long range and that WARSPITE was the only capital ship which got within range of the enemy battleships. MALAYA fired a few salvos which fell some 3,000 yards short. ROYAL SOVEREIGN, owing to her lack of speed, never got into action at all.

7. WARSPITE's hit on one of the enemy battleships at 26,000 yards range might perhaps be described as a lucky one. Its tactical effect was to induce the enemy to turn away and break off the action, which was unfortunate, but strategically it probably has had an important effect on the Italian mentality.

8. The torpedo attacks by the Fleet Air Arm were disappointing, one hit on a cruiser being all that can be claimed, but in fairness it must be recorded that the pilots had had very little practice, and none at high speed targets, EAGLE having only recently joined the Fleet after having been employed on the Indian Ocean trade routes.

9. The enemy's gunnery seemed good at first and he straddled quickly, but accuracy soon fell off as his ships came under our fire.

10. Our cruisers – there were only four in action – were badly outnumbered and at times came under a very heavy fire. They were superbly handled by Vice-Admiral J.C. Tovey, C.B., D.S.O., who by his skilful manoeuvring managed to maintain a position in the van and to hold the enemy cruiser squadrons, and at the same time avoid damage to his own force. WARSPITE was able to assist him with her fire in the early stages of the action.

11. The enemy's smoke tactics were impressive and the smoke screens laid by his destroyers were very effective in completely covering his high speed retirement. With his excess speed of at least 5 knots there was little hope of catching him once he had decided to break off the action. An aircraft torpedo hit on one of his battleships was the only chance and this unfortunately did not occur.

12. The chase was continued under exceedingly heavy bombing attacks until the British Fleet was 25 miles from the Calabrian Coast, and was then reluctantly abandoned, the destroyers being very short of fuel and the enemy fleet well below the horizon.

13. A feature of the action was the value, and in some cases the amusement, derived from intercepted plain language enemy signals.

14. My remarks on the bombing attacks experienced by the Fleet during the course of these operations have already been forwarded.

15. I cannot conclude these remarks without a reference to H.M.S. EAGLE. This obsolescent aircraft carrier, with only 17 Swordfish embarked, found and kept touch with the enemy fleet, flew off two striking forces of 9 torpedo bombers within the space of 4 hours, both of which attacked, and all aircraft returned. 24 hours later a torpedo striking force was launched on shipping in Augusta and throughout the 5 days operations EAGLE maintained constant A/S patrols in daylight and carried out several searches. Much of EAGLE's aircraft operating work was done in the fleeting intervals between, and even during, bombing attacks and I consider her performance reflects great credit on Captain A.M. Bridge, Royal Navy, her Commanding Officer.

Individual pilots and observers have already been rewarded for their work during these operations.

I6. The meagre material results derived from this brief meeting with the Italian Fleet were naturally very disappointing to me and all under my command, but the action was not without value. It must have shown the Italians that their Air Force and submarines cannot stop our Fleet penetrating into the Central Mediterranean and that only their main fleet can seriously interfere with our operating there. It established, I think, a certain degree of moral ascendency, since although superior in battleships, our Fleet was heavily outnumbered in cruisers and destroyers, and the Italians had strong shore based air forces within easy range, compared to our few carrier borne aircraft.

On our side the action has shown those without previous war experience how difficult it is to hit with the gun at long range, and therefore the necessity of closing in, when this can be done, in order to get decisive results. It showed that high level bombing, even on the heavy and accurate scale experienced during these operations, yields few hits and that it is more alarming than dangerous. Finally, these operations and the action off Calabria produced throughout the Fleet a determination to overcome the air menace and not to let it interfere with our freedom of manoeuvre and hence our control of the Mediterranean.

(Signed) A.B. CUNNINGHAM.
Admiral.
Commander-in-Chief,
Mediterranean.

Admiralty footnote:-
* *I Operation M.A.5 – an operation in the form of a sweep by the Fleet in the Central Mediterranean designed to give cover to two convoys on passage from Malta to Alexandria.*

NARRATIVE
FLEET OPERATIONS – PERIOD, 7TH TO I3TH JULY, I940.

The Mediterranean Fleet, less RAMILLIES and the 3rd Cruiser Squadron, left Alexandria on 7th July to carry out Operation M.A.5, the object being the safe and timely arrival at Alexandria of two convoys from Malta with evacuees and Fleet stores.

2. It was intended that the Fleet should reach a position of cover East of Cape Passero p.m. on 9th July, detaching destroyers to Malta, which with JERVIS and DIAMOND, who were already at Malta, would sail p.m. escorting the convoys. It was also intended to carry out operations against the Sicilian Coast on the 9th.

3. The fast convoy, M.F.One, consisted of the Egyptian ship EL NIL, the ex-Italian ship RODI and the British ship KNIGHT OF MALTA. The slow convoy, M.S.One, consisted of the British ships ZEELAND, KIRKLAND and MASIRAH and the Norwegian ship NOVASLI.

4. The Fleet sailed from Alexandria in three groups:-

Force A – 7th Cruiser Squadron * and destroyer STUART.

Force B – Commander-in-Chief in WARSPITE, with destroyers NUBIAN, MOHAWK, HERO, HEREWARD and DECOY.

Force C – Rear-Admiral, Ist Battle Squadron † in ROYAL SOVEREIGN, with MALAYA, EAGLE and destroyers HYPERION, HOSTILE, HASTY, ILEX, IMPERIAL, DAINTY, DEFENDER, JUNO, JANUS, VAMPIRE and VOYAGER.

5. All forces were clear of the harbour by 000I on 8th July and proceeded as follows:-

Force A – To pass through position 35° 00' N, 2I° 30' E.

Force B – To pass through position 34° I5' N, 24° 50' E.

Force C – To pass through position 33° 20' N, 27° 50' E.

6. LIVERPOOL, who was at Port Said, having just arrived there after transporting troops to Aden, sailed to rendezvous direct with Vice-Admiral (D). **

Flying Boat Patrols.

7. The following flying boat patrols were arranged by 20I Group (R.A.F.):-

9th, I0th and IIth July – Continuous patrol on lines Malta-Cape Spartivento and Cape Colonne-Corfu.

8th July – Flying boats on passage Malta-Zante-Malta.

I2th July – Flying boats on passage Malta-Zante-Alexandria.

I3th July – To a depth of 60 miles to the Westward of convoy M.S.One.

8. At 2339/7th July when in position 32° 35' N, 28° 30' E., HASTY sighted an Italian U-boat on passage on the surface at I,000 yards range. A full pattern depth charge attack was made and the U-boat was probably sunk. At 0I00/8 when rejoining Rear-Admiral, Ist Battle Squadron, another attack was carried out on a confirmed contact. It is considered that this attack damaged a second U-boat.

9. The night passed without incident, the Commander-in-Chief with Force B setting a mean line of advance of 305 degrees at 20 knots. At 0800/8 IMPERIAL was sighted returning to harbour with a burst feed tank.

I0. At 0807 a report was received from PHOENIX of two enemy battleships and four destroyers in position 35° 36' N, I8° 28' E., steering I80 degrees at 05I5. She attacked at extreme range but the attack was apparently unsuccessful.

As it was suspected from this report that this force might be covering an important convoy, Vice-Admiral, Malta, was ordered to arrange for a flying boat to locate and shadow this force. The course of the Fleet was maintained pending further information.

Two submarines were sighted by EAGLE's A/S patrols, one of which was attacked with bombs.

II. In the meantime all forces were subjected to heavy bombing attacks by aircraft which appeared to come from the Dodecanese. Seven attacks were delivered on WARSPITE between I205 and I8I2, about 50 bombs being dropped. There were no hits.

12. Between 095I and I749 six attacks were made on Force C, about 80 bombs being dropped. There were no hits.

I3. Most ships experienced some very near misses but the only hit was on Force A, GLOUCESTER being hit by one bomb on the compass platform causing the following casualties:-

Officers, killed 7 (including Captain F.R. Garside, C.B.E.), 3 wounded.

Ratings, II killed and 6 wounded.

The damage caused to the bridge structure, and D C.T.‡ necessitated gun control and steering from aft.

I4. At I510 flying boat L.5803 reported two battleships, 6 cruisers and 7 destroyers in position 33° 35' N, I9° 40' E., steering 340 degrees, and at I6I0 that this force had altered to 070 degrees. This flying boat had to return to Malta at I7I5 and no relief was available to continue shadowing. However, the enemy was resighted by another Sunderland from Malta early the following morning.

I5. At the time, it was suspected that these two battleships were in fact 8" cruisers. The intensive bombing which had been experienced had already given the impression that the Italians had some special reason for wishing to keep us out of the Central Mediterranean.

This, in conjunction with these enemy reports, made it appear that the Italians might be covering the movement of some important convoy, probably to Benghazi, and it was decided temporarily to abandon the operations in hand and to move the fleet at best speed towards Taranto to get between the enemy and his base.

Force B maintained a mean line of advance of 3I0 degrees at 20 knots during the night.

I6. There were no incidents during the night and at 0440 EAGLE flew off three aircraft to search to a depth of 60 miles between I80 and 300 degrees.

The Approach Period 9th July, I940 (0600-I430).

I7. At 0600 the fleet was concentrated in position 36° 55' N, 20° 30' E., and cruising disposition No. I was ordered. The 7th Cruiser Squadron and STUART were in the van 8 miles ahead of Commander-in-Chief in WARSPITE, who was screened by NUBIAN, MOHAWK, HERO, HEREWARD and DECOY. The Rear-Admiral, Ist Battle Squadron, in ROYAL SOVEREIGN, with MALAYA and EAGLE, screened by HYPERION, HOSTILE, HASTY, ILEX, DAINTY, DEFENDER, JUNO, JANUS, VAMPIRE and VOYAGER, was 8 miles to the rear of WARSPITE. The mean line of advance was 260 degrees, speed I5 knots.

I8. At 0732 flying boat L.5807 reported the main enemy fleet consisting of 2 battleships, 4 cruisers and I0 destroyers in position 37° I4' N, I6° 5I' E., steering 330 degrees at I5 knots, and at 0739 that 6 cruisers and 8 destroyers were stationed 080 degrees 20 miles from the main fleet, steering 360 degrees, and that at 0805 the main fleet had altered to 360 degrees. At this time the main enemy fleet were about I45 miles 280 degrees from our own fleet.

At 0810, as a result of these reports, the mean line of advance of the fleet was altered to 305 degrees at 18 knots in order to work to the Northward of the enemy fleet and if possible get between him and his base.

At 0858 three aircraft from EAGLE were flown off to search a sector between 260 and 300 degrees to maximum depth.

Between 1026 and 1135 reports were received from flying boats 5807 and 9020 and EAGLE'S Duty B and Duty C, which, though they differed considerably, yet gave an indication of the movements of the enemy.

19. At 1105, EAGLE's Duty D reported 2 battleships and one cruiser in position 38° 07' N, 16° 57' E., with 4 other cruisers near. At 1115 flying boat L.5807 reported the enemy battlefleet in position 38° 06' N, 17° 48' E., steering 360°.

It is probable that if in this latter report these ships were correctly identified, the real position should have been considerably further to the Westward. Reports up to this time indicated that the enemy forces consisted of at least 2 battleships, 12 cruisers and 20 destroyers, and that during the forenoon they were dispersed over a wide area. It seems probable that the cruisers and destroyers reported at 0739 took a wide sweep shortly afterwards to the North-eastward and that they were joined by other cruisers and destroyers, possibly those which had been with the main fleet,

20. Acting on reconnaissance reports received up to 1115. EAGLE's striking force was flown off at 1145 to attack the enemy fleet, which at this time was believed to be in position 295 degrees 90 miles from WARSPITE, steaming North.

This position seems to have been approximately correct but, owing to an insufficiency of aircraft in EAGLE, touch was lost at 1135 and, in the event, the enemy battlefleet altered course to the Southward about this time and the striking force failed to find them.

21. WARSPITE's noon position was 37° 30' N, 18° 40' E.

22. At 1215 flying boat 5803 reported 6 cruisers and 10 destroyers in position 37° 56' N, 17° 48' E., steering 220 degrees, at 25 knots, and at 1220 three 8" cruisers in position 37° 55' N, 17° 55' E., steering 225 degrees.

23. At 1252 the striking force, having missed the battlefleet, sighted a large number of enemy ships steering to the Southward and, assuming that the battlefleet last reported steering North had altered to the Southward, worked round to the Westward of this force and attacked the rear ship of the enemy line at 1330. At the time this was presumed to be a battleship, but from the high speed and rapid turning which was observed it was almost certainly a cruiser. The two battleships were by this time considerably further to the Southward. No hits were observed. Heavy A.A. fire was encountered from the cruisers and attendant destroyers but the aircraft received only superficial damage. The striking force landed on at 1434.

24. A search by EAGLE's aircraft Duty C reported no enemy ships between bearings 334 and 291 degrees to a depth of 60 miles from 38° N, 18° E., at 1330. It was now clear that at about 1200 the main enemy battlefleet had turned Southward and that the cruiser forces which had been sweeping to the North-eastward had turned South-west to effect a concentration in approximately 37° 45' N, 17° 20' E. (See Diagram No. 1.). [*diagrams not published*]

25. At I340, flying boat 9020 reported 3 battleships and a large number of cruisers and destroyers in position 37° 58' N, I7° 55' E., steering 220 degrees, and at I4I5 that the enemy's course and speed was 020 degrees, I8 knots. It was now clear that after concentrating the enemy had turned Northward again and that our Fleet was rapidly closing the enemy.

At this time the impression was growing that the enemy intended to stand and fight, albeit on his own ground and with more than one road of escape left open to him.

Course was maintained to the North-westward to cut him off from Taranto until it became clear at I400 that this object had been achieved, when course was altered to 270 degrees to increase the rate of closing.

26. Speed of approach was limited by the maximum speed of ROYAL SOVEREIGN, with WARSPITE acting as a battle cruiser to support the 7th Cruiser Squadron, who, being so few and lacking in 8" ships, were very weak compared with the enemy's cruiser force.

At I430 the Commander-in-Chief in WARSPITE was in position 38° 02' N, I8° 25' E., steering 270 degrees at 22 knots. The 7th Cruiser Squadron were 8 miles ahead, with ROYAL SOVEREIGN, MALAYA and EAGLE I0 miles astern. EAGLE's striking force landed on at I434. At I435, EAGLE's Duty C reported the enemy course and speed as 360 degrees I5 knots and at I439 that the enemy centre was 260 degrees 30 miles from WARSPITE. This ended the approach period and surface contact was made soon afterwards.

Weather during the Approach.

27. During the forenoon the wind veered from North-west to North by West, force 5, but later back to North-west again. The sea was slight, visibility I5 to 20 miles. The sky was clear up to 0800 but was 2/I0ths clouded at noon.

The Fleet Action.

28. At I452 NEPTUNE reported two enemy vessels in sight bearing 238 degrees.

At I455 ORION sighted 3 destroyers bearing 234 degrees, 3I,000 yards.

At I500 ORION sighted three destroyers and 4 cruisers between 240 and 270 degrees.

29. At I500 (See Diagram No. 2) the 7th Cruiser Squadron, except the damaged GLOUCESTER who had been ordered to join EAGLE, was I0 miles 260 degrees from WARSPITE and were formed on a line of bearing 320 degrees and steering 270 degrees at I8 knots. NUBIAN and 4 destroyers were screening WARSPITE.

EAGLE, screened by VOYAGER and VAMPIRE, was proceeding to take up a position I0 miles to Eastward of WARSPITE and was shortly joined by GLOUCESTER who, by reason of her bomb hit the previous day, was unfit to engage in serious action.

30. The cruisers were then rapidly closing the enemy forces which were distant I2 to I8 miles between bearings of 235 and 270 degrees. At I508 NEPTUNE sighted 2

enemy battleships bearing 250 degrees I5 miles, and the course of the 7th Cruiser Squadron was altered to 000 degrees and then to 045 degrees at I5I0 to avoid getting too heavily engaged until WARSPITE was in a position to give support. At I5I4 the 7th Cruiser Squadron's line of bearing was altered to 350 degrees and the enemy cruisers marked "C" in the diagram opened fire at a range of 23,600 yards. At I5I6 the 7th Cruiser Squadron altered course to 025 degrees and at I520 to 030 degrees to open "A" arcs.§

3I. At I5I2 the 7th Cruiser Squadron was ordered by Vice-Admiral (D) to engage an equal number of enemy ships. NEPTUNE and LIVERPOOL opened fire at a range of 22,I00 yards and SYDNEY opened fire at the fourth cruiser from the right, thought to be of the ZARA class. ORION opened fire first on a destroyer (Z in Diagram No. 2) then on the right hand cruiser bearing 249 degrees, range 23,700 yards.

32. In the meantime the enemy advanced forces were sighted from WARSPITE who opened fire on an 8" cruiser bearing 265 degrees at a range of 26,400 yards. This was a cruiser in "C" Squadron (Diagram No. 2) which was then engaging and being engaged by the 7th Cruiser Squadron. Ten salvos were fired and a hit possibly obtained with the last salvo. One of the WARSPITE's aircraft was on the catapult preparing to fly off but it became so urgent that fire should be opened in support of the heavily outnumbered cruisers that delay could not be accepted. The aircraft was damaged by the blast of "X" turret and subsequently jettisoned.

33. At I530 the enemy turned away making smoke and fire was checked. WARSPITE turned through 360 degrees and made an "S" bend to enable MALAYA, who had been ordered by the Commander-in-Chief to press on at utmost speed, to catch up. The 7th Cruiser Squadron also made a 360 degree turn to starboard to conform. The enemy fire during this time was ineffective (I5I4 to I530) but our cruisers were straddled several times and at I524 splinters from a near miss damaged NEPTUNE's catapult and aircraft. The latter was jettisoned soon after as it was leaking petrol. No hits were obtained on the enemy.

34. Between I533 and I536 WARSPITE fired 4 salvos at each of two 6" cruisers. These cruisers were evidently of the starboard wing column which had been coming up from the Southward, but were now steering to the Eastward apparently trying to work round to get at EAGLE. At I545 EAGLE again flew off her striking force.

35. At I548 WARSPITE's second aircraft was catapulted for action observation, Duty Q.

36. At I55I the 7th Cruiser Squadron was on a course of 3I0 degrees to close the enemy again and WARSPITE was steering 345 degrees. Six enemy cruisers were in sight ahead of the enemy battlefleet. This squadron is presumed to be the Port wing column "A" in diagram No 3.

37. At I553 WARSPITE opened fire on the right hand of the two enemy battleships of the CAVOUR class, bearing 287 degrees, range 26,000 yards WARSPITE was under fire from both enemy battleships and was shortly afterwards straddled. MALAYA was now in station on a bearing of I80 degrees from WARSPITE and fired 4 salvos at the enemy battleships at extreme range but these fell short. The enemy fired with moderate accuracy, the majority of the salvos falling within I,000 yards

but nearly all having a large spread. Only one closely bunched salvo was observed which fell about 2 cables on WARSPITE's port bow. At I600 the enemy was straddled and one hit observed at the base of the foremost funnel. The enemy then started to alter course away making smoke and WARSPITE altered to 3I0 degrees, speed I7 knots.

38. WARSPITE ceased firing at I604 after firing I7 salvos, the enemy being obscured in smoke. MALAYA fired 4 more salvos, all short and ceased fire at I608.

At I605 EAGLE's striking force attacked a cruiser of the BOLZANO class and it is believed that at least one hit was obtained. No report of this hit was received until I7I5.

39. At I609 WARSPITE opened fire on an enemy cruiser bearing 3I3 degrees, range 24,600 yards. This was presumably one of "A" squadron which had drawn ahead of the battleships and appeared to be working round to the Northward. Fire was checked after 6 salvos as the enemy turned away making smoke.

40. In the meantime the destroyers, who had been released from WARSPITE at I525, MALAYA at I545 and ROYAL SOVEREIGN at I552, had concentrated and at I600 were on the disengaged bow of the battlefleet and steering a similar course at 25 to 27 knots. JUNO and JANUS joined the I4th Flotilla, HERO and HEREWARD the 2nd Flotilla and DECOY the I0th Flotilla. Some of these destroyers were narrowly missed by heavy shells when passing to the Eastward of WARSPITE at I554. At I602 the I0th and I4th Flotillas came under heavy fire from enemy cruisers but were not hit. ROYAL SOVEREIGN in the meantime was pressing on at the maximum speed her engines could give, but never got within range at all.

4I. At I605 enemy destroyers were observed from WARSPITE to be moving across to starboard from the van of the enemy fleet and at I6I0 the tracks of three or more torpedoes were seen by the I4th Flotilla passing close to them. These were evidently fired at very long range.

42. Our destroyers were ordered at I6I4 to counter attack enemy destroyers and at this time were 4 miles East-north-east of WARSPITE and turning to the North-west.

43. At I6I9 the I0th Flotilla opened fire on the enemy destroyers at a range of I2,600 yards. STUART's first salvo appeared to hit. At this time the three flotillas were disposed with guides on a line of bearing 220 degrees, destroyers disposed I80 degrees from guides, course 300 degrees. The 7th Cruiser Squadron were also engaging the enemy destroyers.

44. Between I6I5 and I630 a number of enemy destroyers, probably two flotillas, having worked across to starboard of their main fleet, delivered a half-hearted attack. As soon as they had (presumably) fired torpedoes they turned away Westward making smoke. It was observed that the second flotilla to attack retired through the smoke made by the first flotilla. Spasmodic firing was opened by all forces during the short intervals in which the enemy was in range and not obscured by smoke. No hits were observed by WARSPITE's aircraft.

45. Between I630 and I640 enemy destroyers were dodging in and out of their smoke screens and spasmodic firing by our flotillas was opened. Two torpedoes were seen to cross NUBIAN's stern at I640. WARSPITE fired a few salvos of 6" and

MALAYA one salvo, at enemy destroyers between 1639 and 1641 when they disappeared in smoke.

46. During this period of the action (i.e. between the time CAVOUR was hit and the time our own fleet approached the smoke screen) P/L signals from the enemy were intercepted saying that he was "constrained to retire," ordering his flotillas to make smoke, to attack with torpedoes, and also a warning that they were approaching the submarine line.

These signals, together with my own appreciation of the existing situation, made it appear unwise and playing the enemy's own game to plunge straight into the smoke screen.

Course was therefore altered to work round to the Northward and windward of the smoke screen, course having been altered to 340 degrees at 1635. Our destroyers were well clear of the smoke by 1700 but the enemy were out of sight, evidently having retired at high speed to the Westward and South-westward.

47. Between 1640 and 1925 a series of heavy bombing attacks were made on our fleet by enemy aircraft operating from shore bases. WARSPITE was bombed at 1641, 1715, 1735, 1823 and 1911. EAGLE was bombed at 1743, 1809, 1826, 1842 and 1900. These two ships received the most attention but the 7th Cruiser Squadron received numerous attacks and many bombs fell near the destroyers. In some cases attacks were made from a considerable height. There were no hits and the fleet suffered no damage but there were numerous near misses and a few minor casualties from splinters. MALAYA claimed to have damaged two aircraft with A.A. fire but no enemy machines were definitely seen to crash.

48. From 1700 the fleet steered 270 degrees, the destroyers forming Cruising Order No. 3 in company with the 7th Cruiser Squadron to the Northward of WARSPITE. By 1735 the fleet was within 25 miles of the coast of Calabria and course was altered to 200 degrees. When, however, it became clear that the enemy had no intention of resuming the fight and could not be intercepted before making Messina, course was altered to 160 degrees at 1830 to open the land and to 130 degrees at 1930

49. After the action, as subsequently reported by WARSPITE's aircraft, the enemy fleet was left in considerable confusion, all units making off at high speed to the South-west and Westward towards the Straits of Messina and Port Augusta. It was not until 1800 that they sorted themselves out, the cruiser squadrons taking station to the South-eastward of their battleships and destroyers to the North-west and astern of them. The last enemy report was received from WARSPITE's aircraft at 1905 and the enemy fleet was then in position 37° 54' N, 16° 21' E, i.e about 10 miles off Cape Spartivento, steering 230 degrees at 18 knots.

They were attacked by their own bombers at 1705 and again at 1857. No hits were observed.

50. At 2115 course was altered to 220 degrees for a position South of Malta. There were no incidents during the night.

51. The following destroyers were detached so as to arrive at Malta at 0500 – STUART, DAINTY, DEFENDER, HYPERION, HOSTILE, HASTY, ILEX, JUNO. (STUART arrived with only 15 tons of fuel remaining).

52. At 0800 the fleet was in position 35° 24' N, 15° 27' E., steering West, and remained cruising to the South of Malta throughout the day while destroyers were fuelled.

53. An air raid took place on Malta at 0855 but no destroyers were hit. Three or four enemy aircraft were shot down.

54. The first batch of destroyers completed fuelling at 1115 and rejoined the Commander-in-Chief at 1525. HERO, HEREWARD, DECOY, VAMPIRE and VOYAGER were then sent in, the last three to sail with convoy M.S.One after refuelling. At 2030 ROYAL SOVEREIGN with NUBIAN, MOHAWK and JANUS were sent in, and GLOUCESTER and STUART were detached to join convoy M.F.One which had been sailed from Malta by the Vice-Admiral, Malta, at 2300 on 9th July escorted by DIAMOND, JERVIS, and VENDETTA.

55. Flying boat reconnaissance of Augusta had located 3 cruisers and 8 destroyers in harbour and at 1850 EAGLE's striking force was flown off to carry out a dusk attack. Unfortunately these forces had left harbour before the striking force arrived. One flight, however, located a destroyer of the NAVIGATORI class in a small bay to the Northward and sank it. The other flight returned without having dropped torpedoes. The striking force landed at Malta on completion of the operation.

56. At 2000 the 7th Cruiser Squadron was detached to search to the Eastward in the wake of convoy M.F.One.

57. At 2100 the fleet was in position 35° 28' N, 14° 30' E., steering 180 degrees. There were no incidents during the night.

Thursday, 11th July.

58. At 0130 course was altered to 000 degrees so as to be in position 35° 10' N, 15° 00' E., at 0800. ROYAL SOVEREIGN, with HERO, HEREWARD, NUBIAN, MOHAWK and JANUS, rejoined from Malta at this time and EAGLE landed on the striking force from Malta.

59. At 0900 the Commander-in-Chief in WARSPITE screened by NUBIAN, MOHAWK, JUNO and JANUS, proceeded ahead at 19 knots to return to Alexandria. The Rear-Admiral, 1st Battle Squadron, in ROYAL SOVEREIGN, with EAGLE and MALAYA and remaining destroyers, proceeded on a mean line of advance of 080 degrees at 12 knots to cover the passage of the convoys.

60. The fleet was again subjected to heavy bombing attacks. Between 1248 and 1815 five attacks were made on WARSPITE and attendant destroyers, 66 bombs being dropped. Between 1112 and 1804, twelve attacks were carried out on the forces in company with the Rear-Admiral, 1st Battle Squadron, about 120 bombs being dropped, and four bombing attacks were carried out on convoy M.S.One. There was no damage and no casualties. It was noted that the ship was shadowed by aircraft who transmitted "longs" by W/T at intervals in order to direct attacking aircraft.

61. At 1500 convoy M.S.One was passed and VAMPIRE relieved JANUS on WARSPITE's screen, JANUS remaining with the convoy.

62. WARSPITE was in position 34° 22' N, 19° 17' E., steering 110 degrees at 2100.

63. There were no incidents during the night. Course was altered from time to time during the day to throw off shadowing and attacking aircraft. At 0700, Vice-Admiral (D) with the 7th Cruiser Squadron rejoined the Commander-in-Chief and was then detached with ORION and NEPTUNE to join convoy M.F.One, LIVERPOOL and SYDNEY remaining in company with WARSPITE.

64. The following bombing attacks took place during the day:-

Between 0850 and 1150 seventeen attacks were made on WARSPITE, about 300 bombs being dropped.

Between 1110 and 1804 three attacks were made on the 1st Battle Squadron and EAGLE, 25 bombs being dropped.

There were no hits but several near misses.

As a result of these attacks a course was set to close the Egyptian coast and No. 252 Wing requested to send fighters. Fighters were sent later in the afternoon but no more attacks developed.

65. The Rear-Admiral, 3rd Cruiser Squadron in CAPETOWN, and CALEDON, sailed from Alexandria to rendezvous with convoy M.S.One at 1000/13th in the vicinity of position 33° 50' N, 23° 00' E.

66. The Commander-in-Chief in WARSPITE, with the 7th Cruiser Squadron and escorting destroyers, arrived Alexandria at 0600 and convoy M.F.One and escort at 0900. RAMILLIES, screened by HAVOCK, IMPERIAL, DIAMOND and VENDETTA, was then sailed to escort convoy M.S.One.

67. The force with Rear-Admiral, 1st Battle Squadron, was subjected to bombing attacks between 1056 and 1623. During this time EAGLE's three Gladiators shot down a shadowing aircraft and 2 bombers and another was so severely damaged that it probably did not reach home. Blenheim fighters were sent out during the afternoon to provide protection.

68. Force C entered harbour at Alexandria at 0815 on 14th July, and the 3rd Cruiser Squadron, convoy M.S.One and escort, and RAMILLIES, at 0900 in the 15th.

Admiralty footnotes:-

The 7th Cruiser Squadron consisted of ORION, NEPTUNE, SYDNEY, GLOUCESTER and LIVERPOOL.

† *Rear-Admiral 1st Battle Squadron – Rear-Admiral H.D. Pridham-Wippell.*

** *Vice-Admiral (D) – Vice-Admiral J.C. Tovey, C.B., D.S.O.*

‡ *D.C.T. – Director Control Tower.*

§ *"A" arcs – the arcs on which all guns of a ship's main armament will bear, thus allowing them to fire simultaneously at the enemy.*

2

FLEET AIR ARM OPERATIONS AGAINST TARANTO

11 November 1940

The following Despatch was submitted to The Lords Commissioners of the Admiralty on the 16th January, 1941, by Admiral Sir Andrew B. Cunningham, K.C.B., D.S.O., Commander-in-Chief Mediterranean.

Be pleased to lay before Their Lordships the accompanying report of the Fleet Air Arm operations against Taranto on 11th November, 1940.

2. An attack on the Italian fleet at Taranto by the Fleet Air Arm with torpedoes had been under consideration for many months and long before the outbreak of war with Italy. The bridge between planning and execution was, however, a wide one, since several requirements had to be met before the operation could be undertaken with a reasonable prospect of success.

3. The most important of these requirements was good and timely photographic reconnaissance, since to plan the attack it was necessary to know not only that the battleships were in harbour but also their position and berthing with some accuracy. It was not until the Glenn Martins arrived at Malta that such reconnaissance was possible, war experience having shown that flying boats are too vulnerable and slow to approach defended ports with impunity.

4. In the event, the success of the Fleet Air Arm attack was due in no small degree to the excellent reconnaissances carried out by the Royal Air Force Glenn Martin Flight (No. 431) from Malta, under very difficult conditions and often in the face of fighter opposition.

5. An undetected approach to the selected flying off position was also most important, and to achieve this, the use of long range tanks in the Swordfish aircraft was very desirable. These were not available until ILLUSTRIOUS arrived on the Station early in September.

6. A considerable amount of night flying training was also necessary before the pilots and observers could be regarded as fully competent to undertake the long flight

required for this hazardous enterprise and it was not until mid-October that the necessary state of training was reached.

7. The attack was first planned to take place on the night of 2Ist October, but owing to a fire in ILLUSTRIOUS' hangar a few days before, which destroyed and damaged a number of aircraft, the operation had to be deferred. It was considered again for the night of 30th/3Ist October, when the fleet was operating off the West coast of Greece, but it was decided not to attempt it as there was then no moon and the attack would have had to be carried out with flares, in the use of which the aircraft crews had had little practice.

8. In the meantime further photographs had been taken of the outer anchorage at Taranto by the Glenn Martins, and close examination revealed the presence of balloons and of nets surrounding the battleships. This discovery was most fortunate as these defences naturally affected the method of attack very considerably.

9. It had always been intended that both ILLUSTRIOUS and EAGLE should take part in this attack. Two days before the fleet sailed for the operation EAGLE developed serious defects to her petrol system, caused undoubtedly by the many near bomb misses she had experienced in the early days of the Italian war, and she therefore had to be left behind. Six of her T.S.R.* aircraft and crews, however, were embarked in ILLUSTRIOUS, so that the EAGLE, whose squadrons had reached a high state of efficiency, was to some extent represented in the attack.

I0. The operation is well described in ILLUSTRIOUS' report and needs no elaboration. It was admirably planned and the determined and gallant manner in which it was carried out reflects the highest credit on all concerned.

II. The results achieved,** as disclosed by subsequent photographic reconnaissance, appear to have been:-

One CAVOUR class battleship beached and apparently abandoned.

One CAVOUR class battleship heavily damaged and beached.

One LITTORIO class battleship damaged and subsequently docked in the Taranto graving dock.

There is no definite evidence of damage to cruisers and small craft as a result of the bombing attacks but it seems probable that two cruisers may have been hit.

I2. This was the first occasion on which Duplex pistols were used in the Mediterranean. It is considered that the results achieved have proved the value of this weapon and that the many years of research and experiment devoted to its development have been well repaid.

I3. There can be little doubt that the crippling of half the Italian Battlefleet is having, and will continue to have, a marked effect on the course of the war. Without indulging in speculation as to the political repercussions, it is already evident that this successful attack has greatly increased our freedom of movement in the Mediterranean and has thus strengthened our control over the central area of this sea. It has enabled two battleships to be released for operations elsewhere, while the effect on the morale of the Italians must be considerable. As an example of "economy of force" it is probably unsurpassed.

(Sgd.) A.B. CUNNINGHAM.

Admiral.
* Admiralty footnote:-T.S.R. = Torpedo/Spotter/ Reconnaissance.
**Admiralty footnote:-
From subsequent information it was confirmed that the results were:-
Battleship CAVOUR – Hit by one torpedo abreast No. 2 turret. Bulkheads gave and after some hours ship sank.
DUILIO – Hit by one torpedo near No. 2 turret. Sank by the bows.
ITALIA – Hit by three torpedoes – two on the starboard side forward and one port side aft. Sank.
Cruiser TRENTO – Hit by one bomb which perforated the deck and side but failed to explode.
Destroyer LIBECCIO and PESSAGNO – Slight damage from near miss bombs.

From:- The Commanding Officer, H.M.S. ILLUSTRIOUS.
Date:- 13th November, 1940.

INTENTION.

It was intended to carry out this operation as proposed in Rear-Admiral Aircraft Carriers, Mediterranean's 00478/97 of 28th October, 1940, as amended by Rear-Admiral Aircraft Carriers, Mediterranean's 00478/106 of 6th November, 1940.

2. The proposed plan was as follows:-

(i) H.M.S. ILLUSTRIOUS and escort to be in position 270 degrees Kabbo Point (Cephalonia) 40 miles at 2000 on November 11th and fly off the first range of 12 aircraft at that time. The second range of 12 aircraft to be flown off in about the same position at 2100.

(ii) The first attack to be made at about 2245 and the second at about 2345 and aircraft to be landed on in position 270 degrees Kabbo Point 20 miles.

(iii) Both attacks to be carried out in the following form:-

"The squadron of 12 aircraft to pass up the centre of the Gulf of Taranto and approach the harbour from the southwest. The primary attack to be by six torpedo aircraft against the battleships in the Mar Grande. This attack to be immediately preceded by two aircraft dropping flares (and bombs) along the eastern side of the Mar Grande in order to illuminate the targets arid distract attention from the torpedo aircraft, and by four aircraft making a dive bomb attack on the attractive target presented by the line of cruisers and destroyers in the Mar Piccolo. It was expected that this attack would also distract attention from the torpedo attack."

NARRATIVE.

Preliminary Movements.

3. ILLUSTRIOUS had left Alexandria on November 6th with the Mediterranean Fleet in order to carry out Operation "Coat" (M.B.8)*.

4. Before sailing from Alexandria, in order to provide the maximum number of aircraft that could be flown off in two ranges with no surface wind (24), and as EAGLE, to their great disappointment, was unable to take part in the operation due to defective petrol tanks, eight pilots and eight observers were embarked in ILLUSTRIOUS from EAGLE, all being experienced in night flying. Five of EAGLE'S Swordfish were also embarked.

5. All Swordfish aircraft embarked were fitted with the 60 gallon internal auxiliary petrol tanks.

6. The only incidents that affected the operation during the preliminary movements were, that three Swordfish forced landed in the sea on November 9th, I0th and IIth respectively and the aircraft were lost, thus reducing the number available for the Striking Force to 2I. The crews were, however, picked up, two crews returning to ILLUSTRIOUS at Malta, the third being picked up by GLOUCESTER and flown on board in GLOUCESTER'S Walrus in time to take part in the operation.

7. While at Malta the opportunity was taken to discuss with Air Officer Commanding, Mediterranean, the reconnaissance and meteorological forecasts required, and on the morning of November IIth one aircraft was flown to Malta to collect some extremely good photographs of Taranto taken by the Royal Air Force on the previous day. Further reports were received from Air Officer Commanding, Mediterranean and Royal Air Force reconnaissance aircraft during the day confirming that no important movements had taken place, and a Royal Air Force aircraft carried out a patrol of the Gulf of Taranto until 2230 to ensure that the Italian Fleet did not leave harbour unobserved.

Flying Off Aircraft.

8. At I800 on the IIth in position 37° 33' N I9° 35' E. ILLUSTRIOUS and escort comprising 3rd Cruiser Squadron GLOUCESTER (C.S.3) BERWICK, GLASGOW, YORK, HYPERION (D.2) ILEX, HASTY and HAVOCK were detached by Commander-in-Chief and steered as requisite for the flying off position.

9. At 2035 the first range commenced to fly off, course 060° speed 28 knots and all twelve aircraft of the first striking force were off by 2040. The surface wind at this time was light and variable, the upper winds westerly and about ten knots and 8/I0 thin cloud at 8000 feet. The moon was threequarters full.

I0. The second range of nine aircraft commenced flying off at 2I28 and 8 aircraft were off by 2I34. The ninth aircraft (Clifford/Going) was accidentally damaged and had to be struck down to the hangar for repairs to the wing fabric. It was at first considered that this aircraft could not be flown off in time for the attack but in view of the confidence of the crew that they could catch up, and their keenness to take part in the attack, it was flown off at 2158.

Narrative of First Attack.

II. The first striking force having taken off formed up in a position 8 miles 015° from the position of ILLUSTRIOUS at the time of flying off, and at 2057 set course for Taranto then distant 170 miles.

12. At 2115 when at a height of 4,500 feet the squadron entered the base of a cumulus cloud and some aircraft became separated with result that the whole squadron of twelve did not arrive at Taranto simultaneously.

13. The squadron commander continued with eight aircraft (5 torpedo, 2 flare droppers and one bomber). They sighted flashes of H.E. at 2252. At 2256 the flare droppers were detailed to lay their flares along the eastern side of the harbour. The other four aircraft having lost their leader, all made their attacks independently.

14. INDIVIDUAL NARRATIVES.

(i) *Williamson/Scarlett.*

Task: Torpedo attack on the battlefleet. Did not return. Last seen by Sparke at 4,000 feet over San Pietro Island.

(ii) *Sparke/Neale.*

Task: Torpedo attack on battleship.

Came in at 4,000 feet over San Pietro Island with Williamson (4A), who was last seen at 4,000 feet over the centre of the Mar Grande. At this point the pilot broke away and started his dive. The aircraft was down on the water about half way across the Mar Grande and the Taranto shoal breakwater was crossed about 2/3rds of its length from the shore at a height of 30 feet and the floating dock was observed to starboard. The original intention had been to strike at the more southerly LITTORIO (B in Plan I) [*plans not published*] but the pilot was unable to identify it. He saw, however, the most easterly CAVOUR (E in Plan I) directly ahead and he dropped his torpedo at a range of approximately 700 yards. An explosion, probably that of the torpedo, was observed at the ship about a minute later. "Get away" was made by a sharp 180° turn to port over the Taranto shoal breakwater. Intense A.A. fire was experienced from the batteries at the entrance to the harbour both during the approach and the "get away." The aircraft landed on at 0120.

(iii) *Macaulay/Wray.*

Task: Torpedo attack on battleship.

This aircraft was part of the Sub-Flight led by Williamson and its narrative follows closely that of Sparke/Neale, the most easterly CAVOUR (E in Plan I) being the target in this case also. The torpedo was dropped at approximately 600 yards range. While making a "get away" balloons were seen by the observer in a line outside the Taranto shoal breakwater at 1,000 feet. A.A. fire was experienced from the batteries on the eastern side of the harbour and from the southern batteries during the "get away." The aircraft returned without incident and landed on at 0125.

(iv) *Kemp/Bailey.*

Task: Torpedo attack on the battleships.

Came in from the west over the westerly breakwater at a height of 4,000 feet. At that time A.A. fire was met from Rondinella point on the mainland and from Lo Scanno on San Pietro Island. Fire was continued from batteries along the shore as the aircraft dived down to a position midway between Taranto Island and the most northerly cruiser, where the pilot flattened out on a line for the more northerly battleship of the LITTORIO class (A in Plan I). Prior to reaching the water level intense A.A. fire was met from the cruisers and from small merchant vessels lying inshore off Taranto Island. Projectiles from the cruisers were observed to hit the merchant vessels and the fire only ceased when the aircraft passed between the merchant ships. The torpedo was dropped at 2318 in a position estimated at 1,000 yards from the LITTORIO and the pilot was satisfied that the aim was accurate. The observer saw the torpedo running correctly. Immediately after the drop, fire was re-opened from the cruisers. The pilot then turned to starboard and passed slightly to the westward of the end of the breakwater which extends from the eastern shore to Taranto Shoal. He continued flying a southerly course until clear. A fire was observed in the direction of the seaplane hangars. The aircraft then returned to the ship without incident.

(v) *Swayne/Buscall.*

Task: Torpedo attack on battleships.

Having got detached from the leader this pilot waited off the harbour for ¼ hour for the arrival of the other aircraft. The first flare was seen and the pilot came in at 1,000 feet over the westerly breakwater, encountering severe A.A. fire from the ships and batteries at the entrance. Flying easterly across the Mar Grande and losing height until reaching the end of the Taranto Shoal breakwater he made a sharp turn to port so as to approach the more northerly LITTORIO (A in Plan I) from the east. The torpedo was dropped at about 2215 at a range of approximately 400 yards and the aircraft continued passing directly over the LITTORIO. A column of smoke was observed to arise suddenly from directly abaft the funnels of the LITTORIO. The "get away" was made past the cruisers who fired at the aircraft and over San Pietro Island when severe A.A. fire was encountered. Three balloons round the harbour were observed to catch fire, probably as a result of the enemy's own A.A. fire. ILLUSTRIOUS was sighted at 0140 and the aircraft landed on 10 minutes later.

(vi) *Maund/Butt.*

Task: Torpedo attack on battleships.

Came in over land north of Rondinella Point encountering A.A. fire from the end of the point, followed by fire from the cruisers and from the entrance to the canal while gliding down to the torpedo dropping position approximately 4 cables S.S.W.

of the mouth of the Canal. When the aircraft reached the water the fire was passing overhead and the pilot was able to flatten out and make an accurate drop at the more southerly LITTORIO (B in Plan I) at a range of approximately 1,300 yards. The observer saw the torpedo run. After dropping, the pilot made a sharp turn to starboard, doubled back amongst the merchant ships off the commercial basin and then over the northern end of San Pietro Island out to sea encountering severe A.A. pom-pom fire from Lo Scanno point on the northern extremity of the island. The aircraft then returned to the ship without incident.

(vii) *Kiggell/Janvrin.*

Task: To drop flares along the eastern shore and S.A.P. bombs on any convenient target.

The aircraft was detached by the Squadron Commander off Cape San Vito and came in at 7,500 feet. Over Cape San Vito and the promontory H.E. A.A. fire was encountered. Commencing at 2302 a line of eight flares was dropped at half mile intervals set to burn at 4,500 feet. After the flares had been dropped and appeared to be providing satisfactory illumination, the pilot turned to starboard and cruised around for 15-20 minutes looking for a target, and then made a dive bombing attack on the most southerly oil storage depot (See Plan I) from which a pipe line leads to the new jetty. No results were observed. "Get away" was made at 2325 in a southerly direction. ILLUSTRIOUS was sighted at 0112 and the aircraft landed on at 0120.

(viii) *Lamb/Grieve.*

Task: Stand by flare dropper.

Came in astern of Kiggell/Janvrin but as the first flares appeared satisfactory no flares were dropped. The course flown and the A.A. fire experienced was the same as that by Kiggell/Janvrin and the same oil storage depot was the target for a dive bombing attack but no results were observed.

(ix) *Patch/Goodwin.*

Task: Dive bombing attack on the line of cruisers and destroyers moored stem on against the quay side on the south of the Mar Piccolo.

The aircraft came in at 8,500 feet over San Pietro Island at 2306, encountering fire from both Islands and from Rondinella Point, crossed the Mar Grande and the canal and to the middle of the western portion of the Mar Piccolo. Difficulty was experienced at first in identifying the target which appeared to be in a shadow but two minutes after crossing the canal the target was identified and a dive bombing attack was made from 1,500 feet obliquely across two cruisers from N.W. to S.E. at 2315. Pom-pom fire from a number of points along the quay side, and from the cruisers in the Mar Piccolo (See Plan I) was encountered. The pilot then turned east and about five minutes later a large fire was observed from the direction of the seaplane base. Further anti-aircraft fire was met from a point near the village of San Gorgio but this was avoided by diving behind the neighbouring range of hills. The aircraft crossed the coast in a southerly direction some 8 miles east of Taranto harbour. ILLUSTRIOUS was sighted at 0135 and landed on at 0155.

(x) *Sarra/Bowker.*

Task: Dive bombing attack on cruisers and destroyers in the Mar Piccolo.

Coming in at a height of 8,000 feet over the western mainland and diving to 1,500 feet over the Mar Piccolo, the pilot was unable to identify the target. He accordingly continued along the southern shore of the Mar Piccolo and delivered an attack on the seaplane base (See Plan I) from a height of 500 feet. A direct hit on one hangar and further hits on the slipways were observed and a large explosion occurred in the hangar. Much pom-pom and machine gun fire was met, it being particularly intense just after the attack. The aircraft made its "get away" to the south and went out to sea about 5 miles east of the harbour and returned to the ship without incident.

(xi) *Forde/Mardel-Ferreira.*

Task: Dive bombing attack on cruisers and destroyers in the Mar Piccolo (See Plan I).

This aircraft was separated from the leader and arrived as the first flare was dropped and came in east of Cape San Vito a large fire being observed on the oil storage depot previously attacked by the flare dropping aircraft. No A.A. fire was met until that from a position 1,400 yards N.W. of the oil storage depot. On reaching the Mar Piccolo the pilot turned to port and delivered his attack on the target from N.E. to S.W. releasing at 1,500 feet. The first bomb hit the water short of two cruisers but the remainder should have hit the cruiser although no immediate results were observed. Intense A.A. fire from the cruisers moored in the Mar Piccolo was met throughout the dive. The pilot was uncertain whether his bombs had released and circled the western basin of the Mar Piccolo and repeated the attack. The "get away" was made to the northwest, the aircraft going out to sea about 5 miles west of the harbour. While going out a flash and big fire was seen near the seaplane hangar.

(xii) *Murray/Paine.*

Task: Dive bombing attack on cruisers and destroyers in the Mar Piccolo (See Plan I).

This aircraft arrived when the attack was in progress and came in east of Cape San Vito while the flares were dropping. The pilot continued until the eastern end of the Mar Piccolo was reached and turning to port flew along the southern shore. The attack was delivered from 3,000 feet, the bombs dropping in a line running from E. to W. commencing by the most eastern jetty and extending across four of the destroyers to the most westerly cruiser in the line. The pilot made his "get away" turning sharply 180° to port over the land and returning by the way he had come. A big fire near the seaplane hangar was observed. The aircraft returned to the ship without incident.

SECTION II.
NARRATIVE OF SECOND ATTACK.

I5. The second striking force formed up in position 8 miles, I30 degrees from H.M.S. ILLUSTRIOUS at a distance of I77 miles from Taranto and took departure at 2I45 at a height of 3,000 feet.

I6. Morford-Green were in an aircraft which was fitted with an external overload petrol tank. At 2205 the tank fell off and the securing straps began to bang on the fuselage; the pilot was therefore forced to return to the carrier. On approaching the position of the ship the observer fired a Red Verey Light to indicate that the aircraft was returning in distress, but as it was not expected H.M. Ships ILLUSTRIOUS and BERWICK opened fire. The aircraft then fired a 2 star identification light and gunfire ceased. The aircraft remained outside gun-range for another I5 minutes, then made a further approach and was landed on.

I7. At 2250 the Squadron commenced to climb and at 23I5 sighted flares and anti-aircraft fire from Taranto, a distance of 60 miles, and intermittent firing continued until at 2350, when at 8,000 feet, the northwest shore of the Gulf of Taranto was sighted and the Squadron turned to the north-east. At 2255 the flare droppers were detached and the remainder continued into attack.

I8. INDIVIDUAL NARRATIVES (SECOND FORCE).

(i) *Hale-Carline.*

Task: Torpedo attack.

Considerable fire was experienced from San Pietro Island during the last stages of the approach, and the aircraft came in I mile north of Rondinella Point at 5,000 feet, and glided down over the commercial basin, being fired at from the eastern corner of the basin. The pilot then steered directly for the more northerly battleship of the LTTTORIO class (A in Plan I), the torpedo being dropped at a range of approximately 700 yards. The "get away" was made to starboard and the aircraft passed just north of the Taranto Shoal Breakwater. The observer saw balloons at approximately 3,000 feet and the pilot, seeing mooring barges, avoided them. Anti-aircraft fire was met intermittently throughout attack – particularly from destroyers on leaving. H.M.S. ILLUSTRIOUS was sighted at 0I55 and aircraft landed on at 0200.

(ii) *Bayly-Slaughter.*

Task: Torpedo attack.

This aircraft is missing. It was last seen following the Squadron Commander over Rondinella Point.

(iii) *Lea-Jones.*

Task: Torpedo attack.

Came in astern of the Squadron Commander over Rondinella Point, gliding down to a point 2½ cables south of the canal. The torpedo was dropped at the most northerly

CAVOUR (C in Plan I) at a range of approximately 800 yards. "Get away" was made by turning sharply to starboard between two cruisers and over Lo Scanno Point on San Pietro Island. Severe anti-aircraft fire was received from batteries on each side of the southern end of the Canal, and from cruisers and destroyers in the Mar Grande. When leaving, a fire and petrol smoke were observed near the power station on the mainland behind Rondinella Point. Aircraft landed on at 0230.

(iv) *Torrens-Spence – Sutton.*

Task: Torpedo attack.

Came in over Cape Rondinella, astern of the Squadron Commander, and glided down to a point 5 cables south of the canal. Anti-aircraft fire was experienced from three positions on Taranto Island from the cruisers and the largest battleship. It is probable that the aircraft was silhouetted to the cruisers by the light of the flares. The torpedo was dropped at the more northerly LITTORIOs (A in Plan I) at a range of approximately 700 yards. "Get away" was made by turning to starboard, out between San Paolo Island and the submerged barrier running from the eastern mainland. Pom-pom and machine gun fire was met from San Paolo, San Pietro, and from small gate vessels in the gap on the way out. The aircraft landed on at 0215.

(v) *Welham-Humphreys.*

Task: Torpedo attack.

Came in astern of the Squadron Commander over Rondinella Point, over Mar Piccolo, and the town of Taranto, and turned to starboard to the centre of the Mar Grande. Encountering a balloon which was avoided, the pilot then dived down to attack, during which period the aircraft received hits from machine gun bullets, one of which hit the outer aileron rod, putting the aircraft temporarily out of control. Control was however regained and the torpedo was dropped at a range estimated at 500 yards on the port quarter of one of the LITTORIOs (B in Plan I). "Get away" was made by turning sharply to starboard and the aircraft went out to sea over the northern point of San Pietro.

Intense anti-aircraft fire was directed towards the aircraft during the "get away" and a hit was received on the port wing, probably from a 40 mm. explosive projectile.

Aircraft landed on at about 0205.

(vi) *Hamilton-Weekes.*

Task: Dropping Flares.

Came in over Cape San Vito at 7,500 feet, and dived to 5,000 feet, dropping a line of flares at intervals of 15 seconds to the eastward of the harbour. Pom-pom fire was experienced when coming over Cape San Vito and H.E. while releasing the flares.

After dropping all flares successfully, this aircraft delivered a dive bombing attack from a height of 2,500 feet on the oil storage depot. A small fire was caused. The aircraft made a "get away" well to the eastward and landed on at 0230.

(vii) *Skelton-Perkins.*

Task: Dropping Flares.

Approach course was similar to Hamilton-Weekes' except that the flares were dropped south-east of the harbour. Eight flares were dropped at between 6,500 feet and 5,000 feet, set to burn 3,000 feet lower. Bombs were dropped near the oil storage depot, but it is not considered that hits had been secured. Anti-aircraft fire similar to that of Hamilton-Weekes' was experienced, some of the bursts during the dive bomb attack being particularly close. The aircraft landed on at 0200.

(viii) *Clifford-Going.*

Task: Bombing Cruisers and Destroyers in Mar Piccolo (See Plan I).

This aircraft started ½ hour late as stated in paragraph I0 and arrived at Taranto when the second attack was already in progress. The aircraft came in over the land about 5 miles east of the harbour entrance, and steered straight over the dockyard to the far side of the Mar Piccolo.

Turning to port a dive bombing attack was made from 2,500 feet along the line of cruisers and destroyers from west to east. A stick of 250-lb. S.A.P. bombs was dropped across the cruisers. The pilot then turned north across the Mar Piccolo, later swinging to starboard and returning over the mainland and out to sea about 5 miles eastward of the harbour entrance.

A large fire in one of the battleships was seen to be raging for over 5 minutes.

Anti-aircraft fire was experienced the whole time the aircraft was over the land, the pom-pom fire being particularly intense during the bombing attack.

Aircraft landed on at 0250.

I9. All aircraft, except the two missing, were landed on by 0250, and the Force rejoined the Commander-in-Chief at 0730.

20. It is noteworthy that the enemy did not use the searchlights at all during either of the attacks.

RESULTS OF THE ATTACKS.

2I. The only information so far available of the results of the attacks are in Vice Admiral, Malta's 203I-I2 and 2345-I2, as follows:-

> *To: – C. in C., From: – V.A.M.*
> *(R) R.A.A.*
> *F.O.H.*
> *Admiralty.*

Have examined Taranto photographs carefully and until enlarged I do not wish unduly to raise your hopes but definitely appears that:-

(*a*) One LITTORIO class is down by the bows with forecastle awash and a heavy list to starboard. Numerous auxiliaries alongside.

(*b*) One CAVOUR class beached opposite entrance to graving dock under construction. Stern including "Y" turret is under water. Ship is heavily listed to starboard.

(*c*) Inner harbour: 2 cruisers are listed to starboard and are surrounded by oil fuel.

(*d*) Two auxiliaries off commercial basin appear to have stern under water.

2. Hearty congratulations on a great effort. Our small contribution to-day one Macchi 200 and one Corpse.
   T.O.O. 203I – I2th November.

> *To: – C. in C., From: –V.A.M.*
> *(R) Admiralty,*
> *R.A.A.*
> *F.O.H.*

My 203I-I2. The stem only of northern CAVOUR class battleship shows on photograph but by fix from entrance of Passagio Picolo which also just shows the bows is in about 4 fathoms. There is oil round the stem and it seems certain the ship has been beached. The remaining one LITTORIO and two CAVOUR class battleships appear undamaged.
   T.O.O. 2345 – I2th November.

Royal Air Force Co-operation.

22. The excellent photographic reconnaissance promoted by the Royal Air Force was a most important factor in the success of this operation, the accurate meteorological forecast from Malta was also most useful.

Repetition.

23. It was proposed to repeat the operation on the following night and a Striking Force of I5 aircraft comprising 6 torpedo aircraft, 7 dive bombers and 2 flare droppers was prepared, but the operation was cancelled owing to the unfavourable weather report.

General Remarks.

24. *Duplex Pistol.*
There was considerable debate as to the wisdom of using Duplex pistols in such constricted waters. It was decided to run off I00 yards of the safety range and the battery resistance was removed to ensure that the torpedoes would remain dangerous on completion of their run. The decision to use them was indeed fortunate as the results could not have been obtained by any other weapon.

To those whose faith in this weapon has remained unshaken the greatest honour is due and their faith has been amply justified by 3 battleships being either sunk or crippled by 9 – or possibly II – I8 inch torpedoes.

25. *Spirit in which the attack was made.*

This attack was carried out under somewhat difficult conditions. Owing to the heavy Fleet programme no rehearsals had been possible. Aircraft from H.M.S. EAGLE were embarked the day before leaving harbour and had had no previous experience of landing on H.M.S. ILLUSTRIOUS deck or of our controlled landing and the use of the barrier. A third obstacle was presented by the discovery that our petrol was contaminated, three Swordfish being lost on the preceding days from this cause. In spite of this the zeal and enthusiasm of everyone to carry out this great enterprise was unabated and it is impossible to praise too highly those who in these comparatively slow machines made studied and accurate attacks in the midst of intense anti-aircraft fire.

26. *The Fleet Air Arm.*

Although the proper function of the Fleet Air Arm may perhaps be the operation of aircraft against an enemy in the open sea it has been demonstrated before, and repeated in no uncertain fashion by this success that the ability to strike unexpectedly is conferred by the Fleet Air Arm.

It is often felt that this arm which has had a long struggle with adverse opinions and its unspectacular aircraft is underestimated in its power. It is hoped that this victory will be considered a suitable reward to those whose work and faith in the Fleet Air Arm has made it possible.

(Sgd.) D.W. BOYD.
Captain.

* *Admiralty footnote:-*
Operation "Coat" was an attack by Naval aircraft from H.M.S. ARK ROYAL on Cagliari (Sardinia), on 9th November, I940.

The Commander-in-Chief, Mediterranean.

Forwarded, concurring with Commanding officer, H.M.S. ILLUSTRIOUS report.

From information at present available this attack has achieved considerable success.

Recommendations under Mediterranean Confidential Memorandum II5 are being forwarded separately.

(Sgd) A.L. ST. G. LYSTER.
Rear-Admiral Commanding
Mediterranean Aircraft Carriers.
H.M.S. ILLUSTRIOUS.
26th November, I940.

3

ACTION BETWEEN BRITISH AND ITALIAN FORCES OFF CAPE SPARTIVENTO

27 NOVEMBER 1940

The following Despatch was submitted to the Lords Commissioners of the Admiralty on the 18th December, 1940, by Vice-Admiral Sir James F. Somerville, K.C.B., D.S.O., Flag Officer Commanding, Force "H".

H.M.S. RENOWN.
18th December, 1940.

Be pleased to lay before Their Lordships the attached narrative of an engagement which took place on 27th November, 1940, during the execution of Operation "Collar", between forces under my command and an Italian Naval force in the area to the South of Sardinia.

Object of Operation "Collar".

2. The object of this operation was to secure the safe and timely passage through the Mediterranean of the following:-
    I,400 Royal Air Force and Military personnel,
    Two SOUTHAMPTON Class Cruisers,
    Three M.T. ships,
    Four Corvettes.

Composition of British Force.

3. The British force was composed as follows:-

Force "B".

Battleship:-
RENOWN.
(Flag Officer Commanding, Force "H").

Aircraft Carrier:-
ARK ROYAL.

Cruisers:-
SHEFFIELD.
DESPATCH.

Destroyers:-
FAULKNOR.
FIREDRAKE.
FORESTER.
FURY.
DUNCAN.
WISHART.
ENCOUNTER.
KELVIN.
JAGUAR.

Force "F".

Cruisers:-
MANCHESTER (C.S.I8).*
SOUTHAMPTON.
(Carrying approximately 700 R.A.F. and Military personnel each.)

Destroyer:-
HOTSPUR. (With no asdics and speed limited.)

Corvettes:-
PEONY.
SALVIA.
GLOXINIA.
HYACINTH.
(Corvettes fitted with L.L. sweeps†and asdics. Maximum speed – I6 knots.)

S.S. CLAN FORBES.
S.S. CLAN FRAZER.
S.S. NEW ZEALAND STAR.
(M.T. ships carrying mechanical transport, etc., maximum speed I6 knots.)

Force "D".

Battleship:-
RAMILLIES.

Cruisers:-
NEWCASTLE.
COVENTRY.
BERWICK.

Destroyers:-
DEFENDER.
GREYHOUND.
GRIFFIN.
HEREWARD.

Method of Execution.

4. Forces "B" and "F" to escort and cover the passage of the M.T. ships and corvettes through the Western Mediterranean, being met to the South of Sardinia at approximately noon on 27th November by Force "D" proceeding from the Eastern Mediterranean. Forces "B", "F" and "D" then to proceed in company to a position West of Skerki Bank, which would be reached at dusk. After dark, Force "F", the corvettes and COVENTRY with destroyers of Force "D" to part company and proceed through the Narrows to the Eastern Mediterranean, Force "B", with RAMILLIES, NEWCASTLE and BERWICK, proceeding to Gibraltar.

Condition of Ships taking part.

5. RENOWN, ARK ROYAL and SHEFFIELD were in good fighting condition with the exception that ARK ROYAL had an unduly high percentage of inexperienced pilots and observers, and the efficiency of her torpedo striking force was low, owing to lack of opportunity for exercise.

6. MANCHESTER and SOUTHAMPTON would each be carrying some 700 Royal Air Force and Military personnel.

7. BERWICK (so I had been informed by her Commanding Officer) was not capable of more than 27 knots owing to the removal of some rows of turbine blades and to the higher water temperature in the Mediterranean affecting her vacuum.

8. NEWCASTLE's boilers had developed defects, and judging from signals received, could not be considered entirely reliable.

9. The destroyers of the 8th and 13th Flotillas had been running very hard, but there was no reason to anticipate any definite defects developing during the operation. HOTSPUR was without asdics, had been temporarily repaired and her speed was

limited, though in fine weather it was hoped she could reach 20 knots or possibly more.

10. The condition of RAMILLIES, COVENTRY and the Mediterranean Fleet destroyers was satisfactory so far as was known.

11. The corvettes were incapable of making a speed of advance of 14 knots except in fair weather.

12. With the exception of RENOWN, SHEFFIELD, ARK ROYAL and the destroyers of the 8th and 13th Flotillas, the ships taking part in this operation had not worked together as a squadron.

13. Doubts had been expressed by Vice Admiral L.E. Holland, C.B. (Vice Admiral Commanding, 18th Cruiser Squadron) concerning the advisability of MANCHESTER and SOUTHAMPTON being included, in Force "F", for the following reasons:-

(i) Extreme importance was attached to the safe and timely arrival of the R.A.F. personnel at Alexandria. The best way to ensure this was for the cruisers to proceed independently and rely upon their high speed and mobility, for the achievement of their object.

(ii) With so many additional on board, the ships were not in a fit condition to fight. If obliged to engage, casualties amongst the R.A.F. personnel might be heavy and the object of this part of the operation compromised.

14. I agreed that these ships would not be in a satisfactory state to fight an action and that the achievement of part of our object, namely, the safe arrival of the personnel, would be assured with greater certainty if the cruisers proceeded independently.

On the other hand, achievement of our complete object, which included the safe passage of the M.T. ships and corvettes, was more likely to be accomplished if we made a show of force, since this might deter the Italians from attempting to interfere with the operation.

15. At Admiral Holland's request I asked the Commander-in-Chief, Mediterranean, whether the safe passage of personnel or the M.T. ships should receive priority, if circumstances arose which made a decision necessary after Force "F" had parted company for the passage of the Narrows. The Commander-in-Chief, Mediterranean, replied "Personnel," but subsequent instructions were received from the Admiralty that this must be subject to the overriding consideration that if Italian forces were in sight action taken by the cruisers must be the same as if personnel were not embarked.

Admiralty footnotes:-
C.S. 18 – Vice Admiral Commanding, 18th Cruiser Squadron.
†*L.L. sweep – anti-magnetic mine sweep.*

ESTIMATE OF ENEMY FORCES LIKELY TO BE ENCOUNTERED AND NEED FOR REINFORCEMENT.

16. Prior to the commencement of Operation "Collar" I informed the Admiralty that I considered the inclusion of ROYAL SOVEREIGN (undergoing repairs in Gibraltar) in my force was desirable in view of a possible Italian concentration in the Western Mediterranean which I estimated could reach a total of :-

Three battleships,

Five to seven 8" cruisers,

Several 6" cruisers and other light forces.

The Admiralty reply indicated that some doubt was entertained concerning the necessity for this reinforcement, but approval was eventually given for the inclusion of ROYAL SOVEREIGN in Force "B" if I considered this essential.

The Commander-in-Chief, Mediterranean, was frankly sceptical and considered I was unduly pessimistic. In his opinion, the probability of an Italian concentration in the Western Mediterranean was more remote now than at any time since Operation "Hats" (30th August-5th September).

Since defects in ROYAL SOVEREIGN could not be completed in time she was unable to take part in the operation.

EXECUTION OF OPERATION "COLLAR".

17. The M.T. ships included in Force "F" passed through the Straits of Gibraltar during the night of 24th/25th November and were joined by the corvettes to the East of Gibraltar a.m. 25th November. The remainder of Forces "B" and "F" sailed at 0800 on 25th November.

The operation proceeded according to plan and without incident until the morning of 27th November. The corvettes had been detached on the evening of 26th November, as they were unable to keep up with the convoy. A detailed account of the situation at 0800 on 27th November and subsequent events on that day are given in the attached narrative.

POINTS OF INTEREST.

Enemy Intelligence prior to 27th November.

18. So far as I am aware, reliance was placed entirely on shore based air reconnaissance to locate the position of enemy units in the Western Mediterranean prior to 27th November. This reconnaissance proved quite inadequate for the purpose and there was insufficient information concerning the location of Italian naval forces prior to the 27th November and no report of enemy ships being at sea in the Western Mediterranean until they were sighted by carrier reconnaissance a.m. 27th November.

Enemy Intelligence on 27th November.

19. With the exception of a Sunderland flying boat operating from Malta to cover the area in which our forces would be operating on 27th November, air reconnaissance was limited to that furnished by ARK ROYAL's aircraft.

ARK ROYAL has a high proportion of young and inexperienced pilots and observers. Some of these had to be employed on the initial dawn reconnaissance, since it was necessary to hold the first air striking force in readiness to attack any enemy force attempting to interfere with the concentration of Forces "B" and "F" with Force "D".

Not only had many of these young observers little or no experience of reporting enemy formations, but the need for maintaining wireless silence, except in the immediate neighbourhood of Gibraltar provides little opportunity to exercise communications in the air. These factors, coupled with variable visibility and the similarity of Italian warships' silhouettes, made their tasks difficult.

Taking the above into consideration, I consider the crews of the reconnaissance aircraft acquitted themselves with credit.

Results obtained by Air Striking Force Torpedo Attacks.

20. The results obtained by torpedo bomber attacks on high speed targets during the present war have fallen far short of the estimates based on peacetime practices adjusted for "opposition."

So far as ARK ROYAL is concerned, this is attributed entirely to lack of initial training and subsequent runner practices.* Skilful, unobserved approaches were made in each case and the attacks pressed home with courage and resolution, but the results obtained were disappointing.

Delay in reporting Result of first Striking Force Attack.

2I. It is not always appreciated that sustained observation on enemy ships by the crews of air- craft in the striking force is impracticable. Observations of "own drop" even in peacetime practices, is very difficult, and under action conditions, quite fortuitous. Succeeding attackers may, or may not, be able to observe hits from preceding attacks, but in general the only definite evidence is the subsequent behaviour of the target. On this occasion it was not until the return of the striking force to ARK ROYAL had afforded an opportunity for the interrogation of all aircraft crews, that the probability of one hit on the Littorio class was established. Subsequent observation of the target indicated that her speed had not been reduced to an extent which prevented her keeping in company with the Cavour class, at about 25 knots, but does not disprove the estimate that one hit was obtained.

Fighting Efficiency.

22. With the exception of RENOWN, ARK ROYAL, SHEFFIELD and the destroyers of the 8th Destroyer Flotilla (the permanent nucleus of Force "H"), the remaining

ships taking part in the engagement had been drawn from various stations and in certain cases, met for the first time just before the action opened.

23. To illustrate the constant changes that have taken place in the composition of Force "H" since Ist of July, it is of interest to note that the following different ships have at some time or other been included in this force for operations, viz.:-

Seven capital ships,

Three aircraft carriers,

Thirteen cruisers,

Thirty three destroyers.

24. The fact that ships carried out their action duties correctly and with the minimum of signalled instructions is a tribute to the soundness of our tactical training, in peace and to the "Fighting Instructions."

Decision to discontinue the Chase.

25. My reasons for deciding that a continuance of the chase offered no reasonable prospect of inflicting damage on the enemy and was not justified are contained in the Narrative. Had I received timely information before breaking off the action that some of the enemy ships appeared to have sustained damage, I should have felt justified in continuing the action for a short period. But I was not prepared to hazard the achievement of my main objective, the safe passage of the convoy, unless there was substantial assurance. I could inflict material damage on the enemy by the destruction of one or more of his battleships. The policy I followed was in general accordance with the accepted principles of war and the "Fighting Instructions". I do not suggest that a rigid adherence to these principles and instructions is either necessary or desirable, but on the other hand I consider that the interests of the country are best served by general adherence to established principles, and instructions based on those principles.

Conduct of Officers and Men.

26. Both from personal observation and reports I have received, I am able to state that the conduct of officers and men taking part in this engagement left nothing to be desired. It was a pleasure to observe the enthusiasm with which the ship's company of RENOWN closed up at their action stations on hearing that enemy forces were in the vicinity and their subsequent disappointment when it was clear that the enemy did not intend to stand and fight was obvious.

(Signed) J.F. SOMERVILLE.

Vice-Admiral,

Flag Officer Commanding,

Force "H".

Admiralty footnote:-

* *Runner practices – practice firings with torpedoes not fitted with warheads.*

NARRATIVE OF THE ACTION BETWEEN BRITISH AND ITALIAN FORCES ON 27TH NOVEMBER, I940.

Movements Prior to the Action.

Sunrise on the 27th November was at 0824 (zone-2) and at 0800 the situation was as follows:-

(*a*) RENOWN in company with ARK ROYAL, SHEFFIELD and 4 destroyers(Group I) were in position at 37° 48' N, 07° 24' E, steering at 083° at I6 knots, a position of cover, I0 to 20 miles ahead and to the North Eastward of the convoy having been maintained throughout the night.

(*b*) Vice Admiral Commanding I8th Cruiser Squadron in MANCHESTER with SOUTHAMPTON, DESPATCH and 5 destroyers (Group II) were in company with the M.T. convoy in position 37° 37' N, 06° 54' E. The 4 corvettes were about I0 miles to the Westward of the convoy, having been unable to keep up with the latter.

2. At this time ARK ROYAL flew off a section of fighters, one A/S patrol, one meteorological machine and a reconnaissance of 7 T.S.R.s* designed to cover the area to the West of Sardinia, and between Sardinia and Africa; the depth of this reconnaissance to the Eastward being just sufficient to cover Force "D" which was approaching from Skerki Bank. The fighter section on their return to ARK ROYAL reported that they had shot down a Cant Z.506 – I0 miles North West of Bona at 0930.

3. Group I continued to the Eastward so as to be ready to concentrate with Force "D" should air reconnaissance reveal the presence of important enemy units in the vicinity of that Force. C.O.S. Alexandria's signal timed 0330/27 indicated, that the presence of Force "D" might be known to the enemy.

4. At 0900, in the absence of any report from air reconnaissance, which by that time was expected to have reached a depth of 90 miles from Group I, course was shaped to the South West to join the convoy in accordance with the prearranged plan and provide additional A.A. defence by the time the first bombing attack was likely to develop.

5. The first sighting of the enemy from the air took place at 0852 when one of ARK ROYAL's reconnaissance aircraft sighted a group of warships and closed to investigate. At 0906 an Alarm Report was made of four cruisers and six destroyers but this report was not received by any ship.

6. At 0920, Group I sighted the convoy and course was adjusted to pass astern of it in order to place Group I to the South of the convoy, and up sun from the latter, whilst carrying out flying operations and thus in the probable direction of air attack.

7. At 0956, whilst Group I was still on the Port quarter of the convoy, an aircraft report (T.O.O.**0920) of the presence of 5 cruisers and 5 destroyers was received by V/S***from ARK ROYAL.

8. It seemed possible that this might be a report of Force "D", and ARK ROYAL was asked to confirm that this was an enemy report. Steam for full speed was,

however, at once ordered and Captain (D), 8th Destroyer Flotilla, directed to detail 2 destroyers, to screen ARK ROYAL and 2 to screen the convoy.

9. By I0I6, as a result of further reports from aircraft, and confirmation from ARK ROYAL, the presence of enemy Battleships and Cruisers was established. RENOWN altered course to 075° to join RAMILLIES and speed was increased as rapidly as possible to 28 knots.

I0. The composition and relative position of the enemy forces was far from clear, the situation, as viewed on the Plot at I035 being shown in Diagram I.[*Diagrams not published*]

II. I decided:-

(i) That the convoy should continue towards its destination but on a South Easterly course in order to keep well clear of any action that might develop.

(ii) To limit the escort of the convoy to DESPATCH, COVENTRY and 2 destroyers.

(iii) To proceed with all remaining forces to concentrate with Force "D" and then attack and drive off the enemy.

I2. To implement these decisions ARK ROYAL was instructed to prepare and fly off a T/B†striking force and to act independently under cover of the battle fleet. DESPATCH was placed in charge of the convoy which was ordered to steer I20° at full speed. Cruisers and destroyers of Force "F" were ordered to join Flag Officer Commanding, Force "H", COVENTRY was ordered to join the convoy, and RAMILLIES was informed of Flag Officer Commanding, Force "H"'s position, course and speed.

I3. MANCHESTER, SHEFFIELD and SOUTHAMPTON were now concentrating in the van, cruisers and destroyers being stationed 050° 5 miles from RENOWN, i.e. on the estimated bearing of the enemy. This position was subsequently adjusted as requisite.

I4. At I032 I made a signal to Malta W/T reporting the position of 2 enemy battleships.

I5. At I058 a Sunderland flying-boat closed RENOWN and reported the position of Force "D" as being 34 miles, 070°. The flying-boat was ordered to shadow and report the composition of the enemy bearing 025°, 50 miles.

I6. Reconnaissance aircraft from ARK ROYAL had meanwhile sighted and reported two groups of cruisers and 2 battleships. There were, however, a number of discrepancies between the reports both as to position and composition so that it was not possible to get a clear picture of the situation. It seemed certain that five or six enemy cruisers were present but it was doubtful whether the number of battleships was one, two or three. But, whatever the composition of the enemy force, it was clear to me that in order to achieve my object – the safe and timely arrival of the convoy at its destination – it was essential to show a bold front and attack the enemy as soon as possible.

17. The enemy, who had originally been reported as steering to the Westward, were now reported as altering course to the Eastward at 1115.

18. An Observer who witnessed this alteration of course reported that the Eastern group of cruisers appeared to be thrown into a state of confusion. The leading ship turned 180° whilst the two following ships turned only 90°. Collisions appeared to have been narrowly averted and at one time all three ships appeared to be stopped with their bows nearly touching each other.

19. Based on the Sunderland's report of the position of Force "D", junction with that Force now appeared to be assured. Speed was therefore reduced to 24 knots to maintain a position between the estimated position of the enemy battle fleet and the convoy.

20. At 1128 Force "D" was sighted bearing 073° approximately 24 miles. Shortly after this ARK ROYAL flew off the first T/B Striking Force.

21. Aircraft reports now available appeared to show that the enemy's force consisted of 2 battleships, about 6 or more cruisers and a considerable number of destroyers. RAMILLIES was therefore ordered to steer 045° so as not to lose ground as the action appeared likely to develop into a chase. BERWICK and NEWCASTLE joined Vice Admiral Commanding, 18th Cruiser Squadron, who had been placed in command of all cruisers in the van.

The Approach.

22. At 1134, acting on the latest estimate of the enemy's bearing and distance, speed was increased to 28 knots and at 1140 course altered to 050° to close the enemy.

23. At this time MANCHESTER, SOUTHAMPTON and SHEFFIELD were in single line ahead about five miles fine on the Port bow of RENOWN with BERWICK and NEWCASTLE joining Vice Admiral Commanding, 18th Cruiser Squadron, from the Eastward.

24. Two miles astern of the cruisers, Captain (D), 8th Destroyer Flotilla in FAULKNOR was gradually collecting the Eighth Flotilla and ENCOUNTER, some of whom had been screening the convoy. The four destroyers of Force "D" were also joining Captain (D), 8th Destroyer Flotilla, and were eventually stationed 3 miles, 270° from FAULKNOR. Ten miles fine on the Starboard bow of RENOWN, RAMILLIES was just turning up to a parallel course. ARK ROYAL had dropped well astern and was between our main force and the convoy carrying out flying operations.

25. At 1154 the Sunderland flying-boat returned and reported 6 cruisers and 8 destroyers bearing 330° 30 miles from RENOWN, and that no battleships had been sighted. Unfortunately her report gave no course or speed of the cruisers and she had disappeared from sight before this information could be obtained. This report which was the first visual link received appeared to show that one group of the enemy forces was considerably further to the West than the groups previously reported by aircraft

and that it was in a position to work round astern to attack ARK ROYAL and the convoy if the course of our forces to the North East was maintained.

26. No further report of this group was received during the action and I was consequently in doubts as to its whereabouts and intentions. ARK ROYAL was however between my main forces and the convoy and I considered that returning aircraft would sight and report this group should they attempt to work round to a position from which to attack the convoy.

27. Course was however altered to North so as not to get too far to the Eastward.

28. The situation as it appeared to me from the Plot just before noon is shown in Diagram 2. The number of enemy battleships and cruisers present was still not definitely established, but I judged that in all probability only two battleships were present.

29. At this time the prospects of bringing the enemy to action appeared favourable.

(i) We had effected our concentration of which the enemy appeared to be unaware, since no shadowers had been sighted or reported by R.D/F, and his speed had been reported as between I4 and I8 knots, which suggested he was still awaiting the reports of reconnaissance.

(ii) The sun was immediately astern and if remaining unclouded would give us the advantage of light.

(iii) There seemed every possibility of a synchronised surface and T/B attack if the nearest position of the enemy was correct, and providing he did not retire at once at high speed.

30. My intentions at this time and throughout the ensuing chase were as follows:-

(i) To drive off the enemy from any position from which he could attack the convoy.

(ii) To accept some risk to the convoy providing there was a reasonable prospect of sinking one or more of the enemy battleships.

To achieve (ii) I considered the following conditions must be fulfilled:-
   (*a*) A reduction of speed of the enemy to 20 knots or less by T/B attack.
   (*b*) Engagement of enemy battleships by RENOWN and RAMILLIES in concert.

3I. At I207 RENOWN was reported as having a hot bearing on one shaft. Revolutions on this shaft had to be reduced. This, combined with a dirty bottom and paravanes, limited her speed to 27½ knots.

32. At the same time as this report was received puffs of smoke were observed on the horizon bearing 006° and cruisers in the van sighted masts and ships between the bearings of 346° and 006°.

33. At I2I3 ARK ROYAL's signal timed II47 was received reporting the composition of the enemy as 2 battleships and 6 cruisers accompanied by destroyers.

This however did not disprove the Sunderland's information that a further group of 6 cruisers and destroyers was still further to the Westward.

34. By this time our cruisers were concentrated in the van and had formed a line of bearing 075°-255°, in sequence from West to East, SHEFFIELD, SOUTHAMPTON, NEWCASTLE, MANCHESTER and BERWICK. NEWCASTLE could not maintain the speed of the remainder and never quite reached her ordered station.

35. At II58 BERWICK signalled that as his speed was limited to 27 knots he proposed to join RENOWN. Vice Admiral Commanding, I8th Cruiser Squadron ordered BERWICK to join him but by that time the BERWICK had already turned to implement his proposal and consequently lost ground. BERWICK took station on the Starboard bow of MANCHESTER but owing to lack of speed dropped back during the action.

36. During the approach the 9 destroyers in company, (three being detachable with the convoy and two with ARK ROYAL) were moving up to a position 5 miles 040° from RENOWN. This position was selected so that they would be available to counter attack any destroyers attempting to launch an attack on RENOWN or RAMILLIES.

37. The situation as seen from the cruisers immediately before the action commenced was as follows:-

(i) 3 enemy cruisers and some destroyers – hereafter referred to as the Western group – were visible between the bearings of approximately 340° and 350°, at a range of about II miles hull down and steering a Northerly course.

(ii) A second group of cruisers also accompanied by destroyers – hereafter referred to as the Eastern group – to the right of the Western group, were further away and steering approximately I00°.

Evidence as to the movements of the Western group immediately before action was joined is conflicting. It appears probable however that the Western group was in line ahead on a Southerly course until I2I0 when they turned together to a Northerly course. Between I2I0 and I220 further alterations of course may have been made, as, when first observed from RENOWN they appeared to have a fairly broad inclination to the Eastwards.

The Action.

38. At I220 the enemy opened fire and immediately afterwards our advanced forces replied. The enemy's first salvo fell close to MANCHESTER being exact for range but a hundred yards out for line.

39. At I223 I informed Commander-in-Chief, Mediterranean, that I was engaging the enemy.

40. Immediately fire was opened by our advanced forces on ships of the Western group, they made smoke and retired on courses varying between N.W. and N.E.

Behind their smoke screen they appeared to make large and frequent alterations of course becoming visible at intervals – sometimes almost end on, and sometimes at quite a broad inclination – remaining in sight for a few minutes before again becoming lost in their smoke.

41. Just before opening fire at the Western group, who were already wreathed in smoke, RENOWN sighted two ships, who were not making smoke, at extreme visibility, bearing 020°. It was thought at the time that these might be the enemy battleships but they later proved to be cruisers of the Eastern group.

42. At I224 RENOWN opened fire at the right hand ship of the Western group at a mean range of 26,500 yards. Six salvos were fired before the latter was lost in smoke.

43. At I226, RAMILLIES fired two salvos at maximum elevation to test the range. Thereafter RAMILLIES – proceeding at 20.7 knots – dropped astern and followed in the wake of RENOWN throughout the action.

44. When RENOWN'S target became obscured, course was altered to Starboard to close the supposed battleships and to bring the Western group of cruisers broader on the bow. Shortly afterwards two salvos were fired at a fleeting glimpse of the centre cruiser of the Western group.

45. Course was then further altered to Starboard to open "A" arcs‡on the left hand ship of the Western group which now bore 356°. Eight salvos were fired at her when she next appeared, but at I245 she too was lost to sight in smoke.

46. During this time our cruisers had been hotly engaged with the Western group at ranges varying between 23,000 and I6,000 yards. Many straddles were obtained but smoke rendered spotting and observation generally extremely difficult.

47. MANCHESTER, SHEFFIELD and NEWCASTLE all opened fire initially on the right hand ship of the Western group, BERWICK engaged the left hand ship of the same group whilst SOUTHAMPTON engaged the left hand ship of the Eastern group.

48. No concentration of fire was ordered owing to the speed with which the situation changed and to the large selection of targets available. Moreover, as Vice Admiral Commanding, I8th Cruiser Squadron, states in his report, it is doubtful what the results of an attempt at concentration would have been, as ships of the I8th Cruiser Squadron had not been in company for a considerable time and assembled on the battleground from Rosyth, Reykjavik, Malta and the vicinity of the Azores.

49. MANCHESTER and SHEFFIELD continued firing at the same cruiser until I236 and I240 respectively but NEWCASTLE after I8 broadsides shifted to BERWICK'S target, whilst SOUTHAMPTON, after 5 salvos at her original target engaged a destroyer for eleven minutes. This destroyer was seen to be hit. At least one other destroyer is believed to have been hit during this phase and FAULKNOR at I227 and NEWCASTLE at I233½ report seeing a hit on a cruiser – in the case of NEWCASTLE the left hand ship of the Western group – by what appeared to be a large calibre shell. These hits were not observed in RENOWN.

50. The enemy's fire was accurate, particularly in the early stages, and MANCHESTER was exceptionally lucky not to have received damage. His rate of

fire was however extremely slow and when he was fully engaged his spread became ragged and his accuracy deteriorated rapidly. BERWICK was hit at I222 by an 8-inch shell, Y turret was put out of action and some casualties were incurred.

5I. By I234 the Western group were almost lost in smoke and Vice Admiral Commanding, I8th Cruiser Squadron, decided that the Eastern group should in future form his target. MANCHESTER accordingly shifted to the left hand ship of the Eastern group, 30 degrees on his Starboard bow at a range of 2I,000 yards. This ship was identified as an 8-inch cruiser, probably of the Zara class.

52. Between I233 and I240 all ships of the I8th Cruiser Squadron shifted target on to the Eastern group of the enemy. BERWICK was again hit at I235, officers' cabins being damaged and the Port After Breaker Room wrecked, but without further casualties. At this time she had just started to engage a ship of the Eastern group which was thought to be an 8-inch cruiser of the Pola class, 47 salvos were fired at this target between I238 and I308.

53. In order to ensure that the Eastern group should not be able to work round ahead and attack the convoy, Vice Admiral Commanding, I8th Cruiser Squadron altered the course of the Squadron from North to 090° bringing the Eastern group on to his Port bow. To counter what appeared to be an attempt of the Eastern group to cross the T of the I8th Cruiser Squadron; the course of the latter was altered to the Southward. The enemy however immediately resumed their North Easterly course and the I8th Cruiser Squadron led back to 070° at I256 and to 030° at I258.

54. During, this period the rear ship of the enemy line was observed by MANCHESTER, NEWCASTLE and SOUTHAMPTON to be heavily on fire aft. Between I252 and I259 this ship appeared to lose speed, but thereafter picked up again and drew away with her consorts. No report of this damage to the enemy was received by Flag Officer Commanding, Force "H" until after the action. Subsequent reports indicate that at least one enemy destroyer with the Eastern group was frequently straddled and possibly hit.

55. Whilst the action between the I8th Cruiser Squadron and the Eastern group was starting, the first T/B Striking Force was nearing its objective. On their way they had first sighted the Western group retiring in a rather scattered state to the N.E., and then the Eastern group steaming to the South East at high speed in line ahead. Shortly after this, 2 battleships were observed 20 to 30 miles further to the Eastward and steering a South Easterly course. As the Striking Force manoeuvred to get up sun from the enemy the latter were seen to turn in succession to S.W. and then a few minutes later they turned together into line ahead on a North Easterly course.

56. Shortly after this last turn had been completed, the Striking Force attacked the enemy battlefleet. They dropped their torpedoes inside the screen of 7 destroyers at a range between 700 and 800 yards. The leader of this Striking Force slightly overshot his target – the leading battleship which was of the Littorio class – and therefore swung away and attacked the second ship which was of the Cavour class. The remaining ten pilots attacked the leading ship. Immediately after the attack the leading ship hauled round to the Northward and it was thought that the Cavour class ship went ahead of her, but there was no apparent loss of speed. As a result of careful

comparison of notes on return to ARK ROYAL it was considered that one hit had probably been obtained on the Littorio class battleship. As the Striking Force turned away from their "drop" they machine gunned the bridges of the capital ships and destroyers. The Eastern group of cruisers had tried to attract the attention of the battle fleet to the impending attack by firing at the Striking Force – though well out of range – as they approached. These bursts were seen in RENOWN. Nevertheless, the attack was not observed in the battleships until the leading aircraft had dropped to about 1,500 feet, when an intense but mainly ill directed fire was opened.

57. As the Striking Force completed their attack at about 1245 the Eastern group of cruisers coming up at high speed from the Westwards opened a heavy and accurate fire on them, but fortunately without success, and all returned safely to ARK ROYAL.

58. At the same time as the Striking Force made their attack on the enemy battle fleet RENOWN had lost sight of her final target of the Western group in the smoke and was looking for a further target. At this moment two large ships steering to the Westward emerged out of the smoke cloud left by the Western group. Turrets were trained on to the new targets but fortunately before fire was opened they were identified as three-funnelled French liners.

59. As RENOWN was no longer engaged, and with the information then available it appeared that action with the battleships might be imminent, I decided to concentrate on RAMILLIES. Shortly after starting to turn however, the Eastern group of cruisers was seen to present a possible target and as the Plot indicated that the enemy battleships were heading North East, course was steadied on 070° to engage these new targets.

60. At 1300, after a swing to Starboard to avoid a reported submarine, course was altered to 045° to close the position of two battleships which had just been reported on that bearing by Vice Admiral Commanding, 18th Cruiser Squadron.

61. At 1311 RENOWN fired two ranging salvos at the left hand of the two ships believed at the time to be battleships. It is now considered that they were more probably two of the Eastern group of cruisers. Both salvos fell well short and the range was opening rapidly.

62. When sighted by Vice Admiral Commanding, 18th Cruiser Squadron at 1300 the two enemy battleships were steering to the South West and closing the range rapidly. At 1305 the 18th Cruiser Squadron therefore turned to work round the flank of the enemy battleships and to close the gap on RENOWN, but, at the same time the battleships altered course to the North Eastward and appeared to be retiring at high speed, whereupon the 18th Cruiser Squadron was turned back to a course of 050°.

63. During this short phase of the action large splashes, confirming the presence of capital ships, fell in the vicinity of BERWICK and MANCHESTER.

64. The relative position of my forces and those of the enemy as given by the Plot at 1315 is shown in Diagram 3. The situation was as follows:-

(i) Firing had practically ceased owing to the enemy drawing out of range.

(ii) The heavy smoke made by the enemy had prevented accurate fire during the chase and so far as could be ascertained, no damage had been inflicted.

(iii) In reply to a signal from me to C.S.18 at 1308 "Is there any hope of catching cruisers?" I was informed "No". (A later message from C.S.18 estimated the enemy had three knots excess speed.)

(iv) It was known that the Striking Force had attacked. No report of results had been received, but it was evident that the speed of the enemy had not been materially reduced and was certainly not as low as 20 knots. It was presumed that the attack had been unsuccessful and this was not unexpected.

65. In view of our rapid approach to the enemy coast I had to decide whether a continuance of the chase was justified and likely to be profitable. The arguments for and against continuing the chase appeared to be:-

For Continuing the Chase.

(i) The possibility that the speed of the enemy might be reduced by some unforeseen eventuality.

(ii) He might appreciate that his force was superior to mine and decide to turn and fight.

Against Continuing the Chase.

(i) There was no sign that any of the enemy ships and especially his battleships had suffered damage, nor was there reasonable prospect of inflicting damage by gunfire in view of their superior speed. Unless the speed of the enemy battleships was reduced very materially he could enter Cagliari before I could bring him to action with RENOWN and RAMILLIES.

(ii) I was being led towards the enemy air and submarine base at Cagliari and this might well prove a trap. His appearance in this area appeared to be pre-meditated since it was unlikely that this was occasioned solely by the information he had received the previous night of Force "D"'s presence in the Narrows.

(iii) The extrication of one of my ships damaged by air or submarine attack from my present position would certainly require the whole of my force and must involve leaving the convoy uncovered and insufficiently escorted during the passage of the Narrows.

(iv) The enemy main units had been driven off sufficiently far to ensure they could no longer interfere with the passage of the convoy.

(v) A second T/B attack could not take place until 1530 to 1600 by which time the convoy would be entirely uncovered and the enemy fleet could be under the cover of the A/A batteries and fighters at Cagliari. I entertained little hope that the attack would prove effective as I knew that the second flight was even less experienced than the first.

(vi) I had no assurance that the cruisers reported to the North West might not be working round towards the convoy and ARK ROYAL.

(vii) It was necessary for contact to be made with the convoy before dark to ensure the cruisers and destroyers required for escort through the Narrows should be properly formed up. It was also necessary to provide the fullest possible scale defence against T/B and light surface force attack at dusk. To effect this a retirement between 1300 and 1400 was necessary.

Decision to Break Off the Chase.

66. After reviewing these pros and cons I had no doubt in my mind whatsoever that the correct course was to break off the chase and rejoin the convoy as soon as possible. I consequently ordered a course of 130° to be steered.

67. At approximately 1335 I received a report of an enemy damaged cruiser in position about 30 miles from me and ten miles from the enemy coast. I considered the desirability of detaching two cruisers to search for and attack this cruiser. It was obviously undesirable to use MANCHESTER or SOUTHAMPTON. SHEFFIELD'S R.D/F was required to deal with the bombing attacks which would inevitably develop and this left BERWICK and NEWCASTLE.

68. I considered this most carefully but decided against such a detachment for the following reasons:-

(i) It would involve my main forces remaining in a position to support these cruisers and prevent them from being cut off by enemy forces.

(ii) Action as in (i) would cause an unacceptable delay in rejoining the convoy.

(iii) Isolated ships in such close proximity to the enemy coast would be singled out for air attack. BERWICK was most vulnerable to this form of attack and her disablement would have involved all my force to effect her extrication.

(iv) There was no evidence to indicate that the damaged ship would remain stopped and she might well effect an escape before she could be overtaken.

A subsequent air search failed to locate this cruiser, so it appears that the stoppage was, in fact, only temporary.

69. I therefore ordered Vice Admiral Commanding, 18th Cruiser Squadron, to join the convoy with MANCHESTER and SOUTHAMPTON and instructed ARK ROYAL to attack the damaged cruiser if he considered it feasible.

70. At 1410 ARK ROYAL flew off the second T/B Striking Force. This Force

consisted of the T.S.R.s who had carried out the morning reconnaissance. The Squadron Leader was given the enemy battlefleet as his objective but with full liberty to change the objective if a successful attack was impracticable and if by so doing he considered he had more chance of achieving successful results.

71. The second T/B Striking Force located three cruisers screened by four destroyers 12 miles off the S.E. coast of Sardinia and steering to the Eastward at high speed. Some 8 miles ahead of the cruisers the two battleships were also seen now heavily screened by ten destroyers.

72. In view of the total absence of cloud cover it was considered essential to attack out of the sun if any surprise was to be achieved. An attempt to reach such a position on the battleships would inevitably have led to the cruisers sighting and reporting the position of the Striking Force. It was therefore decided to attack the cruisers.

73. As the first aircraft reached the dropping position the cruisers turned together to Starboard. This caused several of the following flights, who were already committed to their drop, to miss their targets, but one hit was observed on the rear cruiser and another possible hit on the leading cruiser.

74. The attack was unobserved until very late, only two salvos being fired before the first torpedo was dropped. After this the gunfire was intense but appeared to be quite regardless of direction or danger to their own ships. One large projectile was seen to hit the water close to the rear cruiser and shells from close range weapons were seen to burst close alongside all ships.

75. Two of our aircraft were hit by shrapnel but neither was unserviceable and all returned safely to ARK ROYAL.

76. A striking force of 7 Skuas which flew off from ARK ROYAL at 1500 failed to locate the damaged cruiser but attacked 3 cruisers of the Condottieri class steering North off the South West corner of Sardinia. An unobserved attack was carried out on the rear cruiser and two near misses may have caused some damage. On the way back to the carrier an Italian R.O.43 was shot down.

Enemy Air Attacks.

77. At 1407 whilst our surface forces were proceeding at 19 knots to rejoin the convoy R.D/F gave indications of enemy bomber formations in the vicinity. The line was staggered.

78. The first visual indication of the attack was bomb splash on the horizon. This was the result of an attack by the Fulmar Fighter Patrol which caused several of the enemy formation to jettison their bombs.

79. As soon as the enemy aircraft, which consisted of 10 S.79 in V formation, were sighted a Blue Turn[§] was executed to bring all guns to bear. The enemy maintained a steady course and dropped their bombs well clear of the heavy ships, their bombs falling close to the screening destroyers.

80. Two further attacks were made, each by squadrons of 5 aircraft. In both cases ARK ROYAL who had been engaged in flying operations and was not actually in the line, was the objective. In these attacks, apart from a few bombs which were jettisoned as a result of interception by our fighters, most accurate bombing was carried out. ARK ROYAL was completely obscured by bomb splashes two at least

of which fell within 10 yards of the ship. No hits were however obtained and no damage resulted.

81. The complete failure of either fighter attack or gunfire to break up the formation flying of the Italian squadrons was most noteworthy.

82. No further bombing attacks took place, and the convoy was sighted at 1700.
Remarks on the Movements of Enemy Forces after the Action.

83. The movements of enemy units from the time when surface action ceased at 1312 until he was finally lost to sight by air reconnaissance at 1655 are not fully established. From analysis of various reports the following appear most probable:-

(*a*) Immediately after surface action ceased the enemy battlefleet, which consisted of 1 Littorio and 1 Cavour class screened by 7 destroyers, steered for Cagliari at about 25 knots. At about 1500 they turned to the Eastward and at about 1520 to the North Eastward round Cape Carbonira. When last seen at 1655 they were steering North up the East coast of Sardinia. At some time between the attacks of the first and second T/B Striking Forces they are reported to have increased their destroyer screen from 7 to 10 destroyers. There is no indication that their speed was ever materially reduced below 25 knots.

(*b*) The Eastern group of cruisers had closed to about 8 miles from the battlefleet at 1240 and thereafter probably followed astern of them. When attacked by the second T/B Striking Force at 1520 they were on an Easterly course South of Sardinia and at that time were screened by 4 destroyers. After the attack it seemed probable that one cruiser became detached and may have proceeded to Cagliari. One ship of this group had been heavily hit aft by 6-inch fire.

(*c*) When the action ceased the Western group were a considerable distance to the North and West of their own battlefleet and the Eastern group, due to the direction of their retirement. It is probable that they then turned towards Cagliari and rejoined their battlefleet, but their movements are very uncertain.

Admiralty footnotes:-
*T.S.R. – Torpedo / Spotter / Reconnaissance aircraft.
**T.O.O. – time of origin.
***V/S – visual signal.
† T/B – Torpedo Bomber.
‡ "A" arcs – the arcs on which all guns of a ship's main armament will bear, thus allowing them to fire simultaneously at the enemy.
§ Blue Turn – ships turning together to the course ordered by the signal.

4

BATTLE OF MATAPAN

27-30 MARCH 1941

The following Despatch was submitted to the Lords Commissioners of the Admiralty on the IIth November, I94I, by Admiral Sir Andrew B. Cunningham, G.C.B., D.S.O., Commander-in-Chief, Mediterranean Station.

Mediterranean,
11th November, I94I.

Be pleased to lay before Their Lordships the attached reports of the Battle of Matapan, 27th- 30th March, I94I. Five ships of the enemy fleet were sunk, burned or destroyed as per margin.* Except for the loss of one aircraft in action, our fleet suffered no damage or casualties.

2. The events and information prior to the action, on which my appreciation was based, are already known to Their Lordships. Long and anxious consideration had been given to the disposition of available forces, important factors being the necessity to maintain the flow of "Lustre"† convoys to Greece, and the difficulty of finding sufficient destroyers for a fleet operation when demands for convoy escorts were so heavy.

The disablement of H.M.S. YORK at Suda Bay at the outset of these deliberations was a serious blow.

3. The disposition described in paragraph 7 of the Commander-in-Chiefs narrative was adopted with the intention of countering a possible cruiser raid into the Aegean. It was designed to give flexibility and allowed for a quick change of plan if more intelligence came to hand to clarify the situation.

I was concerned to avoid any movement which might alarm the enemy and cause him to defer any operation he might have in mind. To allow a state of suspense to continue, with Operation "Lustre" in full swing, would have imposed an increased strain on the light forces of the fleet.

4. The disposition originally ordered left the cruisers without support. The battlefleet could if necessary have put to sea, but very inadequately screened. Further consideration led to the retention of sufficient destroyers to screen the battlefleet. The

moment was a lucky one when more destroyers than usual were at Alexandria having just returned from or just awaiting escort duty.

5. It had already been decided to take the battlefleet to sea under cover of night on the evening of the 27th, when air reconnaissance from Malta reported enemy cruisers steaming eastward p.m./27th. The battlefleet accordingly proceeded with all possible secrecy. It was well that it did so, for the forenoon of the 28th found the enemy south of Gavdo and the Vice-Admiral, Light Forces (Vice-Admiral H.D. Pridham-Wippell), with Force "B"*** in an awkward situation which might have been serious had the support of the battlefleet been lacking.

6. The situation at 0812 (Diagram No. I), when surface contact was first made did not appear unsatisfactory although in fact at this time Force "B" was very uncomfortably placed with a second and powerful enemy cruiser squadron out of sight to the north-east and well placed to cut Force "B" off from the battlefleet. This squadron had actually been sighted and reported by H.M.S. GLOUCESTER'S spotting aircraft (see paragraph I0 and Report of V.A.L.F., paragraph II) but fortunately for everybody's peace of mind this report did not get beyond H.M.S. GLOUCESTER'S T.S. ‡ (see diagrams I and 2).

7. Aircraft from H.M.S. FORMIDABLE had sighted and reported a further force to the northward of the cruisers and in one case had reported battleships, but the situation was not very clear. The aircraft were not at this time using duty letters which made for confusion: previous experience had taught us how often cruisers of the Italian Navy are reported as battleships from the air. The situation did not, therefore, appear unduly alarming, but the air striking force was made ready and H.M.S. VALIANT ordered ahead to join V.A.L.F.

8. The sighting by Force "B" of a battleship at I058 (see diagram No. 3) put a very different complexion on affairs. The enemy was known to be fast and H.M.S. GLOUCESTER had been reported only capable of 24 knots. Force "B" looked like being sandwiched between the VITTORIO VENETO and the 8 inch cruisers they had already engaged. It was with great relief that it was realised that Force "B" was able to make 30 knots and that the range was not closing.

V.A.L.F. handled the squadron with great skill, holding the range open and taking every advantage of his smoke screen as he worked round to south-east to close the battlefleet; but there were some unpleasant minutes with I5 inch salvos straddling the cruisers before the intervention of the Torpedo/Bomber striking force which gained a hit on the VITTORIO had caused her to turn away (see paragraph I5 and diagram No. 4).

9. It had always previously been my intention, if contact were made with the enemy's fleet, to hold back the torpedo air striking force until the battlefleets had closed within about 50 miles of each other, or until the enemy had definitely turned away. On this occasion owing to the exposed position of the cruisers it was necessary to launch the striking force unduly early. Few things could have been more timely than their intervention but it had the effect I had always feared, that the damaged enemy turned for home with a lead which could not be closed to gun range in daylight.

I0. Meanwhile the battlefleet was pressing on fast to close the enemy. V.A.L.F.'s signal timed I2I0 reporting he had lost touch actually reached me as Force "B" hove in sight at I230. It might be argued that Force "B" should have followed and maintained touch when the enemy turned westward, but with the considerable chance which then existed of being cut off by superior force, and adequate air reconnaissance being available, it is considered that the Vice-Admiral, Light Forces, was correct in his decision to gain visual contact with the battle fleet and check respective positions before resuming the chase. His force had been outranged and outgunned by all enemy vessels with which he had so far made contact.

II. The attacks carried out by Royal Air Force Blenheim bombers from Greece were most welcome as giving the enemy a taste of his own medicine, this being the first time that our bombing aircraft had co-operated with the fleet at sea. In actual fact it is not thought that any hits were scored, certainly no appreciable damage was done, but the attacks must have worried the enemy and made him even more chary of approaching our coasts. The work of 230 Fighter/Bomber Squadron was, as ever, invaluable.

I2. It cannot be said for certain how many, if any, further hits were obtained on VITTORIO by the successive Fleet Air Arm attacks during the afternoon (diagram No. 5) and evening. All that is certain is that the POLA was hit and stopped in a dusk attack, but, whatever the result, the gallantry and perseverance of the aircraft crews and the smooth efficiency of deck and ground crews in H.M.S. FORMIDABLE and at Maleme are deserving of high praise.

An example of the spirit of these young officers is the case of Lieutenant F.M.A. Torrens-Spence, Royal Navy, who, rather than be left out, flew with the only available aircraft and torpedo from Eleusis to Maleme and in spite of reconnaissance difficulties and bad communications arranged his own reconnaissance and finally took off with a second aircraft in company and took part in the dusk attack.

I3. In spite of continual air sighting reports the situation towards the end of the afternoon had become rather confused. This was due to the presence of both ship borne and shore based reconnaissance aircraft, a considerable change of wind, the presence of several separate enemy squadrons and finally the ever present difficulty of distinguishing the silhouettes of enemy warships. It was difficult to decide the tactics for the night.

The situation was however rapidly cleared up by about I800. V.A.L.F.'s cruisers were just gaining touch ahead and two aircraft, Duty V of H.M.S. FORMIDABLE and Duty Q from H.M.S. WARSPITE had made contact. Mention must here be made of the excellent work of H.M.S. WARSPITE'S catapult aircraft (Lieutenant-Commander A.S. Bolt, D.S.C., Royal Navy, Observer). This aircraft had, by a fortunate mistake, returned to the ship instead of going to Suda Bay as ordered. It was recovered, refuelled and catapulted as Duty Q at I745. Within an hour and a half this experienced observer had presented me with an accurate picture of the situation which was of the utmost value at this time (diagram No. 6).

I4. The last report, however, showed that a difficult problem was before us. The enemy had concentrated in a mass which presented a most formidable obstacle to attack by cruisers and destroyers. By morning he would be drawing under cover of dive bombing aircraft from Sicily. The question was whether to send the destroyers in now to attack this difficult target or wait until morning in the hope of engaging at dawn, but with the certainty of exposing the fleet to a heavy scale of air attack. Decision was taken to attack with destroyers and to follow up with the battlefleet.

I5. Meanwhile the Vice-Admiral, Light Forces, was also faced with difficult decisions. As dusk fell he was drawing up on the enemy with his cruisers spread, to maintain contact. In the last of the afterglow it appeared that an enemy squadron was turning back towards him which obliged him to concentrate his force. This was undoubtedly a right decision, but from then onward every time he wished to spread his cruisers to resume the search he was foiled by some circumstances, not least of which was the decision of Captain (D) I4th Destroyer Flotilla to lead the destroyer flotillas round the northern flank of the enemy before attacking. This decision of Captain D.I4 was most unfortunate, as it cramped the cruiser squadron and left the southern flank of the enemy open for escape (diagram No. 6). It is thought that the enemy did in fact "jink" to the south about this time and thus get away.

I6. The battleship night action (diagram Nos. 7 and 8) presented no novel aspect, apart from the employment of Radar and the outstanding success of the indirect illumination provided by H.M.S. GREYHOUND, but a curious contrast of opinion has arisen over the actual targets engaged. The technical records of the action show that H.M.S. WARSPITE engaged the rear-most ship first and subsequently shifted target *left* to the second ship in the enemy line (the leading ship is now thought to have been a destroyer).

My ***own opinion supported by the Chief of Staff, the Captain of the Fleet and several Staff Officers, is that H.M.S. WARSPITE engaged the leading 8 inch cruiser (2nd in the line) and subsequently shifted fire *right* to the rear ship. It is a point which cannot be absolutely decided until the full story of this action from both sides is known, but it appears that the Gunnery Records must be wrong.

I7. On conclusion of the battlefleet action, the signal was made "All forces not engaged in sinking the enemy, retire north-east". The order was intended to ensure withdrawal on parallel tracks clear of the destroyer melee, and was made under the impression that cruisers and striking force were in contact with the enemy. Heavy fighting had been observed to the south westward which supported this belief. Unfortunately the cruisers were not in fact engaged and the Vice-Admiral, Light Forces, accordingly withdrew to the north-east. He had sighted a red pyrotechnic signal some distance to the north-west 40 minutes earlier and was at this time about to spread to investigate (see report of V.A.L.F., paragraph 35). This red light signal was sighted simultaneously by Captain D.I4 bearing 0I0 degrees, who seeing it in the direction of the 7th Cruiser Squadron and knowing from their G.A.B.††signal they had seen it, forebore to investigate.

There seems little doubt, from subsequent analysis, that this, must have been the remainder of the Italian Fleet withdrawing to the north-west (see diagram No. 9). I am of the opinion that the course I selected for withdrawal led the fleet too far to the eastward, and that a more northerly course should have been steered.

18. I hoped when ordering the eight destroyers of the striking force to attack that the cruisers would regain touch to assist Captain D.I4 to launch his attack. The bearing and distance of the enemy given to the striking force when detached (286 degrees 35 miles from H.M.S. WARSPITE) was based on the plot and was in fact approximately correct but the enemy's course appears to have been 45 degrees further to the north-westward than that estimated. In spite, therefore, of Captain D.I4's intention to pass to the northward of the enemy, the striking force apparently passed under the stern of the enemy to his southern flank whilst the cruisers were steering on an approximately parallel course on the enemy's northern flank (see diagram No. 7). The red pyrotechnic was shown between these two British forces.

19. The mistake made by H.M.S. HAVOCK (paragraph 38) in reporting the POLA as a LITTORIO class did not actually bring about any ill effect, since the flotillas had by then missed the VITTORIO and did useful work in polishing off the damaged cruisers (diagram No. I0). The movements and the results achieved by H.M.A.S. STUART's division during the night remain most obscure. H.M.S. HAVOCK certainly sank an enemy destroyer.

They had an exciting night and did considerable execution, but the presence of undamaged enemy cruisers in the area at that time seems unlikely and it is not improbable that the ships so reported by H.M.A.S. STUART were in fact some of the others of his own division.

20. It seems that the enemy must have been able to increase speed again during the night, since although extensive reconnaissance was flown next morning, he remained unsighted and must by then have been nearing the Italian coast. The search for survivors was interrupted by the appearance of German aircraft and it was decided to withdraw the fleet before the expected heavy air attacks developed, as no more useful work appeared to remain to be done. The fleet was in fact subjected to a fairly severe dive bombing attack by Ju 88s at I530, when H.M.S. FORMIDABLE was narrowly missed by several bombs.

2I. The mistake which prevented the Greek destroyer flotilla taking part in the action was perhaps not unfortunate (see paragraph 39). These destroyers had been sent through the Corinth Canal to Argostoli with admirable promptitude to a position where they were well placed to intercept the retreating enemy fleet, a task which they would certainly have undertaken with characteristic gallantry. Nevertheless the presence of yet another detached force in the area, and that force one with which I could not readily communicate, would have seriously added to the complexity of the situation. It was, however, disappointing for the Greeks.

22. The results of the action cannot be viewed with entire satisfaction, since the damaged VITTORIO VENETO was allowed to escape. The failure of the cruisers and destroyers to make contact with her during the night was unlucky and is much to be regretted. Nevertheless substantial results were achieved in the destruction of the three ZARA Class cruisers. These fast well armed and armoured ships had always been a source of anxiety as a threat to our own less well armed cruisers and I was well content to see them disposed of in this summary fashion. There is little doubt that the rough handling given the enemy on this occasion served us in good stead

during the subsequent evacuations of Greece and Crete. Much of these later operations may be said to have been conducted under the cover of the Battle of Matapan.

(Signed) A.B. CUNNINGHAM,
Admiral.

Note: – UNLESS OTHERWISE STATED REFERENCES ARE TO PARAGRAPHS IN THE COMMANDER-IN-CHIEF, MEDITERRANEAN STATION'S NARRATIVE.
*Admiralty footnote:- 10,000 ton cruisers: – ZARA, POLA, FIUME.
1,500 ton destroyers, two, probably: – GIOBERTI, MAESTRALE.
† Admiralty footnote:- Operation "Lustre" was the transport of British troops and supplies to Greece.
** Admiralty footnote:- Force "B" consisted of H.M. Ships ORION (Flag of V.A.L.F.), AJAX, PERTH and GLOUCESTER, the 2nd Destroyer Flotilla comprising ILEX (Captain D.12), HASTY, HEREWARD and VENDETTA.
‡ Admiralty footnote:- T.S. Transmitting Station.
***Admiralty footnote:- Subsequent analysis tends to show that WARSPITE first engaged FIUME, the second cruiser, and that she then shifted target and with VALIANT fired at ZARA the leading cruiser.
†† G.A.B. signifies General Alarm Bearing.

NARRATIVE OF THE COMMANDER-IN-CHIEF, MEDITERRANEAN.

Preliminary Intelligence.

From the 25th March onwards various indications were noticed of increasing activity on the part of German and Italian forces. Features of the activity noticed were an increasingly active sea reconnaissance by aircraft to the south and west of Greece and Crete and daily attempts to reconnoitre Alexandria harbour.

2. These activities together with the obvious imminence of the German attack on Greece and Yugo Slavia led to belief that some important step by the enemy was impending. The unusual keenness with which the enemy was watching the movements of the Mediterranean Fleet made it appear possible that an operation by enemy surface forces was intended.

The most probable actions by enemy surface forces appeared to be:-

(*a*) An attack on our convoy routes in the Aegean.
(*b*) The escorting of a convoy to the Dodecanese.
(*c*) A diversion to cover a landing either in Cyrenaica or in Greece.
(*d*) The possibility of an attack on Malta could not be excluded.

3. The Commander-in-Chief was therefore faced with the problem of meeting a threat which he knew to exist, but whose nature he could not foretell. Our most vulnerable

point at this time lay undoubtedly in the convoys carrying troops and material to Greece. They were moving, at the time, comparatively lightly escorted, under the rather inadequate cover of the Seventh Cruiser Squadron in the Aegean.

It was important to avoid interruption in the passage of these convoys if possible.

4. The obvious course to prevent enemy surface action against the convoys would have been to move the battlefleet into the area west of Crete. It was, however, almost certain that, had this been done, the fleet would have been sighted on its way, in which case the enemy would have only deferred his operation until the fleet was obliged to return to harbour to fuel.

5. After consideration it appeared most undesirable to defer this unknown threat which was impending. It was accordingly decided that the best course would be to clear the threatened area of convoys and merchant shipping so that the enemy's blow would be struck in a vacuum, at the same time making such disposition of available forces as would enable us to engage enemy surface forces should they appear.

6. At the same time it was important to maintain an appearance of normality in the area concerned, lest the enemy should "smell a rat". It was lucky that only one convoy was actually at sea, A.G.9 bound for Piraeus with troops, which was then south of Crete. This convoy was ordered to maintain its course until nightfall 27th and then turn back in its tracks. A southbound convoy from Piraeus was ordered not to sail.

In the meantime authorities in the Aegean were warned at the last possible moment to clear the area of shipping.

Dispositions.

7. The following dispositions were then ordered:-

(*a*) Force B, consisting of Vice-Admiral, Light Forces, with four cruisers and four destroyers to be south-west of Gavdo Island at daylight 28th March.

(*b*) Force C, consisting of five destroyers to join him at that time.

(*c*) T.S.R.* Squadrons in Crete and Cyrenaica to be reinforced.

(*d*) Royal Air Force requested to exert maximum effort of reconnaissance and bomber aircraft in Aegean and to west of Crete on 28th March.

(*e*) H.M. Submarines ROVER and TRIUMPH ordered to patrol off Suda Bay and Milo respectively.

(*f*) Force D, consisting of H.M. Ships JUNO, JAGUAR, and DEFENDER, who were at Piraeus, to be at short notice.

(*g*) H.M.S. CARLISLE ordered to Suda Bay to augment A.A. defences.

(*h*) Greek Naval forces warned to be at short notice.

Air Reconnaissance Report.

8. This plan was adhered to in the main but at noon/27th three enemy cruisers and one destroyer were sighted by air reconnaissance in position 36 degs. 30 mins. N., I6 degs. 40 mins. E., steering I20 degs. This position was later amended to 36 degs. 54 mins. N., I7 degs. I0 mins. E. Visibility was bad and the flying boat could not shadow. The Commander-in-Chief decided to take the battlefleet to sea, cancelled the move to Cyrenaica of the T.S.R. aircraft, and made the following re-dispositions:-

Force "B," consisting of the Vice-Admiral, Light Forces in ORION, AJAX, PERTH, GLOUCESTER, the Captain (D), Second Destroyer Flotilla in ILEX, HASTY, HEREWARD and VENDETTA (all from operations in the Aegean) were to rendezvous and be in position 34 degs. 20 mins. N., 24 degs. I0 mins. E., at 0630/28th. GLOUCESTER'S speed was reported down to 24 knots due to trouble with a plummer block.

Force "C" was to remain with the battlefleet.

Royal Air Force reconnaissance was arranged for 28th over the southern Ionian Sea, the south-west Aegean, and south of Crete.

Fleet Sailing from Alexandria.

9. Enemy reconnaissance planes were over the fleet at Alexandria at noon and again p.m. 27th. At dusk, I900/27th, the Commander-in-Chief sailed the Fleet from Alexandria. WARSPITE, BARHAM, VALIANT and FORMIDABLE were in company, the Rear- Admiral, First Battle Squadron, being in BARHAM, and the Rear-Admiral, Mediterranean Aircraft Carriers, in FORMIDABLE. The fleet was screened by Captain (D), Fourteenth Destroyer Flotilla in JERVIS, JANUS, NUBIAN, MOHAWK, the Captain (D), Tenth Destroyer Flotilla in STUART, GREYHOUND, GRIFFIN, HOTSPUR and HAVOCK. Course was set 300 degs. at 20 knots.

28th March, I94I – First Sight and Contact with the Enemy – Forenoon Action.

I0. A dawn air search was flown off from FORMIDABLE and at 0739 an aircraft reported four cruisers and six destroyers (to be known as Force "X") about 30 miles south of Gavdo Island steering I60 degs. This was at first thought to be an inaccurate report of Force "B" which was known to be in that area, but at 0827 the Vice-Admiral, Light Forces' first sighting report of three cruisers and destroyers was received. The Commander-in-Chief increased speed to 22 knots, maintaining course 300 degs. The Vice-Admiral, Light Forces, was estimated to bear 267 degs. 90 miles from the battlefleet and the enemy were reported 009 degs. I8 miles from him steering first I00 degs. and then I60 degs. At 0900 the enemy were reported turning back to 300 degs. with the Vice-Admiral, Light Forces, also turning to the north-westward. The Commander-in-Chief detached VALIANT to proceed ahead at maximum speed with

NUBIAN and MOHAWK; WARSPITE (who was having slight condenser trouble) and BARHAM remained in company with FORMIDABLE.

II. FORMIDABLE'S aircraft were not using "Duty Letters" so that it was difficult to follow the series of reports. Their positions were also being omitted from reports as in the case of aircraft 5H report timed 0905. An enemy force was being reported to the northward of the cruisers, but it was not clear to the Commander-in-Chief whether this was in fact another force or either of those already in contact. The term "battleships" was used on one occasion. On balance it seemed probable that there was another enemy force containing battleships, on which the cruisers were retiring; the Commander-in-Chief, therefore, decided to keep the air striking force back until the doubt about this had been cleared up. The aircraft, however, lost touch with the enemy and at 0939 the Commander-in-Chief ordered the air striking force to attack the cruisers in contact with the Vice-Admiral, Light Forces; if another squadron was sighted first, it was to be attacked instead.

I2. At this time Force "X" was estimated to be 75 miles 300 degs. from the Commander-in-Chief, being reported I6 miles 320 degs. from the Vice-Admiral, Light Forces. In order to increase the speed of the fleet, BARHAM was ordered to follow in the wake of the screen independently of flying operations. VENDETTA was sighted ahead having been detached by the Vice-Admiral, Light Forces to join the battlefleet on account of engine trouble. The Commander-in-Chief ordered her to proceed independently to Alexandria.

I3. By I030 there was still no further news of the enemy to the northward and it seemed possible that Force "X" in contact with the Vice-Admiral, Light Forces, was after all the only enemy squadron in the vicinity; but at I058 the Vice-Admiral, Light Forces reported two battleships bearing 002 degs. I6 miles from him and steering I60 degs. The Vice-Admiral Light Forces turned away to the south-eastward making smoke, but was evidently placed in a most uncomfortable position with the cruisers on his starboard quarter and the battleships (to be known as Force "Y") to port. The Commander-in-Chief ordered FORMIDABLE to put the air striking force on to the battleships and decided to close the Vice-Admiral, Light Forces as quickly as possible rather than work round between the battleships and their base. The doubt as to whether GLOUCESTER would be able to maintain the Vice-Admiral, Light Forces' reported speed of 30 knots weighed in favour of this decision, but the Vice-Admiral, Light Forces' II23 showed that he was still keeping the battleships at a range of I6 miles.

I4. The Vice-Admiral, Light Forces was estimated to bear 280 degs. 65 miles from the Commander-in-Chief at II35 steering I20 degs. But there was some doubt as to the accuracy of this owing to possible difference in reference positions. In order, therefore, to be certain of making contact with the Vice-Admiral, Light Forces as early as possible, the Commander-in- Chief altered course to 290 degs. at II35 and to 270 degs. at I200. FORMIDABLE was detached with two destroyers to operate aircraft independently, VALIANT was still in company and BARHAM had been keeping up well.

Surface contact lost – First air attack.

15. At 1200 Force "Y", which was now reported to consist of only one LITTORIO class battleship with destroyers, was estimated to bear 290 degs. 45 miles from the Commander-in- Chief; the destroyer screen was detached ahead to join the Captains (D), but at 1210 the Vice-Admiral, Light Forces reported having lost touch with the enemy battlefleet and five minutes later the air striking force returned with the news that the battleship had last been seen at 1145, steering 270 degs. with cruisers 20 miles to the south-east. The striking force reported one probable hit on the battleship. A JU.88 had been shot down by a Fulmar.

Second heavy Enemy Force reported.

16. A new force (to be known as Force "Z") was now sighted to the northward by Flying Boat Duty V. It was reported to consist of two CAVOUR class battleships, one POLA and two ZARA cruisers and five destroyers in position 35 miles west of Gavdo Island steering 315 degs. 25 knots.

Contact made with the Vice-Admiral, Light Forces.

17. At 1230 the Vice-Admiral, Light Forces was sighted bearing 220 degs. 12 miles with all his force undamaged. The Commander-in-Chief altered course to 290 degs. and ordered the second air striking force to attack the LITTORIO battleship. The Vice-Admiral, Light Forces' signal timed 1245 was the first intimation to the Commander-in-Chief that the enemy had turned northward, but this was later assumed to be a signal error and the enemy to have turned westward as reported by the striking force.

By 1250 it was evident that Forces "X" and "Y" had turned back and there was no prospect of overtaking them unless the speed of the LITTORIO was reduced by air attack. The destroyers were, therefore, ordered to reform a battlefleet screen, the Captain (D), Second Destroyer Flotilla and two destroyers being sent to the assistance of FORMIDABLE who was now a long way astern and seen to be engaging two Torpedo-Bomber aircraft. Speed was reduced at 1306 to 22 knots and at 1325 to 21 knots to allow FORMIDABLE and BARHAM to keep up. Force B was now in position 230 degs. 6 miles from the battlefleet.

The Chase.

18. At 1350 course was altered to 310 degs. as it was thought probable that Forces "Y" and "Z" were trying to make contact with each other. An air search was also ordered to the north-westward since no further reports had been received of Forces "X" and "Y". Doubts whether Duty "V" might in reality be reporting Force "Y" were cleared up when his position was checked by a landfall and at 1342 the Commander-in-Chief signalled the positions of the three forces to the fleet. 201 Group were instructed to concentrate all flying boats in the area south and west of Crete to maintain touch with the enemy. JUNO and Force D were ordered to patrol the Kithera Straits.

19. During the forenoon a strong breeze from the north-east had made flying operations delay the fleet, but in the afternoon the wind dropped altogether and the heavy cloud dispersed. This change in the wind probably also affected the accuracy of the reported positions of the shore based aircraft.

20. Force "Y" was sighted again at 1515 when FORMIDABLE's aircraft 4 N N reported one battleship and four destroyers steering 270 degs. in a position 290 degs. 65 miles from the Commander-in-Chief. The second air striking force which had been in the air since 1235 attacked the battleship with torpedoes; they reported three hits and that her speed was reduced to 8 knots. The Commander-in-Chief altered course to 300 degs.

21. Shortly afterwards aircraft 4 N N reported Force "X" consisting of three cruisers and four destroyers stationed 25 miles 250 degs. from the LITTORIO battleship which was steering 280 degs. about 10 knots. Duty "V" also reported three 6 inch cruisers and two destroyers bearing 155 degs. from Force "Z" both steering 300 degs. at 30 knots.

22. At this time Maleme Fleet Air Arm reported that three Swordfish had attacked the cruisers of Force "X" with torpedoes at 1205 scoring one possible hit and that another striking force was being despatched. YORK was instructed to arrange with Maleme for a dusk attack to be carried out in conjunction with the flying boat reports.

23. At 1600 the two CAVOUR battleships with Force "Z" were estimated to bear 305 degs. 120 miles from the Commander-in-Chief still steering north-westward at 30 knots. The damaged LITTORIO with Force "X" was estimated at 60 miles 289 degs. from the Commander-in-Chief; it soon became apparent that she must be making good 12 to 15 knots and would not be overhauled by the battlefleet before dark. So at 1644 the Vice-Admiral, Light Forces, was ordered to press on and gain contact. NUBIAN and MOHAWK were also sent ahead to form a V/S† link with the Vice-Admiral, Light Forces. Soon afterwards a third air striking force was flown off to attack the LITTORIO at dusk.

Night Intentions.

24. Duty "V's" admirable reports of Force "Z" still showed it to be in two groups, each making 30 knots, the battleships steering 310 degs. and the cruisers about 60 miles to the south-east of them, steering 325. It was always possible, however, that this second force of cruisers was in reality Force "X" which at 1727 was seen to turn back and take station five miles south of the LITTORIO. The situation was still, therefore, somewhat confused when at 1810 the Commander-in-Chief signalled his night intentions; if the cruisers gained touch with the damaged battleship the destroyers would be sent in to attack, followed if necessary by the battlefleet; if the cruisers failed to make contact then the Commander-in-Chief intended to work round to the north and west and regain touch in the morning.

Situation at dusk.

25. At 1745 WARSPITE's aircraft was catapulted for the second time and at 1831

made the first of a series of reports which rapidly cleared up the position. By 1915 it was clear that the damaged battleship was about 45 miles from the Commander-in-Chief, steering 290 degs. at 15 knots. Another cruiser force had joined it from the north-westward and the enemy fleet was now in five columns. The LITTORIO was in the centre with four destroyers screening ahead and two astern; to port of her there were three 6-inch cruisers in the inner column and three NAVIGATORI class destroyers in the outer column, to starboard there were three 8-inch cruisers in the inner column and two 6-inch cruisers (later found to have been large destroyers) in the outer column. In addition Force "Z" was still to the north-westward and apparently consisted of two CAVOURs, the three ZARAs and five destroyers. The second force reported by Duty "V" of two SAVOIAs, one DIAZ and two destroyers, was probably that which had just joined the LITTORIO.

26. At 1925 the Vice-Admiral, Light Forces, reported two unknown ships and concentrated his cruisers. Almost immediately afterwards he reported enemy ships 9 miles to the northwest of him engaging aircraft and making smoke. Duty 4 N N reported that the enemy's centre bore 310 degs. 14 miles from four destroyers in the van (probably the Vice-Admiral, Light Forces' four cruisers). At the same time WARSPITE's aircraft reported the enemy altering course to 230 degs. 15 knots, but no indication was given that this was a compass turn of the whole fleet.

Decision to engage at night.

27. At 1935 the air striking force reported "probable hits" but no definite information of damage, and the Commander-in-Chief considered whether he would be justified in taking the fleet at night through a screening force of at least six cruisers and 11 destroyers, with another force of two battleships, three cruisers and five destroyers, in the vicinity. On the other hand if the enemy were able to continue at 14 or 15 knots during the night they would be well under cover of the JU.87 dive bombers at daylight being already only 320 miles from their base; if they were intercepted at dawn, our forces would almost certainly be subjected to a very heavy scale of air attack throughout the day. The Commander-in-Chief decided to accept a night action and at 2040 ordered the destroyers to attack.

28. The attacking force was formed of eight destroyers under Captain (D), Fourteenth Destroyer Flotilla, organised into two divisions (the second under the Captain (D), Second Destroyer Flotilla), while the remaining four destroyers under Captain (D), Tenth Destroyer Flotilla formed the battlefleet screen. The enemy fleet was estimated to bear 286 degs. 33 miles from the Commander-in-Chief, steering 295 degs. at 13 knots. Captain (D), Fourteenth Destroyer Flotilla decided to pass to the northward of the enemy and attack from the van and signalled his intentions at 2115.

29. At 2111 a Radar report was received from the Vice-Admiral, Light Forces, of an unknown ship stopped about five miles to port of him; the Commander-in-Chief at once altered course to 280 degs. to pass nearer to the position. The Vice-Admiral, Light Forces, continued to the north-westward without investigating this report and at 2215 reported that he was steering 340 degs. with his cruisers concentrated and

would keep clear to the northward of the destroyers. The Vice-Admiral, Light Forces, did not again make contact with the enemy and no further reports were received from him.

Night action.

30. At 2210 what was apparently the same ship was detected by VALIANT's Radar six miles on the port bow. The Commander-in-Chief decided to investigate and at 2213 the battlefleet altered course together to 240 degs., the destroyer screen being ordered over to the starboard side.

31. At 2225 two large cruisers were unexpectedly sighted on the starboard bow, with a smaller vessel, thought at first to be a 6-inch cruiser, ahead of them. The battlefleet were turned back to 280 degs. into line ahead, and at 2228 when the enemy were on the port bow at a range of about 4,000 yards, GREYHOUND illuminated one of the enemy cruisers with her searchlight, and WARSPITE opened fire. FORMIDABLE hauled out of the line to starboard and the battlefleet engaged. The enemy were seen to be two cruisers of the ZARA Class on an opposite course; they were apparently completely taken by surprise and their turrets were fore and aft. WARSPITE'S first 15-inch broadside hit the rear cruiser with devastating effect, five out of six shells hitting. Both cruisers were thereafter repeatedly hit, set severely on fire and put out of action. A destroyer was seen passing behind the burning cruisers; this was probably the smaller vessel originally sighted ahead of them.

32. Except for flashing signals seen on the port quarter, nothing further was seen of the original damaged ship which the battlefleet had been closing to investigate. (BARHAM was unable to carry out searchlight sweeping procedure on the port quarter owing to damage to her searchlights by blast.)

33. At 2230 three enemy destroyers were sighted on the port bow closing from a position astern of their cruisers and were engaged. At 2232 they were seen to turn away making smoke and one at least fired torpedoes.

The battlefleet was turned 90 degs. to starboard together by Fixed Light Manoeuvring Signal to avoid torpedoes and at 2233 steadied on course 010 degs. At this time FORMIDABLE was acting independently on the starboard bow.

34. During the engagement with enemy destroyers, the leading destroyers had been hit by 6-inch fire from WARSPITE, and some confusion was caused by HAVOCK being closely engaged with the enemy destroyers and failing to burn fighting lights. As a result WARSPITE fired two salvos at her. HAVOCK was not damaged although it was thought at the time that she had possibly been hit.

35. The battlefleet ceased fire at 2235 and was re-formed into line ahead on a course 010 degs.; FORMIDABLE was ordered to rejoin the line at 2310. The four screening destroyers (STUART, HAVOCK, GREYHOUND and GRIFFIN) were released at 2238 and ordered to finish off the two cruisers seen to be on fire and then bearing 150 degs. four miles.

36. At 2245, when the burning cruisers were still seen right astern (190 degs.), starshell and heavy firing with tracer ammunition could be seen bearing 230 degs., and this continued for 10 minutes or a quarter of an hour. Since none of our ships

were on that bearing it was thought possible that the Italians were engaging their own forces. Firing was seen to continue in the vicinity of the damaged cruisers for some time and at 2300 a heavy explosion was seen and thought to be the torpedoing of one of them.

Withdrawal – Light Forces Engagement.

37. The Commander-in-Chief then decided to withdraw to the north-eastward in order to avoid the possibility of our own forces engaging each other and to return to the battle area in the morning. He, therefore, ordered all forces not engaged in sinking the enemy to withdraw to the north-eastward, and at 2330 altered course to 070 degs., speed 18 knots. The Captain (D), Fourteenth Destroyer Flotilla, was told not to withdraw until after the striking force had attacked. Firing and occasional heavy flashes were still seen intermittently until about 0100 on a bearing of 190 degs. to 200 degs.

38. At 0020 HAVOCK reported contact with a LITTORIO battleship in the position of the damaged cruisers. The Captain (D), Fourteenth Destroyer Flotilla, with the striking force reported that he was joining HAVOCK, as did GREYHOUND and GRIFFIN, but at 0110 HAVOCK altered the report to that of an 8-inch cruiser. At 0036, the Captain (D), Tenth Destroyer Flotilla, had reported leaving three cruisers stopped and on fire and two other cruisers in the vicinity as well as two damaged destroyers. At 0314 HAVOCK reported being alongside POLA and asked whether "to board or blow her stern off with depth charges," the Captain (D), Fourteenth Destroyer Flotilla then reported having sunk ZARA and being about to sink POLA.

29th March, 1941.

39. At 0006 the Commander-in-Chief had ordered the fleet to rendezvous at 0700 in position 35 degs. 54 mins. N., 21 degs. 38 mins. E., and requested air reconnaissance the following morning. JUNO, JAGUAR and DEFENDER were ordered to join the Commander- in-Chief, and also BONAVENTURE, who had left Alexandria the previous afternoon. A Greek flotilla of seven destroyers had been sent through the Corinth Canal to await orders on the first reports of the engagement, but owing to a cyphering error they were not ordered to join the Commander-in-Chief until 0350. The Naval Attache,** Athens, reported that 23 Blenheims had attacked the northern force of enemy ships between 1445 and 1655/28th March and had stopped one cruiser with two direct hits and a destroyer with one direct hit. Maleme also reported at least one torpedo hit on the LITTORIO battleship at 1940/28.

Fleet Re-formed.

40. At 0430 the Commander-in-Chief altered course to 250 degs. and informed the fleet that he was keeping W/T silence. At daylight an air search was flown off from FORMIDABLE and between 0600 and 0700 all units of the fleet rejoined the

Commander-in-Chief. It was thought that at least one of our destroyers must have been seriously damaged in all the firing subsequent to the main action, but no ship reported either damage or casualties. One Swordfish was later reported missing.

41. At 0800 the Commander-in-Chief was in position 35 degs. 43 mins. N., 21 degs. 40 mins. E., and course was set 220 degs. to sweep the area of the action. Between 0950 and 1100 many boats and rafts with Italian survivors were seen and a large number of survivors were picked up by destroyers, but at 1100 enemy aircraft were sighted and as there was no report of enemy surface ships anywhere in the vicinity, course was set 120 degs. for Alexandria. A signal was broadcast to the Chief of the Italian Naval Staff giving the position of the remaining survivors. The Greek flotilla was ordered to return to Athens.

42. The fleet was shadowed during the forenoon and at 1530 a dive-bombing attack was made by about 12 JU.88s, the main attack being directed on FORMIDABLE. There was no damage, however, the fleet "umbrella barrage" proving effective. One JU.88 was shot down and one Fulmar crashed in the sea just before landing on. There were shadowers during the rest of the day but no further attack developed. STUART, GRIFFIN and HEREWARD were detached at 0920 to Piraeus as escort for Convoy G.A.8, and AJAX, PERTH, DEFENDER and HASTY at 1930 to Suda Bay in order to cover Aegean convoys. BONAVENTURE was also detached at this time to join convoy G.A.8 at daylight 30th March.

Damage Inflicted on the Enemy.

43. It was not at all clear to the Commander-in-Chief what ships had been sunk, and the fate of the LITTORIO battleship was in doubt. But it seemed certain from the 900 survivors on board ships of the fleet that POLA was the damaged cruiser that had been detected stopped and that she had been sunk; that the two 8-inch cruisers engaged by the battlefleet were ZARA and FIUME and that they were both sunk; that HAVOCK had sunk one destroyer and the battlefleet possibly another; in addition there might be further losses due to the Royal Air Force bombing attacks. It was also a possibility that the enemy had suffered damage in an encounter between their own forces.

30th March, 1941 – Fleet Return to Alexandria.

44. The fleet continued to Alexandria and arrived there at 1730. An S.79 shadower was shot down by fleet fighters at 0834. A submarine was reported just as the fleet entered the Great Pass and the destroyer screen were ordered to clear the area ahead of the fleet with depth charges. This operation had no result apart from creating a marked impression on the Italian survivors.

Admiralty footnote:-T.S.R. – Torpedo/Spotter/Reconnaissance.
† *Admiralty footnote:-V/S signifies Visual Signal.*

** *Admiralty footnote:-Subsequent information has established that the report of the Naval Attache, Athens, was incorrect in that no ship was hit in these attacks by R.A.F. aircraft although some near misses were scored.*

From: THE VICE ADMIRAL, LIGHT FORCES, MEDITERRANEAN, H.M.S. ORION.
To: THE COMMANDER-IN-CHIEF, MEDITERRANEAN.

Date: I0th April, I94I.

ORION, AJAX, PERTH, GLOUCESTER, VENDETTA and HEREWARD, having fuelled, left Piraeus at I300 on 27th March, I94I.

2. GLOUCESTER had, on the previous day, run a plummer block bearing and had replaced it with a spare while in Piraeus, but at the same time divers had found excessive slackness in one "A" bracket and her maximum safe speed had to be regarded as 24 knots.

3. ILEX and HASTY were ordered to leave Suda Bay so as to join the cruisers thirty miles south of Gavdo Island (in position 34 20 N., 24 I0 E.) at 0630 on 28th March.

4. On the way HEREWARD examined an A/S contact in approximate position 0I2 degs. Phalconera I5 miles. This may have been the wreck of the U-Boat attacked by VENDETTA on I8th March in this position. Light oil was still to be seen on the surface in the vicinity.

5. The passage to the rendezvous was made without incident and at 0607 on 28th March two destroyers were sighted to the northward which proved to be ILEX and HASTY.

6. The course of 200 degs. at 0645 was selected to take the squadron further from the likely area of enemy air reconnaissance, while remaining in a position suitable for any eventuality.

PHASE I (0630-I230).

7. As soon as the enemy aircraft shadowing was identified, at 0633, as a type that is sometimes carried in catapult ships, it was realised that enemy surface forces might be in the vicinity. But when the first enemy report from one of FORMIDABLE'S aircraft reported four cruisers and four destroyers (a force identical in composition with my own), some 35 miles to the north-east of my position, steering a course similar to my own, I was in some doubt whether it was not, in fact, my own force that was being reported. Enemy warships were sighted astern before any further aircraft reports had been received and decoded.

8. The enemy sighted were at once suspected of being ZARA class, since cruisers of this class had been reported at sea on the previous day by flying boats. This suspicion soon proved correct. Knowing that vessels of that class could outrange my squadron and that, having superior speed, they could choose the range I decided to try to draw them towards our own battlefleet and carrier.

9. The enemy followed and opened fire at 25,500 yards at 0812. At the same time one of the enemy cruisers was seen to catapult one aircraft. The fire was accurate to begin with and the enemy appeared to be concentrating on GLOUCESTER. She snaked the line to avoid hits.

10. At 0829, when the range had closed to 23,500 yards, GLOUCESTER opened fire with three salvos, but they all fell short. The enemy made an alteration of some 35 degs. away after the first salvo and put himself outside our gun range. After this time, although the enemy resumed a course similar to my own and continued to fire till 0855, all his salvos fell short.

11. GLOUCESTER flew off her aircraft at 0830 and it carried out action observation, but her reports were not received in ORION owing to her not using the frequency ordered.

12. During this action VENDETTA soon began to lag behind and caused some embarrassment. By 0834 she was about three miles astern and I ordered her to steer to the southward clear of the action.

13. At 0855 the enemy turned away to port and ceased fire. He eventually steadied on a course of about 300 degs. I decided to follow and endeavour to keep touch. VENDETTA, by cutting off corners, rejoined at 0925. She was ordered to join the battlefleet.

14. At 0854 a signal from aircraft 5F had been received, reporting 3 enemy battleships at 0805 in a position which was seven miles from my own position at 0805. Though this report was manifestly incorrect as regards position, it prepared me for a meeting with enemy battleships at any moment.

15. H.M.S. FORMIDABLE reported that at about 1045 or 1100, her striking force was fired at by my squadron. This may have been so. Fire was opened on various unidentified single aircraft at long range about this time.

16. A battleship was sighted to the northward at 1058. Half a minute later she opened an accurate fire from about 32,000 yards and no time was lost in altering to the southward, increasing to full speed and making smoke. ORION was the target for the first ten minutes and the first salvos fell over. ORION was straddled and suffered minor damage from a near mass.

17. When the smoke began to take effect, GLOUCESTER, being to windward, was the only ship in view to the enemy battleship and she became the target. She was repeatedly straddled. The destroyers could hardly keep up at the speed of about 31 knots which the cruiser was maintaining. Only one destroyer, HASTY, succeeded eventually in reaching a position from which her smoke was of any benefit to GLOUCESTER.

18. At 1127 our own aircraft attacked the enemy with torpedoes and she turned away and ceased fire, though owing to the smoke, I did not know this until GLOUCESTER'S signal reporting this fact got through the smoke at 1138.

19. Information for the enemy's movements during this 28-minute action is very scanty, as the battleship was only occasionally sighted from GLOUCESTER and PERTH. She appears to have steered a course approximately 160 degs. at 31 knots or more. Nothing could be seen to the north and west on account of smoke and I felt sure that the enemy cruisers which I had been following would now be closing my force from the north-west.

20. When certain that the enemy had ceased fire, I ordered ships to stop making smoke. This took some time to clear, and when the horizon could be seen (at 1148) there was nothing in sight. The enemy cruisers evidently proceeded to join the battleship.

21. Course was now steered to make contact with our own battlefleet. When touch was gained at 1230, it was found that my position, which had been confirmed within one mile by a fix at noon, was 10 miles 342 degs. from that which the battlefleet had been using.

PHASE II (1230-1800).

22. ILEX, HASTY and HEREWARD were detached to join the battlefleet, and the cruisers drew ahead on a bearing of 290 degs. from the battlefleet to maximum V/S distance, as ordered in your 1305.

23. At 1651 I received your 1644 ordering me to press on and gain touch with the damaged enemy battleship. Speed was increased to 30 knots.

PHASE III (1800/28-0700/29).

24. I decided to spread the cruisers by 2000 in order to locate the damaged enemy battleship. Orders to start spreading were given at 1907, but when, seven minutes later, three or four ships were sighted ahead against the afterglow, these were taken to be enemy cruisers dropping back to drive off shadowers and I concentrated my squadron to deal with them.

25. At 1935 and 1945 the enemy's retaliation to the dusk torpedo attack by our own aircraft could be distinctly seen from my squadron some 12 miles away. The sky was filled with streams of tracer ammunition of various colours and they must have been very gallant men who went through it to get their torpedoes home.

26. As it was evident that a large number of ships was in close company I decided to close concentrate. Speed was kept down to reduce bow waves.

27. At 2015 ORION obtained a deflection by Radar of a vessel six miles ahead. At the same time GLOUCESTER saw a dark object low in the water on the port bow about a mile away. This was not seen from ORION and was not reported by GLOUCESTER at the time. Speed was reduced to 15 knots, and over a period of eighteen minutes, Radar ranges were plotted, proving that the vessel was stopped or moving very slowly. She was thought to be a large vessel, bigger than any cruiser,

and without other vessels in the vicinity unless they were alongside her. AJAX reported the same object by W/T.

28. By 2033 ORION was within three and a half miles of this vessel, which I thought at the time to be the damaged battleship because of her size. She still could not be seen.

29. At this juncture I decided to lead the squadron clear to the northward and then continue in search of the remaining ships. If this ship was the battleship she was "fixed," and, if not, it was necessary to regain touch.

30. The Commander-in-Chief, acting presumably on AJAX'S report, ordered the I4th and 2nd Destroyer Flotillas to attack the battleship, giving her position exactly as reported by AJAX, but giving her speed as I3 knots on a course of 295 degs.

3I. At 2040, I reported the same vessel as stopped, and supposed that Captain (D), I4th Destroyer Flotilla, would attack her in that position.

32. I was considering spreading the cruisers to find the remainder, when I realised that, if Captain (D), I4th Destroyer Flotilla, went further west on the assumption that the enemy was moving at I3 knots, he would almost certainly encounter our cruisers. Furthermore, the enemy had been reported as having altered course to 230 degs. during the dusk torpedo attack and it seemed that he might now be steering, if anything, to the northward of 295 degs., if, as I suspected, he was making for Messina.

33. At 2I55 AJAX reported deflection by Radar of three vessels, five miles to the southward of us. This would be rather farther west than our flotillas were likely to have reached at the time but I decided to keep concentrated and steer more to the north so as to keep clear of them, and later to alter course and increase speed so as to intercept any part of the enemy force that might have continued towards Messina, on a course of about 300 degs.

34. I kept on to the north-west so as not to be silhouetted against the star shell that were being used during the night action then in progress astern.

35. During this time a red pyrotechnic signal was sighted to the north-west at what seemed a long range, though it was difficult to judge its distance. I was about to spread when your signal was received ordering all forces not actually engaged to withdraw to the north-east.

(Signed) H.D. PRIDHAM-WIPPELL,
Vice-Admiral.

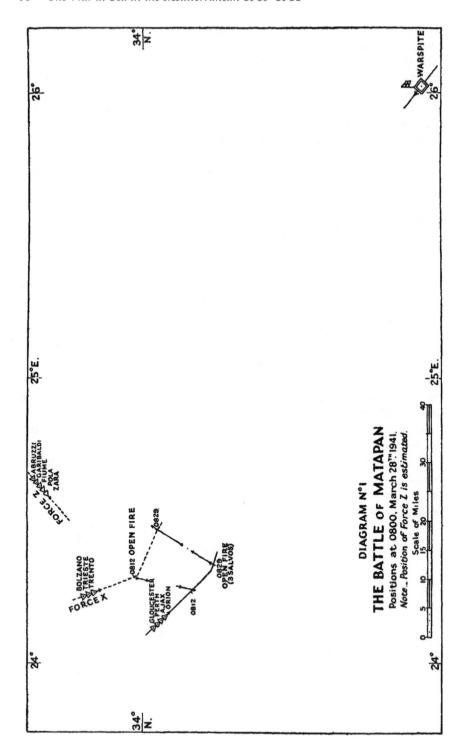

DIAGRAM Nº1

THE BATTLE OF MATAPAN

Positions at 0800, March 28ᵀᴴ 1941.

Note.- Position of Force Z is estimated.

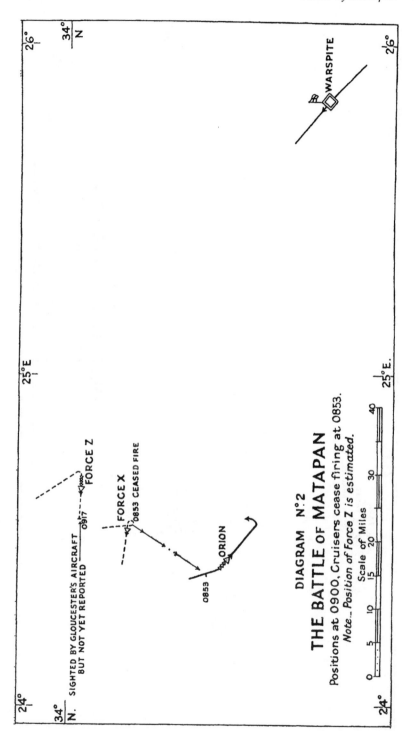

DIAGRAM Nº 2
THE BATTLE OF MATAPAN
Positions at 0900, Cruisers cease firing at 0853.
Note.. Position of Force Z is estimated.

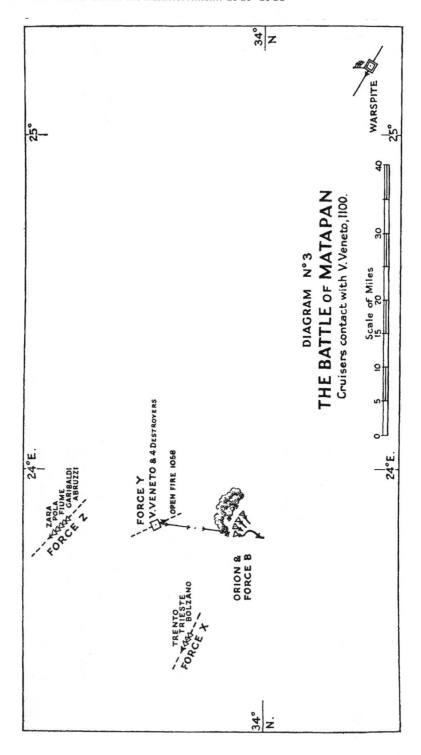

DIAGRAM N° 3
THE BATTLE OF MATAPAN
Cruisers contact with V.Veneto, 1100.

Scale of Miles
0   5   10   15   20   30   40

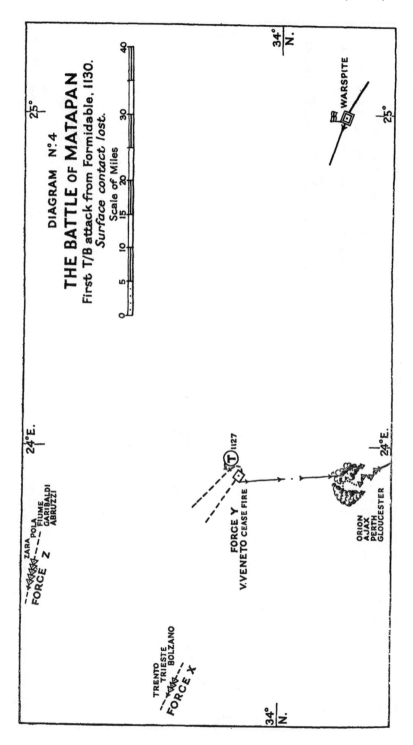

DIAGRAM N°4
THE BATTLE OF MATAPAN
First T/B attack from Formidable. 1130.
Surface contact lost.

Scale of Miles
0 5 10 15 20 30 40

WARSPITE

ZARA
POLA
FIUME
GARIBALDI
ABRUZZI
FORCE Z

TRENTO
TRIESTE
BOLZANO
FORCE X

FORCE Y
V. VENETO CEASE FIRE

1127

ORION
AJAX
PERTH
GLOUCESTER

25°
24°E.
34° N.
25°
24°E.
34° N.

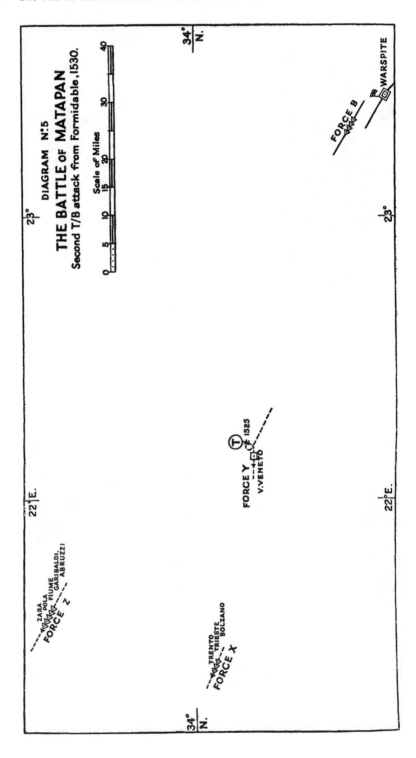

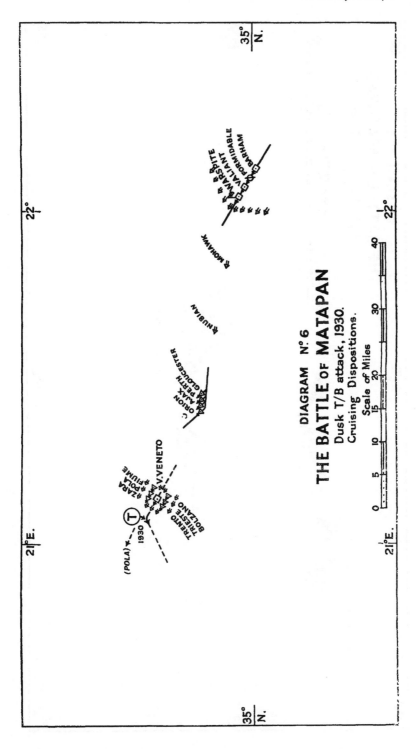

DIAGRAM N.º 6

THE BATTLE OF MATAPAN

Dusk T/B attack, 1930.

Cruising Dispositions.

Scale of Miles

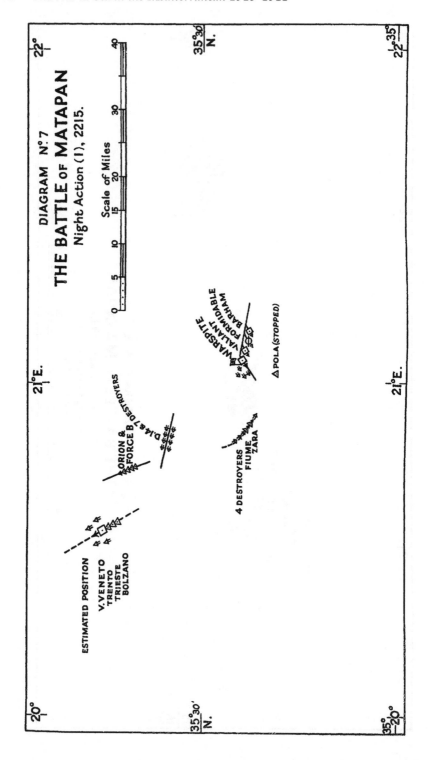

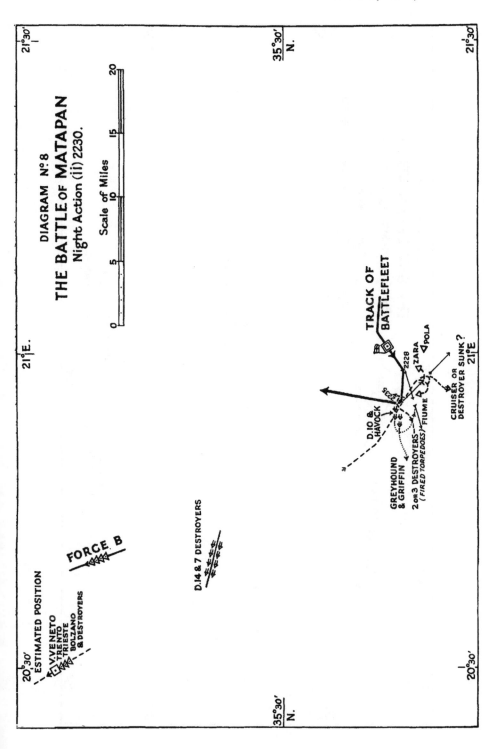

DIAGRAM N°8
THE BATTLE OF MATAPAN
Night Action (ii) 2230.

Scale of Miles

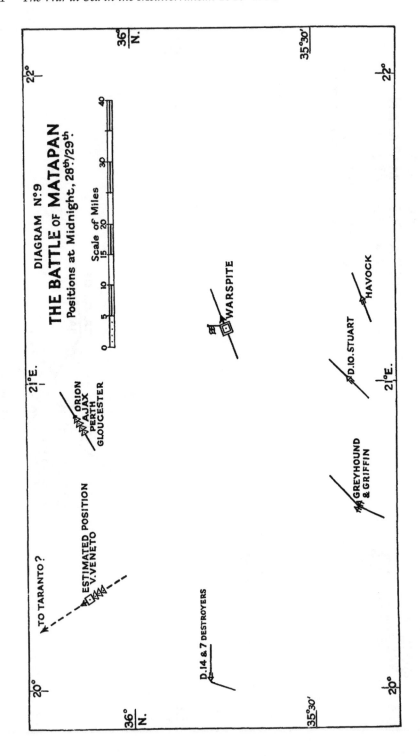

DIAGRAM Nº 9
THE BATTLE OF MATAPAN
Positions at Midnight, 28th/29th.

Scale of Miles

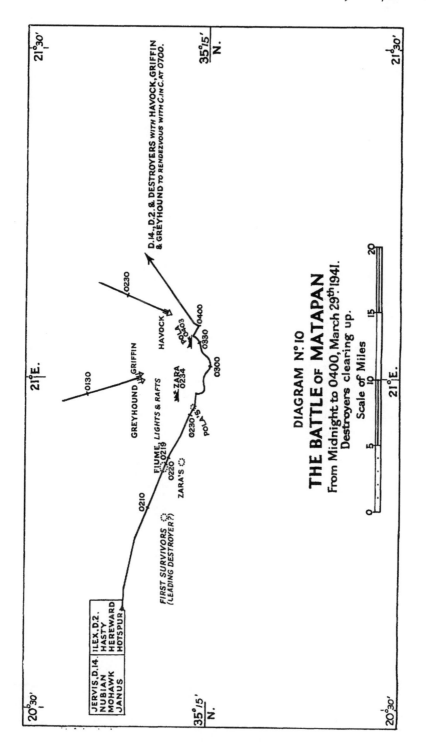

DIAGRAM Nº 10

THE BATTLE OF MATAPAN

From Midnight to 0400, March 29th 1941.
Destroyers clearing up.

Scale of Miles

5

REPORT OF AN ACTION AGAINST AN ITALIAN CONVOY

15/16 APRIL 1941

The following Despatch was submitted to the Lords Commissioners of the Admiralty on the 8th June, 1941, by Admiral Sir Andrew B. Cunningham, G.C.B., D.S.O., Commander-in-Chief, Mediterranean Station.

Mediterranean.
8th June, 1941.

Be pleased to lay before Their Lordships the attached report by Captain (D), Fourteenth Destroyer Flotilla of the successful action fought by the division of destroyers under his command against an Italian convoy on the night of the 15th/16th April, 1941.

2. The search for the convoy was conducted skilfully and with sound appreciation. The action itself was conducted by all concerned with determination and gallantry and was completely successful, resulting in the annihilation of the convoy and escort.

3. These results reflect the highest credit on Captain P.J. Mack, Royal Navy, and the forces under his command. The fighting spirit and high standard of training of the ships concerned is amply demonstrated by this incident.

4. The loss of such a fine fighting unit as H.M.S. MOHAWK is much to be regretted but such losses by chance torpedoes in a mêlée are only to be expected, and it can be counted fortunate that Commander J.W. Eaton, Royal Navy, and a large proportion of his ship's company were saved.

(Signed) A.B. CUNNINGHAM,
Admiral,
Commander-in-Chief.

Office of Captain (D),
Fourteenth Destroyer Flotilla,
H.M.S. JERVIS.

19th April, 1941.

FOURTEENTH DESTROYER FLOTILLA – LETTER OF PROCEEDINGS 15TH-16TH APRIL, 1941. SKIRMISH OFF SFAX.

I have the honour to submit the following report of the sinking of the Tripoli-bound convoy and escort on the night of 15th-16th April, 1941.

2. At 1800 on 15th April, 1941, JERVIS, NUBIAN, MOHAWK and JANUS* slipped and proceeded from Malta by the eastern searched channel to intercept the convoy reported in a signal from an aircraft timed 1157Z of 15th April, 1941.†

Single line ahead in the order JERVIS, JANUS, NUBIAN and MOHAWK was formed.

3. At a speed of 26 knots I could reach Kerkenah No. 4 buoy well before the convoy, assuming its speed to be 8 knots. At 1915, when clear of the searched channel, course 248 degs. was steered.

4. At 1925, I received Vice-Admiral, Malta's signal timed 1836 of 15th April, 1941‡ confirming the convoy's course and speed of 8 knots.

5. At 0044, when in a position 114 degs: No 4 Kerkenah buoy 6 miles; course was altered to 310 degs. and speed reduced to 20 knots.

6. At 0100, I altered course to 333 degs., this being the reciprocal of the enemy's probable course and, at 0110, started normal night zigzag.

7. At 0142, I passed the enemy's expected position, assuming that his speed was still 8 knots, and increased to 25 knots. At 0155, had the enemy proceeded at 7 knots, he should have been only three miles ahead; it was therefore clear that he had steered some other course.

There were two possibilities:-

(*a*) He might have altered to the Northward on realising that he had been reported.

(*b*) He might have kept closer inshore.

If he had done (*a*) it would have been a hopeless task to attempt to find him. My only chance, therefore, was to work under the assumption that he had done (*b*). Therefore, at 0155, I altered course to 214 degs. to close Kerkenah No. 1 buoy.

9. Attached are narratives of the subsequent action of H.M. Ships JERVIS,

NUBIAN and JANUS, together with a copy of the Commanding Officer's report on the sinking of H.M.S. MOHAWK.

(Signed) P.J. MACK,
Captain (D).

Admiralty footnotes:-
*JERVIS – Capt. P.J. Mack, R.N. (Captain (D), 14th Destroyer Flotilla).
NUBIAN – Comdr. R.W. Ravenhill, R.N.
MOHAWK – Comdr. J.W.M. Eaton, R.N.
JANUS – Comdr. J.A.W. Tothill, R.N.
† Signal 1157 of 15th reported five enemy merchant ships, escorted by three destroyers, off the Tunis Coast in the vicinity of Cape Bon and on a southerly course at an estimated speed of nine knots.
‡ Signal 1836 of 15th gave the position of the convoy and escort at 1700, its cruising disposition, and its course and speed as south, 8 knots.

SKIRMISH OFF SFAX – NARRATIVE OF H.M.S. JERVIS.
Wind – N.W., Force 5.
Sea – 31.*
Moon bearing 135 degs.-140 degs.
Course 214. degs. Speed – 25 knots.
Single line ahead in sequence JERVIS, JANUS, NUBIAN and MOHAWK.
Time-Zone -2.

0158   Sighted ships bearing 170 degs. about 6 miles.
0159   Made signal "Enemy in sight to port".
0200   *Altered, course to 140 degs.*
0201   *27 knots.*
0202   Made signal "Train torpedo tubes to starboard".
0203   *Altered course to 210 degs.* to bring enemy between me and the moon.
0205   Made signal "Train torpedo tubes to port".
0207   Able to count 5 ships in all.
0210   Enemy bearing 140 degs. 4 miles.
0211   7 ships counted. *Altered course to 170 degs.*
0212   Enemy bearing 135 degs.-150. degs., 2½-3 miles.
0213   *Altered course to 160 degs.* Enemy now seen to consist of 5 merchant Vessels, 1 large destroyer, 2 small destroyers.
0214   *Altered course to 150 degs.*
0215   Enemy bearing 128 degs.-140 degs.
0218   *Altered course to 140 degs.*
0220   Opened fire on enemy destroyer bearing 100 degs., range 2,400 yards.
0222   Enemy hit by pom-pom and 4.7-in. Enemy appeared to return fire with Breda and probably 3.9in. with flashless, cordite.
0225   1 merchant vessel on fire.

0227   Checked fire. Destroyer sinking. From now on a general mêlée ensued. Fire was opened with 4.7-in. pom-pom, Breda, 0.5-in. and Hotchkiss at many enemy ships at ranges varying from 50 to 2,000 yards. I merchant vessel of about 3,000 tons attempted to ram me, but I just crossed his bows in time by going full speed ahead on both engines.

Fighting lights were switched on. One large destroyer passed down the line to starboard and was heavily engaged, hit with the first salvo and set on fire amidships.

0240   Fired one torpedo at large enemy destroyer, probably obtaining a hit aft.

0244   Fired one torpedo at merchant vessel stopped and on fire, but missed.

0250   An ammunition ship blew up with an enormous explosion, smoke and flames rose to a height of 2,000 feet and JERVIS who was I,500 yards away was showered with pieces of ammunition, etc, weighing up to 20 lbs.; the sea around appeared as a boiling cauldron. Inspection reveals that the ammunition was of German manufacture.

0252   Received a signal from NUBIAN reporting that MOHAWK had been sunk by torpedo. I ordered NUBIAN to burn masthead lights and I proceeded towards her.

03II   A torpedo track passed directly under the bridge, apparently fired from the large destroyer previously engaged, which was stopped and burning and thought to be out of action. Opened fire on this destroyer, scoring several hits, and as the bearing drew too far aft ordered JANUS to finish her off, which she did.

0326   The situation was now as follows:-

I destroyer sunk; 2 destroyers and 4 merchant vessels burning fiercely; the fifth merchant vessel (the ammunition ship) sunk; MOHAWK sunk in about seven fathoms lying on her side with about 50 feet of her forecastle above water. NUBIAN picking up MOHAWK's survivors.

0323   Went alongside wreck of MOHAWK and took off two survivors. I then picked up more survivors and ordered JANUS to sink the remains of MOHAWK which she did by gunfire having no torpedoes left. Position of MOHAWK's wreck 34 degs. 56.5 mins. North, II degs. 42.4 mins. East by fix from Kerkenah Nos. 3 and 4 light buoys. Whilst picking up survivors I merchant vessel was seen to turn over and sink.

0403   Set course *080 degs. 20 knots.*

0418   *29 knots.*

0420   Normal night zig-zag (I0 degs: either side of mean course).

Admiralty footnote:-
* *"Wind force 5" signifies "fresh breeze (16-20 miles per hour)".*
  "Sea 3I" signifies "moderate sea with short, low swell".

SKIRMISH OFF SFAX – NARRATIVE OF H.M.S. NUBIAN.

0045   *Altered course to 330 degs. 20 knots.* Snaking the line.
About 0I20. Sighted dark shapes on the port bow, which were thought to be land.

0I43   *Increased speed to 25 knots.* Altered course as required to close shapes from northward, towards moon. Ships in line ahead, approaching convoy bearing Red 20,* inclination to the right.

02I0 approx. Opened fire on rear merchant vessel. This vessel was hit about third salvo, there was an explosion and a large fire broke out aft. Shifted target to second from rear; and again to a small ship turning away to port. Both these ships were also repeatedly hit and were on fire. Checked fire to allow smoke to clear. Proceeded to head of convoy.

0223   Sighted I destroyer (Navigatori class) on opposite course, range about I,000 yards on starboard beam.

0225   *Increased speed and altered course* towards and then away. Engaged destroyer with pom-pom, 0.5 M.G. and 4.7. Destroyer fired back and there was a short engagement which had to be terminated as MOHAWK passed between NUBIAN and the enemy. Hits were definitely obtained under the bridge and on the hull aft.

0230   Crossed bow of leading merchant ship.

0236   Received V/S signal from MOHAWK (astern of NUBIAN about 4 cables†) "Have been hit by torpedo".

0237   Made signal to Captain (D) I4 re MOHAWK. Sighted destroyer (I funnel) on port bow and engaged, several salvos were fired and she was repeatedly hit and caught fire. Turned and pursued merchant vessel making off to south westward. Engaged with 4.7-in and hit, setting on fire. Turned to port and closed MOHAWK.

0300   Stopped among MOHAWK survivors.

030I   Proceeded 27 knots on report of sighting unknown vessel to the westward.

0307   Reported this unknown vessel to Captain (D) I4. JERVIS and JANUS closed. Turned to port and engaged unknown vessel, now identified as merchant ship. From subsequent information I consider this was probably an old wreck. Ceased fire when vessel was seen to be on fire, and closed MOHAWK.

JANUS closed merchant vessel to investigate.

03I3 to 0405 Engine movements as required to pick up survivors.

0405   *Proceeded I5 knots,* increasing to 29 knots, course 080 degs.

(Signed) R.W. RAVENHILL,
Commander-in-Command.

Admiralty footnotes:-
*Bearing Red 20 signifies 20 degs. from right ahead on the port side.
† I Cable = 200 yards.

SKIRMISH OFF SFAX – NARRATIVE BY H.M.S. *JANUS*.

0140   Obtained contact by R.D.F.* at a range of 12,000 yards on a westerly bearing.

0220   JERVIS opened fire on a small one funnel destroyer.

0222   Opened fire on this destroyer with an R.D.F. range of 2,400 yards and hit with the opening salvo. This was the only time that an R.D.F. range could be used as later the targets became too numerous and confused.

As soon as this destroyer was seen to be well hit fire was shifted to the rear merchant ship. Hits were obtained at a range of 4,000 yards with the second salvo and, after about 5 salvos, a fire was started. Fire was then shifted to the next merchant ship, a fire started in her too, and the order check fire given. One torpedo was fired at the destroyer which had previously been engaged and this missed.

0230 approx. Opened fire, on the largest merchant ship in the leading group of three and obtained hits.

Fired three torpedoes at this same group of merchant ships. Results not observed from the bridge but tubes' crews claim that one hit was clearly seen.

0231 approx. A Navigatori-class destroyer passed through the line from port to starboard at high speed, between JERVIS and JANUS. Two torpedoes were fired which missed astern. The 4.7-in. guns could not train fast enough to catch up the target but the pom-pom claimed to have hit this ship.

0241   Having altered round to port to the northward, opened fire on a large merchant vessel on fire to the eastward.

0242   Fired one torpedo at this ship, which blew up at 0243.

0246   Sighted a Navigatori class destroyer ahead steaming north and making smoke. Increased to 30 knots and hauled out to port clear of the smoke. As soon as his bow could be seen, fire was opened and 3 hits with the first salvo spotted through his smoke.

0247 to 0259 Engaged the LUCA TARIGO on various to courses at speed varying between 16 and 30 knots, mostly at fixed sight range. During this time two torpedoes were fired in bridge control and one in local control, all of which missed. The Italian gunnery was poor, their tracer could be seen going high and wide.

A great many hits were scored on the LUCA TARIGO and by 0259 she was stopped, on fire, and had ceased firing. I considered that she was in a sinking condition and withdrew to the eastward to join Captain (D). Ordered by Captain (D) 14 to finish off the LUCA TARIGO. Fire was opened at 2,000 yards, many hits were scored, and an explosion occurred amidships. A very fierce fire broke out, and the ship could be seen listing over to starboard.

0326   Obtained R.D.F. contact range 10,000 yards bearing 330 degs. Increased to full speed and closed.

0320 I realised that I was in extremely shallow water and hauled off to the eastward.

This contact was two ships about 1,500 yards apart, and obviously aground.

0333 Ordered by D.I4 to finish off the MOHAWK. About I00 feet of her keel was showing, and the maximum height above water was about 6 feet. Fire was opened with one gun of "B" mounting in quarters firing and 4 hits obtained. This released air from inside the hull and the wreck slowly sank.

One survivor from the MOHAWK was picked up near the wreck. No sign was now left of the LUCA TARIGO.

There were two merchant vessels left afloat, heavily on fire, and one small destroyer with her fore end completely ablaze. Nothing else was afloat and one of these blew up about 04I5. JANUS suffered no damage from enemy action.

(Signed) J.A.W. TOTHILL,
Commander, R.N.

Admiralty footnote:- R.D.F., i.e. radar.

H.M.S. ST. ANGELO.
I7th April, I94I.

I have the honour to submit the following report in regard to the circumstances which led up to the sinking of H.M.S. MOHAWK at 024I on I6th April, I94I.

2. At 0045, MOHAWK was in company with JERVIS (Captain (D), Fourteenth Destroyer Flotilla), JANUS and NUBIAN, steering 330 degrees, speed 20 knots.

At 0I30, suspicious objects were sighted on the port bow and course was altered to close from northward, speed being increased to 25 knots.

3. At 0I45, these objects were made out to be a convoy of five merchant ships, screened by three destroyers, and JERVIS led round so as to close on the starboard quarter, opening fire on the nearest screening destroyer at 0205.

This destroyer was quickly hit and disabled and MOHAWK engaged the rear merchant ship, opening fire a few minutes later. This ship was hit at the second salvo and burned fiercely and fire was checked after firing about eight salvos.

4. Fire was opened spasmodically for the next few minutes, as the merchant ships were being repeatedly hit by the destroyers ahead of MOHAWK and I did not wish to waste ammunition. At 0223, an enemy destroyer of the Navigatori class was sighted on the starboard bow, steering an opposite and parallel course at high speed. She was immediately engaged by NUBIAN and MOHAWK, hit and set on fire and was last seen stopped and on fire about a mile astern.

5. At 0230, NUBIAN led round to port across the bow of the leading merchantman, who immediately altered course to starboard and tried to ram MOHAWK. This ship appeared to be quite undamaged and on avoiding her and crossing over to the port side, I turned to starboard with the object of engaging and sinking her.

6. As the ship was still under helm and turning to starboard, a torpedo struck on

the starboard side abreast "Y" gun, blowing away the after part of the ship from just forward of this gun. The ship was at once stopped and I ordered the Engineer Officer to report to me as to the extent of the damage.

The foremost group of guns then opened fire on the merchant ship in Director firing and hits were at once obtained, the ship catching fire and stopping. No ship could be seen in the vicinity which could have fired this torpedo, apart from the enemy destroyer who was stopped and on fire over a mile astern of MOHAWK, and I came to the conclusion that it must have been a stray torpedo fired by this vessel, possibly with the object of getting rid of top-weight.

7. The Engineer Officer then reported to me that although most of the stern had been blown away, the propeller shafts and propellers were still in place and that he would try to move them and get way on the ship.

About five minutes after the first torpedo had struck, a second one struck MOHAWK on the port side approximately on the bulkhead separating Nos. 2 and 3 boiler rooms. The ship commenced to settle rapidly on an even keel and I ordered all hands on deck.

Less than a minute after this order had been given, the ship took up a very heavy list to port and settled on her beam ends with the after parts submerged as far as the after end of the torpedo tubes. The order was then given to abandon ship as I considered that it was only a matter of minutes before the ship sank.

8. Six Carley floats were got out and manned, the remainder of the hands jumping into the sea. It was not possible to lower the boats owing to the rapid listing of the ship but the hands abandoned ship in an orderly manner and I consider that under the circumstances it was not possible to get out the remainder of the Carley floats.

The approximate position in which the ship was torpedoed was 34 degs. 56 mins. North, II degs. 42 mins. East. The depth of water in this position was seven fathoms.

9. The survivors were eventually picked up by JERVIS and NUBIAN and the forepart of the forecastle of the MOHAWK which still remained above water was sunk by JANUS.

I0. I cannot pay too high a tribute to the way officers and men behaved, during the action. The foremost group fired rapidly and accurately after the ship had been torpedoed and the spirit of the men in the water was admirable.

(Signed) J.W. EATON,
Commander, R.N.

6

MEDITERRANEAN CONVOY OPERATIONS

JANUARY 1941

OPERATION "EXCESS"

The following Despatch was submitted to the Lords Commissioners of the Admiralty on the I9th March, I94I by Admiral Sir Andrew B. Cunningham, G.C.B., D.S.O., Commander-in-Chief, Mediterranean Station.

Mediterranean,
I9th March, I94I.

OPERATIONS M.C.4 AND M.C.6

Be pleased to lay before Their Lordships the enclosed reports on Operation M.C.4 (which included Operation "Excess") and Operation M.C.6,* carried out between 6th and I8th January, I94I.

2. These operations marked the advent of the German Air Force in strength in the Mediterranean, and included the damaging of H.M.S. ILLUSTRIOUS on I0th January and the loss of H.M.S. SOUTHAMPTON on IIth January.

3. The incident reported in paragraph 7 of Enclosure No. 6** illustrates the difficulty of passage through the Narrows during periods of bright moon when, in order to avoid the known minefields, it is necessary to pass within gun and visibility range of Pantellaria.

4. With regard to the dawn action reported in Enclosures Nos. 6 and 9,*** it is thought that this must have been a chance encounter, as so small an Italian force would hardly have been sent unsupported to attack a heavily defended convoy. The heavy expenditure of ammunition by BONAVENTURE, largely incurred in an effort

to sink a crippled ship, serves to emphasise the importance of using the torpedo at close range on such occasions.

5. I fully concur with the remarks of the Vice-Admiral, Light Forces[†] concerning the towing of GALLANT by MOHAWK (Enclosure No. II[††]), and consider that this was a most ably conducted operation.

It cannot be satisfactorily determined whether GALLANT was mined or torpedoed, but the absence of tracks and failure by the enemy to claim her sinking lend probability to the supposition that it was a mine.

6. The dive bombing attacks by German aircraft were most efficiently performed and came as an unpleasant surprise. The results of short range A.A. fire were disappointing, though it has been subsequently learned that this fire was in fact more effective than it appeared, and the Germans suffered considerable loss.

Nevertheless, it is a potent new factor in Mediterranean war and will undoubtedly deny us that free access to the waters immediately surrounding Malta and Sicily which we have previously enjoyed, until our own air forces have been built up to a scale adequate to meet it.

7. The dive bombing attacks on the 3rd Cruiser Squadron on the afternoon of IIth January – resulting in the loss of SOUTHAMPTON – were a complete surprise, delivered at a time when the ships concerned believed themselves to have drawn clear of the threat of air attack, and when officers and men were doubtless relaxing their vigilance to some extent after a very strenuous four days.

This damaging attack served to emphasise the importance of including an R.D.F. ship[‡] in detached units whenever possible.

8. The remarks of the Commanding Officer, H.M.S. JAGUAR are of considerable interest, in particular his practice of firing 4.7-inch barrage over the stern of a ship attacked by dive bombers. The idea is now under development in the Mediterranean Fleet with a view to the destroyer screen putting an "umbrella barrage" over the fleet.

9. Force X[§] had originally put to sea to take part in the offensive operations intended in Operation M.C.6, which had to be abandoned. It was most unfortunate that persistent bad weather prevented the Rear-Admiral, Ist Battle Squadron [§§] from delivering any of the attacks which he intended, and which would have been a most useful counter to the undoubted set back which the fleet as a whole had received.

I0. It is satisfactory to record that Convoy "Excess" whose safe passage had been the main object of the operation, reached its destination safely.

(Signed) A.B. CUNNINGHAM,
Admiral,
Commander-in-Chief.

Admiralty footnotes:-
* *Operations M.C.4 and M.C.6 – see paragraph I of Commander-in-Chief's narrative.*
** *This enclosure is not included. The incident referred to was the apparent detection of GLOUCESTER and SOUTHAMPTON by the defences of Pantellaria on the night of 8th/9th January.*

***These enclosures are not included. The action referred to was a brief encounter at dawn on 10th January by ships escorting Convoy "Excess" with two unidentified enemy vessels which delivered a torpedo attack on them.
†Vice-Admiral, Light Forces – Vice-Admiral H.D. Pridham-Wippell, C.B., C.V.O.
††This enclosure is not included. The Vice-Admiral, Light Forces remarked that he considered that the Commanding Officer of MOHAWK "showed determination and good judgment in continuing the tow."
‡R.D.F. ship – ship fitted with radar equipment.
§Force X at Alexandria – BARHAM and EAGLE, screened by 5 destroyers.
§§Rear-Admiral, 1st Battle Squadron – Rear-Admiral H.B. Rawlings, C.B., O.B.E.

OPERATIONS M.C.4 AND M.C.6.
NARRATIVE OF THE COMMANDER-IN-CHIEF, MEDITERRANEAN.

Operation M.C.4 was devised, in co-operation with the Flag Officer Commanding, Force H,* to cover the passage of the much delayed Convoy "Excess". It was intended to continue at sea in the Central Mediterranean after the passage of the convoy and to conduct a further operation (M.C.6), which was to have consisted of offensive operations against shipping on the Italian coasts.

2. Operation M.C.6 was brought into force by the Commander-in-Chief's message 1039/9th January, but the offensive operations in the Central Mediterranean had to be cancelled after the damage to ILLUSTRIOUS described in paragraphs 29 and 30, and although the Rear-Admiral, 1st Battle Squadron remained at sea with Force X intending to deliver F.A.A.** attacks against the Dodecanese and the Cyrenaican coast traffic, the weather prevented these operations.

Tuesday, 7th January, 1941.

3. *Force H,* consisting of RENOWN, MALAYA, ARK ROYAL, SHEFFIELD, BONAVENTURE and destroyers, left Gibraltar, Convoy "Excess", consisting of ESSEX for Malta, and CLAN CUMMING, CLAN MACDONALD and EMPIRE SONG for Piraeus, having sailed the previous evening.

4. *Force A,* consisting of WARSPITE, VALIANT, ILLUSTRIOUS, JERVIS, NUBIAN, MOHAWK, DAINTY, GREYHOUND, GALLANT and GRIFFIN, sailed at 0500.

5. The Commander-in-Chief's position at 0800 was 31° 33' N., 29° 16' E., on a mean line of advance of 345° at 17 knots. There were no incidents until 1640 when an enemy aircraft was located by R.D.F.*** bearing 037°, 32 miles. The aircraft itself was sighted, and ILLUSTRIOUS's fighters which were standing by on deck were flown off but were too late, and Force A was reported. The aircraft then sighted BRAMBLELEAF and the corvettes. In view of this sighting the Commander-in-Chief sent an aircraft to PEONY to order her to make a drastic alteration of course so as to

throw off torpedo bombers. Two groups of aircraft approached the fleet during the afternoon but retired on sighting the Fulmars. The second group sighted and reported the fleet at 1720.

6. The Commander-in-Chief's position at 1800 was 33° 33' N., 27° 25' E., steering 290° at 19 knots.

Shortly after dark, at 1828, enemy aircraft were reported bearing 130° by R.D.F. This aircraft, however, crossed astern and never got nearer than 15 miles to the fleet. There were no further incidents and the Commander-in-Chief's position at midnight was 34° 13' N., 25° 26' E.

7. *Force B,* consisting of GLOUCESTER, SOUTHAMPTON, ILEX and JANUS, left the Aegean for Malta.

8. *Force C,* BRAMBLELEAF and corvettes passed the Kaso Strait without incident. Several floating mines were sighted south of the Kaso Strait, two being sunk by PEONY.

9. Convoy M.W.5½, consisting of BRECONSHIRE, CLAN MACAULAY escorted by CALCUTTA, DIAMOND and DEFENDER, sailed from Alexandria for Malta at 1400.

10. *Force D,* ORION and YORK left Alexandria at 0300 to cover the passage of BRAMBLELEAF through the Kaso Strait. AJAX and PERTH left Piraeus to rendezvous with Vice-Admiral, Light Forces at Suda Bay at 0800/8th.

11. Five floating mines were sighted during the day. There were no further incidents and course was set to pass south of the Medina Bank at 2200 in position 34° 30' N., 14° 50' E., and the mean line of advance was altered to 320°.

Wednesday, 8th January, 1941.

12. The Commander-in-Chief's position at 0800 was 35° 30' N., 23° 12' E., and the Anti-Kithera Channel was entered at 0900. Force D and the corvettes were met leaving Suda Bay, which was entered at 1230. After fuelling destroyers Force A sailed again at 1400, passing through the Anti-Kithera Channel at 1800. The Commander-in-Chief's position at midnight was 35° 54' N., 21° 44' E , on a mean line of advance of 280°.

13. *Force B,* arrived at Malta a.m., fuelled, and sailed again p.m. to rendezvous with Force H, JANUS remaining at Malta to dock. SYDNEY and STUART sailed from Malta p.m. to join Force A, routed south of the Medina Bank through position 34° 56' N., 17° 20' E.

14. *Force C,* BRAMBLELEAF arrived Suda a.m., the corvettes fuelling and proceeding to Malta independently.

15. *Force D,* AJAX and PERTH joined Vice-Admiral, Light Forces at Suda Bay at 0800, and the force then sailed to cover the passage of the corvettes.

16. *Air reconnaissance.*

Taranto – 1 Cavour, 4 cruisers and 2 destroyers. (The dry dock was not visible.).

Naples – I Littorio and 2 Cavours (indicating that the enemy again have 3 battleships in commission).

Messina – 3 cruisers and 3 destroyers.

Cagliari – 2 destroyers.

Trapani – 4 destroyers.

17. At 1537 a flying-boat of 201 Group located a convoy of 4 merchant ships and I hospital ship in position 33° 06' N., 22° 04' E., steering 270°. These were unfortunately out of range of ILLUSTRIOUS's striking force.

18. There were no incidents during the night. Course was altered to 260° at 0300, and at 0730 aircraft were flown off to search a sector 280°-310°. The Commander-in-Chief's position at 0800/9th was 35° 51' N., 19° 05' E.

Thursday, 9th January, 1941.

19. At 1030, Vice-Admiral, Light Forces, with Force D, and SYDNEY and STUART from Malta, joined the Commander-in-Chief. At about this time a reconnaissance aircraft was detected by R.D.F. and also sighted from the fleet. The Fulmars unfortunately failed to intercept owing to low cloud, and at 1140 the aircraft made a sighting report.

20. On the return of the first air search, which sighted nothing, an armed reconnaissance consisting of 6 Swordfish was flown off at 1130 to search the Tripoli-Benghazi route from a position 50 miles east of Tripoli to 60 miles east of Ras Misurata. The Commander-in-Chief's noon position was 35° 40' N., 17° 45' E., on a course of 230°. SYDNEY and STUART were detached to Alexandria at 1240 and Vice-Admiral, Light Forces with Force D at 1330 to cover the convoys and to provide A.A. support for Convoy M.E.6 on the 10th January.

Friday, 10th January, 1941.

21. At 0430, when in position 35° 56' N., 13° 20' E., course was altered to 290° to rendezvous with Convoy "Excess". At 0741 a report was received from BONAVENTURE, who was in position 36° 29' N., 12° 10' E., that she had sighted two enemy destroyers bearing 010°, 3 miles, and at 0756 the Rear-Admiral Commanding, 3rd Cruiser Squadron[†] reported that SOUTHAMPTON, BONAVENTURE, JAGUAR and HEREWARD were engaging.

22. The gun flashes at the commencement of this action were seen from WARSPITE, and Force A continued westward to close the scene of the action, passing close to the southward of Convoy "Excess" at 0800. By this time, BONAVENTURE and HEREWARD were in sight against Pantellaria, still firing heavily at close range into the crippled and burning Italian.

SOUTHAMPTON and JAGUAR were rejoining the convoy.

23. At 0810 one enemy destroyer blew up, having been torpedoed by

HEREWARD, the second having escaped to the north-west at high speed. The destroyer sunk is believed to have been the VEGA.

24. In the meantime a rendezvous had been, made with Convoy "Excess" in position 36° 28' N., I2° II' E. A fighter patrol of 6 and an air search in sector 280°-3I0° was flown off at 08I5, and the mean line of advance altered to I40° at 0820 in the wake of the convoy.

25. At 0834 when in position 36° 27' N., I2° II' E., GALLANT was torpedoed or mined, her bows being blown off. She was taken in tow by MOHAWK, and BONAVENTURE and GRIFFIN were detached to stand by her, HEREWARD and JAGUAR joining the fleet screen. GLOUCESTER and SOUTHAMPTON were also detached to stand by GALLANT at I000, the fleet remaining close to the convoy for the remainder of the forenoon.

26. One of the A/S[††] patrol aircraft sighted a Spica class destroyer about 5 miles from Pantellaria and attacked with A/S bombs, reporting a near miss. Two enemy aircraft unsuccessfully attacked BONAVENTURE with torpedoes.

27. The movements of Malta convoys were as follows:-

M.W.5 arrived Malta at 0800.

M.E.6 escorted by PEONY, SALVIA and HYACINTH, sailed at 0700.

M.E.5½ escorted by DIAMOND, sailed at II30 to join Convoy "Excess".

JANUS left Malta at I200 and joined the fleet screen, and CALCUTTA joined M.E.6.

28. In the meantime the fleet had been located by enemy aircraft at 0930 and reported at I0I5, and at II27 a shadower was shot down over Linosa Island by Fulmars. At I223, two S.79s dropped two torpedoes which missed astern of VALIANT. These aircraft were engaged in good time by the close range weapons of the battlefleet, without effect.

29. At I235 large formations of aircraft were sighted approaching from the north. These were identified as JU.87 and 88 aircraft with German markings.

A very heavy, determined and skilful dive bombing attack developed on the fleet, mainly directed on ILLUSTRIOUS, and lasting for some ten minutes.

ILLUSTRIOUS was hit by six heavy bombs, and hauled out of line heavily on fire and with her steering gear out of action, but with her armament still in lively action.

WARSPITE sustained slight damage to her starboard bower anchor and hawsepipe.

At least two enemy aircraft were seen to be shot down by gunfire.

30. ILLUSTRIOUS reported that she was "badly hit" and making for Malta; but it was not until I530 that she was got under control and steering steadily for Malta at I7 knots. In the meantime she was turning circles while the battlefleet was manoeuvred to maintain supporting distance from her. HASTY and JAGUAR were detached to screen her.

3I. ILLUSTRIOUS's aircraft in the air (8 Swordfish and 5 Fulmars) had in the meantime been ordered to Malta and all arrived with the exception of one Swordfish and one Fulmar, the crew of the Swordfish and pilot of the Fulmar being picked up. The air gunner of the Fulmar was killed.

32. Between 1600 and 1700, a second attack developed on ILLUSTRIOUS and the battlefleet by about 20 aircraft. ILLUSTRIOUS's Fulmars, who had been refuelled at Malta, were able to intervene and shot down 6 or 7 JU.87s, damaging others. The attack on the battlefleet was mostly concentrated on VALIANT who had one killed and two wounded from splinters.

33. ILLUSTRIOUS passed Filfla at 1730, making good 17 knots, though the fire was still burning at this time.

34. ILLUSTRIOUS was met in the swept channel by a tug from Malta and arrived safely at 2145.

35. In the meantime, GALLANT and escorting forces were making good 6½ knots, their position at 1600 being 36° 11' N., 12° 56' E. The convoy movements proceeded according to plan, and ESSEX escorted by HERO arrived safely at Malta at 2045. Owing to the delays to the battlefleet, Vice-Admiral, Light Forces was ordered to remain to the northward of Convoy "Excess" in position 34° 35' N., 14° 52' E. Convoy M.E.6 was at this time making good 9½ knots.

36. The Commander-in-Chief with Force A then proceeded to the eastward without further incident, passing through position 35° 40' N., 14° 10' E., at 1800, and 35° 18' N., 13° 35' E., at 2200, on a mean line of advance of 090°.

Saturday, 11th January, 1941.

37. The Commander-in-Chief's position at 0001 was 35° 20' N., 15° 26' E., steering 080°, and at 0800 was 35° 52' N., 18° 09' E. Convoy "Excess" was in position 35° 28' N., 18° 00' E., at 0800.

38. The fleet remained close to "Excess" for the remainder of the day, passing through position 36° 06' N., 19° 27' E., at noon.

39. At 1500, C.S.3,‡ who had left GALLANT off Malta at 0500, reported that SOUTHAMPTON and GLOUCESTER had been attacked in position 34° 54' N., 18° 24' E., by 12 dive bombers who achieved a surprise attack down sun, and both ships had been hit. SOUTHAMPTON was making good a course of 105° at 22 knots.

At 1605, C.S.3 reported that SOUTHAMPTON was stopped in position 34° 54' N., 18° 24' E.

40. Course was therefore altered to 210° at 1630 to close C.S.3, and at 1645 ORION, PERTH, JERVIS and JANUS were detached to his assistance. Owing to lack of fuel, JUNO and NUBIAN were detached to join the convoy and HERO joined the fleet screen. MOHAWK and GRIFFIN, who had seen GALLANT safely into Malta, were sailed by Vice-Admiral, Malta, at 1700, to close C.S.3 at high speed.

41. At 1819, however, C.S.3 reported that SOUTHAMPTON saw little prospect of getting the fires over the engine room and 'X' magazine under control, and at 1906 that he was forced to abandon ship and would sink her. The Commander-in-Chief approved this action and at 2100, when in position 35° 12' N., 19° 44' E., course was

altered to 100° to reach rendezvous for all forces at sea in position 34° 40' N., 23° 10' E. at 0800/12.

42. At about 1800, when in position 36° 08' N., 20° 50' E., Convoy M.E.5½ parted from Convoy "Excess" to pass south of Crete, "Excess" proceeding through the Elaphonisos Channel.

43. C.S.3 later reported that the first attack was carried out by 12 or more dive bombers and was a complete surprise from the sun in the clear blue sky. The speed of advance of the squadron at the time was 24 knots. The attack was well pressed home in spite of gunfire from both ships. High level bombing attacks continued intermittently until about 1630 and the squadron was shadowed until sunset.

GLOUCESTER's forward 6-inch director was damaged by an unexploded bomb through the roof of the director tower. One aircraft was unserviceable from machine-gun bullets; the other was in the air at the time and force-landed near DIAMOND. GLOUCESTER's casualties were 1 officer and 8 ratings killed and 1 officer and 13 ratings wounded.

SOUTHAMPTON survivors were embarked in GLOUCESTER and DIAMOND after abandoning ship, GLOUCESTER taking 33 officers and 678 ratings, of whom 4 officers and 58 ratings were wounded, and DIAMOND taking 16 wounded ratings.

Sunday, 12th January, 1941.

44. The Commander-in-Chief's position at 0001 was 35° 05' N., 20° 40' E., and at 0800 all forces, including Force X, made a rendezvous in position 34° 40' N., 23° 10' E.

45. The Commander-in-Chief in WARSPITE, with VALIANT, GLOUCESTER, JERVIS, JANUS, GREYHOUND, DIAMOND, VOYAGER, HERO and DEFENDER, proceeded to Alexandria.

46. Vice-Admiral, Light Forces, 7th Cruiser Squadron, YORK, MOHAWK, GRIFFIN and Force X then all proceeded to Suda Bay to fuel.

Convoy "Excess" arrived at Piraeus at 1200.

Monday, 13th January, 1941.

47. At 0230 ORION and PERTH arrived at Piraeus and embarked passengers from Convoy "Excess", sailing again for Malta at 0600 Vice-Admiral, Light Forces informed the Vice-Admiral, Malta that their route would be through the Kithera Channel, north of the Medina Bank, through position 33° 30' N., 14° 10' E., and requested fighter protection.

48. *Air reconnaissance.*

Naples – 2 cruisers, 3 destroyers.

Two convoys in positions 37° 39' N., 11° 44' E., and 35° 02' N., 11° 46' E. No. 830

Squadron was not despatched from Malta to attack owing to an adverse weather report.

Tuesday, 14th January, 1941.

49. ORION and PERTH arrived at Malta a.m. Owing to machinery defects PERTH remained at Malta and ORION sailed with BONAVENTURE and JAGUAR. The latter two ships were brought to Alexandria to reduce the concentration of ships subject to air attack in Malta.

Wednesday, 15th January, 1941.

50. Rear-Admiral, Ist Battle Squadron, with Force X, made a rendezvous with Vice-Admiral, Light Forces in ORION, with BONAVENTURE and JAGUAR, and proceeded to Suda Bay.

Admiralty footnotes:-
* *Flag Officer Commanding, Force H – Vice-Admiral Sir James F. Somerville, K.C.B., D.S.O.*
** *F.A.A. – Fleet Air Arm.*
*** *R.D.F. – radar.*
†*Rear-Admiral Commanding, 3rd Cruiser Squadron – Rear-Admiral E, de F Renouf, C.V.O.*
†† *A/S – anti-submarine.*
‡*C.S.3 – Rear-Admiral Commanding, 3rd Cruiser squadron.*
OPERATION "SUBSTANCE"

The following Despatch was submitted to the Lords Commissioners of the Admiralty on the 4th August, 1941 by Vice-Admiral Sir James F. Somerville, K.C.B., D.S.O., Flag Officer Commanding, Force H.

H.M.S. NELSON,

4th August, 1941.

REPORT ON OPERATION "SUBSTANCE"

Be pleased to lay before Their Lordships the following report, on Operation "Substance",* which includes the covering of Convoy M.G.I**from Malta to Gibraltar.

2. On the 3rd July, the Admiralty notified the authorities concerned the names of the ships taking part in the operation. These were: LEINSTER (personnel ship), MELBOURNE STAR, SYDNEY STAR, CITY OF PRETORIA, PORT CHALMERS, DURHAM and DEUCALION (M.T. ships***). Ocean Escorts: NELSON, MANCHESTER, AURORA, ARETHUSA with 3 destroyers, of the 4th

Destroyer Flotilla and 3 destroyers[†] from the Home Fleet. S.S. PASTEUR would convey to Gibraltar the personnel not already embarked in H.M. and M.T. ships, for subsequent transfer to H.M. Ships together with naval and military details for Gibraltar.

3. On the 8th July, the Admiralty issued certain decisions[††]and instructions. These were as follows:-

(*a*) M.G.I was to proceed by the westward route.

(*b*) The order of importance of the three objects of the operation was to be taken as:
   (i) The safe arrival of Convoy "Substance" at Malta.
   (ii) The subsequent safe return to Gibraltar of the warships forming the escorting forces.
   (iii) The safe arrival at Gibraltar of M.G.I.

(*c*) In view of the above it would not be possible to provide close escort for M.G.I and it was preferable for this convoy to leave Malta on D.3.[‡]

(*d*) The advantage claimed for sailing M.G.I on D.3 with the subsequent dispersal was that the enemy would be presented with a multiplicity of targets.

(*e*) It was essential for warships to carry troops, and an additional carrier would not be available.

I was instructed, after consultation with Vice-Admiral, Malta, to issue detailed orders for the whole operation.

4. On the 9th July, the Vice-Admiral Commanding, North Atlantic Station asked for as many additional flying-boats as possible to be made available at Gibraltar from p.m. D. -4 to D.3 in order to provide cover for the operation.

5. Special instructions were issued by me on the I0th July to conceal the object of the operation.

6. On the 8th July, I had asked Commander-in-Chief, Mediterranean if arrangements could be made for the following submarine dispositions:-

(*a*) 2 off Naples.
(*b*) I off Palermo.
(*c*) 2 in southern approaches to Messina.
(*d*) I off Marittimo.
(*e*) I off Cagliari.

Of these, (*a*) and (*e*) could be provided from the Western Mediterranean.

Outline Plan of Operation.

7. On the I3th July, I informed the Commander-in-Chief, Mediterranean and other authorities that in view of the priorities assigned by the Admiralty and the routes advocated by Vice-Admiral, Malta, I considered that M.G.I should sail a.m. D.3, splitting into three groups after dark, each group proceeding at best speed. The route

to be followed to be close inshore by Cape Bon and subsequently through the Galita Channel.

Subject to no enemy forces being present, cruisers and Hunts of Force X[§] to part company from "Substance" at 0700 on D.4 and proceed to Malta so as to discharge and refuel before arrival of "Substance".

The destroyer escort of "Substance" to be refuelled by 2000 on D.4 at latest and sailed so as to reach the eastern end of Skerki Channel about 0430 on D.5, the remainder of Force X having passed this point about 0400.

Force H[§§] to withdraw to the westward on reaching the entrance of the Skerki Channel on D.3 remaining if possible out of range of shore-based fighters during D.4 but with the object of distracting attention from M.G.I.

Forces H and X to rendezvous shortly after dawn on D.5. Providing no enemy surface forces were in the vicinity, 6 Swordfish to be flown off to Malta, early a.m. on D.5.

Admiralty footnotes:-
* *"Substance" – a convoy from U.K. to Malta via Straits of Gibraltar.*
** *M G.I – a convoy of 7 empty M.T. ships.*
*** *M.T. ships – Military Transports.*
† *Subsequently reduced by one destroyer.*
†† *The reference to "decisions" concerns previous discussions between the Admiralty, Commander-in-Chief, Mediterranean, Flag Officer Commanding, Force H and Vice-Admiral, Malta on the planning of this operation.*
‡ *The calendar date on which an operation is to be carried out is often not fixed until the last moment. For this reason, as well as for reasons of security, it was at this time customary, in writing advance orders, to designate the day on which the operation was to start as "D.I", and the second and subsequent days, as "D.2", "D.3", etc.*
It is now more usual to refer to the starting day as "D.day", subsequent days "D.+I", "D.+2" and the days preceding it as "D.-I", "D.-2", etc.
§ *Force X was composed of H.M. Ships EDINBURGH (Rear-Admiral Commanding, 18th Cruiser Squadron), MANCHESTER, ARETHUSA, MANXMAN, COSSACK (Captain (D), 4th Destroyer Flotilla), MAORI, SIKH, NESTOR, FEARLESS, FOXHOUND, FIREDRAKE, FARNDALE, AVON VALE and ERIDGE.*
§§ *Force H was composed of H.M. Ships RENOWN (Flag Officer Commanding, Force H), NELSON, ARK ROYAL, HERMIONE, FAULKNOR (Captain (D), 8th Destroyer Flotilla), FORESIGHT, FURY, FORESTER, LIGHTNING, and DUNCAN.*

Preliminary Movements.

8. The first movement of destroyers from Gibraltar in connection with the operation took place on the 14th July. These movements, which it is unnecessary to describe in detail, were designed to enable all personnel to be transferred under cover of darkness, all destroyers to have the maximum amount of fuel on board after passing through the Straits, and for the cruiser escorts to arrive at Gibraltar in pairs relieving one another on successive nights in the hope that the change of ships would not be too noticeable.

9. All these movements were carried out according to plan and by 2000 on the 20th July, the situation was as follows:-

(a) *In harbour at Gibraltar –*
PASTEUR accommodating balance of troops for transfer to H.M.
Ships. MANCHESTER, ARETHUSA, LEINSTER, COSSACK,
MAORI, SIKH, waiting to embark troops after dark and then sail to
eastward to join convoy.

Force H consisting of RENOWN, ARK ROYAL, HERMIONE,
FAULKNOR, FEARLESS, FOXHOUND, FIREDRAKE, DUNCAN.

(b) *Due in at Gibraltar at* 2130 –
FORESIGHT, FURY, FORESTER to refuel and sail to the eastward.

(c) *Approaching the Straits from the westward and due to pass Europa at*
0145/21– EDINBURGH (Rear-Admiral Commanding, 18th Cruiser
Squadron*), NELSON, MANXMAN, NESTOR, LIGHTNING,
FARNDALE, AVON VALE, ERIDGE with 6 M.T. ships forming the
convoy.

Departure from Gibraltar.

10. At 0140 on 21st July just before ships in harbour were due to sail, heavy Levant
squalls sprang up combined with dense fog. These conditions made departure difficult
and the programme was considerably delayed. Force H destroyers should have
slipped at 0240, but at this time MANCHESTER and LEINSTER were still at their
berths, though ARETHUSA had slipped from the north end of the detached mole.
Fog was very patchy and MANCHESTER at the south end of the detached mole was
invisible from RENOWN at the north end of the south mole.

11. About 0320 the squalls decreased in intensity and the fog cleared sufficiently
to allow MANCHESTER to sail, followed by LEINSTER. RENOWN, preceded by
ARK ROYAL and destroyers, slipped at 0426, 1¼ hours late on the programme
arranged. By this time the harbour and bay were clear of fog though it persisted south
of Europa.

12. Owing to the fog, ships were ordered at 0412 to proceed independently to the
eastward until daylight. The course and speed of advance of all ships were laid down
in the Operation Orders, a copy of which had been supplied to the Naval Liaison
Officer in LEINSTER. At 0530 a merchant ship passed two miles to starboard of
RENOWN on opposite courses. Half an hour later all ships which were to form on
RENOWN were in station and proceeding eastward at 20 knots to draw abreast of
the convoy in order to exchange destroyer screens.

Movements on 21st July (D.1).

13. Three Swordfish from North Front arrived over ARK ROYAL at 0630, but before
landing on were ordered to search ahead to a depth of 40 miles to locate and report

the position of all ships taking part in the operation. These aircraft reported having sighted all units including LEINSTER.

14. Hereafter ships formed on RENOWN will be referred to as Group 4, and those formed on the M.T. ships as Group 5. The three Tribals, COSSACK, MAORI and SIKH, who should have escorted LEINSTER to join Group 5 overtook and joined Group 4. Having failed to locate LEINSTER in the fog they proceeded independently in accordance with the instructions referred to in paragraph I2. Speed was increased to 20 knots at 0830. Visibility improved and by noon was normal.

15. At 0915 information was received from the Vice-Admiral Commanding, North Atlantic that the personnel ship LEINSTER was ashore near Cape Tarifa. This seemed an improbable position and since LEINSTER had been reported by the air reconnaissance it was not at first accepted. Further interrogation of Swordfish crews revealed that visibility from the air at the time was poor and the vessel reported as LEINSTER was probably BROWN RANGER. Subsequently Vice-Admiral Commanding, North Atlantic corrected the position to read Carnero Point and added that military ranks had been disembarked.

16. I considered it impracticable to take any steps to transfer the personnel from LEINSTER. HERMIONE was a possibility, but her return to Gibraltar at this stage would have inevitably compromised secrecy. In any case, she could not have taken more than 500 men without seriously affecting her fighting efficiency and I considered her presence with Force H on D -4 most necessary in view of possible eventualities. A signal to this effect was passed to Vice-Admiral Commanding, North Atlantic, by means of a returning Sunderland.

17. Clocks were advanced one hour at 1000 to Zone -2.** By 1230 Group 4 was abeam and to the northward of Group 5 and the destroyer screens were readjusted leaving three Tribals, NESTOR, FOXHOUND and FIREDRAKE, all of whom were destined for and could refuel at Malta with Group 4, and the remainder with Group 5 so as to economise fuel.

18. At 1500 Group 4 altered course to 060° to open from Group 5 and at 1600 reduced speed to 18 knots. The two groups were then approximately 30 miles apart.

19. During the day ARK ROYAL kept a fighter section ranged on deck whilst Sunderlands operating from Gibraltar provided A/S patrols ahead of both groups to avoid the use of Swordfish which would have suggested the presence of ARK ROYAL. No hostile or unidentified aircraft were sighted or detected throughout the day but two merchant ships were sighted by Group 4. The first passed westbound at 1255 some 15 miles to the northward of RENOWN who was then 32 miles south-west of Almeria. The second was sighted at 1900 when 35 miles south of Cape Palos, this ship bore E.S.E., 10 miles, and appeared to be northbound from Oran.

Movements during Daylight Hours, 22nd July (D.2).

20. At 0400 Group 4 altered course to 070° when 36 miles S.E. of Formentera, and to 130° at 0700 when 75 miles east of Formentera with the object of covering Group

3 from air observation. Fighter and A/S patrols were flown off for Group 4 at 0715 and maintained during the day.

21. At 0810 aircraft reported a southbound ship 18 miles south-west of the group. It was estimated she would pass 13 miles ahead of Group 5 at 1230.

22. An unidentified floatplane was sighted at 0850 low down to the northward of Group 4 and about 10 miles away. Owing to low air to air visibility the fighters were unable to intercept and the aircraft disappeared to the eastward. A few minutes later an Italian signal was intercepted, timed 0850, which appeared to refer to Group 4.

23. At noon Group 4 reversed course to the westward for two hours to close the distance from Group 5 and turned east again at 1400. One or two aircraft were detected passing 25 miles north of RENOWN at 1430; ARK ROYAL flew off six fighters but these failed to intercept.

24. The Sunderland A/S aircraft was instructed by V/S*** at 1453 to locate Group 5 and to inform Rear-Admiral Commanding, 18th Cruiser Squadron that Group 4 would remain 20 miles to the eastward of the convoy during the night and close at daylight. This Sunderland returned at 1732 reporting Group 5 bearing 240°, 25 miles from RENOWN. Rear-Admiral Commanding, 18th Cruiser Squadron reported via this aircraft that one French merchant ship had passed northbound 9 miles ahead of the convoy at 1300, that all destroyers had been fuelled during the day from BROWN RANGER and that Group 5 would pass through position 37° 40' N., 6° 25' E., at 0300/23.

25. During the day the sea was calm with fair surface visibility and a light easterly wind which enabled ARK ROYAL to operate independently for flying inside the screen.

26. Group 4 streamed paravanes at 1800 in position 37° 49' N., 05° 04' E., and at 2030 again turned west till 2200 to maintain a distance of about 20 miles to the eastward of the convoy during the night. As far as I am aware Group 5 had not yet been sighted by the enemy.

Submarine Attack on Force H on Night 22nd/23rd July.

27. At 2315 when in position 38° 03' N., 05° 45' E., proceeding at 15 knots on a course 085°, NESTOR, who was the starboard wing destroyer of the screen, reported a torpedo approaching from starboard. Immediate avoiding action was taken by means of a drastic turn to port. After a short period three heavy explosions were felt at regular intervals followed a little later by a fourth explosion about a cable ahead of RENOWN. Subsequent reports from NESTOR indicated that a submarine on the surface had fired a salvo of four torpedoes and that NESTOR had counter-attacked.

Movements, early a.m. 23rd July (D.3).

28. At 0648 ARK ROYAL flew off the first fighter patrol and Group 4 closed Group

5. At 0657 RENOWN reported a shadowing aircraft in sight ahead of Group 4. Fighters were sent out 10 miles but owing to the low sun and mist were unable to sight and the shadower made good her escape. A second shadowing aircraft was reported at 0729 ten miles to the northward but owing to low visibility and the fact that the aircraft was too low for R.D.F. reports, no contact was made by the fighters.

29. It became apparent that both groups had been sighted. At 0745 Group 4 was formed as a flexible port column of the convoy with the object of providing A.A. protection whilst still remaining free to manoeuvre for flying. This formation was maintained during the day. The sea was calm with a clear sky and good visibility but a very light and variable wind made flying operations difficult since high speed had to be used on each occasion and the flying-off course could not be predetermined with any accuracy.

Torpedo Bombing and High Level Bombing Attack
on Fleet, a.m. 23rd July (D.3).

30. The first group of enemy aircraft was detected at 0910 bearing 055°, 60 miles. This developed into a well synchronised torpedo bomber and high level bombing attack which commenced at 0942 and was completed in approximately four minutes. Six torpedo planes attacked from ahead and concentrated on the convoy while eight high level bombers crossed from south to north dropping their bombs amongst the convoy.

31. The torpedo bombers approaching low down from ahead were engaged with barrage fire by the destroyer screen. This fire appeared effective and on coming within range the enemy split into two groups of three, one group altering course to port, the other to starboard. One of the starboard group followed by one of the port group attacked FEARLESS who was stationed in the starboard bow position on the screen. The remaining two aircraft of the port group pressed home their attack on the port bow of the convoy which took avoiding action. There is no clear record of any torpedoes having been dropped by the remaining two aircraft of the starboard group, but MANCHESTER observed two tracks from port and one from starboard before a final torpedo approaching from port hit her.

Loss of FEARLESS.

32. The two aircraft which attacked FEARLESS released their torpedoes from a height of 70 feet at a range of about 1,500 and 800 yards respectively. Avoiding action was taken and the first torpedo passed about 90 yards ahead. The torpedo from the second aircraft ran shallow. Course was shaped to comb the track but when abreast the stem on the port side, at a distance of about 30 feet, the torpedo broke surface, altered course to port, and hit the ship abreast the 3-inch gun.

33. Both engines were put out of action, the rudder was jammed at hard-a-port,

all electric power failed due to the switchboard being demolished and an extensive fuel fire was started aft. One officer and 24 ratings were killed outright or died later. FEARLESS reported she was entirely disabled. As she was badly on fire and I did not consider the detachment of a second destroyer to attempt towing was justified under the circumstances, I ordered FORESTER to take off survivors and then sink the ship. This was effected by one torpedo at 1055.

Damage to, and Detachment of, MANCHESTER.

34. Meanwhile, MANCHESTER who was to starboard of the convoy, sighted torpedoes approaching and turned to port to comb the tracks. Two torpedoes were seen to pass down the port side and another one passed astern from starboard. In order to avoid collision with PORT CHALMERS a turn to starboard was then commenced. At this time another aircraft released a torpedo from a position between the first and second M.T. ships of the port column. Wheel was immediately reversed in an endeavour to avoid this torpedo, but it struck MANCHESTER aft on the port side.

35. The immediate effects of the torpedo hit were to cause a list of 12° to port with large reduction of speed and steering gear out of action. Steering was changed over to the after position and a reasonable degree of control was obtained. Subsequently the steering motors failed and hand steering had to be used. The explosion had travelled upwards through the decks to the upper deck, driving large quantities of oil fuel upwards into all the compartments affected. Water and oil fuel flooded the after engine room, after 4-inch magazine, main W/T office, 'X' magazine and various other compartments between 179 and 209 bulkheads. Many ratings were overcome by fumes from the oil fuel but most of these recovered after treatment and were able to resume their duties. Only the starboard outer shaft remained serviceable. A speed of 8 knots was at first obtained which very gradually increased to 12 knots. Emergency leads were run to the steering motors and mechanical steering was again in use by 1315.

36. MANCHESTER's initial signal informed me that she could steam 8 knots so I ordered her to return to Gibraltar escorted by AVON VALE. Her casualties were 3 naval officers, 5 military officers, 20 naval ratings and 7 other ranks killed, 3 naval ratings missing, and 1 military officer, 1 naval rating and 4 other ranks wounded.

37. MANCHESTER had approximately 750 military personnel on board but as the sea was calm I decided to limit her escort to one destroyer in the hope that a single cruiser and destroyer might either escape detection by enemy aircraft or else avoid attack in view of the better targets offered by the convoy and its escort.

High Level Bombing Attacks on Fleet, a.m. 23rd July (D.3).

38. The high level bombing attack carried out simultaneously with the T/B[†] attack was ineffective. The approach was made clear of the sun, and the aircraft were heavily

engaged by all ships. Fire appeared to be accurate although no aircraft were seen to be hit. Bombs fell harmlessly amongst the convoy.

39. At I0II a second wave of 5 high level bombers (probably B.R.20s) approached from north to south and dropped two groups of bombs, the first of which fell clear of the screen to port and the second close to SIKH and FOXHOUND on the port bow of the screen. This was rather a half-hearted attack and the aircraft which were at a height of over I7,000 feet were not engaged by the fleet until after the first bombs had fallen. The presence of 5 Fulmars I,000 feet below and astern, endeavouring to overtake the bombers, may have induced them to get rid of their bomb loads as soon as possible.

40. In the first high level attack, Fulmars shot down two S.79s and two more probably failed to return. Three T/B aircraft (S.79s) were shot down by gunfire, AVON VALE picking up six Italians (2 officers, I warrant officer and 3 ratings) from one of these in a rubber dinghy. Three Fulmars were lost, all of which force-landed in the sea, but all crews were picked up, uninjured by destroyers.

4I. These attacks, which took place I05 miles S.S.W. of Cagliari, appeared to be unsupported by enemy fighters, none of which was seen throughout the day.

Torpedo Bomber Attack on MANCHESTER and AVON VALE, p.m. 23rd July (D.3).

42. At I805 MANCHESTER and AVON VALE were attacked by three torpedo bombers. These approached from astern and proceeded well inside territorial waters to reach a position up sun. AVON VALE, anticipating an attack from out of the sun, moved in that direction to a distance of about two miles from MANCHESTER. The aircraft then approached low down on the starboard bow and were subjected to a heavy flanking fire from AVON VALE and to a barrage from 'A' and 'B' turrets backed up by the starboard 4-inch battery in MANCHESTER. The enemy appeared so deterred by the volume of fire that they did not press home the attack. One torpedo was dropped at AVON VALE and the other two were dropped at such long range that MANCHESTER had no difficulty in taking avoiding action. One torpedo was seen to surface at the end of its run and detonated shortly afterwards.

Abortive Torpedo Bomber Attack on Fleet, p.m. 23rd July (D.3).

43. At I643 a group of aircraft was detected bearing 338°, 43 miles, closing the convoy. Fifteen minutes later five S.79s led by a Cant were sighted low down on the port quarter. Fighters intercepted this group which consisted of torpedo planes and shot down two S.79s and damaged the Cant. The remainder retired without attacking.

Detachment of Force X.

44. By I7I3 the convoy and escort had reached the entrance to the Skerki Channel and HERMIONE was ordered to take MANCHESTER's place in Force X. Group 4

parted company and withdrew westward with the intention of covering MANCHESTER and affording such protection to M.G.I on D.4 as was practicable. A section of fighters remained with the convoy until I830, when they were relieved by Beaufighters from Malta. The Fulmars returned to ARK ROYAL at I922. At I833 Force H encountered the wreckage of one of the S.79s shot down by the fighters at I658. FORESIGHT picked up four survivors including one officer from a rubber dinghy. The officer thought they had been shot down by a Hurricane.

Passage of Force X through the Narrows
on the Night of 23rd/24th July (D.3/D.4).

45. While Force H returned to the west, Force X and the convoy continued through the Skerki Channel towards Malta, one destroyer with T.S.D.S.[††]streamed and locked in the low speed setting being stationed ahead of each column of the convoy. They were attacked at I900 by four T/Bs which approached from the starboard beam and were heavily engaged. One aircraft was seen by FARNDALE to crash. Avoiding action was taken but two torpedoes passed close to EDINBURGH and one close to HERMIONE. The Beaufighters failed to intercept this raid.

High Level Bombing Attack on Force X, I945 on 23rd July (D.3).

46. At I945 a high level bombing attack developed from I2,000 feet. Two Beaufighters at 8,000 failed to intercept. They had been instructed by R/T[‡] from EDINBURGH to circle at I0,000 feet, 5 miles, 070° from the convoy, in a position to intercept the incoming aircraft. They failed to do this and approached from the same direction as the enemy without identifying themselves and were engaged by the gunfire of the fleet. They then withdrew as the enemy approached, 3,000 feet above them. About 20 heavy bombs fell and one either hit or very near missed FIREDRAKE who was towing T.S.D.S. ahead of the port column. At the same time one torpedo passed astern of EDINBURGH but as no T/B aircraft were seen this torpedo may have come from a U-Boat.

Damage to, and Withdrawal of, FIREDRAKE.

47. FIREDRAKE was holed in Nos. I and 2 boiler rooms and temporarily immobilised, but suffered no serious casualties. ERIDGE having been ordered by the Rear-Admiral Commanding, I8th Cruiser Squadron to stand by and escort her to Gibraltar, FIREDRAKE reported that she hoped to have steam in one boiler shortly. In the meantime ERIDGE took her in tow, this being successfully accomplished by 2038. FIREDRAKE's steering gear being out of action, considerable difficulty was experienced in turning to the course for the Galita Channel, and equal difficulty in maintaining that course. Fortunately the steering gear was repaired by midnight, and no further difficulties arose; speed being slowly worked up to I0 knots. The hopes

that had been raised regarding the possibility of steaming the one remaining boiler proved false, for this boiler primed so badly that FIREDRAKE reported she would be unable to steam for some considerable time.

48. The two ships were shadowed by aircraft almost continuously throughout the next day. Air attack was expected at any moment, but for some reason or another, no attack developed. Possibly the shadowers failed to observe the tow, or it may be that the aircraft preferred to attack the merchant ships of Convoy M.G.I.

49. At dark on the 24th, the third degree of readiness was assumed, both ships having then been at action stations for 37 hours. ERIDGE reports that there seemed to be a feeling of genuine regret when darkness fell without any offensive action having been taken against them.

50. At 0930/25 FIREDRAKE slipped, after being in tow for 37 hours ERIDGE then towed her alongside for 2 hours, during which 10½ tons of feed water and 2 tons of drinking water were transferred. FIREDRAKE then cast off and proceeded at 9 knots under her own power.

5I. The damage to FIREDRAKE was doubly unfortunate in that it deprived the port column of the convoy of T.S.D.S. protection. FEARLESS and NESTOR had been detailed as spare T.S.D.S. ships. FEARLESS having been sunk, NESTOR only remained. The delay which would have resulted while NESTOR streamed her sweep could not be accepted. Furthermore, in the absence of FEARLESS, FIREDRAKE, AVON VALE and ERIDGE, the screen was already undesirably thin. The Rear-Admiral Commanding, I8th Cruiser Squadron, therefore, decided to accept the increased risk of damage by mines and to press on without further delay, retaining NESTOR on the convoy screen.

Enemy Aircraft Search for Convoy.

52. At 2000 Force X and the convoy altered course to the northward in accordance with the pre-arranged route. The latter had been selected solely from the point of view of safety from enemy mines, but the alteration to the northward at this time had another and unexpected advantage, for just over an hour later enemy aircraft were reported on the starboard bow. These split into two groups and made an abortive attempt lasting half an hour to locate the convoy.

53. There is no doubt that the enemy expected the convoy to take a more or less direct route from the Skerki Channel to Pantellaria. In fact, they must have felt certain of this since they made no attempt to keep the convoy under air observation during the critical period before and just after sunset, and in consequence the alteration of course to 075° at 2000 was unobserved, and the anticipated attack at dusk, which was most to be feared, never materialised.

54. At 2250 Force X altered course to I05° and a quarter of an hour later to I33°. From this time until midnight aircraft were observed searching with flares to the southward of the convoy. The flares appeared to be towed, but no opinion could be formed of the effectiveness of this method of search.

55. The period between 2250 and 00I3/24, when the convoy entered the Italian convoy route, was probably the most dangerous from the point of view of mines, and

in view of the absence of the T.S.D.S. destroyer ahead of the port column and of two M.T. ships being without paravanes, it was with considerable relief that C.S.18 turned to 160° at 0013/24 into the Italian convoy route.

56. At 0046, FOXHOUND, 5 cables ahead of the starboard column, reported a mine in her sweep and moved over to port to clear it. Except for a distinct bump felt earlier at 2017 on the bridge and in the engine room of NESTOR, followed by a report of an object like a mine in the wake, this was the only evidence of the presence of mines throughout the passage.

E-Boat Attack on Force X, 0300 24th July (D.4).

57. The convoy passed through Position K (36° 57' N., 12° E.) at 0230. A quarter of an hour later three unidentified objects were detected by COSSACK, stationed 5 cables ahead of the port column, on her R.D.F.

58. At 0250, short flashes of light followed by the sound of motor engines starting up indicated to COSSACK and EDINBURGH (leading the port column) the presence of E-Boats.[§] One was promptly illuminated by searchlight and heavily engaged by these two ships. MANXMAN found the target perfectly illuminated by cross searchlight beams and also opened fire. After firing torpedoes, one of which passed under the stern of COSSACK, the E-Boat retired at high speed but not before she had been repeatedly hit. Two torpedoes, either from the same or another E-Boat, passed down the port side of EDINBURGH.

59. Shortly afterwards, ARETHUSA the rear ship of the port column, sighted another E-Boat, which had apparently passed down between the port column of the convoy and the destroyer screen. This boat was engaged by both ARETHUSA and FARNDALE (the rear ship of the port screen), and hits were observed. One officer in ARETHUSA was confident that the boat was stopped; there is no evidence, however, that she was sunk.

60. Shortly after these attacks, one ship of the convoy was observed by NESTOR (the rear ship of the starboard screen) to be dropping astern.

Subsequent action by NESTOR is referred to later in this narrative.

61. At 0305 the noise of an E-Boat was heard by EDINBURGH on the port side, and immediately afterwards its wake was seen. It was promptly illuminated, and raked with pom-pom, 0.5-inch and Oerlikon fire at 1,500 to 2,000 yards range, the target appearing to be enveloped in a hail of tracers. The E-Boat stopped out of control, and at this moment the main armament fired a broadside of 12 guns at fixed sight range. When the splashes subsided nothing was seen.

62. Meanwhile, COSSACK detected hydrophone effect by asdic in several positions ahead, and at 0315 sighted another E-Boat on the port bow. Speed was increased and endeavour made to ram, but the boat passed across COSSACK's bows too close for searchlight to follow. Fire was opened and sounds like splintering of wood heard. A torpedo was fired by this boat, and it is estimated to have passed

immediately under the stem of COSSACK, who was only 100 yards from the enemy at the time.

63. For the next 20 minutes further sounds of motor engines were heard, by COSSACK and EDINBURGH, but no further contacts were made, other than a fleeting glimpse from COSSACK of a boat withdrawing under cover of smoke. Discretion on the part of the surviving E-Boat Commanders was apparently allowed to suppress their valour.

64. The result of these encounters was that of the 6 to 12 E-Boats present, one was sunk, one possibly sunk, and two others damaged.

65. This meeting with E-Boats might have had different results had their attacks been carried out more resolutely. It seemed that they were not expecting surface forces, and the surprise discounted their tactical advantage.

The E-Boats were difficult to see and their presence was not disclosed until they went ahead on their engines at high speed. Possibly they would have achieved more success and suffered less damage had they kept quiet during and after the firing of their torpedoes. The handicap of not having a flashless propellant for starshell was again keenly felt.

Torpedoing and Escorting of SYDNEY STAR.

66. NESTOR, who at 0255 had observed one ship of the convoy dropping astern, proceeded to investigate, and on closing, it was seen that the ship, identified as S.S. SYDNEY STAR, was moving slowly through the water on an opposite course to that of the convoy. On closer approach, it was observed that the starboard boats were being lowered; the ship however appeared undamaged, with no list and at normal trim.

67. Some time elapsed before NESTOR could obtain a reply to repeated requests for information, but eventually SYDNEY STAR reported that she had been torpedoed in No. 3 hold, and that she had 30 feet of water in that hold and appeared to be sinking.

68. NESTOR therefore decided to embark the troops numbering 470, and proceeded alongside for this purpose. Planks were rigged from SYDNEY STAR's gunwale to NESTOR's forecastle, and Jacob's ladders employed aft. Transfer occupied 50 minutes, and was completed by 0405.

69. Throughout this operation both ships were lying stopped in a position 4 miles from Pantellaria. Three E-Boats were observed whilst the transfer of troops was proceeding, but no attacks developed. On completion of the transfer, personnel on board NESTOR numbered 774 (231 ship's company, 56 army passengers, 487 ex SYDNEY STAR).

70. Whilst alongside, NESTOR impressed on the Master of the SYDNEY STAR the absolute necessity of keeping his ship afloat and getting her under way again. At 0410 NESTOR cast off and SYDNEY STAR was able to follow her at 12 knots. It subsequently transpired that her No. 1 and No. 2 holds had also made water, and that the damage was caused by a projectile from one of the escort during the E-boat *mêlée*.

71. At 0615 two T/B aircraft were sighted by NESTOR on the port quarter. Barrage fire was opened and the aircraft crossed astern making off in the general direction of

the convoy. At 0650 two more T/Bs were sighted, this time on the port bow. Barrage fire was again opened and the aircraft crossed ahead and made off towards the convoy. Thinking that SYDNEY STAR was about to be attacked, NESTOR made a "Help" signal, in consequence of which HERMIONE was detached by Rear-Admiral Commanding, 18th Cruiser Squadron at 0700 to join NESTOR and SYDNEY STAR.

Approach to, and Arrival at Malta, 24th July (D.4).

72. At 0705 when some 60 miles west of Gozo, a half-hearted attack was carried out by 3 T/B aircraft on the main convoy and escort. Torpedoes were released at long range when the destroyer screen opened fire. Ships took avoiding action, but no tracks were seen.

73. In order to afford time for the cruisers and destroyers of Force X to discharge personnel and stores and refuel, it had been arranged that Rear-Admiral Commanding, 18th Cruiser Squadron should proceed ahead with the cruisers and Hunts at high speed at about 0700, provided the situation as regards enemy surface forces was considered satisfactory. At this time, although all enemy surface units had been reported in their respective harbours on the previous day, no morning reconnaissance report had been received from Vice-Admiral, Malta.

74. There appeared to be little likelihood of enemy surface forces making contact with the main convoy, a greater source of worry being the SYDNEY STAR. At 0730 the situation appeared easier, and realising that any further delay might jeopardise the arrangements for getting the convoy into Grand Harbour and for sailing Force X to rejoin Force H, Rear-Admiral Commanding, 18th Cruiser Squadron, with ARETHUSA and MANXMAN, parted company from the convoy and proceeded at 25 knots to Malta. At 0830 a reconnaissance report was received from Vice-Admiral, Malta, stating that no enemy surface forces were in the vicinity. This removed what little fears yet remained of an attack by surface forces.

75. At 1000, SYDNEY STAR, HERMIONE and NESTOR were attacked by 8 JU.87 dive bombers with German markings and 2 high level bombers. The attacks were well synchronised, and in the case of the dive bombing attack, well pressed home. One bomb fell 20 yards to port, and another 20 yards to starboard of NESTOR; others fell close to HERMIONE – but no ship was hit. One JU.87 was shot down by A.A. fire. One Beaufighter was in company but failed to make an interception.

76. EDINBURGH, ARETHUSA and MANXMAN entered Grand Harbour at 1130 with ships' companies fallen in and bands playing. A great reception was accorded them by the people of Malta.

77. HERMIONE, NESTOR and SYDNEY STAR, having taken the route north of Malta, arrived at 1400. The safe arrival of SYDNEY STAR reflects great credit on the Commanding Officer of NESTOR, Commander A.S. Rosenthal, R.A.N., who showed judgment, initiative and good seamanship in handling a delicate situation so close to the enemy's coast and in the presence of enemy E-Boats. It was appropriate that the Commanding Officer and most of his crew should be Australians.

78. The main convoy escorted by COSSACK, MAORI, SIKH, FOXHOUND and FARNDALE continued without further incident and, proceeding by the route south of Malta, entered harbour at 1530.

Movements of Force H, 24th July (D.4).

79. Meanwhile Force H had reached position 37° 35' N., 5° 15' E., at 0615, when two Swordfish were flown off to locate MANCHESTER and three more Swordfish to carry out a search between 000° and 100° to a depth of 50 miles to locate any enemy surface forces that might be in a position to attack MANCHESTER. None was sighted. MANCHESTER was reported to be in position 37° 19' N., 3° 44' E., at 0710 leaving a large oil track, slightly down by the stern and with a slight list to port.

80. At 0816 a Cant was sighted 10 miles to the eastward and was shot down by the fighter patrol.

81. The situation at 1000 was as follows. Force H in position 37° 18' N., 04° 30' E., steering 290° at 18 knots. FIREDRAKE and ERIDGE south of Galita making 8 knots to the westward, having been reported by a shadower at 0710. Convoy M.G.1 in three groups ranging between 40 miles west to 20 miles east of Galita with one ship, the SVENOR, just outside Malta. MANCHESTER and AVON VALE about 65 miles to the westward of Force H proceeding at 11 knots and possibly reported by a reconnaissance aircraft at 0700.

82. I decided that Force H should continue to the westward till about 1330 by which time MANCHESTER would be reasonably clear of enemy air attack, and would have three destroyers in company, Vice-Admiral Commanding, North Atlantic having ordered VIMY and VIDETTE to rendezvous with her. About 1330 I intended to turn east in order to fly off 6 Swordfish for Malta during the night and then rendezvous with Force X in the vicinity of Galita Island about 0730.

83. During the day calls for help were intercepted from all three groups of the M.G. convoy. The first came at 1230 from ENCOUNTER, who was escorting Group 2. She reported a threatening aircraft in the vicinity and later reported an attack by four T/Bs, but all torpedoes missed. The attack was followed about 20 minutes later by high level bombing when some 30 bombs fell between AMERIKA and THERMOPYLAE. At 1345 ENCOUNTER reported 2 unknown ships bearing 283°, 12 miles from position 37° 18' N., 8° 35' E. These were later identified as FIREDRAKE and ERIDGE.

84. At 1342 Group 1 called for help in position 37° 19' N., 8° 00' E. A high level attack resulted in bombs dropping between TALABOT and BRECONSHIRE and half an hour later BRECONSHIRE was near missed by some small bombs from a Caproni. Group 3 called for help at 1711 when in the same position and again at 1815.

85. ENCOUNTER left Group 2 at 1430 and proceeded ahead at 28 knots to join and escort Group 1. At 1740 she was attacked unsuccessfully by 3 high level bombers. ENCOUNTER joined Group 1 at 2140 and thereafter had an uneventful passage. No

further signals were received from any of these ships during the day. Their estimated E.T.A.§§ at Gibraltar as signalled by Vice-Admiral, Malta, was:-

Group I Dawn/26th.
Group 2 I800/26th.
Group 3 0I00/27th.
Group 4 0I00/28th.

86. Force H turned to the eastward at I345 and an hour later a reconnaissance of 5 Swordfish was flown off from position 37° 45' N., 3° 47' E., to search for enemy forces between 000° and I00° to a depth of 90 miles. Nothing was sighted.

87. VIMY and AVON VALE, who with VIDETTE were escorting MANCHESTER, obtained an asdic contact at I500 and carried out several attacks with depth charges but there was no evidence of success.

Admiralty footnotes:-
* *Rear-Admiral Commanding, I8th Cruiser Squadron – Rear-Admiral E.N. Syfret, the Senior Officer of Force X.*
** *Zone 2 – two hours ahead of G.M.T.*
*** *V/S – visual signal.*
†*T/B – torpedo bomber.*
†† *T.S.D.S. – two speed destroyer minesweep.*
‡ *R/T – radio telephony.*
§ *E-Boats – similar to British Motor Torpedo Boats.*
§§ *E.T.A. – expected time of arrival.*

Despatch of 6 Swordfish to Malta.

88. At 0I00 ARK ROYAL flew off 6 Swordfish fitted with long range tanks for Malta from position 37° 42' N., 7° I7' E. These all arrived safely.

Movements of Force H, early a.m. 25th July (D.5).

89. Force H turned back to the westward at 0I30 for two hours and then proceeded east to meet Force X.

90. At 05I2 a flashing light was seen to the north-east and ARK ROYAL was ordered to fly off a Swordfish armed with depth charges to investigate. It was thought this might possibly be a U-Boat homing aircraft. It turned out, however, to be the Italian Hospital Ship SORRENTO searching for survivors, presumably after the air attack on the fleet on the 23rd.

9I. A reconnaissance of 3 Swordfish was flown off at 0556 in position 37° 37' N., 07° 32' E., to make certain there were no enemy forces between Force H and Force X. These aircraft found nothing. The visibility was I0-I5 miles. A fighter patrol was flown off at 06I5.

Departure of Force X from Malta, 24th July (D.4).

92. The cruisers of Force X left Grand Harbour at 1800/24 followed by the destroyers at 1845. All ships received a fine send-off from the Maltese and in particular from the crews of the M.T. ships and the troops who had taken passage. FARNDALE who had developed condenser trouble remained at Malta.

93. Force X had a few air alarms during the evening of the 24th but no attacks developed, probably due to better support from the Malta Beaufighters which, largely due to inexperience, had given me cause for anxiety by their performance on 23rd July during the approach to Malta.*

94. The force followed the same route as that taken the previous day by Convoy M.G.I and had an uneventful passage. This route ran from 20 miles south of Pantellaria to Kilibia light and subsequently in French territorial waters round Cape Bon and south of Zembra Island, thence to a position 030°, ten miles from Cani Rocks.

95. At 0748 the cruisers of Force X were reported by aircraft as bearing 110°, 22 miles from RENOWN with the destroyers six miles astern.

96. Force X joined Force H 26 miles N.W. of Galita Island at 0815 and course was shaped to the westward at NELSON'S best speed.

Movements of Force H and Force X, a.m. 25th July (D.5).

97. There was a light breeze from 150° and considerable ground was lost each time the fleet turned to enable ARK ROYAL to fly on or off.

98. A Cant was sighted at 0715 but fighters failed to intercept due to poor air to air visibility especially up sun. The first combat of the day took place at 0822 when Fulmars shot down a Cant shadower in full view of the fleet. Unfortunately one of the attacking Fulmars was shot down in the encounter and crashed heavily leaving no survivors. Four Italians out of a crew of six were rescued from the Cant by FOXHOUND.

High Level Bombing Attack on the Fleet, a.m. 25th July (D.5).

99. At 1035 a large group of aircraft was detected bearing 080°, 69 miles closing. As the group continued to close fighters were ordered to an intercepting position 095°, 15 miles and at 1100 the first "Tally Ho" was received from the fighters. At 1103 another section of fighters got in touch and reported 8 high level bombers. A few minutes later the fighters also reported T/Bs.

100. The Fulmars attacked with great dash and bombs could be seen being jettisoned far away on the port quarter of the fleet between 1107 and 1110. Three S.79 high level bombers were shot down for certain, one was probably destroyed and two others were damaged.

101. In this encounter we lost two Fulmars. One crew was recovered unhurt by

NESTOR. The other aircraft was seen by SIKH to crash vertically into the sea at high velocity. There were no survivors. No further attacks were attempted by the enemy.

Movements of Various Units, p.m. 25th July (D.5).

I02. At I6I0 a signal was intercepted from FIREDRAKE giving her position, course and speed at I3I5 as 37° I0' N., 4° 00' E., 270°, 9 knots, proceeding under her own steam escorted by ERIDGE and AVON VALE. The latter had joined her after relief by WISHART as escort to MANCHESTER. FIREDRAKE's expected time of arrival at Gibraltar was I700/27.

I03. FORESTER was detached at I720 to proceed at her best speed to Gibraltar to land the wounded and other survivors from FEARLESS.

I04. As it now appeared that no ships would require fuel before arrival in harbour I requested Vice-Admiral Commanding, North Atlantic Station at I922 to recall BROWN RANGER who had been sailed, escorted by BEVERLEY, in case she should have been required.

Movements of Units, 26th July (D.6).

I05. MANCHESTER and Groups I and 2 of Convoy M.G.I arrived safely at Gibraltar at 0239, 0800 and I530 respectively.

I06. ARK ROYAL maintained an A/S patrol of 2 aircraft throughout the day.

Arrival at Gibraltar, 27th July (D.7).

I07. Ships of Group 3 of M.G.I arrived at Gibraltar at 02I5 and 09I5. The remaining ships of Forces H and X, including the damaged FIREDRAKE and her escort, arrived during the day. S.S. SVENOR (Group 4 of M.G.I) arrived at 0500 on 28th.

General.

I08. Outstanding points in this operation were:-

(*a*) *Effective work of Fulmars.* – The Fulmars of ARK ROYAL contributed in no small measure to the safe arrival of the convoy at its destination. On 23rd July formations of enemy aircraft were intercepted on three occasions. On the first occasion, two were shot down for certain and another two probably destroyed, whilst the survivors which reached the fleet were in no state to carry out an accurate attack. On the second occasion, as the Fulmars were about to intercept, the bombers released their bombs on the destroyer screen and immediately withdrew. Finally an attempted T/B attack was completely broken up and driven off, leaving two aircraft shot down with another damaged and possibly lost.

On 25th July the only enemy formations to approach the fleet were once again thoroughly routed. A force of torpedo bombers withdrew before the fighters could reach it and the only high level bombing attack was intercepted about 15 miles from the fleet, when four enemy planes were destroyed for certain with one probably destroyed and two more damaged. All bombs were jettisoned.

One Italian officer survivor stated he had been shot down by a Hurricane. It is evident that the enemy hold our Fleet Air Arm fighters in higher esteem than do our own Fulmar pilots.

(*b*) *Towing of FIREDRAKE by ERIDGE.* – Excellent seamanship and determination were displayed by ERIDGE whilst taking FIREDRAKE in tow in spite of difficulties caused by the latter's steering gear being out of action. The tow was maintained for 37 hours, during the whole of which period the ships were in close proximity to enemy air and surface ship bases and subjected to continuous air observation. The resolution and fine spirit displayed by both ships' companies was most creditable.

(*c*) *Prompt action and initiative displayed by NESTOR on two occasions.* – The successful avoiding action taken by the heavy ships at 2315/22 was only rendered possible by the prompt action taken, and quick and accurate report made, by NESTOR.

The initiative and resolution shown in bringing SYDNEY STAR safely into port after she had been torpedoed on the night of the 23rd/24th and stopped 4 miles from the enemy's base was a noteworthy achievement.

(*d*) *Work of the submarines.* – Information has not yet been received of the results obtained by the submarine patrols co-operating in this operation. There is good ground to believe that the marked inactivity of the Italian surface forces may have been due to the marked activity of our submarines.

(*e*) *Tactical and fighting efficiency.* – Although a great number of the ships taking part had not operated in company previously and some were newly commissioned, it was satisfactory to note the good standard of efficiency displayed. Nevertheless it must be appreciated that the highest standard cannot be achieved unless ships have opportunity to work together in company and to exercise the movements and action required to deal with the situations which arise during operations of this nature.

(*f*) *Behaviour of M.T. ships.* – The Rear-Admiral Commanding, 18th Cruiser Squadron reports "that the operation was successfully carried out is due in no small measure to the behaviour of the merchant ships in convoy. Their manoeuvring and general conduct was excellent and caused me no anxiety whatever. I had complete confidence that orders given to them by me would be understood and promptly carried out. Their steadfast and resolute behaviour during air and E-Boat attacks was most impressive and encouraging to us all. Particular credit is due to S.S. MELBOURNE STAR, Commodore of the convoy,[†] who set a high standard and never failed to appreciate directly what he should do. S.S. DURHAM experienced piston trouble in her port engine and it was evident that her engines required careful nursing. Nevertheless, she was able to maintain a speed of I4 knots throughout the critical period on D.3 and D.4, which was only I knot less than her accredited maximum speed."

I09. The Air Officer Commanding, Mediterranean and Officer Commanding, 200 Group, R.A.F. afforded most valuable air co-operation which contributed in no mean measure to the success of the operation.

II0. It was with considerable surprise that I learned on arrival at Gibraltar that a number of women and children had been embarked in the ships of Convoy M.G.I. Had I known this earlier, I should certainly have sent a destroyer to escort each group.

(Signed) J.F. SOMERVILLE,
Vice-Admiral,
Flag Officer Commanding,
Force H.

Admiralty footnotes:-

*On D.3 the Beaufighters sank an E-Boat and damaged an S 79, and on D.4 they shot down two JU.87s when covering the convoy.

The disappointing initial performance of the Beaufighters from Malta was due to shortage of equipment and to inexperience in co-operation with the Royal Navy. The Beaufighters rendered an important contribution to the safety of the convoy by operating over Sardinia, where they destroyed 52 enemy twin-engined aircraft on the ground and damaged a further 34.

†Commodore of Convoy "Substance" was the Master of S.S. MELBOURNE STAR, Captain D.R. MacFarlane.

OPERATION "HALBERD"

The following Despatch was submitted to the Lords Commissioners of the Admiralty on the 9th October, *I94I* by Vice-Admiral Sir James F. Somerville, K.C.B., D.S.O., Flag Officer Commanding, Force H.

n early engagement in the sea war in the Mediterranean was the Battle of Cape
pada. On 19 July 1940, a combined Australian and British Naval Squadron, patrolling
he Aegean and commanded by Captain John Collins in the light cruiser HMAS
ydney, encountered two Italian cruisers, *Giovanni delle Banda Nere* and *Bartolomeo
olleoni*. Here *Bartolomeo Colleoni*, viewed from one of the British destroyers, is
urrounded by incoming shells. (HMP)

As the rearmost of
the two Italians
cruisers, *Bartolomeo
Colleoni* was hit
hardest of the
Italian warships.
So hard in fact that
she was battered to
a standstill, with
her bows blown
off, damage clearly
visible in this
image. (HMP)

This image is another view of *Bartolomeo Colleoni*, unable to manoeuvre, burning fiercely, her bows having fallen away into the water. The two Italian cruisers had been on route from Tripoli to Leros, at that time an Italian colony in the Dodecanese Islands (HMP)

The original caption to this photograph, another from a series detailing the events of the Battle of Cape Spada, simply states: "The torpedo that finished her off." Taken from HMS *Hyperion*, it is therefore likely to show the torpedo which, fired at close quarters, finally caused *Bartolomeo Colleoni* to sink at 09.59 hours. (HMP)

The *Regia Aeronautica Italiana* also made its presence felt in the Battle of Cape Spada. Ironically, the Italian bombers singled out the destroyer HMS *Havock* for particular attention – at the very moment it was trying to pull survivors from the Italian cruiser *Bartolomeo Colleoni* from the water. This photograph is believed to have been taken from HMS *Havock*. (HMP)

In the early hours on 12 October 1940, the British light cruiser HMS *Ajax* fought an Italian force of torpedo boats and destroyers south-east of Sicily in what is known as the Battle of Cape Passero. This image shows *Ajax*'s shells hitting the Italian destroyer *Artigliere*. (HMP)

The torpedo fired by *Artigliere* at *Ajax* during the Battle of Cape Passero missed, but four rounds struck two of *Ajax*'s secondary gun turrets and disabled her radar. This shot shows the crippled *Artigliere* lying still in the water prior to *Ajax* breaking off the engagement. (HMP)

The disabled *Artigliere* was attacked by HMS *York*. This is the moment when, at 09.05 hours on the morning of 12 October 1940, *Artigliere*'s stern ammunition magazines exploded after the torpedo fired by HMS *York* struck. (HMP)

The aftermath of the first ever major victory for naval air power in the world. This vertical photographic reconnaissance image of the sunken and disabled Italian warships in the inner harbour (Mar Piccolo) at Taranto was taken on the morning following the attack. It is one of a series of photographs of the naval base taken by the Commanding Officer of No.431 Flight RAF, flying from Luqa, Malta. (Fleet Air Arm Museum)

On 25 November 1941, while en route with HMS *Queen Elizabeth* and HMS *Valiant* to cover an attack on Italian convoys, HMS *Barham* was hit by three torpedoes. Fired by *U-331*, from a range of only 750 yards, *Barham* had little or no time for evasive action. The explosion was caught on camera by Gaumont News cameraman John Turner, who was on the deck of the nearby *Valiant*. (HMP)

As HMS *Barham* rolled over to port, her magazines exploded and the battleship quickly sank with the loss of over two thirds of her crew. A Royal Navy Court of Enquiry into the sinking ascribed the ship's final magazine explosion to the detonation *en masse* of 4-inch anti-aircraft ammunition stored in wing passages adjacent to the main magazines, which would have detonated the contents of the main magazines. (HMP)

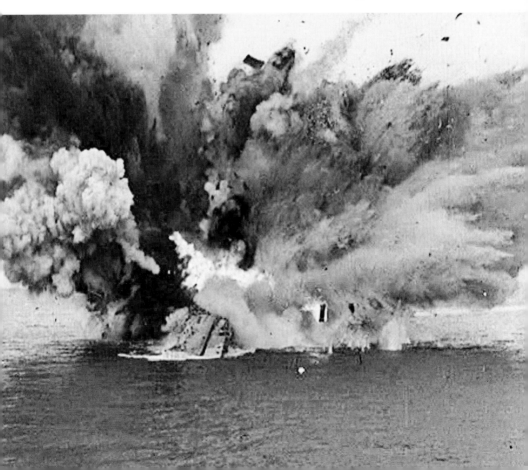

On 27 May 1942, the Type 2 Hunt Class Destroyer HMS *Eridge* was one of three destroyers (the other two being HMS *Hero* and HMS *Hurworth*), from the escort screen of Convoy AT.47, that engaged a German U-boat in the Mediterranean off Tobruk. (HMP)

The captain of *U-568*, *Kapitänleutnant* Joachim Preuss, on surfacing for the second time finally ordered the submarine, be scuttled. In this way the whole crew of forty-seven survived and was subsequently picked up by the three Royal Navy destroyers. In this photograph, some of these survivors can be seen on board HMS *Eridge*. (HMP)

Only a few months after the sinking of *U-568*, on 29 August 1942, HMS *Eridge* would find herself in trouble. Whilst carrying out a bombardment in support of the Eighth Army she was attacked and torpedoed by German E-boats. The damage was extensive, and in this picture *Eridge* can be seen taking water and listing. (HMP)

the month of July 1941 drew to close, a convoy consisting of six fast merchant ships
d their escorts sailed from Gibraltar. Under the code-name Operation *Substance*, the
ips' destination was the besieged island of Malta. One Royal Navy loss during
bstance was the E-class destroyer HMS *Fearless*. On 23 July, whilst screening HMS
k Royal, *Fearless* was torpedoed and heavily damaged by an Italian aircraft. The
ioke rising in the background of this image is from the stricken *Fearless*. (HMP)

The aircraft carrier HMS *Illustrious* under attack sixty miles west of Malta, 10 January 1941. This image is one of a series believed to have been taken by a crewman onboard the escorting battleship HMS *Warspite*. Showing the *Luftwaffe* bombing at its peak, the "wall of water" so vividly recalled by many veterans of Convoy MC4, can clearly be seen. (HMP)

HMS *Eagle* was originally laid down in 1913 as a battleship for the Chilean Navy. But, on 28 February 1918, the hull was purchased by the Admiralty and converted for use as an aircraft carrier. During Operation *Pedestal*, on 11 August 1942, she was hit by four torpedoes fired by the German submarine *U-73*. On fire, and rolling over on to her port side (as evident in this image), she sank in just eight minutes south of the islands of Majorca. A total of 131 officers and men, mainly from the ship's machinery spaces, were lost in the sinking. Sixteen Sea Hurricanes were lost; four from 801 Naval Air Squadron were aloft when the ship was torpedoed, and landed on other carriers. (HMP)

A photograph taken from the aft end of HMS *Victorious'* flight deck showing HMS *Indomitable* and HMS *Eagle* during the early stages of Operation *Pedestal*. A Hawker Sea Hurricane and a Fairey Albacore are ranged on *Victorious'* flight deck. (Imperial War Museum; A11293)

The ships of Operation *Pedestal* under attack on 12 August 1942. Here a bomb explodes astern of HMS *Glenorchy* which was sunk, along with *Empire Hope*, by air attack the following day. (Imperial War Museum; A11171)

In some respects, this is the moment that the siege of Malta in the Second World War is lifted – and at the very least the start of that process. The tanker *Ohio* limps into the Grand Harbour, Malta. Note how low she is lying in the water. She was welcomed by cheering crowds and even a band playing *Rule Britannia*! Not for nothing is the *Ohio* often referred to as "the tanker that refused to die". For his role in seeing the tanker through to Malta, the Master of the Ohio, Captain Dudley William Mason was awarded the George Cross. He was the first merchant seaman to ever receive this gallantry award. (Imperial War Museum; GM1480)

On 13 November 1941, the aircraft carrier HMS *Ark Royal* was torpedoed by *U-81* east of Gibraltar. Gradually, *Ark Royal* began to flood, taking on a list which progressively increased. The list reached 20 degrees some eleven hours and four minutes after the torpedo hit. The angle touched 27 degrees an hour and a quarter later. At this point, the abandon ship order was given. All crew were off the ship at 04.30 hours – twelve hours and nineteen minutes after the hit. At this time the list had reached 35 degrees. *Ark Royal* finally rolled on to her beam ends, paused for about three minutes, before turning right over. She then appeared to break in two, with the aft section sinking first, followed by the bow, all in the space of a couple of minutes. All but one of the crew survived the torpedoing and sinking. (HMP)

The British cruisers HMS *Cleopatra* (making smoke) and HMS *Euryalus* (foreground, elevating her forward 5.25 inch guns) prepare to engage Italian warships whilst protecting a Malta-bound convoy, 22 March 1942. (Imperial War Museum; A8166)

H.M.S. RODNEY.

9th October, 1941.

REPORT ON OPERATION "HALBERD"

Be pleased to lay before Their Lordships the following report on Operation "Halberd". The preliminary discussions, arrangements and movements in connection with the operation, which was designed to secure the passage of H.M.S. BRECONSHIRE* and 8 M.T. ships to Malta, have been dealt with in previous reports of proceedings. This report deals with the period from I800A on 24th September (D. -I) until the completion of the operation.

Situation at I800A on 24th September (D. -I).

2. The situation at I800 on 24th September was as follows:-

(*a*) Convoy W.S.IIX, consisting of H.M. Ships BRECONSHIRE (Commodore), QUEEN EMMA, PRINCESS BEATRIX, ULSTER MONARCH, ROYAL SCOTSMAN, and S.S. IMPERIAL STAR (Vice-Commodore), ROWALLAN CASTLE (Rear-Commodore), CLAN MACDONALD, CLAN FERGUSON, AJAX, LEINSTER, CITY OF LINCOLN, DUNEDIN STAR and CITY OF CALCUTTA, with PRINCE OF WALES (Vice-Admiral, 2nd-in-Command, Home Fleet), EDINBURGH (Rear-Admiral Commanding, I8th Cruiser Squadron), KENYA (Rear-Admiral Commanding, I0th Cruiser Squadron),** EURYALUS, SHEFFIELD, and the destroyers LAFOREY (Captain (D), I9th Destroyer Flotilla), LIGHTNING, ORIBI, COSSACK (Captain (D), 4th Destroyer Flotilla), FURY, FARNDALE and HEYTHROP in company, were to the westward of the Straits of Gibraltar, steering east, to pass south of Europa Point at 0I30A on 25th September.

(*b*) At Gibraltar:- NELSON, RODNEY, ARK ROYAL, HERMIONE, the destroyers ISAAC SWEERS, PIORUN, GARLAND, DUNCAN (Captain (D), I3th Destroyer Flotilla), FORESIGHT, FORESTER, LIVELY, LEGION and the oiler BROWN RANGER with her escort FLEUR DE LYS.

(*c*) Approaching Gibraltar Bay from the westward:- ZULU, GURKHA and LANCE.

3. NELSON, screened by ISAAC SWEERS, PIORUN and GARLAND, sailed to the westward at I8I5. The Flag of the Flag Officer Commanding, Force H, had been

hoisted in RODNEY as a ruse to give the impression that NELSON, on relief by RODNEY, was sailing to the westward for the United Kingdom. Farewell messages were passed between NELSON and RODNEY to assist the deception. This, ruse appears to have created the desired impression.

4. After NELSON had cleared the entrance, GURKHA, ZULU and LANCE, who had been detached by the Vice-Admiral, 2nd-in-Command, Home Fleet to proceed ahead of the convoy to fuel at Gibraltar, entered harbour.

Movements of Forces on the Night 24th/25th September (D. -I/D I).

5. NELSON with her screen proceeded to the westward until 2130, when course was reversed to 090°. After passing south of Tarifa at 1930, several small fishing vessels with bright lights were encountered.

6. BROWN RANGER, escorted by FLEUR DE LYS, sailed from Gibraltar to the eastward at 2030, so as to be in position for oiling destroyers on D.2.

7. RODNEY, ARK ROYAL, HERMIONE, DUNCAN (Captain (D), 13th Destroyer Flotilla), FORESIGHT, FORESTER, LIVELY, ZULU, GURKHA, LEGION and LANCE sailed from Gibraltar at 2300 to simulate a normal sortie of Force H and to rendezvous with the convoy at 0800 the following morning.

8. Force Z, consisting of QUEEN EMMA, PRINCESS BEATRIX, ULSTER MONARCH, ROYAL SCOTSMAN (whose ultimate destination was Freetown) and LEINSTER, escorted by JONQUIL, SPIREA and AZALEA, had been stationed astern of the main convoy at dusk and ordered to proceed into Gibraltar Bay. It was hoped that the presence of these ships in the Bay would allay suspicion, in the event of the convoy having been sighted and reported whilst passing through the Straits.

9. The remainder of Convoy W.S.IIX and escort, organised in two groups one mile apart, and led by the Vice-Admiral, 2nd-in-Command, Home Fleet in PRINCE OF WALES, and the Rear-Admiral Commanding, 18th Cruiser Squadron in EDINBURGH respectively, passed south of Europa Point at 0130.

This disposition was adopted to reduce the frontage of the convoy during its passage through the Straits.

10. At 0730 RODNEY, ARK ROYAL and their screening destroyers were sighted from NELSON at about 10 miles, the limit of visibility at that time. Half an hour later the convoy and its escort were sighted, a few minutes after a Hudson aircraft which was carrying out an A/S patrol had reported them in sight to the westward.

11. NELSON shaped an easterly course while exchanges of destroyers took place in accordance with HAL (short title for Operation Orders), paragraph 21. These exchanges were designed so that destroyers required to accompany the heavy ships after parting company from the convoy on D.3 should be used to screen the convoy on D.I and D.2 and thus economise fuel.

12. The forces then formed two groups, as follows:-

Group I.

NELSON (Flag Officer Commanding, Force H), ARK ROYAL, HERMIONE, COSSACK (Captain (D), 4th Destroyer Flotilla), ZULU, FORESIGHT, FORESTER, LAFOREY (Captain (D), I9th Destroyer Flotilla), and LIGHTNING.

Group II.

PRINCE OF WALES (Vice-Admiral, 2nd-in-Command, Home Fleet), RODNEY, KENYA (Rear-Admiral Commanding, I0th Cruiser Squadron), EDINBURGH (Rear-Admiral Commanding, I8th Cruiser Squadron), SHEFFIELD, EURYALUS, DUNCAN (Captain (D), I3th Destroyer Flotilla), GURKHA, LEGION, LANCE, LIVELY, ORIBI, ISAAC SWEERS, PIORUN, GARLAND, FURY, FARNDALE and HEYTHROP, and the convoy, H.M.S. BRECONSHIRE, CLAN MACDONALD, CLAN FERGUSON, AJAX, IMPERIAL STAR, CITY OF LINCOLN, ROWALLAN CASTLE, DUNEDIN STAR and CITY OF CALCUTTA.

I3. While in V/S touch, Vice-Admiral, 2nd-in-Command, Home Fleet reported that the convoy might have been sighted by a Portuguese merchant ship west of Cape Spartel, but that only fishing boats were seen in the Straits. SHEFFIELD reported that the convoy had not been sighted either by surface vessels or aircraft, whilst in company with her.

Movements of Group I on 25th September (D.I).

I4. In order to give the impression to any shadowing aircraft approaching from the eastward that only the usual Force H was at sea, Group I parted company with Group II, and proceeded to the eastward at I8 knots, with the intention of keeping along the African coast.

I5. Clocks were advanced I hour to Zone -2 at I000A/25 and hereafter times are Zone -2.

I6. ARK ROYAL maintained one A/S patrol aircraft in the air from II05 until dusk. During the day 24 out of the 27 Fulmars carried were flown for exercise, two providing targets for a height-finding exercise. Six Fulmars flew round both groups for recognition purposes.

I7. FLEUR DE LYS and BROWN RANGER were sighted at III5. FLEUR DE LYS reported speed made good was II knots, and she was ordered to make good I2½ knots. It was ascertained after return to harbour that BROWN RANGER intended to convey she was unable to make good more than II knots, due apparently to a foul bottom. This was not appreciated at the time the signal was received.

I8. At I700, when in position 36° 36' N., 0I° 58' W., DUNCAN, in position N in Screening Diagram No. I0, [*Diagrams not published*] obtained a contact bearing I20°, 1,500 yards. She attacked with four charges, the starboard thrower failing to fire. GURKHA co-operated and attacked with a fourteen-charge pattern at I7I6. At I750

DUNCAN fired a second pattern. No further contacts were obtained, and both ships proceeded at 1758 to rejoin the screen. Both ships observed bubbles rising to the surface, possibly from a damaged U-Boat, after DUNCAN's first attack.

Two French merchant ships, MERS EL KEBIR and SIDI ORSA, were sighted about 1800. Several other unidentified ships were reported by aircraft, but did not come in sight of Group I.

Movements of Group II on 25th September (D.I).

19. Group II continued along the track ordered without incident. This track lay to the south of the Balearics through an area which experience suggested was reasonably clear of merchant ships and civil aircraft.

Movements of Group I on 26th September (D.2).

20. One A/S patrol aircraft and 3 or 4 fighters were maintained in the air from daylight until dusk. Speed was reduced to 17 knots at 0920.

21. At 0932 air look-outs in NELSON sighted a shadowing aircraft (probably Cant 506), bearing 150°, 10 miles, and flying very low. This machine was not detected by R.D.F.

Owing to a complete failure of R/T in the fighter leader's aircraft delay occurred in vectoring the fighters, and no interception took place.

22. A Swiss merchant ship, S.S. TUNISIAN, was sighted at 1048.

23. Group I reversed course at 1300, in order to close the distance on Group II. HERMIONE was stationed astern for R.D.F. purposes, and to give A.A. protection to ARK ROYAL.

24. At 1537 two aircraft were sighted low down to the eastward by ZULU, NELSON and HERMIONE. ZULU reported them as probably S.79s, but they appeared to be showing I.F.F.[†] and were thought to be Hudsons by the other two sighting ships and fighters were not vectored. This was an error on my part since there was no information of Hudsons being on passage from Malta to Gibraltar, and the slight I.F.F. reported might well have been due to the proximity of aircraft to one another.

25. To avoid altering course to the eastward before dark, Group I turned to 225° at 1745, paravanes were streamed at 1835, and at dusk a further turn was made to 090°. HERMIONE rejoined the screen for the night.

26. R.D.F. reports at 2030 indicated an aircraft passed 5 miles to starboard of Group I.

A ship burning navigation lights was sighted at 2135, steering 140°. Course was altered to port to avoid.

27. After dark, T.S.R.[‡] aircraft in ARK ROYAL were drained down in order to reduce fire risks during the anticipated enemy air attacks on D.3.

Movements of Group II on 26th September (D.2).

28. Group II proceeded to the north-east until 0700, then to the eastward, and altered course to I07° on passing through 38° 3I' N., 02° 32' E. at noon.

29. The first two destroyers were detached to oil at 0650. Delay occurred owing to BROWN RANGER being 22 miles west of the position ordered and on the quarter of the convoy instead of on the bow. This was due to the unexpected reduction in BROWN RANGER's speed referred to in paragraph I7.

30. During the afternoon an aircraft with Spanish colours and the letters FARM along the fuselage appeared out of the clouds over the destroyer screen and then disappeared in clouds. No other aircraft was sighted or detected. There is reason to believe that this aircraft, or its passengers, reported the presence of the convoy. A merchant ship wearing French colours was passed at I830.

3I. Oiling of the I2 destroyers in company was not completed until dusk. FURY and HEYTHROP rejoined after dark; ORIBI failed to find Group II in the dark and joined up with Group I screen until daylight.

Convoy M.G.2§ – Departure of First Ship from Malta.

32. A signal was received from the Vice-Admiral, Malta at II4I, stating that a few Army and R.A.F. personnel with their wives had been embarked in the three ships of M.G.2 at their own risk, and at the request of H.E. the Governor of Malta. I feel that I should have been consulted about this, since a moral obligation arose to give these ships some degree of close protection. It was my intention, however, not to depart substantially from the priorities laid down by the Admiralty for Operation "Substance", *viz.,* that the safe return of the escorting forces was of more importance than the safe arrival of empty shipping.

33. S.S. MELBOURNE STAR sailed from Malta at noon on 26th September.

Movements, a.m. 27th September (D.3).

34. Group I, which had been steering east during the night, reversed course to 290° at 07I0, sighting Group II right ahead ten minutes later. ARK ROYAL with EURYALUS ahead and HERMIONE astern as close escort operated as requisite for flying off and on inside the screen.

35. The Rear-Admiral Commanding, I0th Cruiser Squadron took charge of the convoy proper and the whole force continued on an easterly course.

36. Four Fulmars were flown off at 0800. This number was increased to ten at I000, to twelve at II00 and again to sixteen at noon, when air attack was expected to follow reports made by enemy shadowers.

37. Indications by R.D.F. suggested that enemy reconnaissance aircraft were in the vicinity of the fleet from 0720, but the first report made by enemy aircraft was not intercepted until 08I0. A second report was intercepted at I056.

A few minutes earlier fighters had been vectored to the southward on an R.D.F. report, but there was some delay due to atmospheric interference with R/T and no contact was made.

38. R.D.F. detected a single aircraft bearing 210°, distant 14 miles at 1158 and two minutes later it was reported by LEGION as a B.R.20. Fighters made contact, but the enemy escaped in cloud. An enemy report was subsequently intercepted, which had probably been made by this aircraft.

Admiralty footnotes:-
*H.M.S. BRECONSHIRE – Ammunition and Store Carrier.
**Commodore of Convoy – Captain C.A.G. Hutchinson, R.N.(Retd).
Vice-Commodore of Convoy – R. Miller (Master).
Rear-Commodore of Convoy – C. Harvey (Master).
Vice-Admiral, 2nd-in-Command, Home Fleet – Vice-Admiral A.T.B. Curteis, C.B.
Rear-Admiral Commanding, 18th Cruiser Squadron – Rear-Admiral E.N. Syfret.
Rear-Admiral Commanding, 10th Cruiser Squadron – Rear-Admiral H.M. Burrough, C.B.
† I.F.F. – a recognition device to identify own craft.
‡ T.S.R. – Torpedo/Spotter/Reconnaissance.
§Convoy M.G.2 – a Malta to Gibraltar convoy.

Air Attacks on the Fleet, p.m. 27th September (D.3).

(a) First Attack (1255–1310).

39. R.D.F. reports at 1255 indicated that two formations were approaching the fleet, one from the north and one from the east, both 30 miles distant. These formations were reported as diving.

Fighters were vectored towards the formations, but as they made contact with the enemy, R.D.F. plots became too confused to be used for fighter direction. One enemy T/B (probably Cant 1007) was shot down by Fulmars at 1300.

40. Six T/Bs (B.R.20) approached from the port bow and beam, and were engaged by the port wing of the screen and the ships on the port side of the fleet. Two T/B aircraft were shot down at 1302, probably by barrage fire from RODNEY and PRINCE OF WALES.

41. An unknown number of torpedoes was dropped about 5,000 yards on the port beam of the convoy, which altered course to 040°at 1304, turning to 075° three minutes later.

Three of the six attackers tried to approach over the port wing of the screen, but unable to face the barrage put up by the destroyers they dropped their torpedoes at the port wing ship, LANCE, who had considerable difficulty in avoiding them, two torpedoes passing very close. The torpedoes were released from about 300feet height, and appeared to take up their depth very quickly, the tracks showing up plainly. ISAAC SWEERS, next in the screen to LANCE, reported one torpedo passed within 30 yards; RODNEY was swung 60° to port to avoid a torpedo which passed 100 yards to starboard.

42. One of these three aircraft was shot down by the destroyers, and crashed in

flames close to LIVELY. Another T/B aircraft was shot down by fighters north of the fleet at about this time.

43. At 1310, a Fulmar which had been among the fighters sent to intercept this attack and which was probably returning damaged from a combat with enemy fighters (C.R.42s), was shot down by barrage fire from PRINCE OF WALES, and the crew were killed. This unfortunate accident occurred through a phonetic misunderstanding between the A.D.P.* and Group Control Officer, and is deeply regretted.

44. On this occasion, and again twenty minutes later when another Fulmar was shot down, both fighters approached low down straight towards the convoy during a T/B attack, and appeared menacing. The considerable amount of smoke from bursting shell added to the difficulties of identification.

45. Three heavy underwater explosions were heard at 1312; these were probably torpedoes exploding at the end of their run.

46. *Result of First Attack.* – The enemy had lost 5 out of the 12 T/Bs which were subsequently reported by Fulmars to have approached in this attack; several others were probably damaged. No ships had been hit, but one Fulmar had been accidentally shot down by the fleet.

(b) *Second Attack* (1327-1337).

47. A group of aircraft splitting into two formations was reported by R.D.F. closing from the eastward at 1327. Destroyers on the starboard wing of the screen opened fire at 1329, when 6 or 7 T/Bs (B.R.20) were seen approaching very low from the starboard bow and beam.

48. Three of the aircraft pressed on through the barrage of the starboard wing destroyers, and carried out a most determined attack on NELSON, who was swinging to starboard to comb the tracks. One aircraft dropped its torpedo about 450 yards 20° on NELSON's starboard bow, passing over the ship at about 200 feet height. This aircraft was almost certainly shot down astern of NELSON by SHEFFIELD and PRINCE OF WALES.

49. The track of the torpedo was not seen until about 150 yards dead ahead of the ship, which had been steadied on a course which proved to be the exact reciprocal of the torpedo. No avoiding action was possible and a second or two after the bubbles disappeared from sight there was a large "crump," the ship whipped considerably and a column of water rose approximately 15-20 feet above the forecastle deck port side. The torpedo had hit on the port bow abreast 60 station, 10 feet below the water-line. NELSON's speed was reduced to 18 knots, pending a report on the damage sustained.

50. A few seconds later another T/B of this formation dropped a torpedo from about 500 feet 1,000 yards fine on the starboard bow of NELSON. This torpedo passed about 100 yards to starboard. The third of this enemy formation was shot down by destroyers just ahead of the screen at 1333. This aircraft was claimed by LAFOREY. FORESTER picked up the W/T operator, the only member of the crew alive. He had a badly broken leg.

5I. Meanwhile, 3 or 4 T/Bs who had split up from this group attacked from the starboard quarter without result.

52. One enemy T/B was shot down by fighters, on the port quarter of the convoy at I336.

A Fulmar was unfortunately shot down by RODNEY's pom-pom, but the crew were rescued by DUNCAN.

53. *Result of Second Attack.* – Three enemy T/Bs out of the 6 or 7 who attacked were shot down. NELSON's speed was reduced by a torpedo hit, but the gun armament remained unimpaired. One Fulmar was shot down but the crew were saved.

(c) *Third Attack* (I345-I405).

54. Six minutes after the end of the second attack, R.D.F. reported a group closing from the S.E. and diving. At I345 a formation of I0 or II S.79s were sighted very low about I0 miles to the southward. These split up into two groups when they came under fire from the escorting ships on the starboard side of the convoy, and 7 or 8 retired to the southwest and disappeared. Three others tried to work round the starboard bow, and the convoy was turned away 60° to port. These aircraft were turned away by the gunfire of the screening destroyers, having dropped their torpedoes well outside the screen. One torpedo narrowly missed LIGHTNING, but they dropped at too great a range to be a danger to the convoy. One of these aircraft was shot down by fighters as it retired.

55. Of the 7 or 8 aircraft who turned away when first fired at, 3 returned from astern of the convoy at I354, two of which retired again on being fired at. The third pressed on to attack ARK ROYAL, but was shot down by the combined fire of that ship and NELSON, while still I,000 yards from ARK ROYAL and before he had dropped a torpedo.

56. At I358 one aircraft, seen right ahead of NELSON, dropped a torpedo outside the screen. COSSACK was able to avoid this torpedo by the warning given by hydrophone effect on her A/S set.

57. At this time (I359) one C.R.42 was seen to be diving on the starboard wing destroyers, and performing aerobatics over them, evidently to make a diversion for the T/Bs. In so far as the destroyers expended a large amount of ammunition he succeeded, but after six minutes was either shot down or failed to pull out from a dive. None of the destroyers reported being machine-gunned.

58. *Result of Third Attack.* – Two more enemy T/Bs and one C.R.42 fighter were shot down, and no further damage inflicted on H.M. Ships or convoy.

It was most noticeable that this attack was not pressed home with the same determination as the first two attacks. Of the I0 or II S.79s which originally approached, only four fired torpedoes, and these were dropped at too great a distance to endanger the convoy. The only aircraft of this group to close within effective range was destroyed before its torpedo was dropped.

59. No further actual attacks developed before dark, though on several occasions R.D.F. indicated that enemy aircraft were closing the fleet. Generally by the time they were within I5 miles of the fleet, R.D.F. reported our fighters among them and they were driven off.

An attack threatened from the port bow at I409 and the convoy made an emergency turn towards to 060° but as no attack developed course 096° was resumed a few minutes later.

General Remarks on Day Attacks.

60. So far as can be ascertained 30 T/B aircraft attempted to attack, but not more than I8 came within torpedo range.

Aircraft Destroyed:

6 T/Bs and I fighter certainly destroyed by gunfire.
4 T/Bs and I shadower certainly destroyed by fighters.
I T/B probably destroyed (cause unknown).
Total: Certain I0 T/Bs, I fighter, I Cant 506 float plane.

We lost 3 Fulmars, two crews being saved.
One torpedo hit was inflicted on NELSON.
6I. H.L.B.** attacks had been expected, synchronised with T/B attacks, but none developed at the time and no bombs were dropped.

Attempt to Intercept Enemy Battle fleet, p.m. 27th September (D.3).

62. Reports of air reconnaissance from Malta carried out on D.2 (26th September), indicated that main units of the Italian fleet were located as follows:-

Taranto – I Cavour in floating dock,
    2 Littorios and I Cavour,
    6 Cruisers,
    5 Destroyers.

Naples – 2 Cavours,
    I Cruiser,
    I2 Destroyers or Torpedo-Boats.

Messina – Bolzano.

Palermo – Nil.

63. While the third T/B attack was still in progress at I404, an emergency report was re-received from aircraft B (R.A.F. Malta) of 2 battleships and 8 destroyers in position 38° 20' N., I0° 40' E., steering I90° at 20 knots at I340.

64. NELSON's position when this report was received was 37° 46' N., 09° 04' E.; the enemy unit was therefore 74 miles, 076° from NELSON assuming it had

continued at the same course and speed. At this time NELSON, with gun armament unimpaired, was thought to be capable of 18 knots or possibly more.

65. My appreciation of the enemy's intentions was that either he did not realise I had more than one battleship with the convoy and that he would attempt to intercept the convoy near the western entrance to the Skerki Channel, or that he wished to draw away my escorting force to the north-eastwards, thus leaving the convoy open to attack by light surface forces in the Skerki Channel at dusk.

66. I therefore decided:-

(i) To proceed towards the enemy at best speed with NELSON, PRINCE OF WALES, RODNEY and 6 destroyers, leaving KENYA, EDINBURGH, SHEFFIELD and 10 destroyers with the convoy; ARK ROYAL escorted by EURYALUS, HERMIONE, PIORUN and LEGION to continue operating in the vicinity of the convoy.

(ii) To fly off two Swordfish from ARK ROYAL to take over shadowing duties and keep the enemy under observation until the striking force could attack.

(iii) To fuel, arm, range and fly off an air striking force as soon as possible.

67. These dispositions would place the battleships between the enemy and the convoy and enable the enemy to be brought to action should he persist in attempting to intercept the convoy.

68. At 1408 I ordered ARK ROYAL to prepare an air striking force. This involved a delay of at least an hour before the striking force could be flown off since as stated previously the Swordfish had been drained of fuel to reduce fire risks during air attacks. Two minutes later I ordered ARK ROYAL to fly off two shadowers and at 1427 to fly off the striking force as soon as ready. The shadowers took off at 1448, being delayed by ARK ROYAL's main armament being in action and two Fulmars having to land on short of fuel.

69. At 1425 a further signal (timed 1350) was received from aircraft B reporting 4 cruisers and 8 destroyers some 15 miles W.S.W. of the enemy battlefleet and steering the same course and speed. Ten minutes later a signal was received (timed 1425) that the total enemy force consisted of 2 battleships, 4 cruisers and 16 destroyers.

70. Meanwhile the battleships had been ordered at 1417 to form on NELSON who had increased speed to proceed ahead of the convoy. At 1433, however, it became necessary for NELSON to reduce to 15 knots to avoid further flooding due to the damage sustained.

71. I therefore modified my previous instructions, informed Vice-Admiral, 2nd-in-Command, Home Fleet that NELSON's speed was reduced to 15 knots and ordered him to proceed with PRINCE OF WALES, RODNEY, EDINBURGH, SHEFFIELD and 6 destroyers at best speed to close and drive off the enemy. The cruisers were ordered to rejoin the convoy before dark if possible. NELSON took station astern of the convoy, as she was becoming sluggish under helm.

72. While these instructions were in transit, a signal from aircraft (timed 1445 and

received at 1506) reported that the enemy fleet had reversed course to 360°. This was followed by a further signal (timed 1503 and received at 1543) that the enemy was steering 060°. A report was also received from Vice-Admiral, Malta, that the two enemy battleships were Littorio class and not Cavours as was originally believed.

73. It was now clear that the enemy intended to avoid contact. I still hoped, however, that the air striking force might be able to materially reduce his speed and allow the Vice-Admiral, 2nd-in-Command, Home Fleet to overtake him before dark.

74. At 1445 an aircraft was seen to fall in flames on the starboard quarter of the fleet. As no combat took place at that time, this must have been one damaged earlier in the action, probably by fighters.

A Fulmar, short of petrol, force-landed astern of ARK ROYAL at 1530. The crew was picked up by PIORUN.

75. About 1525, while ARK ROYAL was ranging her torpedo striking force, she sighted 4 S.79s pass right over the fleet at 17,000 feet, but could not engage because of her aircraft on deck. COSSACK reported them as dive bombers, but they were thought later to be Fulmars and were not engaged. No attack was made by these aircraft. The striking force of 12 Swordfish escorted by 4 Fulmars took departure at 1540.

76. Between 1620 and 1645, Fulmars drove off an attack threatening from the port side of the convoy, and at the later time another section of Fulmars shot down a shadower 10 miles astern.

77. By 1650 there had been no sighting reports from the shadowing aircraft which had taken departure two hours earlier. The last report made by R.A.F. aircraft was timed 1503 and "no change reports" had not been received.

78. With the position of the enemy force in doubt, and since available evidence suggested he was probably retiring at speed to the northeast, I signalled to Vice-Admiral, 2nd-in- Command, Home Fleet at 1658 to rejoin. My appreciation at this time was that even if the striking force succeeded in reducing the speed of the enemy radically it would not be possible for Vice-Admiral, 2nd-in-Command, Home Fleet to make contact until after dark and consequently a successful issue was highly problematical. On the other hand it was essential for the cruisers to return to the convoy before dark, and the destroyers were also required to furnish a screen for NELSON and ARK ROYAL. Any further reduction of Force X destroyers for this purpose was, in my opinion, unacceptable.

Movements of the Force under Vice-Admiral, 2nd-in-Command, Home Fleet while Detached.

79. Vice-Admiral, 2nd-in-Command, Home Fleet's appreciation at 1530 was that it was possible for the enemy:-

(*a*) To continue on his course;

(*b*) To attempt to cut in to the eastward between Marittimo and Skerki Bank, with a view to attacking the convoy under the cover of darkness;

(*c*) To draw the British force northwards in order to cut in to the westward and attack the convoy from rear.

80. Vice-Admiral, 2nd-in-Command, Home Fleet decided to try and close the passage between Skerki and Marittimo, while keeping well placed to fall back on the convoy. Course 080° was therefore set to pass north of Skerki Bank.

81. When recalled at 1659, Vice-Admiral, 2nd-in-Command, Home Fleet was just reaching a position from which he considered a movement either to the eastward or westward feasible without fear of the enemy achieving his object.

82. The air striking force reported to ARK ROYAL at 1740 that they were unable to find the enemy, and I ordered ARK ROYAL to recall them. The cause of this failure to locate the enemy is explained in paragraph 97.

83. At 1800 Vice-Admiral, 2nd-in-Command, Home Fleet's force came in sight to the north-eastward. Two formations of enemy aircraft were detected by R.D.F. at 1820, but they did not approach nearer than 24 miles.

Detachment of Force X.

84. Force A, consisting of the battleships and carrier, with destroyer screen, parted company from the convoy and Force X (cruisers and destroyers) at 1855 on reaching the entrance to the Skerki Channel.

Force A turned to 285°, while Force X and the convoy continued to the eastward under the command of the Rear-Admiral Commanding, 10th Cruiser Squadron.

85. Between 1915 and 1930 some enemy aircraft approached the convoy, but twice turned away when fire was opened. They were probably C.R.42 fighters.

86. Course was altered to 156° at 1915 for flying-on, course 285° being resumed at 1930.

Flying Operations from ARK ROYAL, p.m. 27th September (D.3).

87. At 1200, 16 Fulmars were in the air. It was necessary to land on 4 at 1230, but the number in the air was increased to 15 between 1315 and 1330 when T/B attacks were in progress.

88. At about 1250, one fighter section was vectored to the north of the fleet towards a suspected shadower. They made contact with 12 T/B aircraft (B.R.20 and Cant 1007B) and three more fighter sections were sent to assist.

In the ensuing fight at sea-level, one T/B was shot down, and three others were engaged. An escort of 6 C.R.42 fighters flying at 7,000 feet did not interfere.

One Fulmar section encountered a number of C.R.42s in the clouds, and ARK ROYAL reports that one Fulmar of this section is presumed to have fallen to the enemy fighters. Later information indicates that this Fulmar was probably damaged by the C.R.42s and whilst attempting to reach the protection of the fleet, was shot down by gunfire from the ships (*vide* paragraph 43).

89. Seven Fulmars were flown off at 1315. The wind was very light from the west and flying-off was carried out down wind, to avoid ARK ROYAL becoming detached. Six out of eight fighters already in the air landed on.

90. Fighters were sent to intercept a raid coming from the south-eastward, and one B.R.20 was shot down.

During the subsequent attack, one Fulmar section which was over the convoy, shot down a T/B which had crossed the convoy from south to north without dropping his torpedoes. Another section attacked and damaged one other B.R.20, and about this time one Fulmar attacked 3 C.R.42s from astern, but with no visible result.

91. Between 1330 and 1430, the few remaining fighters in the air were moved from one danger point to another so far as extremely heavy atmospheric interference with R/T would allow. There were continued R.D.F. reports of enemy aircraft on widely different bearings during this period, but no interceptions were made although several potential attacks were turned away.

92. At 1410, ARK ROYAL was ordered to range the striking force and fly off two shadowers to shadow the enemy battlefleet which had been reported by R.A.F. reconnaissance aircraft 74 miles, 076° from NELSON.

The shadowers were ranged as soon as gunfire ceased and two Fulmars who were short of petrol had been landed on; they took off at 1448.

93. When the shadowers took departure, they were informed that the position of the enemy battlefleet was 078°, 60 miles, steering 190°. A report that the enemy had reversed his course to 360° at 1445 was received by ARK ROYAL at 1510, but owing to W/T congestion and bad W/T conditions considerable difficulty was experienced in passing this report to the aircraft.

94. Shadower A, who had not fully received the signal reporting the enemy's course as 360°, turned at 1539 to sight the fleet in order to take a new departure whilst waiting to receive the signal correctly. Subsequently he was attacked and badly damaged by seven C.R.42s and was obliged to return and land on.

Shadower B proceeded initially to the north-eastward, with the object of approaching the enemy on the most suitable bearing for A.S.V.[†] search (*i.e.*, with the enemy bearing between bow and beam). Having reached the anticipated position of the enemy at about 1600, and sighted nothing, he commenced a square search. The report of the enemy's alteration of course to 360° had not been received by this aircraft before ARK ROYAL received and passed on an amended position and new course of 060° of the enemy's battlefleet (R.A.F. aircraft B's signal timed 1503). On receiving this report at about 1630, course was set for the new position, and height increased to 9,000 feet to increase A.S.V. range to fifty miles. When thirty miles short of the enemy's estimated position, A.S.V. failed; a visual search to twelve miles beyond failed to locate the enemy. This aircraft eventually landed on after five hours five minutes in the air.

95. Twelve Swordfish aircraft with torpedoes, escorted by four Fulmars, were

flown off at 1540. When they took departure, the enemy fleet were estimated to be 056°, 54 miles from the carrier, steering 360°.

A few minutes later an enemy report timed 1503 was received, giving a position 14 miles north of the previous ones, M.L.A.†† 060°. This was passed to the striking force by W/T.

96. Having reached the enemy's estimated position, and seen nothing nor obtained any echoes on the ten A.S.V. sets in the formation, the striking force searched to the southward, and were able to obtain a fix by A.S.V. bearing and distance of Marittimo Island. They then proceeded for 40 miles to the north and carried out two complete circles at 5,000 feet, during which the A.S.V. sets should have discovered any large ships within 45 miles. The striking force then reported they were unable to locate the enemy, and were recalled.

97. This failure to locate the enemy is attributed to the fact that no report of the enemy battlefleet timed later than 1503 was received, nor was any report that shadowing had been broken off. Subsequent investigation by the Vice-Admiral, Malta has established that a signal timed 1515 was sent by the shadowing aircraft reporting that the enemy had altered course to the north. This signal was not received by Malta W/T Station, nor by any of H.M. Ships. This alteration resulted in the enemy passing at the extreme limit of the A.S.V. search.

98. While on passage, two formations of enemy fighters were sighted, but did not attack.

The Fulmar escort landed on at 1845, six Swordfish just after sunset, and six after dark; all were very short of petrol.

99. It was not until 1540 that the last of the fighters flown off at 1314 could be landed on; one ran out of petrol and force-landed at 1535.

The fighter situation became acute at 1520 when only three fighters, short of ammunition and fuel, were over the fleet. There were none from 1550 until four were flown off at 1605.

100. Two sections of fighters were vectored on to a Cante 506 shadower at 1630, which they shot down.

Between 1820 and 1920 a formation of 7 C.R.42s twice approached the fleet, but withdrew on the approach of the Fulmars and no combat took place.

101. During the day Fulmars destroyed five enemy aircraft, *viz.,* 4 T/Bs and one Cant 506, without loss by enemy action. Two Fulmars were shot down by the fleet, and one force-landed short of fuel. Two crews were picked up.

Night T/B Attack on Force X and Convoy, 27th September (D.3).

102. After Force A (battleships, ARK ROYAL and 9 destroyers) had parted company at 1855, the convoy and escort were formed in Cruising Disposition No. 17.

103. Between 2000 and 2040, four T/B attacks were made from the port beam, two or three aircraft taking part in each attack.

The moon was bright and on the starboard quarter of the convoy.

SHEFFIELD reports that before and during the early stages of these attacks a considerable amount of signalling with unnecessarily bright lights was taking place in the convoy; this presumably refers to the signals mentioned in paragraph I07 below.

(*a*) *First Attack.*

I04. At I955, when the convoy was steering II4°, COSSACK, stationed on the port bow of the convoy, detected aircraft on R.D.F., and about five minutes later sighted an aircraft on the port side. COSSACK thereupon fired a white and green Very light, the signal for T/B attack.

I05. The Rear-Admiral, I0th Cruiser Squadron ordered an emergency turn of 40° to port together by rapid manoeuvring procedure. KENYA sounded two short blasts and turned, followed belatedly by the port column of the convoy.

This signal was incorrectly transmitted as 45° to starboard and EDINBURGH and the starboard column turned to starboard.

I06. The port screen and the convoy opened fire to port, but only HERMIONE and COSSACK actually saw aircraft.

COSSACK observed the aircraft making white flashes before turning in to attack. As far as is known, no torpedo tracks were observed.

I07. As position V was reached at 20I0, Rear-Admiral Commanding, I0th Cruiser Squadron made the executive signal by V/S to EDINBURGH for the pre-arranged white pendant turn to 07I° and himself altered to the course. At this time the port column was formed on an approximate line of bearing II4° /294°; ships were not ordered to follow in the wake of their guide.

Rear-Admiral Commanding, I8th Cruiser Squadron first turned the starboard column to the original course (II4°) and then led round to 07I°.

(*b*) *Second Attack.*

I08. Aircraft were reported bearing 090°, 3 miles at 20I0 and others were detected on the starboard bow. Both these formations crossed from starboard to port, and attacked from the port beam. Two aircraft were seen by LAFOREY, flying from starboard to port about 2 miles ahead.

ZULU heard 4 separate aircraft distinctly, but only saw one, which passed so close that her guns could not train fast enough to get on.

Again, as far as is known, no torpedo attacks were observed.

(*c*) *Third Attack.*

I09. Three T/Bs attacked from the port beam at 2022. HERMIONE saw a torpedo explode at the end of its run on the starboard quarter of the convoy. Aircraft were sighted and engaged by the port screen and convoy.

II0. At about this time, ROWALLAN CASTLE and CITY OF CALCUTTA, the two rear ships of the port column, were in collision; no serious damage occurred, and both ships proceeded.

(*d*) *Fourth Attack.*

III. COSSACK sighted aircraft on the port side at 2027. A torpedo was dropped on SHEFFIELD'S port bow at 2029, and five minutes later she had to turn to starboard under full rudder to avoid another dropped on her port beam.

II2. At 2032 in position 37° 3I' N., I0° 46' E., IMPERIAL STAR was struck port side aft by a torpedo. The subsequent proceedings of IMPERIAL STAR and the ships which proceeded to her assistance are included later in this report.

HEYTHROP, the rear destroyer of the port screen, sighted and engaged an aircraft at this time, possibly that which torpedoed IMPERIAL STAR.

II3. ORIBI was attacked at 2036, a torpedo being dropped 800 yards just abaft her port beam, which she avoided by turning stern-on and increasing to full speed. This aircraft was shot down with pom-pom and Oerlikon guns by ORIBI.

II4. No further attacks were made, but at 23I2 and again at 2340 R.D.F. detected formations closing to within I0 miles, then subsequently retiring, having failed to find the convoy.

Remarks on Night T/B Attacks.

II5. *Enemy tactics.* – All attacks appear to have been made from the port beam, although this was not directly up-moon, which was on the starboard quarter.

Torpedoes were observed to be dropped from a greater height than that in most of the day attacks.

II6. *Gunfire.* – On several occasions the cruisers leading the columns were prevented from firing a barrage by the destroyers adjacent to them.

Gun flashes probably showed the convoy up to aircraft manoeuvring to attack. Flashless charges would be most useful for barrage fire at night.

ZULU sustained superficial damage from splinters, but no casualties.

Loss of M.V. IMPERIAL STAR.

II7. When IMPERIAL STAR was torpedoed at 2032 it is probable that the explosion blew away both propellers and her rudder; in addition No. 6 hold and the after engine room were both flooded.

II8. HEYTHROP, the rear ship of the port screen, proceeded alongside, but did not attempt to take IMPERIAL STAR in tow as she did not consider she was a suitable vessel to do so.

II9. About 2045 EURYALUS ordered ORIBI to go to the assistance of IMPERIAL STAR. When ORIBI closed, HEYTHROP was already standing by, and while HEYTHROP took off IMPERIAL STAR'S passengers, ORIBI proceeded close alongside to obtain reports from the Master and the N.L.O.‡

They were first insistent that an attempt should be made to tow the vessel back to Gibraltar, but the Commanding Officer of ORIBI (Lieutenant-Commander J.E.H. McBeath, D.S.O., R.N.) realised that the only chance of saving the ship was to tow her the 220 miles to Malta, and prepared to do so.

120. HEYTHROP parted company at 2200 to rejoin the convoy. By 2235 ORIBI had IMPERIAL STAR in tow with 90 fathoms of special 5-inch wire hawser provided by IMPERIAL STAR.

121. For two hours the most determined attempts were made by ORIBI to tow IMPERIAL STAR towards Malta. Although a speed of 8 knots through the water was made, nothing would prevent her steering in circles.

IMPERIAL STAR's normal displacement was 17,000 tons; in her damaged condition she was drawing 38 feet aft, and it is possible that her damaged stern was acting as a rudder.

122. Eventually, at 0120, ORIBI found herself being dragged stern first by her tow sheering off, and was forced to slip the tow.

ORIBI then went alongside to consult again with the Master and N.L.O. It was reluctantly decided that it was impracticable to tow the ship without tugs, which were not available at Malta, and that the remaining 141 persons aboard should be taken off by ORIBI and the ship scuttled.

Scuttling arrangements were not in place, and most of the flooding valves were jammed by the torpedo explosion; ORIBI therefore placed 3 depth charges lashed together just below the waterline abreast a bulkhead, and these were fired by a safety fuse.

123. ORIBI cast off at 0340 and the charges fired 11 minutes later, starting a large fire aft. As this did not spread quickly, ORIBI shelled IMPERIAL STAR with 4.7-inch S.A.P. shell§, and left her at 0452, heavily on fire fore and aft and listing badly.

Aircraft from Malta sent to search for IMPERIAL STAR the next day failed to find any trace, and there can be no doubt that she sank or blew up.

124. ORIBI proceeded along the convoy route at 32 knots, and came up with them off Malta at 1215, having passed unmolested within 7 miles of the Sicilian coast in daylight.

Passage of Force X and Convoy through the Narrows.

125. Meanwhile Force X proceeded through the Narrows by the route previously arranged, *i.e.,* along the south coast of Sicily. During the afternoon I had suggested to Rear-Admiral Commanding, 10th Cruiser Squadron the advisability of taking the Tunisian route owing to the presence of enemy forces in the vicinity. Rear-Admiral Commanding, 10th Cruiser Squadron replied that he preferred the Sicilian route, and in view of the enemy's hurried withdrawal to the north-east I agreed.

126. HERMIONE parted company from the convoy at 2030 to carry out a bombardment of Pantellaria harbour. A detailed account of this operation, which was very skilfully planned and executed by HERMIONE (Captain G.N. Oliver, R.N.) is contained in HERMIONE's report. Rear-Admiral Commanding, 10th Cruiser Squadron reports that the bombardment caused a most spectacular diversion which was clearly visible from the convoy and escort, then distant 50 miles.

127. No opposition was encountered by the convoy after the conclusion of the T/B attacks at 2040. The following lights on the Sicilian coast were seen to be exhibiting

normal characteristics:- Admiralty List of Lights No. I928 Cape San Marco, No. I930 Cape Granitola, No. I962 Cape Grosso.

I28. At some time between 2000/27 and 0030/28, HERMIONE lost her port paravane. From the state of the end of the wire recovered there is little doubt that it was cut by an explosive cutter or other anti-sweep device. The route followed was identical with that taken by HERMIONE during Operation "Substance", on which occasion the starboard paravane towing wire when recovered at Malta was severely crippled and showed signs of having fouled a mine mooring. It therefore appears possible that a minefield exists on the Talbot Bank, the depth there being considerably less than I00 fathoms. This occurrence was reported in my message 093I of 6th October.

I29. HERMIONE rejoined at 06I5/28. At daylight HEYTHROP and FARNDALE were detached to proceed ahead to fuel at Malta.

I30. Although several formations of enemy aircraft were detected between dawn and the arrival of the convoy at Malta, the excellent protection given by shore-based fighters from Malta prevented any attack from developing.

Two Fulmars arrived over the convoy at 06I5, followed at 0700 by 6 Beaufighters, and subsequently Hurricanes. Fighter direction was carried out by EDINBURGH and the cooperation of the fighters left nothing to be desired.

I3I. At 0800 a report that no enemy surface forces were to northward or southward of the convoy's track was received from the Vice-Admiral, Malta. The Rear-Admiral Commanding, I0th Cruiser Squadron consequently detached KENYA, SHEFFIELD, EURYALUS and HERMIONE to proceed ahead to Malta to fuel. The four cruisers were sighted from Gozo at 0845 and entered Grand Harbour at II30 with guards and bands paraded. They were accorded a great welcome by the people of Malta.

I32. The whole convoy, with the exception of IMPERIAL STAR, entered harbour undamaged early in the afternoon of 28th September (D.4).

Movements of Force A from Dusk 27th September (D.3) to p.m. 28th September (D.4).

I33. After landing on all aircraft (*vide* paragraph 86), Force A proceeded to the westward at I4 knots, this being NELSON's best speed at the time. LEGION reported an A/S contact at 00I0/28 (D.4), but this was not confirmed.

I34. In view of the low speed of NELSON I did not consider that action to afford close support of the ships of M.G.2 was justified, since this would have involved an unacceptable reduction in the destroyer screen then available. I wished also to convey the impression that a general withdrawal of forces to the westward was in progress and would be continued.

I35. ARK ROYAL flew off I A/S patrol and 3 fighters at 0725. The latter carried out a search to a depth of 40 miles astern, but nothing was sighted. At 08I2 an enemy shadower was sighted, but escaped into cloud.

I36. An enemy report made by an R.A.F. aircraft received at 0958 indicated that 2 enemy battleships, 5 cruisers and I3 destroyers were 70 miles, I05° from Cagliari at

0940, steering 195°. These ships, which were not in a position to menace the convoy, manoeuvred in this area throughout the day.

137. NELSON sighted a Cant 506 very low down at 1025, and fighters were vectored. After a chase to the south-east he was shot down 55 miles from the fleet and only 200 yards from the Algerian shore, near Cape de Fer. This was a fine example of fighter control and relentless pursuit which reflects the greatest credit on those concerned. Although there were no survivors from the Cant the occurrence may have been witnessed by occupants of the lighthouse at Cape de Fer, a small house in the vicinity and from a small vessel also in the vicinity.

138. Shadowers were again reported at 1640, and yet again an hour later, but due to a failure of ARK ROYAL's R/T transmitter, it was not possible to vector fighters in time to intercept. An enemy report made by Italian aircraft was intercepted at 1720.

139. DUNCAN in position M in Screening Diagram No. 7 reported a contact on the port bow at 1942, in position 37° 30' N., 3° 45' E. She reported "definitely submarine" and carried out two attacks with no apparent result. LEGION closed to co-operate but did not gain contact. Both ships left the area at 2012 to rejoin the screen.

140. Speed was reduced to 12 knots at 2010 to reduce the strain on bulkheads and decks in the wake of flooded compartments in NELSON. At this time NELSON was approximately 8 feet down by the bows, and it was estimated that 3,500 tons of water had entered the ship.

141. At 2100, Group 2 of Force A, consisting of PRINCE OF WALES (Vice-Admiral, 2nd-in-Command, Home Fleet), RODNEY, ARK ROYAL and 6 destroyers were detached to proceed to the eastward and rendezvous with Force X a.m. on D.5. Group 1, consisting of NELSON and 3 destroyers, continued towards Gibraltar.

142. By keeping the battleships concentrated until dark, I hoped to have concealed damage to NELSON, and that consequently enemy surface vessels would keep clear while Force X made the passage westward from Malta.

Submarine Attacks on Force A, a.m. 29th September (D.5).

143. At 0555, in position 37° 30' N., 06° 25' E., PRINCE OF WALES obtained an R.D.F. surface echo ahead, and an emergency turn of 40° to port together to 050° was carried out at 0609. Three minutes after the turn, GURKHA (in position A, Screening Diagram No. 6) sighted a torpedo track approaching from an approximate bearing of 330°, and at a speed estimated at 40 knots. It was too late to alter course to avoid, and a second track followed a few seconds later; both appeared to pass under the ship.

GURKHA turned to port in the direction from which the torpedoes had approached, and ISAAC SWEERS joined in hunting for the submarine. No A/S contact was obtained and no depth charges were dropped.

At 0622, ten minutes after the tracks had been sighted, a double explosion was heard and felt.

GURKHA and ISAAC SWEERS rejoined the screen at 0700. Owing to the absence of these ships from Gibraltar it has not yet been possible to ascertain why no depth charges were dropped, but this will be investigated on their return.

144. GURKHA obtained an A/S contact, classified as a submarine, bearing 102°, in position 37° 26' N., 07° 14' E. at 0810, two hours after the previous attack. The contact was nearly ahead and a deliberate attack with a 14-charge pattern was carried out at 0815. Six minutes later a heavy underwater explosion was heard and felt – this was similar to that felt after the successful attack on a U-Boat next day.

GURKHA was ordered by the Vice-Admiral to rejoin the screen at 0841, and the hunt was abandoned. No torpedo tracks were seen.

Westward Passage of Force X from Malta, 28th/29th September (D.4/5).

145. After fuelling, FARNDALE and HEYTHROP sailed from the Grand Harbour at 1500, followed at 1615 by KENYA, EDINBURGH and ORIBI. The remainder of Force X sailed at 1830.

146. At 1745, the Rear-Admiral Commanding, 18th Cruiser Squadron was detached in EDINBURGH with ORIBI in company, to search for two enemy destroyers reported northwest of Gozo, steering 180°.

Nothing was seen, and at 2035 these ships joined the Rear-Admiral Commanding, 10th Cruiser Squadron in KENYA. It is probable that these two destroyers were FARNDALE and HEYTHROP.

147. Force X proceeded on a course to make the Tunisian coast, and thence to Cape Bon, keeping close to the coast.

The night was uneventful.

148. FARNDALE and HEYTHROP joined the Vice-Admiral, 2nd-in-Command at 0835/29, and by 1030 the remainder of Force X had rejoined.

Passage of NELSON to Gibraltar, 29th/30th September (D.5/6).

149. At 0700/29 I informed the Vice-Admiral Commanding, North Atlantic Station of NELSON's position, course and speed, and requested additional A/S vessels and escort. This message was purposely delayed until this time, in order to give no indication that NELSON was proceeding independently.

150. A Catalina flying-boat joined at 0730 and a Hudson as fighter escort at 1000. Later in the day a second Catalina joined, and this air escort was maintained until dusk.

151. PIORUN obtained a doubtful A/S contact at 1110 and dropped one depth charge.

A French merchant vessel was sighted at 1415, and observed to alter course away to the south.

152. During the day NELSON ranged bower and sheet cables aft and flooded

certain after compartments in order to reduce the draught forward to the 39 feet required for entering harbour.

Clocks were put back one hour to Z -I at I800; times in paragraphs I53 to I56 are Zone -I.

I53. DUNCAN obtained a doubtful contact at I809 and dropped one depth charge.

I54. The first additional A/S vessel, ROCKINGHAM, joined at I845; she was followed by SAMPHIRE at 2020, JONQUIL at 2040, FLEUR DE LYS ten minutes later, and ARBUTUS at 2240. NELSON's screen now consisted of 4 destroyers and 4 corvettes.

I55. SAMPHIRE and ARBUTUS obtained an A/S contact and dropped depth charges at 0030/30 without result; the contact was probably non-sub. Air escort of one Hudson and one Catalina joined at daylight.

I56. At II00/30 NELSON entered Gibraltar harbour. Tugs were used ahead and astern as the ship was sluggish under helm especially at low speed.

Passage of Forces A and X to the Westward, 29th September (D.5).

I57. After Force X had joined Force A at I030/29 (*vide* paragraph I48), course was shaped to the westward, keeping 40 miles clear of the African coast.

I58. At I645, LIVELY, in position D, Screening Diagram No. 9, sighted an object resembling a ship's lifeboat with mast stepped well forward, bearing 28I°, distant about I,000 yards. LIVELY identified this as a submarine periscope and conning tower momentarily breaking surface, and estimated the course of the submarine as 220°. LIVELY, already under wheel to alter course to 28I° in accordance with the zig-zag, increased speed to 24 knots and altered course to 260°. Two torpedo tracks, course 0I0°, were sighted soon afterwards which confirmed the course of the submarine. The tracks indicated that the submarine was moving at speed, so course was altered to 250° and a counter-attacking I4-charge pattern set to shallow depth was fired at I650. LEGION on the starboard beam of LIVELY and on a parallel course fired a 5-charge shallow pattern about a minute and a half earlier. Action to avoid the torpedoes was taken by the fleet. LEGION then stationed LIVELY on her starboard beam and both ships hunted the submarine.

LIVELY obtained a definite A/S contact on a submarine at I700, and attacked with a I4- charge pattern set medium five minutes later. After opening to I,000 yards, LIVELY turned towards the point at which charges had been fired, and regained contact at I7I5, the plot showing the submarine's speed was about I knot.

Contact was lost at 400 yards, and not regained. The hunt was abandoned at I745 in order to rejoin the screen at I900 as ordered by the Rear-Admiral Commanding, I8th Cruiser Squadron.

I59. PRINCE OF WALES, KENYA, SHEFFIELD, LAFOREY, LIGHTNING, ORIBI, FORESIGHT, FORESTER and FURY parted company from the remainder of the force at I930 and proceeded ahead in order to arrive at Gibraltar p.m. 30th September.

The Rear-Admiral Commanding, 18th Cruiser Squadron took charge of the remainder of the ships of Force X and proceeded towards Gibraltar at 17 knots.

Return of Units under Vice-Admiral Commanding, 2nd-in-Command, Home Fleet to Gibraltar, 30th September (D.6).

160. During the night 29th/30th September, between 0325 and 0408, R.D.F. gave echoes suggesting a U-Boat, and several explosions, assumed to have been torpedoes exploding at the end of run, were heard.

161. No further incidents occurred, and the force arrived at Gibraltar at 1800.

Return of Units under Rear-Admiral Commanding, 18th Cruiser Squadron to Gibraltar, 30th September/1st October (D.6/7).

162. At 0928/30 in position 37° 10' N., 00° 56' E., GURKHA obtained an echo bearing 240°, 2,000 yards, which was confirmed as a submarine.

She immediately attacked, held contact up to 100 yards, and fired a 14-charge shallow pattern at 0933.

A black circular buoy with electric cable attached came to the surface after this attack; at 0945 a loud underwater explosion was heard and felt, and oil started to come to the surface. GURKHA was unable to regain contact.

LEGION, who was hunting with GURKHA, obtained contact, and attacked with a 14-charge pattern set to medium depth at 0955, regaining contact at 1001, and attacking with another 14-charge pattern set deep at 1009.

During LEGION's second attack, wreckage and oil appeared close to where her first pattern was dropped.

Among the wreckage picked up were an Italian dictionary, a mattress pillow, numerous pieces of wood, some with bright screws, and a piece of human scalp attached to a piece of wood by a splinter of metal. The interiors of the dictionary, pillow and mattress were dry. There appears to be no reasonable cause to doubt that an Italian U-Boat was destroyed by GURKHA and LEGION.§§

163. The force entered harbour between 0700 and 0900/I.

Convoy M.G.2. – Passage from Malta to Gibraltar.

164. As stated earlier (paragraph 33) the first ship, S.S. MELBOURNE STAR, sailed from Malta at noon on 26th September (D.2).

The remaining two ships, S.S. PORT CHALMERS and S.S. CITY OF PRETORIA, left Malta at 1030 on 27th September (D.3), escorted until 1930 by GLOXINIA.

165. After an uneventful passage MELBOURNE STAR arrived at Gibraltar at 0700 on 29th September (D.5).

166. PORT CHALMERS and CITY OF PRETORIA were reported by Italian aircraft at 1200/27, shortly after leaving Malta. No enemy surface craft or aircraft were seen until 2320, when what was believed to be an E-Boat was sighted by PORT CHALMERS, who was following in the wake of CITY OF PRETORIA. The enemy craft when first sighted by PORT CHALMERS was lying stopped 3-400 yards on the port beam of CITY OF PRETORIA, who saw nothing except gunfire from her consort.

PORT CHALMERS sheered off to starboard, and 10 minutes after first sighting heard E-Boat engines approaching from the port quarter; she turned to starboard to bring the enemy astern, and opened fire with her 4-inch gun at the enemy's bow wave.

The enemy opened fire at PORT CHALMERS with her machine-gun, but scored no hits, and after PORT CHALMERS had fired six rounds of 4-inch, the enemy crossed astern and made off. PORT CHALMERS then resumed her station astern of CITY OF PRETORIA.

This action took place 15 miles S.S.W. of Pantellaria.

167. At 0535/28 (D.4) the Commodore of the Convoy ordered PORT CHALMERS to part company. The latter then proceeded at full speed, wearing French colours.

168. An Italian reconnaissance seaplane (Cant 506) approached from the direction of the French coast and circled CITY OF PRETORIA at 0915/28, subsequently making off to the westward and paying PORT CHALMERS the same attention. Both ships were wearing French colours and had taken care to keep all service personnel out of sight. They were fully ready for action, but did not open fire as the aircraft took no offensive action.

169. At 1015/28 CITY OF PRETORIA was circled several times by a large 3-engined seaplane, with distinct French markings, which approached from Bizerta. An hour and a half later, when approaching the Galita Channel, CITY OF PRETORIA sighted an Italian twin-engined seaplane stopped on the water, five miles to the north. She lost sight of this aircraft at 1215.

170. PORT CHALMERS sighted neither of these aircraft and was left alone until 1555, when she was circled by an Italian Breda 20, which did not attack, although the Master considers she could not have been deceived by the French colours.

171. CITY OF PRETORIA was attacked at 1725/28 by three T/B aircraft. As these approached with obviously hostile intentions, British colours were hoisted and fire opened as soon as the leader came in range. There is good reason to suppose the leading aircraft was damaged.

By skilful handling, all three torpedoes were avoided. While one aircraft was machine gunning the ship at long range, a submarine periscope was reported on the starboard quarter by two independent lookouts.

Three smoke floats and a depth charge set to 150 feet were dropped, and under cover of smoke CITY OF PRETORIA turned away.

She signalled "Help Major" at 1730, and "Major now all right" three quarters of an hour later.

172. As CITY OF PRETORIA was approaching Cape de Gata at 0200/30 (D.6) an

unidentified vessel, possibly a submarine, was seen to be following. Two or three rapid shots, followed by a dull explosion, were heard. CITY OF PRETORIA made smoke and dropped smoke floats and then made close in to Almeria Bay, into territorial waters, thus shaking off her pursuer.

173. PORT CHALMERS arrived at Gibraltar at 0900/30, followed during the afternoon by CITY OF PRETORIA.

174. The able and resolute handling of both PORT CHALMERS and CITY OF PRETORIA in successfully driving off enemy attacks deserves high praise.

Both Masters showed excellent restraint in withholding fire at enemy aircraft while there was a chance of their false colours being effective, and also in keeping W/T silence when attacked, except on the one occasion when CITY OF PRETORIA was attacked by T/B aircraft, and her report might possibly have brought fighter assistance if ARK ROYAL had been in the vicinity.

Submarine Dispositions.

175. Nine submarines were disposed in suitable areas throughout the operation – 2 south of Messina, 6 to the northward of Sicily, and one off the south-east corner of Sardinia. In some cases submarines were moved by the Vice-Admiral, Malta, to new areas in an attempt to intercept enemy warships.

176. A full report of the operation of these submarines has not yet been received, but as far as is known no successful attacks were made on enemy warships.

General Remarks.

177. *Failure to locate enemy battlefleet.* – The operation orders stated clearly that the primary object of the operation was the safe arrival of the convoy at its destination, and any action taken to deal with enemy surface forces in the vicinity must be related to the achievement of this object.

At no time did the enemy surface forces constitute a serious threat. On the other hand enemy air forces remained a potential and serious threat throughout the day and well after moonset. Under these circumstances the maintenance of fighter patrols assumed an importance which could not be ignored. Light variable winds added to the difficulties with which ARK ROYAL was confronted, and I consider that her Commanding Officer acted throughout with great judgment and a well balanced appreciation of the situation.

Had the shadowing aircraft from Malta been able to maintain observation on the enemy battlefleet for a longer period the two reconnaissance Swordfish should have experienced no serious difficulty in making contact. Unfortunately, communications, due to atmospherics and congestion, were difficult. Congestion was due in part to the damage sustained by NELSON involving a last minute alteration of the pre-arranged plan to deal with the situation. With a force occupying a front of 12 miles the delay caused by V/S communication was unacceptable.

I consider that shadower B acted incorrectly in not approaching the estimated position of the enemy by the shortest route and then carrying out a circular search in order to obtain the full range of his A.S.V. Admittedly it is easier to detect and hold a target at long range if the aircraft is on a steady course and the target is on a bearing which gives maximum range. But against this is the fact that to dispose of errors in position or unknown alterations of course, it is necessary to approach the position of the enemy, as estimated by available data, by the shortest route.

Failure of Malta and H.M. Ships to receive the all important signal timed 1515 on 27th September, referred to in paragraph 97, undoubtedly contributed largely to the failure of the striking force to locate. It appears now that whilst the enemy was at pains to withdraw as quickly as possible he was probably concerned to keep under a C.R.42 umbrella furnished from Cagliari.

178. *Added hazards due to the operation taking place during moonlight.* – It cannot be emphasised too strongly that if operations of this character are carried out during moonlight the hazards are increased to a very considerable extent. Had the enemy concentrated his T/B aircraft in attacking from dusk onwards he might well have succeeded in torpedoing a large proportion of the convoy.

179. *U-Boat activity.* – Once the nature of the operation was disclosed the enemy took vigorous action to station submarines on the expected course of the fleet; not a difficult matter in view of the relatively narrow waters of the Western Mediterranean.

Of the contacts obtained it is considered that there is sufficient evidence to assume the following were submarines:-

*D.*4.

(i) DUNCAN contact. No visible result.

*D.*5.

(ii) PRINCE OF WALES's A.S.V. and torpedo track sighted by GURKHA. No visible result; no A/S contact.

(iii) GURKHA's contact. No visible result; heavy underwater explosion felt six minutes after depth charge attack.

(iv) Periscope and conning tower sighted by LIVELY, also torpedo track. A/S contact but no visible result.
*D.*6.

(v) A.S.V. gave indications. Explosions heard as from torpedoes at end of run. No contact.

(vi) Contact of GURKHA and LEGION. Submarine destroyed.

It is possible that (iii) in addition to (vi) may have become a casualty.

The failures to obtain any contact during (ii) or to obtain results in (iv) are disappointing and cannot be explained. On the whole it is considered that the luck was certainly with us on this occasion.

I80. *R.A.F. air co-operation.* – I wish to place on record my high appreciation of the excellent co-operation furnished by the R.A.F. throughout this operation.

The bombing and machine-gunning of enemy aerodromes in Sicily and Sardinia undoubtedly reduced to a considerable extent the scale of air attack which the enemy intended to launch. Apart from the circumstances attending the sighting and reporting of the enemy battlefleet which may well have been due to circumstances beyond the control of the aircraft in question, the reconnaissance of enemy bases and in particular of the approaches to Malta on D.4 were adequate and most valuable.

Rear-Admiral Commanding, I0th Cruiser Squadron has stated that the co-operation of the R.A.F. fighters on D.4 left nothing to be desired.

I8I. I attribute the immunity from attack experienced by Force X and the convoy after passing Skerki Channel to using the route proposed by the Vice-Admiral, Malta. This well-judged move coupled with HERMIONE's bombardment appears to have deceived the enemy completely.

(Signed) J.F. SOMERVILLE,
Vice Admiral,
Flag Officer Commanding,
Force H.

Admiralty footnotes:-
* *A.D.P. – Air Defence Position.*
** *H.L.B. – high level bombing.*
† *A.S.V. – a radar equipment.*
†† *M.L.A. – mean line of advance.*
‡ *N.L.O. – Naval Liaison Officer.*
§ *S.A.P. shell – an armour piercing shell.*
§§ *The destruction of this submarine, the Italian submarine ADUA, on this occasion has since been confirmed.*

OPERATION "HARPOON"

The-following Despatch was submitted to the Lords Commissioners of the Admiralty on the 24th June, I942 by Vice-Admiral Sir Alban T.B. Curteis, K.C.B., Senior Officer, Force T.

H.M.S. KENYA,
24th June, 1942.

REPORT ON OPERATION "HARPOON"

Be pleased to lay before Their Lordships the following report on Operation "Harpoon" – the passage of a convoy of six merchant ships through the Western Mediterranean to Malta.

Passage from Clyde as far as the Straits of Gibraltar. Thursday, 4th June to Friday, 12th June.

(Times Zone -2 (suffix B))

2. Having hoisted my flag in KENYA at 0900 on 4th June and having that afternoon held conferences with the Commanding Officers of H.M. Ships of Force T present in the Clyde and other officers concerned, Convoy W.S.19Z and escort sailed as required to comply with Admiralty messages, forming up a.m. Friday, 5th June as follows:-

Convoy W.S. 19Z:

TROILUS (Senior Liaison Officer acting as Commodore), BURDWAN, CHANT, ORARI, TANIMBAR.

Ocean Escort:

KENYA (Senior Officer, Force T), LIVERPOOL.

A/S Escort:

ONSLOW (Captain (D), 17th Destroyer Flotilla), BEDOUIN, ICARUS, MARNE, MATCHLESS, ESCAPADE, BLANKNEY, MIDDLETON, BADSWORTH, KUJAWIAK.

3. It early became clear that the merchant ships would not live up to the name of a 14-knot convoy, for BURDWAN claimed to be able to do only 13 knots and CHANT failed to produce much more, while TANIMBAR, a diesel ship, was unable to steam in the range of her critical revolutions, approximately 12.5 to 13.5 knots. However,

favourable weather and a route selected short in anticipation of delay enabled the force to keep to timetable.

4. The passage was uneventful except for

(*a*) heavy oil consumption by KUJAWIAK necessitating detaching her at 0800/9 to refuel;

(*b*) identifying Portuguese VILLA FRANCA – Greenland to Lisbon with cod at 2I00/8;

(*c*) several A/S contacts and attacks all of which were considered to be "non-sub."

5. To allow for refuelling, KENYA, BEDOUIN and KUJAWIAK approached Gibraltar without being visible on the night of the I0th June. KENYA only sailed to be clear of land by dawn IIth June.

Seven destroyers of the Gibraltar force sailed by day on the IIth June and the eight remaining destroyers from Home Waters reached Gibraltar after dark IIth June, though probably sighted from the African coast approaching Spartel. LIVERPOOL should have entered sufficiently late not to be sighted from the shore on the night of IIth June.

Passage from the Straits of Gibraltar to the Point of Separation of Forces W and X.

(Times Zone -3 (suffix C))

Friday, I2th June.

6. The convoy having passed through the Straits during darkness IIth/I2th June was joined by the following units:-

Convoy:

S.S. KENTUCKY (Tanker).

Force T:

MALAYA, EAGLE, ARGUS, CAIRO, CHARYBDIS, Destroyers (who sailed IIth June) WISHART, WESTCOTT, WRESTLER, VIDETTE, ANTELOPE, ITHURIEL, PARTRIDGE.

Minesweepers:

HEBE, SPEEDY, RYE, HYTHE.

Motor Launches:

I2I, I34, I35, I68, 459, 462.

Temporarily Attached:

WELSHMAN.

Separately Routed:

Force Y – BROWN RANGER, GERANIUM, COLTSFOOT.

7. I703. – The Spanish M.V. CABO PRIOR must have seen the convoy.

Saturday, I3th June.

8. Delay in starting the refuelling programme was caused by navigational errors. The same happened on Operation "Halberd" and it is recommended that if possible the refuelling force should be sailed with the remainder. Nevertheless, by using LIVERPOOL and continuing till well after dark CAIRO and I4 destroyers were refuelled.

9. In spite of maintaining a section of Hurricanes in the air from 0845 till dark, and an A/S patrol of Swordfish, the convoy was kept under observation by enemy aircraft and reported at I045, II5I, I405 and at I202 by a U-Boat bearing 090°. Hurricanes made contact with one JU.88, probably killing the rear gunner, and destroyed one Cant Z.I007.

I0. 2245. – Report of cruisers and destroyers leaving Cagliari was received.

Sunday, I4th June.

II. 0242. – The convoy was probably reported by an Italian U-boat.

I2. 0650. – Snoopers were again in company, reporting Force T at 0650 and 0750. Force Y was also reported at I8I0.

I3. 0730. – Paravanes were streamed.

I4. 0830. – One JU.88 was badly damaged by Hurricanes who expended all ammunition.

I5. 0930. – A BR.88 shadower was badly damaged in air combat with a Hurricane.

I6. I009. – A group of aircraft was detected by radar and it became apparent that the enemy were gathering for an attack. All ships assumed the first degree of air readiness.

The wind was still from the west causing me considerable anxiety over the carriers, particularly ARGUS with her small margin of speed.

I7. I020. – A column of white smoke was reported about 20 miles away and some reports suggest that this may have been a homing mark deliberately laid. It is thought more probable that this was from a bomber shot down by EAGLE's Hurricanes at about that time, though why the smoke should have been such an unusual colour cannot be explained.

I8. I028 to I032. – Two and possibly three formations each of 5 or 6 high level bombers in V formation reached the convoy, the bombs falling astern of the convoy and in the neighbourhood of ARGUS. Gunfire was ineffective but ARGUS's Fulmars shot down 2 of the enemy while they were retiring.

I9. II08 to II35. – Torpedo bombing aircraft were seen low over the horizon and the main attack developed. The timing was not very good and resulted in an attack being delivered at about II12 by I5 torpedo bombers from the port beam and at II16-II25 by three small groups of torpedo bombers totalling I3 torpedo bombers from the starboard side. An unknown number of formations of bombers attacked between II15 and II26 scoring no hits. The convoy lines, EAGLE, ARGUS and BADSWORTH appeared to be the target for bombing.

20. The port torpedo bomber attack was severely dealt with by gunfire and it is thought that not more than six aircraft got within 4,000 yards. A turn of 45° to port was made and no torpedo damage resulted.

2I. On the starboard side it was difficult to see what was happening as the wind was holding the cordite smoke on the line of sight. It appears that the three groups forced their attack well home from the bow, beam and quarter obtaining hits on LIVERPOOL and TANIMBAR, setting on fire and sinking the latter.

22. It has been difficult to fix the total enemy losses accurately but it is certain that 6 aircraft were shot down during this period. Aircraft claimed 2 fighters and 3 torpedo bombers certainly and 2 torpedo bombers probably brought down, while one Fulmar was shot down by our own gunfire.

23. II57 to I202. – Several half-hearted attacks were carried out by ones and twos, presumably aircraft which had been turned away by gunfire earlier. None approached within 6,000 yards or endangered the convoy.

24. ANTELOPE followed by WESTCOTT were detached to stand by LIVERPOOL who was retiring on a course 270° at 3 knots*. WELSHMAN took over guide of the starboard column.

25. I2I5 to I8I5. – Peace reigned during the afternoon, the radar screen showing snoopers and some formations which steered clear of us and, from subsequent information, attacked LIVERPOOL.

26. I8I5 to I835. – High level bombers and dive bombers attacked. As is usual in the Mediterranean it was very difficult to see these till they had reached the bombing position and gunfire was ineffective. At least two formations attacked. Our aircraft

formed two JU.88s to jettison their bombs and severely damaged two more who also jettisoned bomb loads. The remainder failed to achieve more than near misses one of which was very near EAGLE, pitching on her port side but going under the ship and bursting on the starboard side.

27. 2000 to 2005. – WELSHMAN was detached to proceed to Malta, being herself attacked at about 2020. KUJAWIAK took her place leading the starboard column.

28. At the same time it was evident that further air attacks were imminent.

2006 to 2032. – About 17 torpedo bombers, 14 high level bombers and 20 single-engined fighters in addition to dive bombers were involved in attacks which began at 2006.

29. During this period no less than four of the screen were out of position either investigating or attacking submarine contacts.

30. During the attacks our fighters met considerable fighter opposition and were therefore unable to assist in breaking up the attacks.

However, in spite of a number of near misses, the attacks were unsuccessful. The majority of the bombs from high level bombers and some of those from dive bombers fell round destroyers on the screen, ICARUS being particularly lucky to escape.

31. A well-delivered attack was made by about 9 of the torpedo bombers who circled round astern out of range and then tried to come in from the starboard beam. Three emergency turns away were made to port to keep the sterns of the convoy towards the enemy, and the aircraft were forced to release their torpedoes at a very poor track angle, though from very close range, and failed to achieve any success.

The gunnery of the force failed to obtain any known kills, but did much in breaking up attacks. I regret that one Fulmar was shot down during these attacks, the crew being picked up by HYTHE. Our fighters claim 2 certains and 3 probables during these attacks.

32. 2055. – SPEEDY attacked with depth charges and claimed to have sunk a U-Boat**.

33. 2056. – Friendly aircraft appeared on the screen. These proved to be Beaufighters from Malta.

34. 2130. – The air being clear at 2037, I formed KENYA as escort to EAGLE and turned the convoy over to CAIRO, and at 2130 Force W turned to the westwards at 16 knots.

35. 2230 to 2350. – Force W was searched for by two flare-dropping aircraft.

36. At about 2315 I received a signal from Vice-Admiral, Malta reporting 2 enemy cruisers and 4 destroyers leaving Palermo at 2125. This report necessitated an immediate decision whether to reinforce Force X by sending one or both of the cruisers in Force W. My reasons for not doing so were:-

(i) I did not consider the Italian force would go west and attack the convoy by night, or that;

(ii) they would go into the area in which the convoy would be by the following dawn, as I have always understood the Italians avoid this area owing to the danger of air attack from Malta.

(iii) Judging from past encounters with the Italians, the convoy escort was large enough to deter them from doing any harm to the convoy, and, with the added danger of air attack, they would keep clear. The original intention was that Force X should consist only of destroyers. I had the CAIRO added.

(iv) Force W would, by dawn on I5th June, still be only I30 miles from the air base in Sardinia, which is within easy striking distance. Also, torpedo bomber attack during the night was quite probable. EAGLE and ARGUS would be extremely vulnerable without the gun support of the cruisers.

(v) By midnight Force W was I62 miles from where the convoy would be by daylight and cruisers would, to be of any use, have to average about 24 knots on courses which included a stretch of quite tricky navigation, in itself a hazardous undertaking.

With the force available, a decision either way was a gamble. If the LIVERPOOL had been present there would have been no doubt in my mind.

Monday, I5th June.

37. Force W was shadowed continuously but only two very half-hearted approaches by torpedo bombing aircraft were made. One SM.79 was shot down by Hurricanes and other aircraft were chased away.

38. I600 to I700. – Reports indicated that the Italian surface ships were retiring northwards and at 0I30/I6 these ships were reported near Marittimo still going north.

Tuesday, I6th June.

39. 0800. – Having taken Force W clear of air attack, I ordered MALAYA, ARGUS, WISHART, WRESTLER, VIDETTE and ESCAPADE at 0850 to Gibraltar and remained in KENYA with EAGLE, CHARYBDIS, ONSLOW and ICARUS in a position from which I could cover the oiling of Force X from BROWN RANGER if required further east on the I7th or I8th. EAGLE's escort was short of fuel and at I7I0 I decided to send her to Gibraltar with ONSLOW and ICARUS to complete with fuel and be ready to sail again if required.

Wednesday, I7th June.

40. Force X, still being intermittently bombed, was met at 20I7, and I returned to Gibraltar with them.

4I. Reports of the proceedings of Force X while detached are being forwarded direct to Admiralty by CAIRO.†

Remarks.

42. *Merchant ships.* – The ships in convoy behaved in an exemplary manner during periods of attack, but the fact that the convoy could not be relied on to keep station at more than 12½ knots added to the difficulties of keeping up to time. With the limitations imposed by darkness on the last 36 hours' run every revolution counted.

43. *Motor Launches.* – I consider the determination of the Captains and crews of these boats worthy of high praise. They had ample excuse for turning back, yet not one of them did so and all arrived safely. They had a few very close shaves with bombs and one torpedo when dropped very nearly landed on one of them.

44. *Fighters.* – The number of fighters in the air never exceeded 6 Hurricanes and 2 Fulmars. This number is quite inadequate and the Hurricane is not sufficiently strongly armed to deal with types such as the JU.88. Twenty fighters armed with cannon in the air would have made a vast difference.

The achievements of the pilots of EAGLE were magnificent while the ground staff deserve high praise for the way in which they managed to keep aircraft in the air in excess of the numbers it had been thought possible to operate.‡

45. *Forces employed.* – If further operations of this nature are undertaken, interference by surface craft must now be considered as probable between the time of the main force parting company and the arrival of the convoy at Malta.

On this assumption there should be sufficient ships in Force X to deal with surface attack, leaving the Fighter Directing Ship and some A.A. screen with the convoy.

Further it is essential to have only really reliable fast ships in the convoy. This will very materially increase the chances of success.

46. I cannot speak too highly of the conduct of all ships under my command. Many were sorely tried and none found wanting. CAIRO and the destroyers of Force X, and EAGLE and LIVERPOOL were outstanding I saw as many of the ships of my force as I could at Gibraltar before sailing, and greatly admired the spirit and enthusiasm I found. I know how pleased they must have been to receive Their Lordships' signal of congratulations.

(Signed) A.T.B. CURTEIS,
Vice Admiral,
Senior Officer, Force T.

Admiralty footnotes:-
*LIVERPOOL in tow of the destroyer ANTELOPE reached Gibraltar safely p.m. 17th June, in spite of further air attacks on her.
**The final assessment of sinking of enemy submarines does not allow this claim.
†Report of Senior Officer, Force X is attached as an appendix to this despatch.
‡ The 16 Hurricanes and 6 Fulmars operated by H.M. Ships EAGLE and ARGUS shot down 13 and damaged at least 11 Italian and German aircraft on the 13th, 14th and 15th June, 1942. This was no mean achievement, especially in view of the persistence of the enemy air attacks and the fact that it was not possible to maintain more than four Hurricanes (six for short periods) and two Fulmars in the air at a time.
Our total fighter losses from all causes were three Hurricanes and four Fulmars, few of which were lost in air combat

APPENDIX

H.M.S. CAIRO,
21st June, 1942.

OPERATION "HARPOON"
REPORT OF PROCEEDINGS OF PASSAGE OF FORCE X AND
CONVOY TO MALTA ON I4TH AND I5TH JUNE, I942.

Sunday, 14th June.

At 2II5 Force X was detached from Force T in position 37° 38' N., I0° I3' E. Merchant ships in convoy formed single line, escort took up screening positions and course was set for Zembra thence to follow the coastal route detailed in the Senior Officer, Force T's orders for Operation "Harpoon".

2. At 2205 a medium dive bombing attack was carried out by about 8 JU.88s. The attack developed during dusk coming from the dark sector ahead of the convoy. One enemy machine was destroyed by gunfire, another was seen to be going away on fire, and a third is known to have been destroyed by a Beaufighter of the escort from Malta.

Monday, I5th June.

3. Dispositions for the coastal passage were formed as detailed in my signal timed I644 on IIth June.

4. During the night a number of parachute flares were observed to be dropped to seaward and it appeared that the enemy was attempting to locate the convoy thinking it had passed to the north of Zembra Island.

Alternatively, his object may have been to indicate to surface forces the relative position of the convoy.

5. While rounding Cape Bon, BLANKNEY reports that he observed signals made from the shore which may have been intended for the enemy. These signals had the appearance of tracer bullets fired into the sky.

6. At 02I2, in the vicinity of Ras-el-Mirh, about two miles north-east of Kelibia Road Light (36° 50' N., II° 08' E.), the IIth Division of destroyers (Fleets) engaged an object to starboard close inshore. BEDOUIN ordered "Cease fire" and it is thought that the object may possibly have been the wreck of H.M.S. HAVOCK which is understood to be in this approximate position. MARNE, however, reports having seen fall of shot ahead of his ship at this time.

7. At 0620 an R/T report was received from a Beaufighter that two Italian cruisers and four Italian destroyers were in a position I5 miles on the port beam of the convoy. Almost immediately these Ships were sighted by CAIRO and destroyers on the port wing of the screen, silhouetted against the eastern sky. The position of the convoy then was 36° 25' N., II° 43' E., course I30°, speed I2 knots. The enemy bore 075°, distance I0 miles, approximate course I50°. CAIRO'S first sighting report at 063I described the enemy as consisting of two cruisers and four destroyers but I am now satisfied that there were two cruisers and five destroyers. The cruisers are believed to have been of the Condottieri class,* "C" type, but it is not certain whether they were "C" or "B" type. The class of the destroyers is not known. The distance of the enemy given in CAIRO'S first sighting report was given as 6 miles and this was considerably in error.

8. On sighting the enemy, BEDOUIN was ordered to act independently with the fleet destroyers. I had previously discussed with the Commanding Officer, BEDOUIN, the action to be taken in such an eventuality which was for BEDOUIN's division to attack while CAIRO and the Hunt destroyers screened the convoy with smoke. BEDOUIN led his division towards the enemy while CAIRO turned to port to cover the left flank of the convoy with smoke, at the same time ordering BLANKNEY's division to make smoke and close.

9. The enemy opened fire at 0640, his first salvo falling short, and the second straddling CAIRO. A number of salvos fell near the convoy until smoke had been laid.

I0. CAIRO opened fire at 0650 and fired intermittently throughout the subsequent action but largely for moral effect as the enemy was never within effective range of the four-inch guns.

II. At 0645, anticipating that the enemy would immediately press home his attack with the full force at his command, my immediate intention was to gain time and to fight a delaying action in the hope that an air striking force could be sent from Malta. I therefore ordered the Commodore to turn away and make for territorial waters and later at 0650 ordered him to steer 240°.

I2. Meanwhile, having covered the port flank of the convoy with smoke, CAIRO turned I6 points and then steered on an approximately parallel course to the enemy, making smoke to cover the convoy from the southward as the enemy cruisers appeared to be working round in that direction.

I3. Meanwhile, BLANKNEY's division of destroyers, on emerging from the smoke, observed two enemy destroyers working round to the northward; these were engaged and driven off turning away under smoke.

I4. By 0700 BEDOUIN's division was hotly engaged with the enemy cruisers and destroyers and about this time BEDOUIN and PARTRIDGE in the van were observed to have been hit and to have had their speed reduced. MARNE, MATCHLESS and ITHURIEL pressed on the attack past these two disabled destroyers engaging the enemy cruisers and destroyers. The Commanding Officer, MARNE reports that fire from MARNE and MATCHLESS was observed to take effect on two enemy destroyers who turned away under smoke. ITHURIEL was at this time engaging the near enemy cruiser. There is little doubt that fire from the IIth Division of destroyers was effective and caused the enemy to keep the range open and continually alter course.

15. Shortly after 0700 the two Italian destroyers originally engaged by BLANKNEY's division made a further threat but turned away again as BLANKNEY manoeuvred his division to engage.

16. During this time CAIRO was on a course roughly parallel to the enemy but kept continuously under wheel to avoid enemy salvos. The enemy's gunnery was good and he appeared at this stage to have split the armament of his cruisers, each cruiser firing four gun salvos at CAIRO while the remainder of the armament engaged our attacking destroyers. At this stage one hit by a six-inch projectile was made on CAIRO but did little damage. The shell hit on the fore superstructure.

17. By 07I5 BEDOUIN and PARTRIDGE were out of the action lying stopped and I decided to concentrate the remaining fleet destroyers on CAIRO.

18. At 0745 the enemy was observed to turn away and open the range; I then turned to port to effect the concentration with the destroyers.

19. By 0822 both Fleet and Hunt classes of destroyer were concentrated on CAIRO; meanwhile the enemy had turned to the northward and was closing the range. At this stage the convoy appeared to be steering on a south-easterly course and I signalled to the Commodore to turn I80° to port at 0834. CAIRO and the destroyers circled between the enemy and the convoy making smoke.

20. The enemy turned on a north-easterly course at about 0840, CAIRO and destroyers steering on an approximately parallel course. At this stage CAIRO received a hit from a six-inch projectile on the starboard side which penetrated an oil tank and the inner bottom. The engine room started to flood but it was possible to keep the water down by using the 790-ton pump working to full capacity. The shell failed to explode and remained lodged in the oil tank where it was discovered later. Had this shell exploded it is more than likely that the ship would have been disabled. At 0848 I detached the I2th Division to return to protect the convoy against air attack and the possibility of enemy destroyers working round from the north or south.

2I. By 0930 the enemy had opened the range and had disappeared to the eastward. I therefore altered to a north-westerly course to rejoin the convoy.

22. At about I000 I had decided to turn the convoy towards Malta as the enemy was no longer barring this route, and made a signal to BLANKNEY to turn but he had already anticipated my wishes and had turned the convoy to I80° soon after I000. A course of I30° was resumed at I030.

23. At 0930, BEDOUIN then in tow of PARTRIDGE, had informed me that he intended steering to the westward but I ordered him to make for the convoy as I

considered that this gave me the best chance of giving him protection.

24. I rejoined the convoy at about 1030 and re-formed the screen. The position then was as follows:- TROILUS, ORARI, and BURDWAN undamaged. KENTUCKY disabled in tow of HEBE screened by RYE and HYTHE. CHANT had been sunk.

25. These casualties to CHANT and KENTUCKY had occurred in an air attack on the convoy at about 0710, which is believed to have been made by 8 JU.87s. CHANT had received three direct hits and KENTUCKY had been near missed. One enemy plane had been brought down by ships' gunfire.

26. Previous reference has been made (paragraph 7) to an enemy report made at 0620 by a Beaufighter escorting the convoy. This aircraft is understood to have returned to its base to make a full report seeing that surface action was imminent. Contact with the other aircraft of this flight, and also the relief flight, was not made and it is not known whether they were in the vicinity. It was not until 0930 that communication was established with a flight of night-flying Beaufighters.

27. From 0930 onwards fighters from Malta provided continuous escort except for two short periods of about 10 minutes when escorting sections, having been in combat, had used up their ammunition and were short of fuel and had had to return to their base before the reliefs arrived. It is unfortunate and probably more than a coincidence that enemy air attacks were made during these two periods.

28. The speed of the convoy was reduced while I considered what to do in regard to KENTUCKY. I had ordered ITHURIEL to take this ship in tow at 1033 hoping it might be possible to obtain a speed of 10 or 11 knots, while the best that could be hoped for with HEBE towing was about 6 knots. I reconsidered and cancelled this order as I came to the conclusion that I could not afford to immobilise one of the three remaining fleet destroyers for this purpose while the threat from enemy surface vessels was considerable.

29. A dive bombing attack by 3 JU.88s developed at 1040 but the enemy were driven off by fighters and gunfire before dropping their bombs. One enemy aircraft was shot down by fighters.

30. At 1120 a heavy high level and dive bombing attack by JU.88s and JU.87s was made. This attack had been detected coming in by radar, but unfortunately the escorting aircraft, having been engaged previously, were short of fuel and ammunition and had had to return to base before being relieved. The relieving section of Spitfires arrived in time to take their toll of the enemy but were too late to enable the fighter directing officers in CAIRO to intercept the attack. In this attack BURDWAN was near missed and reported she was disabled. I ordered BADSWORTH to take her in tow and shortly received reports through BADSWORTH that the merchant ship intended to scuttle. I believe Masters had received instructions regarding scuttling in the event of damage, but I do not know what these orders were.

31. The position then was as follows – Two ships of the convoy intact, TROILUS and ORARI. KENTUCKY in tow some distance astern making from 4 to 6 knots. BURDWAN disabled and preparing to scuttle with BADSWORTH standing by.

BEDOUIN disabled in tow of PARTRIDGE making about 8 knots and approaching the convoy from the east.

32. The convoy was then about 150 miles from Malta and I had to decide whether to continue at a speed of about 6 knots and try and bring in the disabled ships, KENTUCKY, BURDWAN, and BEDOUIN, or whether to accept the loss of the two disabled merchant ships and to proceed at maximum speed with the two undamaged ships both of which had a speed of about 14 knots.

33. In making my decision I considered the following points:-

(*a*) That until reaching a position 50 or 60 miles from Malta the air escort would be limited to long-range Spitfires and Beaufighters and I understood that the numbers of the long-range fighters available at Malta was limited.

(*b*) I had to keep the convoy concentrated owing to the continual threat from enemy surface forces which would undoubtedly have taken action against ships separated from the main force.

I decided to cut my losses and at 1142 ordered BADSWORTH and HEBE to scuttle BURDWAN and KENTUCKY at the same time ordering the remaining merchant ships to proceed at their utmost speed. I informed the Vice-Admiral, Malta of the action I had taken.

34. At about this time PARTRIDGE with BEDOUIN in tow rejoined the convoy and I ordered ITHURIEL to take BEDOUIN in tow as I considered she could make 14 knots and so enable BEDOUIN and PARTRIDGE to remain with the convoy.

35. At 1154 I received a signal from BEDOUIN reporting that she expected to steam on one engine shortly and suggesting that to avoid delay PARTRIDGE should continue to tow. I therefore recalled ITHURIEL to join the convoy which was then opening.[†]

36. At 1315 a dive bombing attack was carried out by 12 JU.87s. Once again the attack developed at a most inopportune moment while escorting Spitfires had been forced to return to their base before being relieved. The attack was detected by radar and the relieving section of Spitfires arrived in time to shoot down two of the enemy.

37. During this time HEBE and BADSWORTH appeared to be having difficulty in sinking KENTUCKY and BURDWAN. PARTRIDGE and BEDOUIN were now out of sight astern and I have since learned from the Commanding Officer, PARTRIDGE, that BEDOUIN, failing to get one engine under way as he had hoped, considered the circumstances changed and made off to the westward with PARTRIDGE.

38. At 1341, heavy gunfire was heard astern and HEBE, then rejoining from astern, reported two enemy cruisers and two enemy destroyers in sight astern.

39. I therefore concentrated the three remaining fleet destroyers and turned back towards the enemy to cover HEBE, HYTHE, and BADSWORTH who were returning after attempting to sink KENTUCKY and BURDWAN, and PARTRIDGE and BEDOUIN who I then believed to be following me.

40. The enemy were observed approaching on the starboard bow soon after I had

turned and appeared to be firing at HEBE and the abandoned merchant ships. The enemy turned to the westward engaging a target enveloped in a pall of smoke which I believed to be PARTRIDGE and BEDOUIN. Shortly the enemy turned directly away.

41. By 1400, having covered BADSWORTH, HEBE, and HYTHE, I decided I could no longer afford to steam away from the convoy which was then about fifteen miles distant. I therefore with great reluctance turned to rejoin the convoy though it meant leaving BEDOUIN and PARTRIDGE.

42. I have since learned that about this time enemy torpedo bombers most conveniently attacked and sank BURDWAN and KENTUCKY, a task which HEBE and BADSWORTH had been striving to accomplish for some time. I understand that both BURDWAN and KENTUCKY were fitted with scuttling charges but I do not at present know why these charges were not used.

43. At 1430 PARTRIDGE reported that BEDOUIN had been torpedoed and sunk by enemy aircraft in position 36° 12' N., 11° 37' E., and at 1515 that enemy destroyers appeared to be picking up BEDOUIN's survivors. From this time until 1645, although unable to steam more than 18 knots, PARTRIDGE with great gallantry continued to shadow the enemy and report this greatly superior force.

44. At 1535 I was informed by the Vice-Admiral, Malta that an air striking force of 3 Albacores had left Malta to attack the enemy. This information was very heartening as I felt that we should see no more of the enemy cruisers and destroyers if he considered himself threatened by air attack.

45. At 1640 an enemy float-plane observed shadowing was shot down by fighters visually directed from CAIRO and about the same time two shadowing JU.88s were detected by radar, intercepted, and destroyed by escorting aircraft directed from CAIRO.

46. At 1700 PARTRIDGE was ordered to return to Gibraltar by the Vice-Admiral, Malta, and at 1730 WELSHMAN joined and ordered me to continue as Senior Officer.

47. At 1910 a heavy dive bombing attack by about 12 JU.88s was made. At this time a large number of Spitfires was patrolling overhead and the radar scan was saturated by I.F.F. signals both from our own fighters and from friendly fighters over Malta. Consequently the enemy's approach was not detected and neither the fleet nor the escorting fighters were given any warning. WELSHMAN and TROILUS were narrowly missed. Escorting fighters were able to intercept and are believed to have destroyed a number of the enemy after the attack had been delivered.

48. At 2040 a light dive bombing attack developed carried out by 3 JU.88s. These were driven off by escorting Spitfires and gunfire, without dropping their bombs.

49. At 2035 I received orders from the Vice-Admiral, Malta that all ships of the convoy and the escort were to enter harbour. Ships were ordered to enter harbour in the order motor launches, minesweepers, CAIRO, merchant ships, and destroyers and at 2006 I ordered the Senior Officer, Minesweepers (SPEEDY) to take the minesweepers and motor launches under his orders and to proceed ahead.

50. By the time CAIRO reached the entrance to the swept channel it was dark and mine-sweepers except for one of the Hythe class were out of sight. This minesweeper

proceeded ahead of CAIRO and appeared to be steering somewhat to starboard of the proper course. On sighting the first mark boat flashing "V", CAIRO hauled round and led the merchant ships up the marked channel until reaching the last mark.

51. TROILUS was then ordered to proceed ahead to comply with the Vice-Admiral, Malta's berthing signal and CAIRO stopped off the entrance. ORARI following closely behind TROILUS also proceeded into harbour ahead of me and was mined about 2 cables from the breakwater. She was able to proceed up harbour.

Air Co-operation.

52. From 0930 on 15th June, long-range fighters from Malta gave continuous cover to the convoy, except for two short periods when fighters had been heavily engaged and had used up their petrol and ammunition and had had to return to base early. To have maintained this escort at such a considerable distance from base, must have entailed a very heavy strain on the resources at Malta. The timing of the relieving flights was excellent. The pilots showed great dash in attacking the enemy, never hesitating to follow through anti-aircraft fire to prevent deliberate attacks being delivered.

53. The passage entails a period of two days and one night when the convoy is within range of heavy scale air attacks. I do not propose to remark on the problem as it affects the protection from surface forces.

54. During Operation "Harpoon" Force T and the convoy were subjected to a series of heavy air attacks on the 14th June. Fighters from the carriers and gunfire from the fleet prevented the enemy scoring more than one success against the convoy (TANIMBAR) but it is emphasised that during this period the force of the enemy attacks was directed more against the carriers than the merchant ships.

55. The most critical period of the passage is likely to be from daylight on the final day until the convoy has reached a position where short-range fighters based on Malta can give it cover. It is important therefore that as many long-range fighters as possible should be provided to protect the convoy during this time.

56. With the heavy scale of air attack which the enemy is capable of launching in this area I do not consider we can rely on fighters, however numerous, being able to prevent a proportion of the enemy's dive bombers delivering attacks. The enemy tactics appear to be to break his formations some distance away and for individual aircraft or small groups to attack from different sectors.

57. It is apparent therefore that merchant ships in convoy must rely on their own close range armament for protection against dive bombing. The enemy evidently has a healthy respect for our fire for he seldom appeared to press home his attacks to a close enough range to ensure hitting, but the danger from near misses is very considerable.

58. During the final day of "Harpoon" three merchant ships in convoy were lost due to enemy air action. Of these, CHANT received three direct hits, but BURDWAN

and KENTUCKY were, I believe, not touched but disabled by near misses. But for the enemy surface force, both of these ships might have been brought in.

(Signed) C.C. HARDY,
Captain, R.N.,
Senior Officer, Force X.

Admiralty footnotes:-
* *Condottieri class were 6-inch gun cruisers.*
† *Opening, i.e., increasing its distance.*

OPERATION "PEDESTAL"

The following Despatch was submitted to the Lords Commissioners of the Admiralty on the 25th August, 1942 by Vice-Admiral E.N. Syfret, C.B., Flag Officer Commanding, Force F.

H.M.S. NELSON,

25th August, 1942.

REPORT ON OPERATION "PEDESTAL"

Be pleased to lay before the Board the following report on Operation "Pedestal" which included Operations "Berserk,"* "Bellows" and "Ascendant."**

2. In compliance with Admiralty instructions I disembarked from H.M.S. CANTON at Takoradi on 7th July, and accompanied by my Staff Officer (Operations), Commander A.H. Thorold, O.B.E., R.N., proceeded by air to the United Kingdom, arriving on 13th July.

3. On arrival at the Admiralty, discussions regarding the planning of the Operations "Pedestal," "Berserk" and "Ascendant" were held with Rear-Admiral A.L. St. G. Lyster, C.B., C.V.O., D.S.O., Rear-Admiral H.M. Burrough, C.B., D.S.O., and the Naval Staff.

4. On the return of NELSON and RODNEY from Freetown my flag was transferred to NELSON and I joined that ship at Scapa on 27th July. This enabled me to convene a conference on 29th July of Flag and Commanding Officers of those naval forces** destined for "Pedestal" which were then assembled at Scapa, at which the orders for the operation were gone through in detail.

5. On 31st July the Rear-Admiral, Aircraft Carriers, Home Fleet sailed from Scapa in VICTORIOUS with ARGUS, SIRIUS and destroyers to rendezvous with EAGLE

and CHARYBDIS from Gibraltar and INDOMITABLE and PHOEBE from Freetown, for Operation "Berserk." "Berserk" was subsequently carried out according to plan and was of the utmost benefit in exercising fighter direction and co-operation between the three carriers.

6. The convoy under a bogus W.S.*** name escorted by NIGERIA (flag of Rear-Admiral Commanding, I0th Cruiser Squadron†), KENYA and destroyers sailed from the Clyde during the night 2nd/3rd August and joined my flag the following morning.

7. Just prior to sailing, but after the "normal" convoy conference, Rear-Admiral Burrough held a meeting with the Masters of the M.T. ships on board his flagship at which the whole plan was explained to them in detail. A meeting with radio operators of the M.T. ships was also held when all details regarding fleet communications and procedure were fully explained. These two meetings were invaluable.

8. Personal messages signed by the First Lord of the Admiralty wishing the Masters "God Speed" and contained in envelopes marked "Not to be opened until 0800/I0th August" were handed to the Masters. This act of courtesy and encouragement was very highly appreciated.

9. Shortly before leaving Scapa the Admiralty decided that FURIOUS should carry out Operation "Bellows," to reinforce Malta with Spitfires, concurrently with "Pedestal." The necessary additions and amendments to the Operation Orders were made and subsequently distributed to all ships and authorities concerned.

I0. Owing to technical difficulties connected with the aircraft's propellers, and FURIOUS's humped flying deck, FURIOUS was unable to sail with the main body. She later proceeded at high speed with MANCHESTER and joined my flag on D minus 3.

II. The passage of the convoy from the United Kingdom to the rendezvous with the aircraft carriers west of the Straits was wholly successful, though there were many alarms over U-Boat contacts en route.

I2. The convoy was repeatedly exercised in anti-aircraft gunnery, in emergency turns and in changing from one cruising disposition to another, using both flags and short range W/T. The risk to security in breaking W/T silence was accepted and as a result of these exercises the convoy attained an efficiency in manoeuvring comparable to that of a fleet unit.

I3. Unfavourable weather conditions coupled with unsuitable equipment and an inexperienced crew in ABBEYDALE, prevented all the ships taking part in "Berserk" completing with fuel at sea. This entailed sending additional large and small ships into Gibraltar on the night of D minus 2 and D minus I, thus throwing further heavy commitments on the already complicated organisation required from the Vice-Admiral Commanding, North Atlantic.

I4. It gives me great pleasure to record the excellent way in which these heavy commitments were met by the Vice-Admiral Commanding, North Atlantic, and all concerned at Gibraltar.

I5. During the afternoon of D minus I, the dummy air attacks on the force, followed by a fly past for identification purposes, were carried out and proved to be of the utmost benefit, for exercising the radar reporting and fighter direction organisation and for giving everyone an opportunity for studying the characteristics and markings of our own aircraft. They did, of course, entail a great volume of W/T and R/T traffic which must have been very apparent to enemy or enemy controlled listening stations. This risk to security was considered acceptable when balanced against the benefit to be derived from the practices.

16. At 1330 when INDOMITABLE joined my flag it is believed to have been the first occasion when five of H.M. aircraft carriers have ever operated in company at sea simultaneously.

17. The passage of the Straits and D.I (10th August) were uneventful. Fishing boats and one merchant vessel were passed at close quarters, but aided by a moonless night and indifferent visibility it is improbable that the force was sighted from the shore. Reports received later, showed however, that the enemy was fully cognisant of our passage of the Straits.

18. D.2 (IIth August) was marked by the following important occurrences:-

(*a*) The successful completion of the large fuelling programme, thanks very largely to the extreme efficiency shown by DINGLEDALE and BROWN RANGER. In previous similar operations it has not been necessary to provide for so large an oiling programme since ships going to Malta have been able to fuel there. In this case Malta had no oil to spare. The problem of oiling 3 cruisers and 26 destroyers at sea, under enemy observation and in U-Boat infested waters, was an anxious one, failure of which could have seriously upset the whole plan.

(*b*) The tragic sinking of EAGLE, which quite apart from the loss to the fleet of a well tried and valuable carrier, at once bereft the force of 25 per cent of its fighter strength.

(*c*) The large number of sightings and reportings of torpedoes and U-Boats, a proportion of which may well have been actualities.

(*d*) The successful execution of Operation "Bellows" whereby 37 much needed Spitfires reached Malta safely.[††]

(*e*) The continuous snooping throughout the day despite all our fighters could do to prevent it; and the heavy, but fortunately unsuccessful, air attack at dusk. Our fighters competed manfully at great height against the snoopers but the speed and the height of the JU.88s made the fighters' task a hopeless one. It will be a happy day when the fleet is equipped with modern fighter aircraft.

D.3 (*12th August*).

19. As the force moved east it was to be expected that the U-Boat and air threat would progressively increase. Additional anti-submarine measures were taken to counter the U-Boat concentration which was believed to have been disposed in an area near Galita and our vigilant A/S screen had the satisfaction of achieving a "kill" of one

Italian submarine.‡ H.M.S. ITHURIEL delivered the *coup de grace* to this submarine by ramming it and in doing so badly damaged herself and put her asdic gear out of action. The submarine when it came to the surface after being depth charged was obviously "all in" and I thought the expensive method chosen by the Commanding Officer, H.M.S. ITHURIEL, to sink it quite unnecessary. Moreover, I was disturbed at the resulting absence of ITHURIEL from the screen when an air attack was impending.

20. Throughout the day the force was under continual observation by aircraft which were protected, progressively more strongly by fighters. During the day the force was subjected to three very heavy air attacks; whilst Force X, after parting company, was attacked at dusk by bombers and torpedo bombers.

2I. During daylight hours our fighters, though frequently greatly outnumbered, continued their magnificent work both in reporting approaching raids and in shooting down enemy aircraft. Success also attended our A.A. guns though more from their deterrent effect than from the accuracy of their fire.

22. In their daylight attacks, the enemy employed every form of air attack, including minelaying ahead of the fleet, which, so far as I know, has not been used before by the enemy.

23. Despite the great numbers of aircraft employed in the four heavy attacks on the fleet up to I900 on D.3, it is gratifying to record that the only casualties were one M.T. ship with her speed reduced by a near miss, one destroyer torpedoed but afloat (though later sunk by own forces), and the INDOMITABLE put out of flying action but capable of steaming at 28½ knots.

24. I had intended that Force Z should turn to the westward on reaching the entrance to the Skerki Channel at I9I5 and had warned the fleet accordingly. The damaged INDOMITABLE, on fire forward and aft, caused me, however, to advance this time by twenty minutes, and at I855 I ordered Force Z to turn and Force X to proceed to Malta. The withdrawal of Force Z was apparently unnoticed by the enemy and its separation from Force X not discovered by him until about 2030.

25. In view of the magnitude of the enemy's air attack at I830 to I850 it seemed improbable that a further attack on Force X on any great scale would be forthcoming before dark, and having reached the Skerki Banks, it was hoped that the submarine menace was mostly over. The dangers ahead of Force X seemed to lie principally in attacks by E-Boats during the night and by aircraft the following morning.

26. Thus the enemy's successful submarine attack at 2000 when NIGERIA, CAIRO and OHIO were torpedoed was unexpected and its effect far reaching. The time was a critical one, for the change from four columns to two columns was being made, and for this manoeuvre the cruisers were much needed as leaders of columns. The torpedoing of H.M. Ships NIGERIA and CAIRO, the temporary non-effectiveness of H.M.S. ASHANTI (Captain (D), 6th Destroyer Flotilla) while embarking Rear-Admiral Commanding, I0th Cruiser Squadron, and the detachment of 4 Hunt destroyers to stand by the damaged cruisers, deprived (*a*) Force X temporarily of its Commander, (*b*) two columns of their leaders, (*c*) the convoy of nearly half its escort, and (*d*) the force of its two Fighter Direction ships. On hearing

that NIGERIA and CAIRO had been torpedoed I ordered CHARYBDIS, ESKIMO and SOMALI to reinforce Force X. From about 2035 to 2100, the convoy was subjected to a very severe dusk air attack by dive bombers and torpedo bombers. ASHANTI and PENN laid a smoke screen to cover the light western horizon, but this did not prevent the attack being effective. EMPIRE HOPE and GLENORCHY were both bombed and sunk, the latter blowing up with no survivors.

A separate torpedo bomber attack sank DEUCALION at 2130 near the Cani Rocks when under escort of BRAMHAM.

The Commanding Officer, H.M.S. KENYA describes the state of the convoy subsequent to these misfortunes as chaotic. I think this may be an exaggeration for though necessarily the convoy was in a confused state there is no evidence to show that any ship of the convoy was steaming other than in the correct direction. Furthermore we know that II of the convoy got safely, though some not undamaged, as far as Kelibia,§ by early morning.

D.4 (13th August).

27. The attenuated line of merchant ships and the reduced number of escort ships provided easy opportunities for attacks by the E-Boats which were lying in wait off Kelibia. Here three of the merchant ships which failed to reach Malta were torpedoed. Of these the WAIRANGI, it is believed, was hit in the engine room and was permanently disabled, but the ALMERIA LYKES was hit before the bulkhead of No. I hold and could well have continued steaming to Malta.

28. In the early morning MANCHESTER was torpedoed, supposedly by an E-Boat or possibly mined, and after the ship's company had abandoned her in the ship's boats and Carley rafts she was scuttled by order of her Commanding Officer.

29. The E-Boat attacks during the night added further to the disorganisation of the convoy and at daylight the scattered ships were comparatively easy prey for enemy aircraft. Three M.T. ships were hit by bombs and sunk. The remaining five M.T. ships reached Malta.

30. That these five ships did make their goal is a magnificent tribute to the resolution shown by all concerned, and a special word of praise is due to the gallant Master of the OHIO (Captain D.W. Mason), to PENN (Lieutenant-Commander J.H. Swain, R.N.), LEDBURY (Lieutenant-Commander R.P. Hill, R.N.) and BRAMHAM (Lieutenant E.F. Baines, R.N.), to the Malta Local Forces, and to the Royal Air Force based on Malta.

31. Having turned over his charges to the Malta Escort Force, Rear-Admiral Commanding, 10th Cruiser Squadron with Force X less H.M. Ships PENN, LEDBURY and BRAMHAM withdrew at 1600/D.4.

32. H.M.S. NIGERIA and three Hunts had already started back, as had H.M. Ships ESKIMO and SOMALI who had been sent by Rear-Admiral Commanding, 10th Cruiser Squadron to help H.M.S. MANCHESTER. H.M.S. TARTAR, who had sunk H.M.S. FORESIGHT at 0955/D.4, was also on her way back to Gibraltar.

33. Throughout D.4 Force Z continued to the westward, apparently unobserved by the enemy, turning to the eastward at 2300/D.4, when H.M. Ships RODNEY and INDOMITABLE with 5 destroyers were detached to Gibraltar.

D.5 (14*th August*).

34. During D.5 I was uncertain of the position of Force X and how it was faring, though from intercepted manoeuvring and radar reporting signals, it was clear that they were being subjected to air attacks to the west of Galita Island. In fact they were undergoing severe attention from the enemy's air forces but fortunately they came through unharmed.

35. With the object of being near at hand if support was required, Force Z cruised to the northward of Algiers until about 1500/D.5, when I was relieved to receive a signal from Rear Admiral Commanding, 10th Cruiser Squadron, giving his noon position, course and speed as 37° 21' N., 06° 27' E., 272°, 20 knots. Course of Force Z was then set to make contact.

36. An Albacore was sent to establish a visual link with Force X and at 1800/D.5 Force Z and Force X met and the combined forces withdrew to Gibraltar, arriving at 1800/D.6.

37. Of the remainder of the forces at sea, H.M.S. FURIOUS and screen arrived Gibraltar at 1900/D.3, H.M. Ships NIGERIA, TARTAR and 3 Hunts at 0010/D.6, and H.M. Ships ESKIMO and SOMALI at 0530/D.6.

38. Force R cruised in the western basin until it was certain that they would not be required to fuel Force X, when they were ordered to return to Gibraltar, arriving a.m./D.7.

39. H.M. Ships PENN, LEDBURY and BRAMHAM arrived at Malta with S.S. OHIO at 0755/D.6. They sailed for Gibraltar at 2030/D.9 and arrived there at 0715 on 21st August.

40. During the return passage of H.M.S. FURIOUS from Operation "Bellows," H.M.S. WOLVERINE, one of her escort, detected, rammed and sank a U-Boat§§ in position 37° 18' N., 01° 55' E. at 0050/D.3. There were no survivors. H.M.S. WOLVERINE severely damaged her bows and was escorted part of the way back to Gibraltar by H.M.S. MALCOLM, who later reinforced H.M.S. NIGERIA's screen.

41. H.M.S. NIGERIA was shadowed continuously on D.4 and was attacked by three torpedo bomber aircraft at 1515. She successfully combed the tracks and was not further molested by aircraft.

When 5 miles south of Alboran, at 1644/D.5, she avoided torpedoes fired by a U-Boat. Prior to this attack her screen had been reinforced by four Western Approaches destroyers despatched by Vice-Admiral Commanding, North Atlantic.

42. H.M. Ships ESKIMO and SOMALI were attacked by a JU.88 and a torpedo bomber aircraft when west of Galita p.m. on D.4, and a near miss on H.M.S. SOMALI caused her to lose steam and stop for five minutes.

43. Force Y sailed from Malta at 2030/D.1. Though aircraft flew over them on D.2, their Italian deck markings seemed to nonplus the enemy's observers. Off Cape Bon on the night of D.2, Force Y encountered and was fired on by a darkened Vichy minesweeper and on D.3 was shadowed occasionally by single aircraft who remained mystified. No incident occurred subsequent to noon on D.3 and the force arrived safely at Gibraltar at 1000/D.5.

General Remarks.

44. *Planning and assembly.* – It was a great advantage that the planning could be done at the Admiralty for the following reasons:-

(*a*) Early decisions could be obtained and questions answered, thus saving signals.

(*b*) Communications were better and there was less chance of loss of security.

(*c*) General views on policy could be obtained.

(*d*) Experts in all branches were readily available.

(*e*) The advice and help of the Naval Staff was always at hand.

45. Assembling and sailing of ships at Scapa Flow not only enabled me to discuss the operation with the majority of Commanding Officers of ships taking part, but also gave many advantages from the security point of view. The use of a telephone, fitted with a scrambler, was invaluable as it enabled many points of detail to be cleared up, up to the moment of sailing. I am sure that the decision to bring NELSON and RODNEY from Freetown to Scapa was fully justified.

It was some disadvantage from the cooperation point of view that INDOMITABLE and EAGLE and their attendant ships should have had to start from Freetown and Gibraltar respectively; from the security point of view, however, this was probably advantageous.

46. *Surprise.* – Our attempt to pass the convoy into the Mediterranean without the enemy's knowledge resulted in a very complicated fuelling programme during dark hours at Gibraltar in the days preceding D.I. Operation "Berserk," invaluable in itself, was a further source of embarrassment from the fuelling point of view. With the efficient intelligence service which it appears the enemy now has in the Gibraltar area it may be argued that the small chance of effecting any surprise is not worth the complications and difficulties of attempting to do so. I think, however, it would be wrong to take this line. Until the enemy's reconnaissance forces actually see us in the Mediterranean he cannot be sure his intelligence is correct, and any uncertainty we can create in his mind must be all to our benefit.

47. It would, however, be better, if circumstances permitted, to carry out the necessary and invaluable aircraft carrier co-operation exercise further away, preferably north of Ireland, on another occasion.

48. *Re-fuelling destroyers on D.2.* – The refuelling of CAIRO and 24 destroyers between 0600 and 2030 on D.2 was an accomplishment redounding very greatly to the credit of BROWN RANGER and DINGLEDALE. But the Masters of these ships would be the first to admit that fortune favoured us. The weather was good and a light easterly wind enabled the desired course to be maintained whilst fuelling was in progress.

Such fortune cannot be expected on all occasions, more particularly in winter months, and the failure or partial failure of fuelling plans must be provided for.

49. Furthermore one must always have in mind the possibility of the oiler(s) being damaged or sunk by enemy action. Hitherto the oilers have borne a charmed life, though on this occasion they experienced alarms on account of both enemy aircraft and submarines.

50. *Co-operation by other Commands.* – Information I received showed that part of the enemy's air forces which attacked the fleet on D.2 and D.3 were operating from Trapani and recently had been based at Heraklion. It seems probable, therefore, that the enemy moved some air squadrons from Greece, and possibly also from Crete, for the occasion.

51. The diversionary convoy from Haifa and Port Said was planned by Commander-in-Chief, Mediterranean, with a view to dissuading the enemy from any such re-disposition of his air forces, and I had hoped that the Army would have helped to further this end by staging an attack in Egypt. In this hope I was disappointed.

52. The attacks on Sardinian and Sicilian aerodromes by bomber forces from Malta and Egypt were valuable contributions to our plan and it is believed they achieved effective results.

53. The losses suffered by Force F were regrettably heavy and the number of merchant ships which reached Malta disappointingly small. But I have no fault to find with the personnel of the fleet because better results were not achieved. On the contrary, Commanding Officers, generally, have praised the fine bearing and spirit shown by their ships' companies, many of whom were very young and to whom battle was a new experience. I am proud to associate myself with these tributes, and in particular give credit to those whose duties kept them below decks during submarine, air and E-Boat attacks.

54. The constant A/S vigilance shown by the destroyers under the leadership of Captain R.M.J. Hutton (Captain (D), 19th Destroyer Flotilla) and Acting Captain R.J. Onslow (Captain (D), 6th Destroyer Flotilla) for a period extending over 14 days is deserving of much praise. It is true that the submarine which sank H.M.S. EAGLE was undetected but I am very sure that their watchfulness foiled many another attack.

55. That 27 emergency turns were made on passage to the Straits and 48 during D.1, D.2 and D.3, consequent on warnings given by the A/S screen, is an illustration of the value of their work. Besides this, their defence of the fleet against torpedo bomber attack was so successful that only one torpedo bomber aircraft managed to get past them.

56. The work of the aircraft carriers (H.M.S. INDOMITABLE, Captain T.H. Troubridge, and H.M.S. VICTORIOUS, Captain H.C. Bovell) under the command of Rear-Admiral Lyster, was excellently performed, while that of their fighters was magnificent. Flying at great heights, constantly chasing the faster JU. 88s, warning the fleet of approaching formations, breaking up the latter, and in the later stages doing their work in the face of superior enemy fighter forces, they were grand. The fact that 39 certainties were shot down by them and the probability that at least the same number were incapacitated is a remarkable measure of the success of the carriers, their teamwork and their fighters and of the able and inspiring leadership of Rear-Admiral A.L. St. G. Lyster, C.B., C.V.O., D.S.O.

57. Tribute has been paid to the personnel of H.M. Ships but both officers and men will desire to give first place to the conduct, courage and determination of the Masters, officers and men of the merchant ships. The steadfast manner in which these ships pressed on their way to Malta through all attacks, answering every manoeuvring order like a well trained fleet unit, was a most inspiring sight. Many of these fine men and their ships were lost but the memory of their conduct will remain an inspiration to all who were privileged to sail with them.

58. The task of Force X was always difficult and hazardous. Unhappily a serious disaster befell them almost at once and heavily tipped the scales in favour of the enemy. Nevertheless they continued undaunted and determined, and fighting their way through many and heavy attacks by U-Boats, E-Boats and aircraft, they delivered five of their charges to Malta and then fought their way back to Gibraltar. In doing this they showed a display of fortitude and determination of which all may be proud and particularly their courageous and resolute leader, Rear-Admiral H.M. Burrough, C.B., D.S.O.

59. In conclusion I think I am speaking for all in saying that we are disappointed at not doing better but we should like to try again.

(Signed) E.N. SYFRET,

Vice-Admiral,

Flag Officer Commanding,

Force F.

Admiralty footnotes:-

* *Operation "Berserk" – an aircraft earner cooperation exercise (vide paragraph 5).*

Operation "Bellows" – a reinforcement of R.A.F. at Malta by Spitfires (vide paragraph 9).

Operation "Ascendant" – the sailing of a small convoy from Malta to Gibraltar under the cover of Operation

"Pedestal" (vide paragraph 43).

** *For composition of these forces see Appendix 'A'.*

****W.S. convoys were normally those from UK to Suez via Cape of Good Hope.*

†*Rear-Admiral Commanding, 10th Cruiser Squadron – Rear-Admiral H.M. Burrough, C.B., D.S.O.*

††*The distance from Malta at which these Spitfires were flown off from FURIOUS was 584 to 555 miles.*

‡*This was the Italian submarine COBALTO. Her destruction on this occasion has been confirmed.*

§*Kelibia – some 20 miles south of Cape Bon in Tunis.*

§§ *This was the Italian submarine DAGABUR. Her destruction on this occasion has been confirmed.*

APPENDIX 'A'

NOMENCLATURE OF FORCES TAKING PART.

Force as a whole	Force F.
Convoy and Escort. U.K. rendezvous.	Force P.
VICTORIOUS, ARGUS and Escort. U.K. rendezvous.	Force M.
EAGLE and Escort. Gibraltar rendezvous.	Force J.
INDOMITABLE and Escort. Freetown rendezvous.	Force K.
Aircraft Carriers and Escort (after rendezvous for Operation "Berserk").	Force G.
BROWN RANGER and DINGLEDALE (Fleet oil tankers) and Escort.	Force R.
ABBEYDALE (Fleet oil tanker for Operation "Berserk") and Escort.	Force W.
Naval forces escorting convoy to Malta.	Force X.
Force F, less Force X.	Force Z.
Convoy and Escort. Malta-Gibraltar.	Force Y.

COMPOSITION OF FORCES.

Force Z.

Battleships.   *NELSON*
(Senior Officer, Force F) and RODNEY.

Aircraft Carriers.
VICTORIOUS (Rear-Admiral, Aircraft Carriers, Home Fleet), INDOMITABLE and EAGLE. (Also FURIOUS for Operation "Bellows").

Cruisers.   *PHOEBE*
SIRIUS and *CHARYBDIS.*

Destroyers.   *LAFOREY*
(Captain (D), 19th Destroyer Flotilla), LIGHTNING, LOOKOUT, QUENTIN, ESKIMO, TARTAR, ITHURIEL, ANTELOPE, WISHART, VANSITTART, WESTCOTT, WRESTLER, ZETLAND and *WILTON.*

Force X.

Cruisers.   *NIGERIA*
*(Rear-Admiral Commanding, 10th Cruiser Squadron), KENYA, MANCHESTER
and CAIRO.*

Destroyers.   *ASHANTI*
*(Captain (D), 6th Destroyer Flotilla), INTREPID, ICARUS, FORESIGHT,
FURY, PATHFINDER, PENN, DERWENT, BRAMHAM, BICESTER and
LEDBURY.*

Convoy W.S.2IS.

M.T. ships (15 knots):-

EMPIRE HOPE
DORSET
WAIRANGI
ROCHESTER CASTLE
WAIMARAMA
BRISBANE STAR
PORT CHALMERS
ALMERIA LYKES
SANTA ELISA
CLAN FERGUSON
GLENORCHY
MELBOURNE STAR
DEUCALION.
Oil tanker (15 knots):- OHIO
Additional escort for Convoy W.S.2IS (U.K. to Straits of Gibraltar):-

Destroyers.
KEPPEL, MALCOLM, AMAZON, VENOMOUS and WOLVERINE.

Force Y.

M.T. ships (14 knots):- TROILUS and ORARI.
Escort: Destroyers *MATCHLESS and BADSWORTH.*

Force R.

R.F.A. BROWN RANGER and DINGLEDALE (Fleet oil tankers).
H.M. Tugs: JAUNTY and SALVONIA.
Escort: Corvettes: *JONQUIL, GERANIUM, SPIREA and COLTSFOOT.*

DIARY OF EVENTS.

PART I.

Passage of Straits of Gibraltar to detaching of Force X and commencement of
Force Z's withdrawal.

Monday, 10th August (D.I).

Cape Spartel was passed at midnight 9th/10th. During the passage through the Straits of Gibraltar a large number of fishing boats was passed between Malabata and Tarifa and also two neutral steamers steaming to the westward.

2. At 0245 fog was encountered. The visibility was at times down to I cable. The fog cleared at 0500. At 0840 the force proceeded eastwards at 13½ knots in Cruising Disposition No. 16.

3. During the day, ships which had been detached to refuel at Gibraltar rejoined, and at 1600 the force was complete with the exception of WRESTLER, who, owing to a mechanical defect, was later replaced by AMAZON.

4. The day was uneventful except that alarms were caused through the I.F.F. of several of the Hudson aircraft provided by Vice-Admiral Commanding, North Atlantic, for A/S patrol not showing. This on one occasion caused the "duty section" of 4 fighters to be flown off from VICTORIOUS to intercept and entailed the breaking of W/T silence on radar reporting and fighter direction waves.

5. At dusk a diversionary convoy was due to be sailed from Port Said to rendezvous at 0800/D.2 with a similar convoy which was to sail from Haifa at 0400/D.2. These convoys were to be escorted by cruisers and destroyers and were due to turn back at dark D.2.

It is believed that these movements took place as arranged though no information was received by me to that effect.

Tuesday, IIth August (D.2).

6. At 0645, ASHANTI (Captain D.6), LEDBURY, ZETLAND, WILTON, BRAMHAM, BICESTER, FORESIGHT and DERWENT made contact with Force R and commencing fuelling, having been detached at 2130 the previous night. SIRIUS, PHOEBE and Tug JAUNTY joined from Force R at 0845. JAUNTY reported his maximum speed as being 12½ knots. Captain (D), 6th Destroyer Flotilla remained with Force R in charge of the oiling until relieved by Captain (D), 19th Destroyer Flotilla at 1800. Thanks to the excellent arrangements on board the oilers, CAIRO and 24 destroyers had been fuelled by 2030.

By the end of the day, BROWN RANGER was down to 100 tons and 1,000 tons of oil were transferred from DINGLEDALE on the morning D.3.

7. At 0800/II, COLTSFOOT, one of the corvettes screening Force R, reported that 2 torpedoes had been observed to break surface in position 37° 56' N., 01° 40' E. There were indications that Force F may have been reported by Italian U-Boats at 0815 when south of Formentera Island.

8. At 1055 I received Vice-Admiral Commanding, North Atlantic's 0902A/II informing me that an aircraft sighting report of Force F at 0620Z/II had been broadcast by Rome to "all units and stations." This followed a previous warning from Vice-Admiral Commanding, North Atlantic (his 0732A/II) that German reconnaissance aircraft were active in the Western Mediterranean.

The first radar contact was obtained at 0815, and from then onwards there was continuous "snooping" of the force by enemy aircraft. Two sections of 4 fighters each were kept in the air throughout the day, being reinforced as necessary. The enemy machines (JU.88s) were flying at 20,000 feet or more and difficulty was experienced by our fighters in intercepting them. Five interceptions were made resulting in one JU.88 shot down and two damaged. One Hurricane and one Fulmar were lost but the crews of both were recovered.

9. At 1128 three distant disturbances on the surface of the sea, as of torpedo discharges, were seen in both NELSON and CHARYBDIS, bearing 200°, about 3 miles. They were described by a submarine officer in NELSON as exactly similar to the torpedo discharges of a carelessly handled submarine, and by CHARYBDIS as a torpedo "break surface". It seems probable that a U-Boat attempted to attack the convoy at this time.

Operation "Bellows".

10. At 1218, FURIOUS screened by LIGHTNING and LOOKOUT moved out to the port quarter of the convoy for Operation "Bellows". The first Spitfire took off at 1229. Two flights of 8 Spitfires were flown off before delay was caused by emergency turns following the sinking of EAGLE.

The third, fourth and fifth flights were flown off between 1350 and 1450. In all 38 Spitfires were flown off of which one, with a defect, landed on INDOMITABLE. I was informed later in the day by Vice-Admiral, Malta that 37 had arrived at Malta.

Sinking of EAGLE.

11. At 1315 in position 38° 05' N., 3° 02' E., EAGLE was hit on the port side by four torpedoes, all within an interval of about 10 seconds At this time EAGLE was stationed on the quarter of the starboard wing column of the convoy, speed 13 knots, and on the starboard leg of zig-zag No. 10, mean line of advance 090°.

12. EAGLE heeled rapidly over to port and sank in about eight minutes. No torpedo tracks were seen and it seems probable that the attack was carried out by a German U-Boat which dived under the screen, passed between columns 3 and 4 and attacked EAGLE at very short range with electric torpedoes There were thirteen destroyers on the screen at this time and none obtained a contact.

13. LOOKOUT, who was screening, FURIOUS for "Bellows", and LAFOREY were ordered to stand by EAGLE. Tug JAUNTY also proceeded immediately towards EAGLE and joined LOOKOUT in picking up survivors. Neither LOOKOUT nor CHARYBDIS, who steamed over the probable position of the U-Boat, obtained a contact. Nine hundred and twenty-seven survivors, including the Commanding Officer, were picked up by LAFOREY, LOOKOUT and JAUNTY.

14. For about one hour and a half after the sinking of EAGLE numerous sightings of submarines and torpedoes and asdic contacts were reported but there is no conclusive proof of a second U-Boat being in the vicinity during this period.

15. At 1429, KEPPEL (Senior Officer), MALCOLM, AMAZON, VENOMOUS,

WOLVERINE and WRESTLER were sighted by Captain (D), I9th Destroyer Flotilla, and ordered by him to carry out an A/S search of the area. After picking up survivors, LAFOREY (Captain D. I9) and LOOKOUT rejoined Force F. KEPPEL, MALCOLM, VENOMOUS, WOLVERINE and WRESTLER joined at I545, AMAZON having been ordered to take JAUNTY under his orders and join Force R.

I then ordered survivors in LAFOREY to be transferred to KEPPEL, those in LOOKOUT to VENOMOUS, and those in JAUNTY to MALCOLM. This was completed by I830 when the five destroyers formed screen on FURIOUS who parted company and returned to Gibraltar.

I6. At I420 enemy aircraft approaching from the starboard beam were detected by radar. They passed directly over the force at a great height at I430, NELSON and RODNEY opening fire in barrage for a few minutes. These aircraft were not seen but it seems possible that a photographic reconnaissance was being carried out by the enemy. This formation remained in the vicinity for some time but no attack developed.

I7. At I545 Rear-Admiral, Aircraft Carriers informed me that one of our aircraft had force landed, bearing 022°, 23 miles away. WESTCOTT was ordered to proceed to search for the pilot and join Force R before dark. The pilot was recovered and WESTCOTT then joined Force R as directed.

I8. Paravanes were streamed by battleships, cruisers and M.T. ships at I635.

The Dusk Attack on the Force.

I9. From about I700 until the attack developed at 2045, Force F was continuously snooped by three or more enemy aircraft and the fighters were kept extremely busy.

20. At I634 I received Vice-Admiral Commanding, North Atlantic's I446A/II warning me that the enemy would probably make a JU.88 attack at dusk. The fleet was by now in the second degree of H.A. readiness and at I854 I ordered Captain (D), 6th Destroyer Flotilla (then the Senior Officer of destroyers in the absence of Captain (D), I9th Destroyer Flotilla, who was oiling) to station Hunt class destroyers close to the flanks of the convoy as in Cruising Disposition No. I7 by sunset; also that the screen were to increase their distance from the convoy to 6,000 yards in the event of an attack.

2I. Radar reports made it evident that a raid was coming in at 2030, and not many minutes later sighting reports of enemy aircraft were received from the screen. The last destroyers to oil, which included LAFOREY (Captain D.I9), joined at this time, thus bringing the force up to full strength.

22. At 2056, I5 minutes after sunset, firing began from destroyers on the port bow followed almost immediately by the cruisers and battleships.

23. The attack was by a number of JU 88s which dived from about 8,000 feet to 2/300 feet and by some torpedo bombers; the latter did not press home their attack though some tracks were seen and avoided. The attack lasted until about 2I30 and the barrage put up by the force was most spectacular. Three enemy aircraft were shot down for certain by ships' gunfire. Force R to the south'ard also came in for attention, one JU.88 dropping two bombs, one of which fell between the oilers and the escort,

another diving on JAUNTY who was about seven miles to the westward endeavouring to join. She claims to have damaged it with Oerlikon fire. No damage was done to any ship in these attacks.

A number of friendly fighters were in the area throughout but were unable to locate the enemy in the failing light. They had to be landed on after dark, and in doing so some were fired on by our own ships.

24. During the above air attack, QUENTIN in position A on the screen confirmed an asdic contact, carrying out three depth charge attacks before rejoining at 2I40.

25. No further incident occurred during the night and the force proceeded to the eastward unmolested.

At dusk Beaufighters from Malta attacked Elmas and Decimomannu aerodromes with results reported by Vice-Admiral, Malta as having been highly satisfactory.

By night two Liberators from the Middle East, operating from Malta, bombed Decimomannu aerodrome.

Wednesday, 12th August (D.3).

26. Radar reports of enemy snoopers began to come in at first light and all ships went to the first degree of readiness for H.A. and L.A.* at 0530. Twelve fighters were flown off at 06I0, and this number was maintained in the air throughout the day, being reinforced as necessary. There were few moments when neither aircraft, submarines, torpedoes nor asdic contacts were being reported. Cruising Disposition No. I7 was formed at 0600.

27. Information having been received of a probable concentration of U-Boats in the area to the northward of Galita, I ordered Captain (D), I9th Destroyer Flotilla, as an additional A/S measure, to reduce the distance apart of destroyers in the ahead and wing positions on the screen while shortening the distance of the screen ahead of the convoy and lengthening the distance apart of destroyers in the beam and quarter positions.

28. The first raid of the day by about 20 high level bombers approached at 0907. They were engaged by I6 of our fighters who were observed to shoot down one. The aircraft came in over the fleet from right ahead at 09I4, dropped their bombs and were away in about six minutes. Two JU.88s were observed to be shot down and a third retired to the south'ard on fire fore and aft and losing height. Our fighters shot down 8 certain, 3 probable and 2 damaged. No damage was done to any ship.

29. FURY on the starboard wing of the screen confirmed an asdic contact at 0935 and was joined in the hunt by FORESIGHT. This was about I2 minutes after LAFOREY in position B had counter-attacked a confirmed contact and it is possible that a U-Boat having escaped from LAFOREY, by diving under the convoy, was detected by FURY.

Soon there were four destroyers investigating contacts on the starboard side and at 0940 all destroyers were ordered to rejoin by Captain (D), I9th Destroyer Flotilla, as the U-Boat, if there was one there, was no longer a danger to Force F.

30. In order to fill gaps in the screen due to destroyers falling out for asdic contacts two Hunts from the convoy close screen were stationed astern of positions B and P to act as reserve destroyers.

3I. Meanwhile spasmodic firing by the screen at snoopers which came within range continued and, of course, the carriers and their "chickens" were, as always, extremely busy.

32. PATHFINDER in position C (port bow) confirmed an asdic contact and heavily attacked it. She was assisted in the hunt by ZETLAND who was in the spare position. The hunt lasted from 1I35 until II50 when both ships lost, contact and rejoined. Seven minutes later the destroyer in position H (on the port quarter) investigated a contact and carried out an attack but reported non-sub. This, sequence of events makes it appear possible that a U-Boat attempted to break through the port screen but was foiled by PATHFINDER.

33. At I200 a raid was reported coming in from ahead. It was intercepted by fighters. One was shot down, the smoke of which could be seen from the fleet. The aircraft were sighted by ASHANTI at I2I0 and cruisers and destroyers in the van opened fire one minute later. This formation was of at least nine aircraft which dropped parachute mines in the path of the fleet. An emergency turn of 90 degrees to port was executed to avoid these. Several explosions some distance to the south-eastward, at about I229 were probably these mines detonating. One minelayer was probably shot down by destroyer. No damage was sustained by any ships.

34. This attack was followed by a large number of torpedo bombers which came in, in formation of 5 or 6 on the port bow, port beam and finally on the starboard quarter. None of these attacks were pressed home and no aircraft penetrated the destroyer screen.

35. All dropped their torpedoes well outside the screen and outside range of the convoy. Several destroyers on the port side were near missed by torpedoes. One torpedo bomber was probably shot down by ships' gunfire.

36. The torpedo attack was closely followed by attacks by a large number of JU.88s which dive bombed and also dropped small canisters with small black parachutes. DEUCALION was near missed and had her speed reduced. BRAMHAM was detailed to stand by her. She reported that No. I hold was half flooded and No. 2 completely flooded, but later added that she could steam at I0 knots. I ordered BRAMHAM to escort her via the coastal route to Malta. NELSON, RODNEY, CAIRO and several M.T. ships were very near missed. One JU.88 was probably destroyed by gunfire and several damaged.

37. At I345 two Italian Reggione fighter-bombers dived on VICTORIOUS. After releasing their bombs, one of which glanced off the flight deck without exploding, they flew low over the convoy. As VICTORIOUS was flying on at the time, these were taken for friendly fighters and they got away practically unfired at. The bombs were estimated at about I00 lbs.

38. Meanwhile TARTAR on the starboard quarter reported a submarine in sight and carried out a depth charge attack. No further report was received.

39. At I4I7 ZETLAND was seen to alter course and steam to the south'ard at high

speed. He reported "submarine on the surface on the horizon, bearing 200 degrees." This submarine was no danger to the force and ZETLAND was ordered back to her station. The information was passed to BRAMHAM, who, with DEUCALION, was near the bearing. The submarine was not seen in NELSON.

40. The following two hours, until the next air attack developed, brought innumerable reports of submarine sightings and asdic contacts. As an additional A/S measure, at Rear-Admiral Commanding, I0th Cruiser Squadron's suggestion, I had ordered Captain (D), I9th Destroyer Flotilla to arrange for a depth charge to be dropped by a destroyer on each side of the screen every ten minutes between I400 and I900.

4I. At I6I6 PATHFINDER in position C (on port bow) reported a confirmed asdic contact which she heavily attacked with two patterns in quick succession. ZETLAND who had joined PATHFINDER remained until the contact was no longer a danger when she rejoined at I64I.

42. At I649 ITHURIEL in position I (port quarter) sighted a periscope and part of a conning tower on her starboard bow and immediately attacked. She obtained contact at 900 yards and carried out a counter-attack by asdics. This attack brought the U-Boat to the surface and ITHURIEL opened fire, turned and finally rammed it. This U-Boat sank before anything of value could be removed from her, although the boarding party managed to reach the conning tower. The U-Boat was the Italian COBALTO: 3 officers (including the Captain) and 38 ratings were taken prisoner. It is probable that this submarine was the one which PATHFINDER so heavily attacked.

43. Meanwhile at I640 TARTAR in position U (starboard quarter) reported "torpedo in sight starboard" and immediately counter-attacked. A few minutes later LOOKOUT in the next position astern of TARTAR (position V) reported submarine in sight. Both these ships obtained asdic contact and hunted until the U-Boat was no longer a menace, each ship having made two deliberate attacks.

44. At I726 I ordered WILTON to join Force X as BRAMHAM was detached escorting DEUCALION and at I8I3 I informed the force that Force Z would turn to the westward at I9I5.

45. Reports of small formations of enemy aircraft were coming in and it became evident before long that the enemy might be expected to make an air attack on a considerable scale. Our fighters made contact with enemy formations at about I736 and reported that they were heavily escorted by fighters.

46. At I749, ITHURIEL, who had not yet rejoined after picking up prisoners and shoring up his foremost collision bulkhead after ramming COBALTO, was attacked by 4 JU.88s and I C.R.42 fighter-bomber. She sustained no further damage but her speed had been reduced to 20 knots by the ramming and her A/S had been put out of action.

47. Course was altered in succession to I2I degrees at I800, this being the course to pass through the Skerki Channel.

48. At I830 the first enemy formation was sighted. It is believed now that there were from I00 to I20 enemy aircraft in the vicinity, many of them fighters. Against

them we had 22 fighters in the air, who continually harassed and broke up the enemy formations.

49. The first attack commenced at 1835 and comprised at least 13 torpedo bombers; simultaneously an unknown number of high level bombers, dive bombers and minelaying aircraft attacked. An emergency turn was made to avoid the mines and torpedoes which had been dropped outside the starboard screen.

Very soon after this 40 torpedo bombers were reported ahead, followed immediately by a Stuka attack on INDOMITABLE who became obscured by splashes and smoke.

The net result of these series of severe attacks was FORESIGHT torpedoed aft, INDOMITABLE 3 hits by large bombs and several near misses, causing two large fires and putting the flight deck out of action. There were many near misses elsewhere in the force but no other ships suffered damage.

The casualties to enemy aircraft are uncertain but INDOMITABLE's fighters shot down 9 certain, 2 probable and 1 damaged, for the loss of 2 fighters, 1 pilot being saved. One JU.87 was probably shot down by ships' gunfire.

50. TARTAR proceeded to FORESIGHT's assistance and subsequently took her in tow.

51. INDOMITABLE reduced speed and turned to the west away from the wind. CHARYBDIS closed her and some of Force Z destroyers were ordered to form a screen on her. As the time was now 1855 and the attack apparently over, Force Z was turned to the westward and Force X was detached.

52. At 1914 LOOKOUT was ordered to close INDOMITABLE to pump water on the fires but soon INDOMITABLE reported "situation in hand" and at 1927 that she could steam 17 knots. Shortly afterwards her steering gear became temporarily disabled, but by 2030 she was in all respects ready to proceed at 20 knots and shortly after reported able to make 28½ knots.

53. Force Z withdrew to the westward at 18 knots, speed being restricted to this by boiler tube defects reported by RODNEY.

PART II.

Detaching of Force X until their rejoining Force Z.

The following account of proceedings of Force X from the time of their detachment at 1900/D.3 until rejoining my flag at 1800/D.5 has been compiled from the reports of Rear Admiral Commanding, 10th Cruiser Squadron and Commanding Officers of ships concerned. In the circumstances prevailing, discrepancies, differences and uncertainties are bound to arise in the recording of incidents.

2. At about 1956, as Cruising Disposition No. 21 was being taken up, H.M.S. NIGERIA leading the port column was hit, supposedly by a torpedo, and within a few minutes H.M.S. CAIRO, S.S. OHIO and another M.T. ship (probably S.S. BRISBANE STAR) were also hit.

3. Rear-Admiral Commanding, 10th Cruiser Squadron is of the opinion that all these casualties were from torpedoes fired by one or more U-Boats, though the possibility of the damage being caused by mines cannot be excluded.

4. No detection of U-Boats by visual, asdic or radar was made. The time intervals between the explosions were such as to make it improbable as being the work of one U-Boat.

5. Whatever the facts, however, H.M.S. NIGERIA at once assumed a list to port of 13° and circled to starboard. By 2010 the ship was under control and at 2015 was stopped to transfer Rear-Admiral Commanding, 10th Cruiser Squadron and his staff to H.M.S. ASHANTI. Very prompt damage control measures had by this time reduced the list to 5° and by 2030 the ship was able to proceed at 14 knots for Gibraltar, despite her being 11 feet down by the head. H.M. Ships BICESTER and WILTON proceeded as escort, later in the night to be joined by H.M.S. DERWENT.

6. S.S. OHIO and BRISBANE STAR were temporarily brought to a stop, but, soon after, gallantly proceeded on their way to the southward.

7. H.M.S. CAIRO whose stern was blown off and engines disabled, was sunk by our own forces as soon as the survivors had been taken off.

8. The effect of this series of disasters was to cause the convoy to become scattered, though they continued on their course for Cape Bon.

9. Meanwhile, Rear-Admiral Commanding, 10th Cruiser Squadron in H.M.S. ASHANTI proceeded to close and direct the convoy. Whilst doing so, H.M.S. ASHANTI with H.M.S. PENN endeavoured to protect the convoy from an impending air attack by laying a smoke screen against the light westerly horizon.

10. At 2038, some 25 minutes after sunset, a severe dive bomber and torpedo bomber air attack developed and lasted until 2100. In this attack several M.T. ships were hit and two, S.S. EMPIRE HOPE and GLENORCHY, blew up or were later sunk.

11. At 2112, H.M.S. KENYA was hit on the fore foot by a torpedo fired by a U-Boat which she saw. One other torpedo passed under her and two more narrowly missed her stern. She was able to proceed, however, and soon after rejoined H.M.S. MANCHESTER.

12. After these attacks, 11 merchant ships were proceeding on their way, of which, however, only three or four were in visual touch with H.M. Ships MANCHESTER, KENYA and ASHANTI in the van.

The three T.S.D.S. destroyers were ahead; H.M.S. PATHFINDER rejoining from H.M.S. CAIRO, and H.M.S. PENN from her rescue work, were overtaking astern.

13. At 2130, S.S. DEUCALION, who had been proceeding separately with H.M.S. BRAMHAM, sank after having been torpedoed by a torpedo bomber aircraft near

the Cani Rocks. Having picked up survivors, H.M.S. BRAMHAM proceeded to overtake Force X.

Thursday, 14th August (D.4).

14. At 2354 the leading ships of Force X passed Cape Bon, and 40 minutes later two E-Boats were detected by radar on the port beam and engaged by all ships. Further running fights with E-Boats, occurred until near Kelibia Light and again at 0330 when some twenty miles from position "R", and during these attacks, H.M.S. MANCHESTER at 0120 and 3 M.T. ships, SANTA ELIZA, ALMERIA LYKES and WAIRANGI, were hit. H.M.S. ASHANTI reports that near Kelibia Light two horned mines, possibly cut by the T.S.D.S. destroyers ahead, were passed within 10 feet. The possibility exists, therefore, that one or more of the above casualties may have been caused by mines and not by torpedo.

15. These E-Boat attacks did not go unpunished, at least one and possibly two E-Boats being destroyed. V.H.F.[†]conversations in Italian intercepted in H.M.S. ASHANTI confirmed this.

16. At about 0140, H.M.S. PATHFINDER went alongside H.M.S. MANCHESTER and after discussion with the Captain embarked about 150 of the ship's company and then proceeded to join Rear-Admiral Commanding, 10th Cruiser Squadron as he had been ordered to do.

17. Subsequently, the Commanding Officer, H.M.S. MANCHESTER decided to abandon and sink his ship. The last of the ship's company left the ship at about 0245 and at about 0550 the ship was seen to sink.

18. At 0245, H.M. Ships CHARYBDIS, ESKIMO and SOMALI joined Rear-Admiral Commanding, 10th Cruiser Squadron.

19. S.S. WAIRANGI was hit in the engine room and S.S. ALMERIA LYKES before No. 1 hold. Both ships were abandoned and their crews picked up some hours later by H.M. Ships ESKIMO and SOMALI. Neither ship was seen to sink though both are reported as left in a sinking condition. Commanding Officer, H.M.S. ESKIMO reports that he did not complete the sinking of the ships because he thought there might be an opportunity later for salving them. S.S. SANTA ELIZA was sunk later in a bombing attack.

20. At dawn D.4, Rear-Admiral Commanding, 10th Cruiser Squadron in H.M.S. ASHANTI had in company with him H.M. Ships KENYA, CHARYBDIS, INTREPID, ICARUS, FURY, ESKIMO, SOMALI and the M.T. ships MELBOURNE STAR, CLAN FERGUSON and ROCHESTER CASTLE. H.M.S. LEDBURY with S.S. OHIO was 5 miles astern, H.M.S. PATHFINDER and H.M.S. BRAMHAM with S.S. PORT CHALMERS were 10 miles to the north-west, while H.M.S. PENN was observed beyond S.S. PORT CHALMERS standing by an M.T. ship – probably S.S. WAIMARAMA – which was on fire and shortly afterwards blew up. Later S.S. DORSET was sighted to the northward and ordered to join the convoy.

21. It was learned later that S.S. BRISBANE STAR spent the night and part of the

day in the Gulf of Hammamet. Whilst in territorial waters his ship was boarded by the French authorities who, after protest, behaved well and took a seriously wounded man ashore to Susa. S.S. BRISBANE STAR eventually reached Malta at 1430 the following day, 14th August.

22. At 0712, Rear-Admiral Commanding, 10th Cruiser Squadron ordered H.M. Ships ESKIMO and SOMALI to return and stand by H.M.S. MANCHESTER. On their way to do so they picked up survivors of S.S. ALMERIA LYKES and WAIRANGI and at 1040 off Kelibia they recovered about 150 of the MANCHESTER's ship's company from Carley floats. They were then only half a mile from the coast and were able to see several hundreds of, apparently, H.M.S. MANCHESTER's ship's company being marched away. Having recovered all survivors, H.M. Ships ESKIMO and SOMALI proceeded for Gibraltar.

23. At 0810, the first of a series of air attacks was experienced by Force X, JU.88s delivering a dive bombing attack, mostly directed at S.S. CLAN FERGUSON, second ship of H.M.S. CHARYBDIS's column. S.S. CLAN FERGUSON received a direct hit and blew up. Her next astern passed through the flames apparently unscathed. H.M.S. CHARYBDIS reports seeing two aircraft diving on S.S. CLAN FERGUSON and only one coming out of the dive, the other presumably being destroyed by the explosion.

24. Further attacks by Stuka dive bombers accompanied by Italian aircraft laying parachute mines ahead and on the flanks of the convoy occurred at 0925. The Stukas made a set at S.S. OHIO who sustained several near misses. One Stuka which was shot down by the combined efforts of H.M.S. ASHANTI and S.S. OHIO dived into S.S. OHIO's side.

25. The Malta Beaufighters and Spitfires were now in sight of Force X and seen to be making contact with the enemy at times. Rear-Admiral Commanding, 10th Cruiser Squadron reports that, observing they had no fighter direction aid from Force X, he considered the fighters performed a magnificent job of work throughout the day.

26. At 0941, H.M.S. KENYA was near missed by further dive bombers, and at 1017 and 1050 similar combined dive bombing and minelaying attacks occurred. In these S.S. DORSET, who was rejoining, and S.S. OHIO, were both near missed and stopped. H.M. Ships PENN, LEDBURY and BRAMHAM stood by S.S. OHIO and DORSET. The latter was eventually sunk at 2014 after being set on fire by more air attacks.

27. At 1120, Italian torpedo bombers carried out an attack combined with the dropping of parachute mines or circling torpedoes. Torpedoes were dropped at long range and except for one which became entangled in S.S. PORT CHALMERS' paravane (subsequently cleared safely) none appeared to endanger the force.

28. Beaufighters and long-range Spitfires were observed to shoot down at least 4 enemy aircraft in the distance but unfortunately one Spitfire was engaged by merchant ships during a dive bombing attack and crashed, the pilot being killed.

29. By 1230, Force X was within range of Malta's short-range Spitfires and thereafter was unmolested.

30. At 1430, the Malta Escort Force under the Senior Officer, Minesweepers, in H.M.S. SPEEDY, reinforced the escort and at 1600, Force X, less H.M. Ships PENN, BRAMHAM, and LEDBURY, who continued to stand by S.S. OHIO and DORSET, retired to the westward. S.S. PORT CHALMERS, MELBOURNE STAR and ROCHESTER CASTLE were turned over to the local escort and eventually entered harbour at Malta safely at 1825.

Friday, 15th August (D.5).

31. After an epic struggle by her gallant Master and escorts, S.S. OHIO entered Grand Harbour at 0755.

32. Force X's withdrawal was uneventful in the initial stages. When off Cape Bon at 0130 they were attacked by E-Boats. These were engaged and an explosion was seen which was believed to be an E-Boat blowing up.

33. At 0450 when off Fratelli Rock a U-Boat attacked the force, H.M.S. ASHANTI being just missed. H.M.S. KENYA sighted the submarine and made an attempt to ram but the submarine was inside her turning circle.

34. At daylight the force was S.S.E. of Galita Island and shortly afterwards the first snoopers appeared.

35. At 0912 the first of a long series of air attacks commenced with a number of JU.88s. H.M.S. KENYA was near missed at 0942 and a small fire in "A" boiler room entailed a short reduction in speed.

36. From 1000 to 1300 attacks were almost incessant, and included dive bombers, high level bombers, torpedo bombers and dropping of mines or circling torpedoes by low-flying aircraft. Fortunately, however, Force X came through untouched and at 1800 joined Force Z in position 37° 29' N., 03° 25' E.

Admiralty footnotes:
H.A. – High Angle armament; L.A. – Low Angle armament.
† *V.H.F. – very high frequency radio telephone.*

7

BATTLE OF SIRTE

22 March 1942

The following Despatch was submitted to the Lords Commissioners of the Admiralty on the 2nd June, 1942, by Admiral Sir Henry H. Harwood, K.C.B., O.B.E., Commander-in-Chief, Mediterranean Station.

Mediterranean,
2nd June, 1942.

Be pleased to lay before Their Lordships the attached reports of proceedings during Operation M.G. One between I9th March and 28th March, 1942.* This operation was carried out with the object of passing a convoy (M.W.I0) of four ships to Malta, where it was most urgently required. In the course of the operation a greatly superior Italian surface force which attempted to intercept the convoy was driven off.

Plan.

2. When running the previous Malta convoy (M.W.9) in February, I942, an attempt was made to escape detection during the first and second days out from Alexandria by splitting the convoy and simulating two normal Tobruk convoys. In the event this proved a failure. Further, an attempt to keep clear of JU.87s from Cyrenaica during the passage of the central basin by keeping well to the northward had little effect owing to the weight of attack from aerodromes in Greece and Crete.

3. It was therefore decided to keep convoy M.W.I0 together throughout, and to use all available forces to fight the convoy through, and to reinforce this escort at dawn D.3 by Force K** from Malta. The route was chosen with a view to:-

(*a*) arriving at Malta at dawn,

(*b*) being as far to the westward by darkness on D.2 as was possible consistent with remaining within range of long-range fighter protection during daylight,

(*c*) taking advantage of a suspected weakness in the enemy's air reconnaissance of the area between Crete and Cyrenaica, and at the same time avoiding suspected U-boat areas,

(*d*) keeping well south during the passage of the central basin to increase the distance to be covered by surface forces attempting to intercept.

4. To reduce the scale of air attack on the convoy, the Eighth Army were to carry out a feint advance (Operation "Fullsize") on D.2. It was hoped that this would focus the attention of the enemy air forces on the land, and so draw off some of the attack from the convoy. In the event this feint achieved its object very successfully.

5. Simultaneously the Royal Air Force were to undertake as heavy attacks as possible on enemy aerodromes in Cyrenaica and Crete. Anti-ship striking forces were to be held in readiness on D.3, when interception by surface forces was a possibility.

6. Covering submarine patrols were established by two submarines in the southern approaches to Messina and four in the Gulf of Taranto.

The Operation.

7. As no adequate escort was available in Malta, it was necessary for part of the escort force from Alexandria to remain with the convoy until arrival at Malta. H.M.S. CARLISLE and five Hunts were selected for this duty.

8. The Fifth Destroyer Flotilla*** left Alexandria at 1130 19th March to carry out A/S sweeps between Alexandria and Tobruk. In the course of these operations H.M.S. HEYTHROP (Lieutenant-Commander R.S. Stafford, R.N.) was torpedoed and sunk by a U-boat.

9. The Flotilla arrived at Tobruk at 1830 20th March, fuelled, and sailed during the night to rendezvous with M.W.10 at dawn 21st March. H.M.S. BEAUFORT was delayed through fouling her starboard screw with a berthing wire, but rejoined the Flotilla by dawn 22nd March.

10. At 0700 20th March, convoy M.W.10 consisting of H.M.S. BRECONSHIRE, and S.S.s CLAN CAMPBELL, PAMPAS and TALABOT (Norwegian) left Alexandria, escorted by H.M.S. CARLISLE and six destroyers. The Fifteenth Cruiser Squadron†and four destroyers followed at 1800 the same day. All these forces were in company by 0600 22nd March, HM. Ships PENELOPE and LEGION from Malta two hours later.

11. It was hoped that the enemy had so far failed to locate the convoy, but at 0131 22nd March, H.M.S. P.36‡reported a force, including heavy ships, leaving Taranto. It was evident that the convoy had been reported, probably by U-boat on the afternoon of 21st March. A flight of five JU.52s had been sighted at 1705 the same day, and it seems certain that these also reported the force.

12. Air attacks began at 0930 22nd, and continued all day at intervals. At 1410 H.M.S. EURYALUS reported smoke to the northward, which by 1434 had resolved itself into enemy surface forces.

Attempted Interception by Enemy Surface Forces.

I3. The ensuing action is graphically described in the report of the Rear-Admiral Commanding, Fifteenth Cruiser Squadron and individual ships. The battle plan which the Rear-Admiral Commanding, Fifteenth Cruiser Squadron, had evolved and practised for this eventuality was, in brief, to lay smoke between the enemy and the convoy, and to attack with torpedoes under cover of the smoke should the enemy attempt to break through in pursuit of the convoy.

I4. The strong south-easterly wind was favourable to the execution of this plan, which was brilliantly executed, and the enemy was driven off. The weather had also caused the enemy to dispense with his destroyer screen in order to maintain the speed necessary to intercept the convoy before dark. As had been anticipated, the enemy was unwilling to risk coming through the smoke, and further played into the hands of the Rear-Admiral Commanding, Fifteenth Cruiser Squadron, by attempting to work round to leeward of the smoke area.

I5. Nevertheless a critical period ensued at about I640, when the enemy which by now included a Littorio battleship, again made contact to the northward of the convoy. The Rear Admiral Commanding, Fifteenth Cruiser Squadron was at the time in search of two enemy ships unaccounted for and thought to be working round to windward of the smoke. It thus fell to H.M.S. SIKH (Captain St. J.A. Micklethwait, D.S.O., R.N.) with H.M. Ships HAVOCK, LIVELY and HERO, to hold off the enemy for half an hour until the return of the Rear Admiral Commanding, Fifteenth Cruiser Squadron. During this remarkable and determinedly fought action, H.M.S. HAVOCK was hit and stopped, but was later able to proceed to Malta.

I6. The situation, relieved, but not saved, was finally turned to our advantage by a most determined torpedo attack carried out by the Fourteenth Destroyer Flotilla[††] supported by H.M.S. CLEOPATRA and H.M.S. EURYALUS. In the face of this attack, the enemy turned away. It is almost certain that the battleship sustained one torpedo hit, and hits from the cruisers' gunfire. H.M.S. LIVELY sustained damage from a 15-inch salvo which straddled and hit her, but she was able to return to Alexandria.

I7. This ended the enemy's attempts to intercept, and he was last seen on a northerly course at I900. It is noteworthy that no attempt was, apparently, made to intercept the convoy after dark. The actual damage to the enemy cannot be accurately assessed but in addition to the damage to the battleship it is known that one cruiser was seriously damaged.

I8. Meanwhile the convoy, making the best of its way westward, had been subjected to heavy and continuous air attack, from which it emerged unscathed. The credit for this must go to the fine gunnery of H.M.S. CARLISLE and the Hunt class destroyers[‡‡]and to the admirable handling of the merchant ships in the convoy. Without in any way wishing to detract from the fine work of the masters, there is little doubt that the presence of naval liaison officers in the merchant ships contributed largely to the defeat of these attacks.

Return of Force B to Alexandria.

I9. Owing to heavy weather during the night 22nd-23rd March, Force B was faced with a long passage through "Bomb Alley"§ in daylight. Shadowing started early, but no attacks developed until the afternoon, when H.M.S. LIVELY, who had dropped astern, was the target. Beaufighters of 20I (Naval Co-operation) Group provided cover from 0800 onwards. They had, on the previous day, also provided cover until 0900; a notable achievement at a distance of over 300 miles from their base.

20. Force B arrived at Alexandria at I230 24th March without further incident of note, and received a deservedly great welcome.

Arrival of the Convoy at Malta.

2I. At I900 on 22nd March the convoy was dispersed by order of H.M.S. BRECONSHIRE, and made for Malta in an attempt to reach harbour by daylight. H.M. Ships PENELOPE, CARLISLE, HAVOCK, LEGION, KINGSTON and the whole of the Fifth Destroyer Flotilla were either escorting or covering.

22. All ships were subjected to heavy air attack shortly after daylight on 23rd March, though under fighter protection from Malta Spitfires and Hurricanes. Several German aircraft were destroyed or damaged by the fighters who also forced other enemy aircraft to jettison their bombs. S.S. TALABOT and S.S. PAMPAS had made good time, and passed the breakwater at 09I5 and 0930 respectively. H.M.S. BRECONSHIRE, having completed all but the last eight miles of this hazardous journey, was, at 0920, hit and stopped. H.M. Ships CARLISLE and PENELOPE both made unavailing attempts to take her in tow, and she eventually anchored off Zonkor Beacon.

23. S.S. CLAN CAMPBELL, who had, all through, been the slowest ship, found herself some 50 miles south of Malta at daylight, escorted by H.M.S. ERIDGE. Attacks soon developed, and, at I030, S.S. CLAN CAMPBELL was hit. Her engine room flooded and she sank shortly afterwards. H.M.S. ERIDGE picked up II2 of S.S. CLAN CAMPBELL's people; a difficult operation which, in the heavy weather prevailing, took 2½ hours. H.M.S. LEGION had been ordered to join H.M.S. ERIDGE and S.S. CLAN CAMPBELL, but herself sustained damage from a near miss and had to be beached in Marsa Xlokk.

24. H.M.S. BRECONSHIRE was eventually got into Marsa Xlokk during the night 24th/25th after a fine piece of towing under most difficult circumstances by H.M. Tug ANCIENT, under the direction of Captain A.D. Nicholl (H.M.S. PENELOPE) and Mr. Murphy, Senior Pilot. Unfortunately during the operations to screen H.M.S. BRECONSHIRE while she was at anchor, H.M.S. SOUTHWOLD was mined. She sank after the most determined efforts to save her had been defeated by the weather. Finally, H.M.S. BRECONSHIRE was again bombed, and sank on her side.

25. Thus two out of the original four ships in the convoy actually arrived in the Grand Harbour.

Dispersal of H.M. Ships from Malta.

26. An extremely heavy scale of air attack was developed on ships in harbour, and it became imperative to get as many ships as possible away before they sustained further damage. Accordingly ships were sailed as follows:-

25th March – CARLISLE, HURWORTH, DULVERTON, ERIDGE and BEAUFORT for Alexandria.

29th March – AURORA and AVON VALE for Gibraltar.

5th April – HAVOCK for Gibraltar.

8th April – PENELOPE for Gibraltar.

27. The sailing of these ships from Malta represents a series of the most determined efforts on the part of both the ships themselves and the dockyard authorities in the face of continuous and heavy attack. H.M.S. PENELOPE actually expended her outfit of A.A. ammunition and had to re-ammunition before she could sail. With the exception of H.M.S. HAVOCK, all ships reached their destinations without further damage. H.M.S. HAVOCK grounded at high speed near Kelibia.§§ She was destroyed by her own ship's company, who were interned by the French authorities.

Unloading of Convoy.

28. In the face of the heavy and relentless air attack which was maintained after the arrival of the convoy, unloading and berthing arrangements proved unsatisfactory. Both the ships which reached Grand Harbour were damaged and eventually sunk. As a result only 5,000 tons of the 25,900 tons of cargo which had been carried to Malta at such risk and price was safely unloaded.

29. It is evident that before another Malta convoy is run, air superiority in the island must be assured. In addition, ships will be berthed in shallow water or beached, and steps are being taken to ensure that there shall be no delay in starting to unload, and that the highest possible rate of unloading is maintained.

Personnel.

30. The behaviour of all personnel throughout the many phases of this hazardous and testing operation was worthy of the highest traditions of the service. In addition to the many outstanding acts already referred to, particular mention must be made of the gallant and devoted endeavours made by the officers and men of the damaged destroyers to save their ships. It is noteworthy that all these efforts were successful except for H.M.S. SOUTHWOLD, and in this case the weather completed the enemy's unfinished handiwork.

31. The loss of H.M.S. BRECONSHIRE, after a long and arduous career running stores to Malta, was particularly galling, occurring as it did, so near the end of the journey. The gallant fight put up by H.M.S. BRECONSHIRE before finally being sunk is typical of the stalwart determination of her Commanding Officer, Captain C.A.G. Hutchison, Royal Navy.

32. The good handling of the merchant ships and the excellent work done by the

naval liaison officers has already been remarked on. There can be no doubt that the defeat of the heavy air attacks on the convoy on 22nd March was due in no small measure to the excellent seamanship and discipline displayed by the merchant ships.

33. During the action on 22nd March, the determination and team-work of all ships more than fulfilled the high standard that had been expected. This, combined with the resolute leadership and masterly handling of the force by Rear Admiral Philip L. Vian, K.B.E., D.S.O., produced a heartening and thoroughly deserved victory from a situation in which, had the roles been reversed, it is unthinkable that the convoy or much of its escort could have survived.

(Signed) H.H. HARWOOD,

Admiral,

Commander-in-Chief.

*Admiralty footnote:- Admiral Sir Andrew B. Cunningham, G.C.B., D.S.O., was Commander-in-chief of the Mediterranean Station at the time when this operation was carried out.

**Admiralty footnote:- Force K – H.M. Ships PENELOPE (Cruiser) and LEGION (Destroyer).

***Admiralty footnote:- Fifth Destroyer Flotilla – SOUTHWOLD (Commander C.T. Jellicoe, D.S.C.), BEAUFORT, DULVERTON, HURWORTH, AVON VALE, ERIDGE and HEYTHROP.

† Admiralty footnote:- Fifteenth Cruiser Squadron – CLEOPATRA (flying the flag of Rear-Admiral P.L. Vian, D.S.O.), DIDO, EURYALUS and CARLISLE.

‡Admiralty footnote:- H.M.S. P.36 – a submarine.

††Admiralty footnote:- Captain (D), Fourteenth Destroyer Flotilla – Captain A.L. Poland, D.S.O., D.S.C.

‡‡ Admiralty footnote:- Destroyers of the Fifth Destroyer Flotilla.

§ Admiralty footnote:- "Bomb Alley" – the waters between Cyrenaica and Crete.

§§ Admiralty footnote:- Kelibia – on N.E. coast of Tunis, south, of Cape Bon.

ENCLOSURE

Office of Rear Admiral Commanding,
Fifteenth Cruiser Squadron.
31st March, 1942.

OPERATION M.G. ONE – REPORT.
(20th March to 24th March, 1942.)

Herewith is forwarded the report on Operation M.G. One, which includes an account of an action against Units of the Italian Fleet in the Gulf of Sirte on 22nd March, 1942.

(Signed) PHILIP VIAN,

Rear Admiral Commanding,

Fifteenth Cruiser Squadron.

PART I – NARRATIVE (GENERAL).

I. The Convoy and Escort arrived in position "N" (Lat. 034 degs. I0 mins. North, Long. 020 degs. 00 mins. East) at 0600, the appointed time, on 22nd March, I942.

Westward Passage – Tactical Problems.

2. The problems presented on passage to this point had been:-

(*a*) To steer such courses, after being reported, which, while keeping the force within fighter range, avoided crossing the track of the last reported line of advance. The track used is shown on the strategical plot: it is known that one U-boat made contact.

(*b*) To afford protection to the A/S Screen from U-boat attack when, through the slow speed of S.S. CLAN CAMPBELL, it became necessary to discontinue the convoy zig-zag. Protection was afforded by a modified form of E.Y. (Conduct of the Fleet); the screen zigzagged as a whole across the front of the units screened.

3. At 0800 on 22nd March, I942, PENELOPE and LEGION having joined, course was set 250 degs. I3 knots.

The southerly course was chosen in view of P.36's 0I3IB of 22nd March, received at 05I8, reporting that the enemy had left Taranto; it was my wish to delay contact until evening, if practicable.

Strategical Background.

4. In the action to follow, the strategical considerations governing the courses of action open to me were:-

 (i) The convoy, if it were to reach Malta at all, must arrive within a very few hours of daylight.

(ii) Force B could not be oiled at Malta.

(iii) Air reconnaissance from Malta could not be expected on Day 3.

Tactical Plan.

5. The tactical plan evolved on 4 (i) above is contained in the Operation Orders, and was based on the consideration that the convoy must steer west, not south, for the greater part of the engagement.

6. From 4 (ii) above it was clear that the enemy must be driven off by dark since, if involved in night operations to the westward, the oil situation for the return passage to Alexandria would be most difficult.

7. The probable absence of air reconnaissance rendered it imperative that Cruisers and Fleet Destroyers should be able to move out from a Cruising Disposition designed

to meet air attack into a disposition suitable for surface action with the least possible delay.

8. The tactical plan was exercised off Alexandria by the cruisers and some of the fleet destroyers about a month before the action.

Air – 22nd March.

9. No air reconnaissance from Malta proved practicable. The enemy commenced shadowing at 0930; air attack began a few minutes later and was continued, with increasing intensity, until dusk. It is estimated that for shadowing, high-level bombing, torpedo bombing, and spotting, the enemy employed 150 aircraft during the day.

First Contact.

10. H.M.S. EURYALUS, as in 1805, first sighted the enemy. Contact was made with 4 ships, range 12 miles, first thought to be 3 battleships, at 1427 – much earlier than was expected. Cruisers and Fleet Destroyers concentrated on their leaders in 5 divisions on a northerly course, and when at a suitable distance from the convoy turned east and laid smoke in accordance with the plan. The gun action commenced at 1436. By 1444 it was clear that the composition of the enemy was in fact one eight-inch and three six-inch cruisers: our force was ordered to steer towards the enemy, who broke off the engagement at 1515 and were lost to sight to the northward.

Second Contact.

11. At 1637, four enemy ships made contact: at 1640, three more. The composition of this force was the battleship LITTORIO, two eight-inch, three six-inch cruisers and one vessel never identified.

The same tactics were pursued as before, our cruisers and destroyers steering easterly and westerly courses to lay smoke, the enemy working round to the southwest to cut off the convoy from Malta.

In view of the weight of the air attack on the convoy, I was forced to order the smoke-laying division – CARLISLE and two Hunts – to rejoin the convoy and join in its air defence.

This meant that Cruisers and Fleet Destroyers had to lay smoke, not only to cover themselves but also to cover the convoy.

Smoke laid for the latter purpose seriously hampered gunfire: while CLEOPATRA, normally at the head of the formation, fired 1,000 rounds in low angle.* PENELOPE, generally in the centre, fired 64, and ZULU, leading a division in the rear, none.

12. CLEOPATRA was hit on the after part of the bridge at 1644, but in turn a palpable hit on the bridge of a Bolzano was obtained, probably by DIDO.

Intervention by Captain (D), Twenty-Second Destroyer Flotilla.

13. By 1730, in search of two enemy ships not accounted for and which I thought might be working round in the rear, I got too far to the eastward: the situation was retrieved by Captain (D), Twenty-Second Destroyer Flotilla, in H.M.S. SIKH, who, with HAVOCK (detached after being hit shortly afterwards), LIVELY and HERO, held off the enemy without other support for nearly half an hour: a remarkable feat. It transpired subsequently that the two enemy ships the search for which had led me astray had been hit hard earlier and had withdrawn from the action.

14. At 1800, on my return, the situation appeared critical: CLEOPATRA fired torpedoes at the enemy line, which turned them away, and I ordered a general attack by torpedoes to be made on the enemy under cover of smoke.

Torpedo Attack.

15. Such an attack presented considerable difficulties owing to great pall of smoke, the falling visibility and the rising wind (force 6) and sea (44)[†] at this time.

Captain (D), Fourteenth Destroyer Flotilla went in to the attack on a broad line of bearing, in the traditional manner at 1840: the attack was pushed home to a range of about 3 miles against very heavy fire and certainly obtained one hit on LITTORIO.

KINGSTON was stopped by a hit and set on fire but was later able to proceed and make Malta.

Gunfire from CLEOPATRA and EURYALUS following the destroyers in started a fire in the after part of LITTORIO which was burning 20 minutes later, and obtained hits forward also.

16. The enemy turned from south to northwest in the face of Captain (D), Fourteenth Destroyer Flotilla's attack: Captain (D), Twenty-Second Destroyer Flotilla, who had reached a good firing position was baulked by the turn and by smoke but in his division LIVELY, who had suffered flooded compartments from a 15-inch straddle, had a funnel on fire and her tubes jammed, so far recovered to fire 8 torpedoes with the right settings before retiring.

Enemy breaks off action and retires.

17. LITTORIO and cruisers were last sighted at 1900 steering north-northwest, the former still with a fire aft; the convoy was dispersed for Malta at this time, and at 1940 Force B shaped course for Alexandria.

Damage suffered by the enemy.

18. In addition to the damage suffered by LITTORIO, it is apparent from intelligence reports that one cruiser was seriously damaged and a second damaged.

Air Attack.

19. During the 28 raids on the convoy made concurrently with the surface action, 4

aircraft were shot down and many damaged by CARLISLE and the Hunts whilst no ship in the convoy or escort suffered damage – a remarkable result.

Concurrent attacks on Cruisers and Fleet Destroyers were less intense; EURYALUS shot down one torpedo-bomber.

Beaufort Striking Force.

20. At 1800, I received your message informing me of the despatch of our air striking force: homing signals were made by EURYALUS, but aircraft did not arrive as the enemy fleet was beyond their range.

Force B – Passage Eastward.

21. The return passage to Alexandria was made against an easterly gale: the scale of air attack developed was only a fraction of what was expected; LIVELY had to act the part when attacked by 6 Stukas.

The immunity from air on Day 2 and relative immunity on Day 4 must be due largely to the work of the fighters of 201 (Naval Co-operation) Group, operating in a storm at great distance from their bases.

*Admiralty footnote:- Low angle – i.e. at ship targets.

†Admiralty footnote:-Wind (force 6) – a reference to the Beaufort scale denoting "Strong Breeze – (21-26 knots)." Sea (44) – a reference to the combined sea and swell scale, denoting "Rough sea and moderate swell."

PART II – NARRATIVE.

Convoy M.W.10, consisting of H.M.S. BRECONSHIRE (Captain C.A.G. Hutchison, R.N.), S.S. CLAN CAMPBELL, S.S. PAMPAS and S.S. TALABOT escorted by the Twenty-Second Destroyer Flotilla (H.M. Ships SIKH (Captain St. J.A. Micklethwait, D.S.O., R.N.), ZULU, LIVELY, HERO, HAVOCK and HASTY), and H.M.S. CARLISLE (Captain D.M.L. Neame, D.S.O., R.N.), sailed from Alexandria at 0800 on 20th March, 1942.

2. In view of the uncertainty of weather and of fuel considerations, Force B consisting of H.M. Ships CLEOPATRA (Captain G. Grantham, D.S.O., R.N.) (Flag of the Rear Admiral Commanding, Fifteenth Cruiser Squadron), DIDO (Captain H.W.U. McCall, R.N.), EURYALUS (Captain E.W. Bush, D.S.O., D.S.C., R.N.), and the Fourteenth Destroyer Flotilla (H.M. Ships JERVIS (Captain A.L. Poland, D.S.O., D.S.C., R.N.), KIPLING, KELVIN and KINGSTON) sailed at 1800 on 20th March, 1942, by a northerly route to rendezvous with M.W.10 at 0800 21st March, 1942.

3. Rendezvous was made with M.W.10 at 0940 on 21st March in position 33 degs. 20 mins. N., 24 degs. 40 mins. E. The Fifth Destroyer Flotilla (H.M. Ships, SOUTHWOLD (Commander C.T. Jellicoe, D.S.C., R.N.), DULVERTON, ERIDGE, AVON VALE and HURWORTH) had also joined the convoy by this time from Tobruk. Cruising Disposition No. 4 was formed slightly amended to meet existing

conditions, and course 294 degs. shaped with the whole force, at 13 knots, carrying out zig-zag No. 12.

4. Owing to lack of facilities at Tobruk and late arrival there owing to the torpedoing of HEYTHROP the day before, DULVERTON, ERIDGE and HURWORTH had left Tobruk with 60 per cent fuel. BEAUFORT was delayed at Tobruk by a fouled propeller.

5. CLAN CAMPBELL had difficulty in maintaining the speed of the convoy. At 1245 zig-zag No. 10 was started, CLAN CAMPBELL maintaining a steady course so as to keep up with the convoy.

6. At 1600, as an intercept had shown that the force might have been reported by enemy aircraft, course was altered to 320 degs. and at 1700 back to 290 degs.

7. At 1705, the force was sighted by 6 JU.52s escorted by one M.E.110 on passage from Libya to Crete, by whom the force was reported. At 1745 course was altered to 270 degs. and at 1900 to 320 degs. and at 2000 to 285 degs. and thence by evasive steering, which avoided crossing the last reported mean line of advance to position "N".

8. At 1900 BEAUFORT closed the convoy from astern having arrived from Tobruk.

9. A speed of 12 knots was made good during the period 0930 on 21st March to 0800 on 22nd March.

10. Fighters were present from 0740 to 1715.

11. The force passed 3 miles south of position "N" at 0600 on 23rd March, steering 290 degs. to make contact with H.M. Ships PENELOPE and LEGION.

12. H.M. Ships PENELOPE (Captain A.D. Nicholl, D.S.O., R.N.) and LEGION were sighted at 0742 bearing 343 degs., and at 0750 course was altered to 250 degs. in view of P.36's report of 3 destroyers and heavy ships south of Taranto.

13. Shadowing by enemy aircraft commenced at 0935 at which time the first torpedo-bombing attack commenced. Raids continued from this time.

14. Own fighters were present from 0810 to 0900.

15. Two groups of enemy aircraft failed to locate the convoy and were searching for it 30 or 40 miles astern.

16. No zig-zag was carried out by the convoy after 0650 as it was considered essential to make the best speed. The escort carried out independent zig-zags.

17. At 0920 course was altered to 270 degs. to make more westing, and at 1220 to 250 degs. to make the probable enemy surface contact as late as possible.

18. At 1332 a JU.88 dropped 4 red flares ahead of the convoy – a probable indication that enemy surface forces were in the vicinity – though it was not thought that they should make contact before 1630 or 1700.

19. At 1410 EURYALUS reported smoke bearing 353 degs. This was not seen from CLEOPATRA. A further signal at 1417 said report was uncertain.

20. At 1230 Organisation No. 4* was assumed as it was decided that the convoy would not turn back but proceed to Malta even if enemy surface forces made contact. Destroyers had been ordered to raise steam for Full Speed at 1400 (they had been at ½ hour's notice for Full Speed).

A signal was made ordering Divisions to form up on a northerly course in the event of a contact being made.

*Admiralty footnote:- Organisation No. 4 was as follows:-
Ist Div. – JERVIS, KIPLING, KELVIN, KINGSTON (Destroyers).
2nd Div. – DIDO, PENELOPE (Cruisers), LEGION (Destroyer).
3rd Div. – ZULU, HASTY (Destroyers).
4th Div. – CLEOPATRA (flag of C.S.15), EURYALUS (Cruisers).
5th Div. – SIKH, LIVELY, HERO, HAVOCK (Destroyers).
6th Div. – CARLISLE (Cruiser), AVON VALE (Destroyer).
The 6th Div. to be employed on smoke laying.

PHASE I.

21. *Reports*
   1427 "4 suspicious vessels bearing 040 degs." received from EURYALUS.
   1427 "I unknown bearing 010 degs. 12 miles" received from LEGION.
   1429 Signal "ZLG" transmitted from CLEOPATRA (C.S.15).
   1432 "4 unknown bearing 015 degs. 15 miles" received from LEGION.
   1434 "3 battleships bearing 010 degs. 12 miles" transmitted from CLEOPATRA (C.S.15).
   1506 "Enemy previously reported as battleships now believed to be cruisers" transmitted from C.S.15.
   22. As soon as the enemy were reported the signal "ZLG" was made and carried out exactly as detailed in the operation orders.
   The convoy turned away from the enemy to 210 degs. while all Divisional Leaders led out to the northward to concentrate by divisions.
   During this phase of the action, LEGION joined the Fourteenth Destroyer Flotilla with the First Division at 1507 and remained with them for the rest of the day.
   23. As soon as divisions were clear of the convoy to the northward, an easterly smoke-laying course was shaped – about 1435. The enemy opened fire at this time and the first splashes were seen well short about 1436.

Enemy disposition.

24. The enemy are believed to have consisted of one eight-inch and three six-inch cruisers disposed abeam about 2 miles apart on a course of 200 degrees.
   They turned beam on, on a southeasterly course about 1436 and away about 1442 and then to the northwest, finally retiring on approximate course 010 degs. about 1501.
   25. CLEOPATRA led the Fourth Division towards the enemy at 1444 and the Rear Admiral Commanding, Fifteenth Cruiser Squadron's signal "Turn towards the enemy" was made at 1445.
   26. CLEOPATRA and EURYALUS engaged one cruiser from 1456 to 1509 when the enemy passed out of range. The remaining divisions were fouled by smoke which was made continuously by all ships from 1433 until 1516. At 1507 a signal was made to Mediterranean Fleet in company "Enemy's course 010 degs."

27. One enemy cruiser turned to the west-northwestward about I509 and engaged the Fourth Division from I5II to I5I5, straddling several times even after the division had retired into smoke. This was probably due to aircraft spotting. A few salvos were fired at this ship from I5II to I5I3 and she turned away at the same time as CLEOPATRA at I5I5.

At I535 the Rear Admiral Commanding, Fifteenth Cruiser Squadron, reported to the Commander-in-Chief: "Enemy driven off".

28. Course was then shaped 235 degs. and Guides of Divisions disposed on a line of bearing 3I0 degs. – I30 degs. I½ miles apart.

The convoy bore 222 degs., 7 miles at I605, steering 270 degs. with CLAN CAMPBELL lagging and being supported by CARLISLE and AVON VALE. At I607 the striking force altered to 270 degs. at 20 knots and were 5 miles abeam of the convoy by I640.

At I450, the Rear Admiral Commanding, Fifteenth Cruiser Squadron, ordered the convoy to steer west, and they had altered to that course at I500.

29. CARLISLE and AVON VALE (the special smoke-laying division) had hauled out to the northeast and laid smoke between the enemy and the convoy, keeping in V/S touch with the Striking Force. When CARLISLE saw the striking force returning towards the convoy she rejoined it but was ordered to keep closer to it by signal from the Rear Admiral Commanding, Fifteenth Cruiser Squadron, at I6I0.

Air Attack.

30. Heavy air attack was made throughout the whole of this period mostly on the convoy but also on the striking force. Whilst the striking force was rejoining the sound of the 4 in. fire from the Hunts and CARLISLE was most impressive, resembling continuous pom-pom fire even though heard at a distance of 8-I0 miles.

3I. In view of this intensive attack CARLISLE was asked at I605 if she had enough ships to cover the convoy from air attack.

CARLISLE replied "No, we have used I/3 of our outfit" at I6II and SOUTHWOLD reported at I633 "Nine attacks so far. Forty per cent. 4 inch ammunition remaining".

Accordingly, at I63I, the Fourteenth Destroyer Flotilla (forming the Ist Division) were ordered to cover the convoy from air and surface attack from the southward in order to back up the H.A. fire.

PHASE II.

32. *Reports*

I637 "4 unknown 042 degs. 9 miles course unknown" received from ZULU.

I640 "3 cruisers 035 degs. I5 miles" received from EURYALUS.

I648 C.S.I5 reported "I battleship and 4 cruisers bearing 035 degs. I5 miles. Course 2I5 degs."

I708 C.S.I5 reported that enemy battleship was accompanied by cruisers and destroyers.

(NOTE. – There is no confirmation that any destroyers were present nor is it considered now at all likely that they were.)

33. At I640, when the second sighting reports were received, Divisional Leaders at once led out to the northward as for carrying out "ZLG" although on this occasion no signal was made except that, at I655, the Convoy was ordered to steer south, which they did.

34. The 4th Division led out on a course 0I0 degs. sighting an 8-inch cruiser ahead which was engaged at I643, opening fire at the same time as 2 enemy cruisers (one 8-inch and one 6-inch) opened fire on 4th Division.

The enemy disposition at that time was 4 cruisers (probably two 8-inch and two 6-inch) on a line of bearing about II0 degs., I mile apart, steering about 230 degs. The battleship and 2 cruisers were farther to the eastward also steering about 220 degs.-230 degs.

CLEOPATRA Hit.

35. At I644 the second salvo from the 6-inch enemy cruiser scored one hit on the starboard after end of CLEOPATRA'S bridge, wrecking the Air Defence Position and starshell sights, bringing down all except one aerial and one set of halyards and killing I officer and I4 men, and wounding I officer and 4 men. CLEOPATRA continued firing until I648, but turned away into smoke to the westward. Straddles continued for a few minutes after this. About this time, the battleship was also firing at the 4th and 2nd Divisions, but was out of range from cruisers' armament. No other hits were obtained on our ships at this time, but one casualty resulted in CLEOPATRA from a near miss.

36. DIDO leading the 2nd Division opened fire at I644 at an enemy cruiser, but results could not be observed owing to smoke and spray. The 2nd Division conformed to the movements of the Flagship.

Smoke.

37. All ships continued to make smoke from I642 until the end of the action about I9I3. There was therefore an enormous area of smoke which lay well in the existing weather conditions of a 25-knot wind from southeast. The enemy tried after this contact to make touch with the convoy by passing round the western end of the smoke (to leeward) and was therefore effectually held away from the convoy as he would not approach the smoke, which was drifting towards him at 25 knots.

38. Captain (D), Fourteenth Destroyer Flotilla with the Ist Division receiving at I640 an incomplete V/S signal I3 from the Rear-Admiral Commanding, Fifteenth Cruiser Squadron, "Feint at . . ." gave up proceeding towards the convoy and made smoke between the convoy and the enemy gradually working to the south westward. Owing to the lack of enemy reports at this time, he did not know the exact position of the enemy from I645 to I745 when he saw gun flashes.

39. ZULU and HASTY (3rd Division) after sighting and reporting the enemy at long range at 1637, made smoke and conformed generally to the movements of the Admiral. No opportunity to fire guns or torpedoes was found during this phase.

40. Captain (D), Twenty-Second Destroyer Flotilla with the 5th Division, sighted what was thought to be two destroyers, but is now believed to have been one cruiser at 1640 and engaged the enemy with gunfire. The enemy was apparently hit, turned away to the northward and was not seen again.

At 1649, he sighted 2 cruisers and the battleship and the 5th Division continued to the westward in the hopes of achieving a favourable torpedo firing position.

41. At 1659, Captain (D), Twenty-Second Destroyer Flotilla, had three cruisers in sight and the 5th Division engaged them on a north-westerly course until the battleship was sighted at 1705, when course was altered away to avoid punishment. At 1720, however, HAVOCK suffered damage, her speed was reduced to 16 knots and she was detached to join the convoy. Shortly afterwards, a further attempt to attain a position of torpedo advantage was made but conditions were unfavourable and a southerly course was continued.

42. Between 1701 and 1712 the 4th Division engaged dimly-seen enemy ships at a range of about 14,000 yards. Enemy gun flashes were seen in this direction (010 degs. to 000 degs.) at this time and splashes were seen round the 4th Division. No results could be observed of this action.

43. Between 1703 and 1710 the 2nd Division engaged the westward of the three cruisers being engaged by the 4th Division, and this ship was identified as Gorizia-type. Nine controlled broadsides were fired from DIDO and hits were seen during the 6th and 7th broadsides. This was also seen by ZULU.

At 1705, the battleship opened fire on the 2nd Division who retired under smoke at 1707.

44. The 4th Division opened fire on an enemy ship at extreme range at 1727 for a few salvos. It appears probable that the enemy was at that time out of range. The 4th, 2nd and 3rd Divisions continued to steer alternate easterly and westerly courses until 1740, covering the convoy with smoke.

ZULU reports sighting 2 Trento class cruisers and 3 destroyers (which were certainly 6-inch cruisers) from the eastern end when clear of smoke, and the battleship and one cruiser from the western end during this period. The enemy were always at long range (outside 4.7" range) and well clear of the smoke.

Convoy.

45. During this phase, the convoy had turned south at 1655 but BRECONSHIRE turned them back to west at 1720. The Rear Admiral Commanding, Fifteenth Cruiser Squadron's 1716 signal to SOUTHWOLD ordering convoy to steer south was transmitted at 1719 and by 1730 they had again been shepherded on to a southerly course.

BRECONSHIRE turned the convoy to 225 at 1745 but SOUTHWOLD repeated Rear Admiral Commanding, Fifteenth Cruiser Squadron's order to steer south and the convoy turned back to south at 1800. This complied also with Captain (D), Twenty-Second Destroyer Flotilla's signal timed 1758.

Air Attack.

46. Continued heavy air attack was made on the convoy throughout phases 2 and 3; and CARLISLE and the Hunts did fine work in keeping up their high rate of accurate fire in the heavy sea then running. Some enemy aircraft were shot down and no damage was sustained by convoy or close escort.

Numerous attacks by single aircraft were also made on the various divisions of the striking force but were hardly noticed in the general melee. Close range weapons combated these attacks whenever they developed and the larger H.A. guns were used when not employed in low angle.† No damage resulted.

* Admiralty footnote:- V/S signal – Visual Signal, in this case by light.
† Admiralty footnote:- Low angle – i.e., at ship targets.

PHASE III.
The enemy endeavouring to work round to Leeward of the smoke.
1740-1820.

47. During this phase of the action, Captain (D), Twenty-Second Destroyer Flotilla in SIKH with the 5th Division bore the brunt of the enemy's fire.

At 1740 SIKH sighted the enemy battleship bearing 330 degs. 16,000 yards, and continued to engage it by gunfire until about 1820. Neither HERO nor LIVELY (the remaining ships in the Division) could know what was happening as SIKH's smoke effectively hid the enemy from them. SIKH was straddled at 1748 and, in Captain (D), Twenty-Second Destroyer Flotilla's words, "in order to avoid sinking with all torpedoes on board" 2 torpedoes were fired at 1750. No result was observed. SIKH broke off this action at 1820 by turning to a northerly smoke laying course.

48. At 1800 Captain (D), Twenty-Second Destroyer Flotilla ordered the convoy to steer south. This confirmed earlier instructions, and the convoy continued to be effectually covered by smoke. The convoy turned to the westward between 1825 and 1840 on receipt of the Rear Admiral Commanding, Fifteenth Cruiser Squadron's signal timed 1819 – but then resumed a southerly course until 1900 when BRECONSHIRE ordered "Carry out Operation "B"."*

49. During this phase the 5th Division's smoke hid the enemy almost continuously from the rest of the striking force. Captain (D), Fourteenth Destroyer Flotilla in JERVIS with the 1st Division maintained a southwesterly course between the enemy and the convoy, making smoke.

The 2nd, 4th and 3rd Divisions also made ground generally to the southwestward, making smoke. The smoke was drifting at over 25 knots to the northwestward and several attempts to cut through it in west-northwesterly direction (towards the enemy) failed. The smoke continued to lie extremely well and for a long time.

At 1759 the general signal was made "Prepare to fire torpedoes under cover of smoke".

50. At 1802, however, CLEOPATRA had worked through the smoke to get a view of the battleship bearing 310 degs. at about 13,000 yards with a slightly closing inclination. Fire was opened and at 1806 she turned to port and fired 3 torpedoes, as the battleship disappeared again behind drifting smoke. No results were therefore observed, but from the later positions of the enemy it is evident that she observed and turned away from this attack, further delaying the moment at which she might sight the convoy and slightly relieving the pressure on the 5th Division.

DIDO leading the 2nd Division found, when she emerged from smoke that the enemy had in fact turned away under cover of smoke and so the 2nd Division was unable to fire torpedoes. ZULU sighted at too long a range and in a disadvantageous position, so the 3rd Division was also unable to fire.

51. Throughout this period, many 15 in. splashes were seen in and around the smoke, mostly near the 5th Division, but also more wildly amongst all other ships.

52. After firing torpedoes, course was continued to the eastward until 1817 to obtain a clear view of the weather end of the smoke and if necessary to cover the convoy from the northeastward. While it was evident that the battleship and some cruisers were attempting to pass to leeward of the smoke, it was equally evident that the enemy's most effective course of action was to pass to windward (east) of it and that all his force was not with the battleship so that some cruisers might be taking this course of action.

53. Between 1816 and 1818 when a clear view was obtained to the northeast and north no enemy ships were seen. It is now evident that by this time 2 or 3 of the enemy 6-inch cruisers must have retired from the battle.

54. At 1817 course was altered to west, still making smoke and to rejoin the 1st and 5th Divisions in beating off the enemy to the westnorthwestward.

* Admiralty footnote:- Operation "B" – Dispersal of convoy to proceed independently to Malta during dark hours.

PHASE IV.

The enemy driven off by Gun and Torpedo.

55. This phase started with all divisions attempting to carry out the torpedo attack ordered at 1759, and all converging on the all important point between the battleship and the convoy about 15 miles southeast of her.

56. Captain (D), Fourteenth Destroyer Flotilla in JERVIS with the 1st Division and LEGION avoided 4 torpedo-bombers at 1823 by a turn to the southward but resumed a northwesterly and then a northerly course 4 minutes later. At 1834 he sighted a large enemy ship bearing 292 degs. about 6 miles, and at 1835 turned his division together to 270 degs. at 28 knots. He identified the enemy as one Littorio class battleship and 3 cruisers widely spaced in line ahead on approximate course 180 degs.

57. During the run in, the 1st Division carried out a concentration shoot on the

battleship and two hits were seen. At the same time CLEOPATRA (the only ship of the 4th, 2nd or 3rd Divisions to get a clear view because of smoke) engaged the battleship when visible and the leading 8-inch cruiser at other times. CLEOPATRA was firing almost continuously from 1831 to 1856 closing to just under 10,000 yards at 1847. Two hits were seen by 1845, one of which started a considerable fire on the battleship's quarterdeck, and appeared to put her after turret out of action and further hits observed after she had turned away at 1845.

58. The enemy returned fire with 15-inch, 8-inch, 6-inch and smaller calibres. The battleship appeared to be in divided control, the forward 15-inch firing at the 1st Division and the after group towards our cruisers. All their fire was erratic and it was hard to say who was the target.

59. At 1841, at a range of about 6,000 yards, the 1st Division turned to starboard to fire torpedoes. It appeared that LEGION (the southernmost ship) actually turned to port, and she was seen to be almost completely covered by a 15-inch salvo as she turned. She emerged from the splashes with speed unimpaired and apparently unharmed.

60. KINGSTON was hit by gunfire during the turn and suffered a fire in a boiler room and the engine room. She stopped but got the fire under control and reported at 1907 that she was able to proceed on one boiler at 16 knots. KELVIN stood by her whilst she was stopped. KINGSTON was accordingly ordered to join the convoy, or, if she could not find it, to proceed independently at her best speed to Malta. This latter in fact she did.

61. At 1840, the leading 8-inch cruiser had altered away, and at 1845 the battleship and the other two cruisers also altered away and to a course of about 340 degs.

62. At 1850, Captain (D), Twenty-Second Destroyer Flotilla in SIKH, who was steering northwest in an endeavour to get into a torpedo-firing position, observed a certain torpedo hit amidships on the battleship.

The 5th Division turned to fire torpedoes from the enemy's quarter at 1855, but smoke interfered with the aim and only LIVELY fired. She fired a full outfit (8 torpedoes) but no result was observed.

LIVELY had been damaged by a 15-inch near miss at 1852 and had her fore lower mess deck flooded.

63. The enemy was now retiring rapidly to the northward. No further opportunities for torpedo or gunfire presented themselves, but smoke was continued until 1913 – on a course to close the convoy.

64. At 1911, course was altered to the northward to concentrate the striking force and all ships joined company by 1920 when a southerly course was shaped again to close the convoy. KINGSTON was detached.

Air Attack.

65. During this phase several torpedo-bomber attacks were made on the striking force, all ineffective, though they might well have used our smoke to their advantage. There were also a number of T/B attacks on the convoy, some combined with high-level

bombing attacks. These also were beaten off without damage. No aircraft were seen after 1925.

Dispersal of the Force.

66. At 1940, the convoy not being in sight and dark fast approaching, it was decided to turn Force B for Alexandria. Accordingly course was shaped 050 degs. at 22 knots, altering to 080 degs. at 2040. At 1949, BRECONSHIRE was ordered to carry out Operation "B". In fact she had already done so at 1900 and the convoy was already dispersed.

At this time (1940) it was known that the enemy was retiring to the northward. He had failed to make contact with the convoy by day, being driven off, and it was thought unlikely that he would attempt a night attack after having his battleship damaged by torpedo.

The weather was strong south-easterly to east-southeasterly gale, with a rising sea and swell. Fuel in the "K" class and Hunt class destroyers was insufficient to allow an extra day to be spent in the central basin west of Benghazi, so it was necessary to get as far east as possible through bomb alley by daylight.

The Return Passage.

67. At 2004, PENELOPE and LEGION were ordered to join the convoy.

AVON VALE had been ordered to proceed to Malta with the convoy, as, in the prevailing weather, it was considered she would hold the rest of Force B back. In accordance with the Commander-in-Chief, Mediterranean Station's message timed 1302 of 22nd March, 1942, CARLISLE was also ordered to remain with the convoy.

68. At 2130, owing to the strong easterly gale speed had to be reduced to 18 knots, and at 0325 on 23rd March, to 15 knots.

Even so, only one destroyer (SIKH) had not lagged by daylight, ZULU had to reduce to 10 knots for half an hour at 0530. At 0630 the cruisers turned to 180 /degs. to collect destroyers, and at 0700 proceeded at 14 knots.

At 0800 force was in position 34 degs. 23 mins. N., 20 degs. 14 mins. E., course 080 degs.; course was altered at 0900 to 100 degs.

69. During 23rd March speed was gradually increased as the weather slowly improved. By 1300, 20 knots was achieved, but at 1535 speed had to be reduced for an hour to enable LIVELY to repair weather and action damage.

Air Attack and Fighter Protection.

70. Two Beaufighters arrived at 0756 and from this time on with a few intervals fighters were present. Fighter Direction was not good because of bad communications.

Shadowing by the enemy aircraft commenced in the forenoon but no attack developed until 1610 when 8 JU.87s attacked. Six of these aircraft attacked LIVELY who was then astern of the cruisers. No damage was sustained.

From this time until dusk, sporadic attacks were made by JU.88s and torpedo-bombers.

7I. At 2200 the weather having moderated considerably, speed was increased to 22 knots. An evasive course well north of the normal track was used during the night.

At 2248 LIVELY reported that she was unable to maintain more than I7 knots and she was detached to Tobruk where it was considered she could repair damage before proceeding to Alexandria.

72. At daylight on 24th March speed was increased to 26 knots.

Air – on 24th March.

73. At 0730 on 24th March an A.S.V.* Sunderland arrived, and at 0735 two more aircraft, thought at first to be Beaufighters, made an almost unopposed torpedo attack. No damage resulted and no further attacks developed. Fighter escort was provided from 0800.

74. The Force arrived at Alexandria at I230 where they were honoured to receive the great demonstration which then ensued.

Admiralty footnote:- A.S.V. – radar equipment.

8

COASTAL FORCE ACTIONS

FEBRUARY 1943

The following Despatch was submitted to the Lords Commissioners of the Admiralty on the 13th March, 1943, by Admiral Sir HENRY H. HARWOOD, K.C.B., O.B.E., Commander-in-Chief, Levant.

Levant,
13th March, 1943.

MOTOR TORPEDO BOATS 6I, 77, 82, 307 AND 3I5 – REPORT OF PROCEEDINGS I5TH/I6TH FEBRUARY, I943.

Forwarded for the information of Their Lordships, concurring generally in the remarks of the Captain Coastal Forces. This operation resulted in a torpedo hit on an enemy merchant ship and damage to other enemy ships by gunfire.* Much valuable experience was gained.

2. The remarks in paragraph 3 of the Captain Coastal Forces' letter are fully concurred in. M.T.B.s 77 and 82 should have fired both torpedoes at their targets.

3. The operation was carried out in the face of strong opposition in a spirited and determined manner, which bodes well for future operations. The diversion by the M.G.B., was well planned and carried out.

4. The freedom from mechanical trouble during the operation reflects credit on all concerned.

(Signed) H.H. HARWOOD,
Admiral,
Commander-in-Chief.

ENCLOSURE I TO C.-IN-C., LEVANT'S LETTER.

FROM ... The Captain Coastal Forces, Mediterranean.
DATE ... 2Ist February, I943.
To ... The Commander-in-Chief, Levant.

The attached report and diagram from the Commanding Officer, 7th Motor Torpedo Boat Flotilla are forwarded, with the following remarks.

I. The composition of this strike was as follows:-

        M.T.B.s 6I }
        77 (Flotilla Commanding Officer on board) } 7th Flotilla
        82 } (Vospers)
        M.T.B.s 307 } I0th Flotilla
        315 } (Elcos).

As the I0th Flotilla boats had been undocked only the same day, it was impossible for them to be ready in time to sail in company with the other boats. It was unfortunate that the two units were not able to join up, as intended; results would probably have been far more effective had a larger number of Motor Torpedo Boats been available to attack the main enemy convoy. The results of this attack were that one merchant vessel of medium size was definitely damaged with an expenditure of two torpedoes. There is now no reason to suppose that this ship was the same as that subsequently sunk by an aircraft.

2. It is considered that Motor Torpedo Boat 77 was well handled by Lieutenant J.B. Sturgeon, Royal Naval Volunteer Reserve. His attacks were pressed home to short range, resulting in a hit with the only torpedo fired, confirmed by Motor Torpedo Boat 82. It was not known to the Commanding Officer that his second torpedo had failed to fire until about twenty minutes later. This misfire and the casualty to the First Lieutenant when about to release a depth charge were two misfortunes which combined to spoil a very spirited attack during which Motor Torpedo Boat 77 was subjected to intense enemy fire.

3. Motor Torpedo Boat 82 fired one torpedo only, which missed. The conclusions (paragraph I3 (viii)) of the Flotilla Commanding Officer are that both torpedoes should be fired whenever a good target presents itself. This is considered, without doubt, to be the correct procedure and has again been impressed on Commanding Officers.

4. Motor Torpedo Boat 6I (Lieutenant T.J. Bligh, Royal Naval Volunteer Reserve), equipped as a gunboat, fought a prolonged and resolute action with the convoy escort, which was greatly superior in fire power. It is considered that this boat did particularly well; her wheel steering was out of order throughout the action, during which she was steered with the tiller from aft.

5. The conclusions of the Flotilla Commanding Officer are considered sound, particularly paragraph I3 (viii), referred to above. The R.D.F.† with which these M.T.B.s are fitted was not used on this occasion, as the enemy convoy appeared before it was expected.

6. Motor Torpedo Boats 307 and 3I5, not having met the others at the rendezvous,

were deprived of their target at the last moment by its being sunk by a Wellington torpedo-bomber. The small fast enemy destroyer which had been escorting the merchant ship was not a suitable torpedo target and these Motor Torpedo Boats are not sufficiently heavily armed with guns to engage such a target with a good chance of success.

7. Mechanically, all the Motor Torpedo Boats ran well and without giving any trouble. This is a far more satisfactory state of affairs than has recently been the case with boats of this type, and the improvement is largely due to the skill and enthusiasm of Lieutenant (E) W.R. Coverdale, Royal Navy, the Coastal Force Base Engineer Officer.

The conduct of officers and ships' companies during this operation is reported to have been excellent.

8. It is considered that this force of Motor Torpedo Boats was well led by Lieutenant R.A.M. Hennessy, Royal Navy, the Commanding Officer of the 7th Flotilla, who was hampered by having only two Motor Torpedo Boats and one Motor Gun Boat, against the enemy escort of four destroyers and three E-boats‡ and merchant ships which were themselves armed. His small attacking force caused great confusion among the convoy, enemy ships firing on one another and some in the air. Under these conditions, a really adequate force of Motor Torpedo Boats should have been able to sink several enemy ships. In this case the main Motor Torpedo Boat striking force had been removed from Malta a few days previously.

(Signed) M.C. GILES,
Lieutenant, R.N.,
for Captain, Absent on Duty.

Admiralty footnotes:-
* *The action took place in the vicinity of Maritimo Island, off the western point of Sicily.*
† *R.D.F. – radar.*
‡ *E-boats – similar to British M.T.B.s.*

ENCLOSURE 2 TO C.-IN-C., LEVANT'S LETTER.

FROM ... The Senior Officer, 7th M.T.B. Flotilla.
DATE ... 17th February, 1943.
To ... The Captain Coastal Forces, Mediterranean.
Submitted:

M.T.B.s 77 (V.7* on board), 82 and 61 sailed from Malta in accordance with previous instructions, and passed the boom at 1500. Having reached the end of the swept channel a course was set for a position 15 miles due south of Maritimo Island. All three boats were carrying a thousand gallons of upper-deck fuel, and as this was the first time of carrying it a speed of 18½ knots was allowed for engine revolutions giving 20 knots under normal load. It was subsequently found that there was no reduction in speed due to the extra load.

M.T.B.s 307 and 315 were due to sail at approximately 1600, and catch us up en route, or failing that to rendezvous in position 15 miles south of Maritimo Island.

2. At 2140, an enemy report was received of one merchant vessel and two destroyers, steering 240 degrees towards Maritimo Island. It was thought that these ships would be our target, and that they would eventually alter course to the southward, in which case our position south of Maritimo Island would be very suitable.

At 2320, M.T.B. 61 signalled that she had a defective dynamo and that it was necessary for her to stop. Boats stopped at 2325 and cut engines. At that moment an enemy report of four merchant vessels and three destroyers to the northward of us was received, and before it could be plotted on the chart M.T.B. 61 reported that she had sighted a large merchant vessel to starboard, about 1½ miles away.

3. All boats were ordered to start up one engine, and M.T.B. 77 followed by M.T.B. 82 proceeded on a north-easterly course with the object of getting the target on the port bow.

On closing it was observed that there were two columns of ships, with a heavy escort of destroyers, and that we were steering on a course almost exactly opposite to the port enemy column.

The starboard column was sighted to port, and consisted of a destroyer with two merchant vessels astern. As we were in an ideal position to attack the leading ship of this column, the signal "Attack with torpedoes" was made, and all three boats acted independently from then on.

4. *M.T.B.* 77 (Lieutenant J.B. Sturgeon, R.N.V.R.) altered course to port to get on the firing course to attack the leading merchant vessel of the starboard column. In order to avoid the port column it was necessary to go on to all three engines and increase to 20 knots.

M.T.B. 77 was now crossing the centre of the convoy and by some miracle remained unobserved until the range of the target had closed to 400 yards, and the port torpedo was fired. The torpedo was seen to run correctly, and we decided to alter course 100 degrees to starboard to attack the rear ship of the port column. The columns were about 5 cables apart. Having turned 100 degrees to starboard, fire commenced on M.T.B. 77, at first from the second merchant vessel of the starboard column, but very soon every ship was firing with machine-guns varying from 40-m.m. to 303-inch, and the destroyers were firing 4-inch H.E. that burst about 50 feet in the air.

An explosion was felt shortly after M.T.B. 77 had altered round.

5. M.T.B. 77 got into position between 300 and 400 yards on the starboard bow of the second merchant vessel of the port column and the starboard torpedo firing lever was pulled. Unfortunately the firing mechanism failed, and owing to the heat of the battle it was not noticed that the torpedo had not left the tube. At about this time a burst of about ten heavy calibre cannon shells aimed at M.T.B. 77 struck the bridge of the merchant vessel.

6. It was then decided to attack the leading merchant vessel of the port column with depth-charges before disengaging. Speed was increased to 27 knots and M.T.B. 77 steered so as to pass close under the stern of the target, Lieutenant D.M.W. Napier,

R.N.V.R. went aft to the port depth-charge to release it when in position, but was killed when abreast of it.

M.T.B. 77 passed right under the stern of the target, and a tray of twelve 20-m.m. S.A.P. incendiary from the Breda gun was fired into the merchant vessel hitting her just above the water line.

We then decided to disengage to the southward as quickly as possible as the enemy gunfire was intense and becoming very accurate; an attempt to lay smoke was unsuccessful as the C.S.A. apparatus had been hit. After about ten minutes, firing on M.T.B. 77 ceased and course was set to the south-east, M.T.B. 82 having joined us. The escort continued to fire, at times in the air, for some time after our withdrawal.

7. *M.T.B.* 82 (Lieutenant P.R.A. Taylor, R.N.R.), when the order was received to proceed on one engine, followed close behind M.T.B. 77 and assumed by the course that M.T.B. 77 was steering that she intended to attack the port column, and consequently altered course to the westward to attack from the convoy's starboard bow. On altering course to port to cross over to the starboard column, M.T.B. 82 sighted the destroyer ahead of the column and decided to steer down between the lines and attack the first merchant vessel of the port column. By this time M.T.B. 77 was crossing between the columns and M.T.B. 82 decided to attack the leading ship of the starboard column. M.T.B. 82 then came under very heavy fire from many directions, and fired one torpedo at the leading ship of the starboard column. M.T.B. 82 altered course to the southward, being engaged by a destroyer and an E-boat.

8. A cloud of black smoke was observed alongside the leading merchant vessel of the starboard column, preceded by a flash. This was certainly caused by M.T.B. 77's torpedo hitting.

During her withdrawal, M.T.B. 82 engaged an E-boat that was keeping station on her starboard beam; this action drew accurate fire from the destroyer. M.T.B. 82 increased to maximum speed and withdrew to the southeast, joining up with M.T.B. 77.

9. *M.T.B.* 6I *(Gun Boat)* (Lieutenant T.J. Bligh, R.N.V.R.) sighted the enemy at 2328, and on receiving the order to proceed on one engine decided to proceed to the stern of the convoy to create a diversion in accordance with pre-arranged tactics.

On hearing M.T.B. 77 start all three engines, M.T.B. 6I did likewise and passed down the port side of the convoy engaging the merchant ships with 20-m.m. gunfire. Having observed the two M.T.B.s disengaging, and M.T.B. 6I being apparently mistaken for an E-boat (or unobserved) she stopped abeam of the stern destroyer. Calcium flares were then dropped in an endeavour to draw off an E-boat, but although a destroyer opened fire on the flares, the E-boats did not leave the convoy.

I0. M.T.B. 6I then proceeded to the starboard beam of the convoy and opened fire, with all bearing guns at a range of about 2,000 yards. As the E-boats still declined action and the merchant vessels showed no inclination to straggle, M.T.B. 6I proceeded to the port beam of the convoy and opened fire on an E-boat at a range of 2,000 yards. Fire was returned by the convoy. M.T.B. 6I then proceeded to the head of the convoy to investigate possibilities of a smoke screen, but as three destroyers were keeping close station there, and the wind and sea were increasing, it was decided to discontinue the engagement at 0100/16.

A course of south 48 degrees east was steered and M.T.B. 61 joined M.T.B.s 77 and 82 at the rendezvous at 0210.

During the whole of the time that M.T.B. 61 was in contact with the enemy she was on hand steering, which made manoeuvring very difficult, and turning at high speed almost impossible.

At 0220/16, M.T.B.s 77, 82 and 61 proceeded on a course of south 48 degrees east for Malta, arriving at 0830/16.

II. It is considered that the following damage was sustained by the convoy:-

One merchant vessel damaged and possibly sunk by torpedo from M.T.B. 77;

One merchant vessel damaged by gunfire from escort;

One merchant vessel damaged by gunfire from M.T.B. 77;

E-boats possibly damaged by our gunfire.

I2. Damage sustained by our own forces:

M.T.B. 77 – shrapnel holes in engine-room, tank-space and crew space, slight damage on deck;

M.T.B. 82 – one cannon-shell hit on the stern;

M.T.B. 61 – no damage.

I3. *Conclusions*.

(i) Due to the fact that the convoy appeared much sooner than we expected, and that we found ourselves right in their track, there were two courses open to us.

(ii) The first was to haul out and return to carry out a silent attack in the hope that the escort would not see us. This course was not adopted as it was considered that we were already too close, and were bound to be observed any moment.

(iii) The alternative was to deliver an attack at once, down the middle of the convoy, as it would not have been possible to get outside the screen without using all engines and making a great deal of noise.

(iv) We adopted the second method, which was made much easier by the very indifferent look-out that the convoy was keeping.

(v) They could not have been using R.D.F. or keeping a listening watch.

(vi) In future, more use could be made of a gunboat diversion astern of the convoy to leave the M.T.B.s a clear run from ahead.

(vii) For this method of attack more gunboats are needed.

(viii) Both torpedoes should be fired at the same target to make certain of sinking it.

(Signed) R.A.M. HENNESSY,
Lieutenant, R.N.

Admiralty footnote:-
*V.7 – the Commanding Officer of 7th M.T.B. Flotilla

The following Despatch was submitted to the Lords Commissioners of the Admiralty on the 12th October, 1943, by Vice-Admiral Sir HENRY D. PRIDHAM-WIPPELL, K.C.B., C.V.O.,

Flag Officer Commanding, Dover.
Dover,
12th October, 1943.

SINKING OF ENEMY SUPPLY SHIP IN A STRONGLY ESCORTED CONVOY EASTBOUND FROM LE HAVRE – NIGHT 26TH/27TH SEPTEMBER, 1943.

Be pleased to lay before Their Lordships the attached reports of an action between three M.T.B.s, supported by three M.G.B.s, and a strongly escorted enemy convoy on passage from Le Havre to Boulogne during the night 26th/27th September, 1943.

2. Aerial reconnaissance had reported the presence in Le Havre of two enemy merchant vessels which were expected to attempt the passage of the Dover Strait.

3. Accordingly, M.T.B.s 202 (Lieutenant J.L. Bommezyn, R.Neth.N.), Lieutenant E.H. Larive, D.S.C., R.Neth.N., Senior Officer embarked, 204 (Lieutenant H.C. Jorissen, R.Neth.N.), 23I (Lieutenant C.H. Vaneeghen, R.Neth.N.) with M.G.B.s I08 (Lieutenant L.E. Thompson, R.N.V.R.), II8 (Lieutenant M.O. Forsyth Grant, R.N.V.R.), II7 (Sub-Lieutenant D.W.B. Woolven, R.N.V.R.), were ordered to patrol the vicinity of Berck Buoy in accordance with my signal timed I545 on 25th September, copy of which is attached.

Albacore patrol between Boulogne and Dieppe had to be withdrawn earlier owing to weather.

4. Paragraphs 2, 3 and 4 of the remarks of the Senior Officer, M.T.B.s are concurred in.

This well planned and skilfully executed attack reflects the greatest credit on Lieutenant E.H. Larive and the officers and men under his command.

It is probable that the enemy's misplaced faith in his recently laid minefields, through which a channel had been swept only two days prior to the engagement, together with the improbability of our Coastal Forces operating in the prevailing weather conditions, contributed to an unusual element of surprise.

The likelihood of this event in no way belittles the success of the M.G.B.s' diversion to seaward which, added to the advantage of the light, no doubt accounted for the unpreparedness of the enemy for a torpedo attack from inshore.

5. This action was fought outside the range of shore-based radar and in consequence considerable risk from enemy minefields to returning craft doubtful of

their position had to be accepted, but had all craft been fitted with Rotet, * valuable assistance could have been given in the later stages of their return.

(Signed) H.D. PRIDHAM-WIPPELL,
Vice-Admiral.

Admiralty footnote:-
*Rotet – a device to increase the range of shore based radar.

ENCLOSURE I TO F.O.C. DOVER'S LETTER.

FROM ... Senior Officer, H.M.M.T.B.s, Dover.
DATE ... 6th October, I943.
To ... Flag Officer Commanding, Dover.

I have the honour to submit the following report of proceedings of the night 26th/27th September, I943, from the Senior Officer, 9th M.T.B. Flotilla.

2. The action was well planned and executed and led to the sinking of the main torpedo target.

3. The handling of the force by the Senior Officer, 9th M.T.B. Flotilla up to the moment of firing torpedoes was excellent and put the M.T.B.s into a perfect firing position. I feel, however, that he would have been better advised to have had the M.T.B.s in Starboard Quarter line instead of Port Quarter line and thus avoided M.T.B.204 crossing the bows of M.T.B.23I just before M.T.B.23I fired. Starboard Quarter line in this instance would have been the usual formation.

4. I consider M.T.B.23I was incorrect in shifting his point of aim to a coaster from the main torpedo target. All Commanding Officers should realise that while the main torpedo target remains afloat that target only should be attacked. Even if the main target has been hit but has not yet sunk, any torpedoes remaining in the force should be used against that target.

5. It has long been the intention to attack from inshore in this area and it is most satisfactory that on this first occasion the attack was successful. This is only possible between the Berck Buoy and the southern limit of the Command. The suggestion in para. I7 of the Senior Officer, 9th M.T.B. Flotilla's report is agreed with and it is hoped to try it out at an early opportunity.

(Signed) B.C. WARD,
Lieutenant, R.N.

ENCLOSURE 2 TO F.O.C. DOVER'S LETTER.

FROM ... Senior Officer, 9th M.T.B. Flotilla.
DATE ... 27th September, I943.
To ... Senior Officer, H.M.M.T.B.s, Dover.

I have the honour to submit the following report of the action on the night of 26th/27th September off Point du Haut Banc between a combined Motor Torpedo Boat and Motor Gun Boat force and an escorted enemy convoy.

Own Forces.

2. *Force A,* M.T.B.s 202 (S.O.), 204 and 23I, and *Force B,* M.G.B.s I08 (S.O.), II8 and II7. S.O. Force A was in command of the combined forces.

Object.

3. To intercept and destroy northbound convoy which was expected to be on passage from Le Havre.

H2:*Weather Conditions.*

4. Visibility moderate to westward, poor to eastward, due to clouds and land giving no horizon; sea moderate; swell short; wind N.W. force 4;* squally.

Narrative.

5. Forces A and B slipped at 2325/26th and proceeded in accordance with Vice-Admiral, Dover's signal timed I545 on 25th September (copy attached). AA buoy was passed at 0046 and course was set through swept channel until Point du Haut Banc was bearing east, when course was altered to east. When forces were 9 miles east of Point du Haut Banc, radar was switched on and M.T.B.s came in single starboard cruising line. M.G.B.s were in single port cruising line. This formation is always used when approaching patrol line as no signalling is allowed by me unless in emergency, and speed can be reduced or increased without danger of collision.

6. Forces stopped in position Point du Haut Banc 5 miles at 0202 and engines were cut. Position was checked with bearings from Etaples and Point du Haut Banc lights and constant radar watch was kept. As the horizon to the westward was far better than to the eastward and it was suspected that northbound convoys used the inshore route, I decided at 0245 to move I½ miles more inshore, where forces stopped and cut engines at 025I. Although the weather was too bad for proper use of hydrophone, watch was kept as well as with radar. A faint "ping" noise was heard in the hydrophone and at 0307 a faint propeller effect was obtained through the interference. By this time the radar as well was giving echoes and "hydrophone up" was ordered. The ship was rolling too much to use the radar echoes for plotting the enemy movements accurately.

7. Enemy was sighted at 0308 when clear of a low dark cloud obscuring the horizon. Immediately after the first radar echoes were obtained fast signalling with a

blue light was seen on the same bearing as given by radar and hydrophone, being south 20 degs. west, thus confirming by visual contact the technical ones. As it could be seen that under the present circumstances the enemy would be passing too close to the seaward of us, I ordered both forces to start up at 0309, and proceeded on course north-east to get more inshore. I steered north-east and not east so as to prevent showing more silhouette than was necessary. Speed at first 12 knots and later increased to 20 knots for reasons of wash. The enemy was expected to do 9 knots. Enemy was kept in radar touch all the time.

8. At 0317 forces were stopped in position 290 degs. Point du Haut Banc 1.8 miles and the ships' heads kept pointing in the direction of the enemy to keep the silhouette small.

At 0319 the enemy was sighted again in the form of several still, small, dark shapes.

9. At 0320 several starshells exploded dead above us. Immediately afterwards a most violent battle started in the direction of the enemy. Radar gave a range of 2,000 yards to the enemy. I ordered the forces to start up and proceeded on course north-west, speed 36 knots, in order to get to the seaward of the enemy forces and the shore batteries. An attack under these circumstances was out of the question. It could not be observed where the starshells were coming from. No small arms fire was directed at us except some stray bullets. Shell fire, however, was experienced. At 0323 speed was reduced to 22 knots so as not to damage the engines. Boats were bumping heavily against the swell.

10. In the light of the starshells the bows and bow waves of nine E or R-boats[†] forming a screen ahead of the convoy could be seen in line abreast, six of which seemed to be pointing in our direction, giving the impression of being in pursuit of us. No fire from these ships however seemed to be directed at us. The whole situation was rather puzzling.

11. When the enemy convoy was south of us the gunboats on our starboard quarter swung into attack to create a diversion, passing astern of the M.T.B.s to the south-west, in accordance with plans discussed previously. When the M.T.B.s had cleared the light arc of the starshells and I considered that the gunboats had attracted the attention of the enemy effectively, course was altered to the north and later to the north-east, speed 30 knots, and east at 0328. Speed varied between 30 knots and 18 knots as convenient. Radar touch was kept all the time. Force was stopped at 0337 in position 350 degs. Point du Haut Banc 4.2 miles, when range was 4,500 yards and M.T.B.s were well inshore of the enemy route.

12. When the inshore position was reached, Force B was ordered to attack from the seaward.

By the time, however, Force A attacked, no diversion from seaward took place. When the enemy came up north the M.T.B.s slowly closed in, keeping well out of sight of the screen ahead. The enemy, however, silhouetted against a fairly light horizon, could be observed with ease from about 1,800 yards. As soon as the screen ahead of the convoy passed, the M.T.B.s increased speed to between 8 and 12 knots, closing in to about 1,400 yards.

13. Having been unable to plot the enemy movements with the radar echoes, I

altered course to parallel with the enemy, speed 10 knots, thus comparing our speeds and in the meantime picking out the main target, which was rather difficult as the longest silhouette that could be seen was rather low and I was expecting something higher for that size of ship. After close scrutiny it was decided that the silhouette mentioned was the main target, but heavily laden, a three island ship. At approximately 0400 course was altered to port. Orders to attack the main target were shouted to M.T.B.s 204 and 231, who were in advanced single port cruising line, and the estimated speed of the enemy passed – 9 knots.

14. The enemy convoy consisted of a big merchant vessel, 6 to 9 E or R-boats ahead, two coaster type vessels on the starboard quarter of the main target, and astern were 6 or more other trawler size vessels. The screen on the port side, being of no interest to us, was not observed properly. No outer screen was present on the starboard side. At 0403, I observed a bright flash and a dark smoke cloud just abaft the funnel of the main target and a distinct shock was felt in M.T.B. 202. Immediately afterwards a siren was heard.

15. The Commanding Officer of M.T.B. 202 had just fired his starboard torpedo and turned to port to disengage according to his instructions. Speed was increased – when very heavy gun and machine gun-fire was opened on us. Starshell was again used with great accuracy; apart from the usual starshell the enemy used floating luminous flares coming down ahead of us, and several grape-shots exploded fairly close ahead and to starboard. Although no hits were received enemy fire was extremely heavy and accurate, causing numerous near misses. Quite a lot of fire went just over.

16. At 0426 M.T.B. 202 was stopped and an investigation was carried out as to the cause of a misfire at the port torpedo tube. When this was cleared I ordered M.T.B. 202 at 0443 to close some lights and an occasional small searchlight which had been observed in the bearing where the action had taken place, to fire her second torpedo. After having closed in at varying speeds for reasons of wash I ordered M.T.B. 202 to stop at 0451, when radar range was 1,200 yards to the centre of activity, where three ships were lying stopped. I considered it unnecessary to reduce the range more as the targets were lying stopped and an outer screen of E or R-boats were circling slowly around them, only 700 yards away, and the attack might have been spoiled if sighted. After two disappointing attempts to fire the port torpedo I ordered M.T.B.202 to return to harbour as it was obvious that the firing system was defective.

Conclusions.

17. Attack from inshore has been proved to be possible at this point of the enemy convoy route. Close co-operation with gunboats to create a diversion, strongly enough armed to fight off a pursuing enemy, again proved its value, particularly under circumstances like these where an attack from the inshore side can be made. The diversion created by the gunboats is of great value, partly because of the starshells fired at them silhouetting the enemy for the inshore attack. Against such a heavy escort, however, it is too risky to do so for a long time. To get the same result as from starshell it would be of great value if the M.G.B.s could drop floating luminous flares to seaward in a case like this, not just abreast of the enemy, but starting from a mile

or half a mile ahead; this making a line of flares which the enemy has to pass, giving the M.T.B.s a fair chance to attack. The possibility that the enemy expects an attack from inshore in this case is acceptable as they probably have no time in the confusion to divert their escorts to their inshore side.

(Signed) E.H. LARIVE,
Lieutenant, R. Neth. N.

Admiralty footnotes:-
**Wind force 4 – moderate breeze (II-I5 m.p.h.).*
†*R-boats – motor launches.*

ENCLOSURE 3 TO F.O.C. DOVER'S LETTER.

FROM ... Senior Officer, M.G.B.s.
DATE ... 29th September, I943.
To ... Flag Officer Commanding, Dover.

I have the honour to submit the following report on the action on the night 26th/27th September by a combined Motor Torpedo Boat and Motor Gun Boat force on an escorted enemy convoy.,

General Narrative.

2. Combined forces were stopped in position 090° Berck Buoy I mile at 0203. Owing to low visibility to shoreward and good visibility to seaward, forces moved I½ miles inshore, stopping in position I00° Berck Buoy 2½ miles at 0250. Engines were cut, and M.G.B.II7 set radar watch, while M.T.B.s kept hydrophone watch.

3. At 0306, some flashing from a blue light was observed, bearing south-west, and immediately afterwards one large vessel and several smaller could be seen. S.O. Force A was informed. At 03I0, combined forces proceeded north-east at I2 knots, gradually increasing speed. At 03I4, starshell were fired over the forces. It could not be seen whether they were fired by the convoy or from ashore, but it is probable that the convoy sighted our wakes.

4. The combined forces altered course northwest and increased speed. Force B altered course to port at 30 knots and engaged the leading enemy escort on opposite courses, opening fire at 03I7. The enemy fire was believed to be from 4-inch and all calibres below. It was intense and mainly accurate, especially from the larger calibre guns. Many near misses were observed by all boats. The enemy starshell also were intense, but promiscuously placed. The blinding effect of the starshell and enemy tracer made it difficult to distinguish targets. M.G.B.II7 observed the nearest escort to be almost stopped with a small fire aft, and her guns temporarily silenced. The Commanding Officer of M.G.B.II7 assumed that this had been caused by the fire of

M.G.B.I08. M.G.B.II7 engaged this target at a range of 300 yards, and observed several hits with Oerlikon shells.

5. At 0330, a 4-inch (?) shell missed M.G.B.I08's port quarter by two yards, and the starboard engine stopped. M.G.B.s, who were in line ahead, disengaged to north-west and stopped at 0335 to investigate damage and casualties. The after Oerlikon gunner of M.G.B.I08 was wounded and his place was taken by the radar operator. The other boats were not damaged, but M.G.B.II7's pom-pom could not be laid owing to the failure of the elevating ram. Force B was still being illuminated by starshell, but was not being actively engaged. It was decided to withdraw to the north and signal the Force A to find out if they had attacked with torpedoes. Accordingly at 0342, Force B proceeded north at 22 knots, and stopped at 0353, where signals were made to Force A, firstly asking if they were all right, and secondly asking if they had completed the attack. At 0357, a message from Force A was received, ordering Force B to attack from seaward.

6. Accordingly, Force B proceeded at 26 knots steering north-east, and at 0406 were again illuminated by starshell. At 0407, Force B engaged the enemy screen on a similar course. Enemy fire was still heavy, especially from larger calibre guns, but was not so intense as during the first attack. Starshell again made it difficult to see the enemy at all clearly, and no results of own gunfire were observed. At 0408 the signal "Attack completed" was received from Force A. At 0410, Force B disengaged to the north-west and stopped at 0413, when the signal "Withdraw" was received from Dover.

7. As however it was obvious that the enemy were by now in a confused state and were firing at each other, it was decided to make a brief attack in order to keep the kettle boiling. Accordingly Force B proceeded at 0415, steering east at 10 knots in single line abreast to port, and at 0418, opened fire. Two T.L.C.* type craft were observed, and several E or R-boats in a formed state were observed by the light of the enemy starshell. A considerable amount of enemy fire was observed, but not very much in our direction, and it appeared as if the kettle was boiling nicely. At 0420, Force B turned 180° and disengaged under smoke. Course was set west at 28 knots and then to Dover by the swept channel.

General Conclusions.

8. It had previously been arranged between the S.O.s of the forces that if possible, M.G.B.s should make diversionary attacks from seaward, in order to draw the attention and fire of the enemy, while M.T.B.s made an unobserved attack on the main target from inshore. In the event, this was carried out successfully, although the M.T.B.s did not attack while the M.G.B.s were carrying out the first diversion.

9. It is estimated that the enemy escort consisted of at least two gun coasters or T.L.C.s and three or more groups of E or R-boats, each group consisting of at least 4 boats. The groups were mainly on the seaward side of the convoy, and were also ahead and astern of the main target. From the intensity of larger calibre fire, there

may have been more larger sized escorts, as it was too accurately placed to have been fired from the shore.

I0. It was interesting and heartening to observe during the first attack that although the enemy fire was intense, and it appeared impossible for boats to live through it, negligible damage was actually sustained.

(Signed) R.B. ROOPER,
Lieutenant, R.N.

Admiralty footnote:
* *T.L.C. – Tank Landing Craft.*

ENCLOSURE 4 TO F.O.C. DOVER'S LETTER.
SIGNAL.

FROM ... V.A. Dover.

Tonight Saturday Force A, M.T.B.s 202 (S.O.), 204, 23I, and Force B, M.G.B.s II4 (S.O.), I08, II6, are to be sailed in company to pass AA buoy at 0045, thence via swept channel to Berck Buoy where patrol is to be assumed in vicinity.

Object to intercept and destroy northbound convoy which may be expected to be on passage from Le Havre.

Albacores of 84I Squadron may be patrolling convoy route to Dieppe with freedom to bomb surface craft south of latitude 50° 20' North.

Unless in action and in absence of other orders, forces are to leave patrol area at 0500 and return by same route at best speed until AA buoy is passed thence to harbour.

I545/25th September.

The following Despatch was submitted to the Lords Commissioners of the Admiralty on the I8th *November,* I943, *by Admiral of the Fleet Sir JOHN C. TOVEY, K.B.E., D.S.O., Commander-in-Chief, The Nore.*

The Nore,

I8th *November,* I943.

DESTROYER AND COASTAL FORCE ACTION WITH E-BOATS ON NIGHT OF 24TH/25TH OCTOBER, I943.

Be pleased to lay before Their Lordships the following report on E-boat operations on the night of 24th/25th October, I943. The forces employed were:-

Destroyers patrolling convoy route:

EGLINTON, WORCESTER, MACKAY, and CAMPBELL.

With F.N. Convoy:

PYTCHLEY.

Coastal Force Units:

Unit P.   M.T.B.s 693, 689.
Unit O.   M.G.B.s 86, 85.
Unit C.   M.L.s II2, II4.
Unit Y.   M.G.B.s 607, 603.
Unit L.   M.T.B.s 444, 445.
Unit V.   M.G.B.s 3I3, 327.
Unit R.   M.G.B.s 609, 6I0.
Unit S.   R.M.L.s* 250, 5I7.
Unit E.   M.T.B.s 438, 443, 440.**
Unit J.   M.T.B.s 442, 439.**

PART I – NARRATIVE.

The Coastal Force dispositions for this night had been made with an eye to a possible attack north of Yarmouth. The dispositions north of Yarmouth are shown in Appendix A. Other patrols and Coastal Force Units operated south of the area shown in the diagram.

2. Soon after 2200A several reports from bombers who had been out "gardening"**** were received. These indicated the possibility of small craft in the vicinity of 52° 50' N. 3° 35' E., steering 300° at about I940. The inference was made that if these were in fact E-boats they were using a route direct from Ijmuiden north of the Ower Bank thence to the convoy route either in the Humber or Cromer area. It was also considered probable that they would use the same route for their retirement. When the action started coastal forces were redisposed accordingly.

3. At about 23I8 H.M.S. PYTCHLEY who was guarding the seaward flank of the F.N. convoy† obtained a radar contact of E-boats. The E-boat warning was at once sent out. At 23I8 H.M.S. PYTCHLEY went into action with 5 or 6 E-boats 4 miles north of 56B buoy†† and drove them off to the north-east, severely damaging one. This timely and well fought action undoubtedly saved the convoy from being accurately located. It appears probable that the E-boats intercepted by Unit Y at 0206 (see paragraph 22) were some of this group escorting the damaged boat back to its base.

4. On receipt of H.M.S. PYTCHLEY's enemy report at 23I8 coastal force units were redisposed as follows:-

(*a*) Units R and V (positions Z56 and Z55‡) were fleeted § 300°, 20 miles.

(*b*) Units L and Y (positions ZI8 and ZI6) were fleeted 020°, 20 miles, to cover the inferred line of retirement to Ijmuiden.

(*c*) Units C, O and P (positions ZI4, ZI2 and ZI0) were fleeted 0I5°, I8 miles to close the gap left by (*b*).

(*d*) Two fast units of M.T.B.s (E and J) were ordered out from Lowestoft to positions ZI0 and ZI2. These were later ordered to the northern end of Brown Ridge, again covering the inferred line of retirement to Ijmuiden.

It is most creditable that all these signals were correctly received and acted upon with promptitude.

5. The shore radar stations now began to get unidentified plots in dangerous proximity to the F.N. convoy – H.M.S. EGLINTON on patrol 3 was therefore ordered to remain with the convoy until further orders, H.M. Ships WORCESTER, MACKAY and CAMPBELL (patrols 4, 5 and 6) being fleeted north to 3, 4 and 5 respectively at 0002.

6. It soon became clear that the E-boats had split into numerous groups which were approaching the outer war channel at a number of points east of 57F buoy. It was remarkably fortunate that all these groups came in astern of the convoy which was in fact never sighted. This convoy happened to be 2 hours ahead of timetable. In addition to the convoy the trawler WILLIAM STEPHEN was a source of anxiety as she had straggled some miles astern of the convoy.

7. The situation at 0002 on 25th October on the convoy route was as follows:-

The rear of the F.N. convoy approximately at 57C buoy – H.M.S. WORCESTER on patrol 4 had by that time reached the eastern end of her patrol, 57 buoy. There was thus temporarily a stretch of 25 miles that was completely open to attack since H.M.S. EGLINTON (patrol 3) had been ordered to remain with the convoy. Radar stations showed unidentified plots close north of 55B buoy and approaching 56B. Another track appeared about 3 miles north-east of 57C moving slowly towards 57F. Shortly after this time yet another track appeared a mile or so north of 56 buoy. At 0002 H.M.T. WILLIAM STEPHEN was near 56 buoy.

8. Between 00I5 and 0II5 there were groups of E-boats at 56, 56B and at 57F buoy after the convoy had passed. Positions of these groups obtained by shore radar were signalled by Commander-in-Chief, The Nore, although no immediate action could be taken to deal with them. These groups were in addition to those engaged by H.M.S. PYTCHLEY at 23I8, H.M.S. WORCESTER at 0027, H.M.S. MACKAY at 0045 and 0I36, and Unit R at 0I40.

Destroyer Actions.

9. *H.M.S. PYTCHLEY (with F.N. 60).* – Already described in paragraph 3.

I0. *H.M.S. WORCESTER (patrol 4).* – At 0027 when 3 miles east of 55B buoy, H.M.S. WORCESTER engaged 4 E-boats, scoring Oerlikon hits on second boat in the line. The E-boats retired on a course of 030°. A cast round after contact had been lost did not locate the possibly damaged boat.

II. H.M.S. WORCESTER passed 56 buoy about 0I00, at which time shore radar placed the group that had been near that buoy about 3 miles north of it. By now the large number of plots made identification and following of units extremely difficult and a clear picture of the situation in this area could not be obtained.

12. At 0117 H.M.S. WORCESTER engaged 3 E-boats 1¼ miles north of 56B buoy. One E-boat was hit by a 4.7-inch shell and close range weapons and was seen to blow up, burning wreckage being passed during the chase to the northward. At 0151 on return to the channel, H.M.S. WORCESTER sighted and engaged 3 E-boats on the scene of the action at 0117. These were stopped when sighted. They were engaged and driven off.

13. *H.M.S. MACKAY (patrol* 5). – At 0005 when "fleet north" signal was received H.M.S. MACKAY was at southern end of patrol 5. At 0036 when at 57 buoy radar detected 3 targets 4 miles to the northward. At 0040 5 E-boats were engaged at 1,700 yards range. These retired to north-eastward, making smoke and dropping delayed action depth charges which were easily avoided. M.G.B. Unit L fleeted 020°, 20 miles from ZI8 obtained H.E. from this group at 0137 but could not intercept. At 0107 H.M.S. MACKAY, then some 14 miles north-east of 57 buoy, shaped course for 54D buoy.

14. At 0136 when 6 miles north of 57 buoy, H.M.S. MACKAY obtained suspicious radar contact 4 miles to the west. At 0148 at least 2 E-boats were engaged and straddled with the twin 6-pdr. The E-boats retired to the north-eastward, dropping depth charges as they went. At 0205 H.M.S. MACKAY in the vicinity of Z23 broke off the engagement and returned to patrol 4.

Admiralty footnotes:-
* *R.M.L.s – Rescue Motor Launches.*
** *At Lowestoft until receipt of first enemy report.*
*** *"Gardening" – laying parachute sea-mines.*
† *F.N. convoys were northbound coastal convoys.*
†† *For positions of numbered buoys, see Appendix A.[not provided]*
‡ *For numbered positions Z56 etc., see Appendix A.*
§ *"Fleet" was a code-word used in signals when re-disposing units on patrol; in this context, "fleeted" means merely "moved".*

Loss of H.M.T. WILLIAM STEPHEN.

15. This trawler did not maintain her station in the convoy though she should have had sufficient speed and had dropped some five miles astern. As soon as the E-boat activity developed it was seen that this unfortunate trawler had E-boats both ahead and astern of her and she ran into the group at 56B buoy, being sunk by torpedo a few minutes before 0100. I regret now that I did order her to steer inshore, but at the time the E-boat situation was not so clear as it became subsequently. The explosion was felt by Unit V to the northward. A German broadcast on the following day mentioned the picking up of survivors.

Coastal Force Engagements.

16. *Unit S – M.L.* 250 *and R.M.L.* 517 *(position* Z22) sighted H.M.S. MACKAY's first action but was not able to intercept the E-boats, the speed of the unit being reduced to 12 knots due to engine failure in M.L. 250. At 0156 a momentary action was fought with the two E-boats driven off by H.M.S. MACKAY in her second action.

17. *Unit V* – M.G.B.s 315 and 327 (position Z55) started to fleet 300°, 20 miles at 2345. The first actions of H.M. Ships WORCESTER and MACKAY were seen in the distance to the southward. An underwater explosion was felt about 0100 which confirms the time of the torpedoing of trawler WILLIAM STEPHEN. H.M.S. WORCESTER's second action (paragraph 14) was also seen and at 0120 radar contact was made with these E-boats. Three boats were heavily engaged from 0138 until 0144, hits being observed on two of them. The last boat in the line may have been considerably damaged. At 0230 three more E-boats were sighted on a north-easterly course at high speed about six miles north of 55B buoy. Owing to their large turning circle Unit V was unable to turn quickly enough to engage the fast moving enemy.

18. *Unit R* – M.G.B.s 609 and 610 (position Z56) started to fleet 300°, 20 miles at 2341. Two unidentified plots were signalled to the unit at 0035 and 0040 some ten miles E.N.E. of Sheringham buoy but Unit R had already investigated radar contacts in this area by the time the signals were received.

19. At 0100 Commander-in-Chief signalled position of Unit R and an enemy plot – Unit R had already obtained hydrophone contact and at 0102 obtained contact by radar. From this time until 0141 Unit R stalked the enemy, keeping between him and the convoy. As soon as the enemy showed signs of closing the convoy, Unit R attacked, twice forcing him to withdraw to the eastward, the second time for good. The second boat in the line on which Unit R concentrated their fire was undoubtedly hit hard and forced to leave the line.

20. This group of E-boats was the only one to operate north of 57F buoy.

21. *Unit Y* – M.G.B.s 607 and 603 (position Z16) together with Unit L (position Z18) was fleeted 020°, 20 miles at 2340 as mentioned in paragraph 4. H.M.S. WORCESTER's first engagement at 0027 and those of H.M.S. MACKAY were observed to the westward. H.M.S. MACKAY's track chart and that of Unit Y indicate that the E-boats engaged by H.M.S. MACKAY at 0148 could not be the same as those engaged by Unit Y as suggested by Senior Officer of Unit Y. From statements by prisoners of war and other sources it is considered that Unit Y's group were proceeding back to their base possibly escorting one E-boat that had been damaged by H.M.S. PYTCHLEY at 2318. The fact that they reached Unit Y approximately at the end of H.M.S. MACKAY's action appears to have been pure coincidence.

22. At 0206 Unit Y engaged a group of E-boats steering an easterly course about 22 miles north-east of Smiths Knoll buoy. The unit pressed home its attack with great vigour and set two E-boats on fire. These E-boats were seen to blow up. M.G.B. 607 (Lieutenant R.M. Marshall, R.N.V.R.) also rammed and sank a third E-boat.

23. At 0400 M.G.B. 603 with 607 in tow obtained radar contact to the northward.

Tow was slipped and at 0418 M.G.B. 603 went into action with six E-boats at a range of under 800 yards. As the result of being the first to open fire M.G.B. 603 obtained many hits on one boat and probably damaged it severely. After a running fight the enemy made off at high speed at about 0445. M.G.B. 603 then rejoined M.G.B. 607.

24. *Unit J* – M.T.B.s 442 and 439. Units E and J which had been ordered out from Lowestoft to positions ZI0 and ZI2 when E-boat activity started, were ordered to the northern end of Brown Ridge (position RB27 and ten miles north of position RB27 respectively) where they arrived at 0300. At 0406 unit went into action with three E-boats and a high speed running fight ensued in which both M.T.B.s scored a number of hits. They also suffered damage and casualties, a hit on the bridge of 442 killing the First Lieutenant. At 0415 M.T.B. 439 lost contact with 442 owing to the failure of the rudder to turn the boat, although hard over – 439 continued to engage the enemy, however, until 0445 when it became necessary to attend to action damage and to wounded. At 0450 M.T.B. 442 also disengaged due to action damage and stoppage of 2-pdr. It is considered probable that considerable damage was inflicted on the enemy in these engagements.

25. At 0545 in position 52° 50' N. 3° 04' E., M.T.B. 439 sighted four E-boats steering E.S.E. As by this time 439 was in no fit state for action, avoiding action was taken. The presence of 439 appears to have confused the enemy sufficiently to induce them to open fire on one of their own boats which was straggling from the line.

26. At 0605, some 12 miles further west, 439 sighted another group of eastbound E-boats who opened fire. This group was also avoided. I consider this avoiding action was justified.

27. Most unfortunately fog at the aerodromes prevented any aircraft of Fighter or Coastal Commands taking advantage of this unique opportunity of attacking E-boats in daylight. A number of these did not reach their base before noon.

PART II – REMARKS.

28. This was probably the most difficult night yet experienced from the radar point of view. The E-boats split up into many small groups thus making identification most difficult.

29. As late as 0540 there were indications that some E-boats were still not far from the coast, almost certainly north of Ower Bank since the area south of it was covered by Coastal Forces. From previous experience it can be inferred that they were looking for missing boats. It is always a sign that our countermeasures have achieved some success. Analysis of the action reports points to the E-boats having come in north of the Ower Bank and then fanned out to the southward in probably three main groups (A, B and C) which in turn split up into smaller groups.

30. Group A operated between 57F buoy and 56B buoy and appears to have been a very large group. Units of it were engaged by H.M. Ships PYTCHLEY and WORCESTER (second action). Group A also provided the unit which remained at 57F buoy between 0050 and 0212. Another unit of this group went north of 57F buoy

in search of the convoy and was only prevented from finding it by the well judged action of Unit R. It was probably some of group A that sank H.M.T. WILLIAM STEPHEN.

31. Group C was the most easterly of the three. Units of it were engaged by H.M.S. WORCESTER at 0027 and HJM.S. MACKAY at 0045 and 0I48.

32. Group B appears to have been between 56B and 55B buoys. Shore radar showed E-boats near 56 buoy and Unit V's second sighting was probably boats of this group. It appears to have merged with group A at times and may have had a hand in the sinking of H.M.T. WILLIAM STEPHEN and therefore in H.M.S. WORCESTER'S second action.

33. From the number of callsigns heard (30) and the number of boats accounted for by radar plots and ships' action reports (see paragraph 8) it is considered that at least 30 E-boats were present on this occasion, a strength of attack that has to be expected with the large number of E-boats known to be based on Dutch ports.

Shore Radar.

34. Shore radar stations did much good work in detecting E-boat units in or near the swept channel. It was their first experience of action conditions and it is considered that great credit is due to them in view of the very large number of both enemy and friendly vessels involved.

Remarks on Ships' Actions and Reports.

35. *H.M.S. PYTCHLEY* (Lieutenant-Commander R.H. Hodgkinson, R.N.). – This timely and well fought action had considerable bearing on the general success of the night's operations in that it prevented the enemy accurately locating the convoy. Throughout the Commanding Officer acted with sound judgment.

36. *H.M.S. WORCESTER* (Lieutenant J.A.H. Hamer, R.N.). – The Commanding Officer's decision at 0I30 to break off the chase of E-boats when five miles north of the swept channel and return to his patrol was correct, especially as the range was such that hits could scarcely be expected. The definite destruction of an E-boat is a most satisfactory indication of the efficiency of the ship. The Commanding Officer handled his ship with determination and sound judgment.

37. *H.M.S. MACKAY* (Lieutenant-Commander J.H. Eaden, D.S.C., R.N.). – Although it is undesirable to lay down any hard and fast rule as to how far from his patrol a destroyer should chase E-boats, in this case H.M.S. MACKAY's patrol was left completely open for a very long time. The object of these patrols is the prevention of minelaying in the channel and on this occasion the enemy would have been able to lay mines at his leisure during a period of two hours.

38. *Unit V (M.G.B.s 3I5 and 327)* (Senior Officer, Lieutenant J.A. Caulfield, R.N.V.R.). – The shore control had great difficulty in identifying Unit V among the

many radar plots that appeared in the area concerned, consequently it was not possible to give this unit much help. It is most satisfactory that the unit was able to get into action with good effect so soon after H.M.S. WORCESTER's engagement and probably with the same boats. The continual harrying of the E-boats is bound to have a discouraging effect. The results obtained by the new type of hydrophone are most satisfactory but the standard of radar performance in M.G.B. 3I5 leaves something to be desired. Had the second enemy unit been picked up by radar the unit might have been able to turn to a similar course to that of the enemy before sighting and thus have got into action.

39. *Unit R (M.G.B.s 609 and 6I0).* – The Senior Officer of this unit, Lieutenant P. Edge, R.N.V.R., showed a quick and sound appreciation of the Commander-in-Chief's object in fleeting the unit, *i.e.*, the defence of the northbound convoy, and throughout handled his unit with tactical ability of a high order. Skilful use of radar gave him an exact picture of the enemy's movements and enabled him to go into action at a moment of his own choosing. The moment he chose was entirely correct and there is no doubt that this well fought action saved the convoy from being located and attacked. The unit was unfortunate in not obtaining a kill especially as a probable one had to be sacrificed in achieving the object.

40. It is not possible to lay down any hard and fast rule as to how far destroyers should be from the convoy route and it is inevitable that they should illuminate any craft approaching them that they cannot identify as friendly. The onus of establishing identity must remain with the coastal forces.

4I. *Unit Y (M.G.B.s 607 and 603)* – Lieutenants Marshall and Lightoller showed admirable judgment and a magnificent fighting spirit in this, the most successful action of the night. It is considered that the claim to have destroyed 3 E-boats is substantiated. Once again the value of 2-pdr. starshell both as illuminants and as incendiary ammunition was demonstrated.

42. This action also shows the devastating effect of the gunpower of the D class M.G.B.s in an attack which is pressed well home. The results obtained give clear proof of the very high fighting efficiency of these two boats.

43. The gallant action fought single-handed by M.G.B. 603 against six E-boats not only showed determination to lose no chance of engaging the enemy but may well have saved M.G.B. 607 from destruction.

44. *Unit J (M.T.B.s 442 and 439)* (Senior Officer, Lieutenant C.A. Burk, R.C.N.V.R.). – Here again good use was made of radar during the action. Considerable damage was undoubtedly done to the enemy and but for action damage a kill might well have resulted.

General.

45. This action gives general proof of a great improvement in the efficiency of the Coastal Forces particularly as regards communications and the use of radar. The small number of material breakdowns also indicates a higher standard of interest and

handling by the Commanding Officers and crews of boats and reflects great credit on the maintenance officers and staffs of the bases. Furthermore, it clearly demonstrates the value and essential need of constant training and practice.

46. The dispositions and movements of forces were controlled by Commander H.A. Taylor, R.N., and the success of the operations was in large part due to his skill and extremely clever and prompt anticipation of enemy movements.

47. In addition to the successful defence of the convoy, it is considered permissible to feel a modicum of satisfaction in the number of times the E-boats were engaged. They were roughly handled six times in or near the convoy route (H.M. Ships WORCESTER and MACKAY twice, H.M.S. PYTCHLEY and Unit R once each), once by Unit V when retiring from H.M.S. WORCESTER's second action, and by Units Y and J on their homeward passage when they probably felt they were clear of our forces. Had the R.A.F. been able to attack them after daylight it would have been a strong deterrent to E-boats leaving their return to their bases till so late.

(Signed) JACK C. TOVEY,
Admiral of the Fleet,
Commander-in-Chief.

The following Despatch was submitted to the Lords Commissioners of the Admiralty on the 9th December, *1944,* by Admiral Sir JOHN H.D. CUNNINGHAM, K.C.B., M.V.O., Commander-in-Chief, Mediterranean Station.

Mediterranean,
9th December, 1944.

ACTION REPORT – H.M. M.G.B. 662, H.M. M.T.B.s 634, 637, 638, ON THE NIGHT OF IITH/I2TH OCTOBER, I944.

Forwarded for the information of Their Lordships, strongly concurring in paragraph 2 of the remarks of the Captain Coastal Forces, Mediterranean.

(Signed) J.H.D. CUNNINGHAM,
Admiral,
Commander-in-Chief.

ENCLOSURE I TO C.-IN-C., MEDITERRANEAN STATION'S LETTER.

FROM ... The Captain Coastal Forces, Mediterranean.
DATE ... I8th November, I944.
To ... The Commander-in-Chief, Mediterranean Station.

The remarks of the Commander Coastal Forces, Western Mediterranean, are fully concurred in.

2. The Senior Officer, 57th M.T.B. Flotilla has written such an excellent report and so ably summed up this prolonged action in his paragraphs 39 and 40, that little remains to be said. To the factors which made victory possible *(vide* paragraph 39 of the Action Report) must unquestionably be added brilliant and inspiring leadership, as the Commander Coastal Forces, Western Mediterranean has indeed already remarked. I have on several previous occasions remarked on Lieutenant-Commander T.J. Bligh's splendid leadership of his flotilla in action. On this occasion he set a seal on his previous performances.

3. In my letter dated 3rd October, 1944, I remarked on the brilliant success of three boats of the 56th M.T.B. Flotilla in a prolonged night action. It is a matter of great personal satisfaction to me, knowing all the officers of both flotillas and having watched the happy mixture of close co-operation and friendly rivalry existing between them, that the 57th Flotilla has now crowned its career with an equally, and possibly even more brilliant success.

(Signed) J.F. STEVENS,
Captain, R.N.

ENCLOSURE 2 TO C.-IN-C., MEDITERRANEAN STATION'S LETTER.

FROM ... The Commander Coastal Forces, Western Mediterranean.
DATE ... 23rd October, 1944.
To ... The Captain Coastal Forces, Mediterranean.
Submitted:
Forwarded:

2. This highly successful action was characterised in its initial stages by skilful anticipation of enemy movements; and later, by the manner in which prevailing conditions and available resources were turned to such good account in securing maximum opportunity for attack, but for which our boats would have undoubtedly incurred greater damage and casualties. Throughout, the engagement was carried out with skill and determination under brilliant leadership, in the face of heavy enemy fire.

(Signed) A.D. McILWRAITH,
Commander, R.N.V.R.

ENCLOSURE 3 TO C.-IN-C., MEDITERRANEAN STATION'S LETTER.

FROM ... The Senior Officer, 57th M.T.B. Flotilla.

DATE ... I5th October, I944.
To ... The Commander Coastal Forces, Western Mediterranean.

The following report of the attack on enemy F-lighter* convoys in the Adriatic on the night of IIth/I2th October, I944, is submitted.

Own Force.

2. His Majesty's M.G.B. 662 (Senior Officer), His Majesty's M.T.B. 634 (Lieutenant W.E.A. Blount, D.S.C., R.N.V.R.), His Majesty's M.T.B. 637 (Lieutenant R.C. Davidson, D.S.C., R.N.V.R.) and His Majesty's M.T.B. 638 (Lieutenant D. Lummis, R.N.V.R.).

Duty on which Force was employed.

3. On patrol, North of Zara, in accordance with instructions from the British Senior Naval Officer, Vis.

4. *Weather* – fine: *Wind force and direction* – north-east, force I-2:** *Sea and swell* – nil: *Moon* – moonrise 0II4: *Visibility* – I,000 yards until moonrise: *Phosphorescence* – slight.

General Narrative.

5. It was arranged that the unit proceed on patrol, north of Zara, on D -I day, lie up at Ist on D day, patrol on the night of D day and either return to Vis on D +I, or wait at Ist for a further night, patrolling on D +2 and returning to Vis on D +3 day.

Accordingly, the unit left Komiza at I300 on I0th October, I944, proceeding northwards at seventeen knots in arrowhead formation. H.M. M.T.B. 634, who had been to Ist before, was sent ahead at nineteen knots to contact the L.R.D.G.*** Officer and the Partisan naval authorities and obtain the latest naval intelligence. At I845, the unit arrived at the rendezvous position just south of Ist harbour, but as H.M. M.T.B. 634 was not there H.M. M.G.B. 662 entered the bay to find her and go alongside.

6. Lieutenant W.E.A. Blount, D.S.C., R.N.V.R., reported that the intelligence he had been given was as follows. A northbound convoy of some four or five ships (mostly F-Boats) had been seen by L.R.D.G. to enter Zara some three or four days ago and it was to be expected that they would endeavour to proceed northwards as soon as possible. Further, no shipping had been seen either northbound or southbound for three days and there was a certainty of something passing near Vir Island during the night. In addition, three Partisan "tigers" † were patrolling the Maon Channel to the northwards (where they had recently sunk one and captured another enemy schooner), and a Ju.88 had machine-gunned a small ship in Ist Bay at dawn two days previously.

7. Accordingly the unit was led between Ist and Mulat (a very narrow but deep channel) at I945 and course was set to close Vir Island on silent engines, the three

"tigers" being sighted on the port beam, forming up into their cruising formation as the leading boat left the channel.

8. At 2040 the unit closed the coast of Vir, and lay stopped, in wait for the promised northbound convoy.

The weather was very dark and thundery, with vivid flashes of lightning to the southwards, but apart from two panics caused by the spire of Zara Church, all was quiet.

9. At 2245, three white flares were seen over Mulat.

At 2347, much tracer was seen coming from Ist, in what appeared to be a land battle, but the L.R.D.G. representatives on board H.M. M.T.B.634 considered that a low flying air attack was being made on the harbour. I myself thought this unlikely, and was of the opinion that an E-boat was firing irresponsibly for some obscure reason known only to the enemy. (I had seen this happen before, in the same place, on the night of 26th June, this year.) The firing then ceased, but ten minutes later broke out further south, near Mulat. This time there were some flares (or starshell) being used, and some large flashes were seen on the land, and the aircraft theory seemed possible: however, some 88-m.m. tracer was identified from the eastern side of Mulat and it was obvious that there was something taking place.

I0. In view of the intelligence reports received earlier in the evening, I was averse to leaving the patrol area – in fact the firing may have been a diversion to draw our craft away from the eastern side of the channel – but it did seem possible that there was at least one F-lighter or siebel ferry[††] over on that side, so at 0039 H.M. M.T.B.634 was detached to go to Ist to contact the L.R.D.G. or Partisans and find out what was happening, whilst the remainder of the unit stayed in the patrol area.

II. At 0223, H.M. M.T.B.634 made R/T[‡] contact with H.M. M.T.B.637 and reported that there had been two destroyers in position 206° 4½ miles Veli Rat Light, having previously sent, a W/T signal to me to the effect that there was heavy firing to seaward, and broadcasting an enemy report. H.M. M.T.B.634 also reported that an F-lighter had been seen by the Partisans in amongst the islands, but was southbound.

The unit at once proceeded to Kok Point to rendezvous H.M. M.T.B.634, torpedoes were set to 3 and 5 feet, radar switched on and a course set to pass between Skarda and Ist, to carry out a sweep outside the islands to try and find the two destroyers. Search was abandoned at 0345, as there was a rising wind and sea, and unit returned to Ist.

I2. It seemed probable that the destroyers had proceeded northwards at high speed, directly after the bombardment and the chance of catching them was remote.

My opinion is that I was justified in staying off Vir and not leaving my area, but that I should have detached H.M. M.T.B.634 earlier, when I might have been able to have contacted the enemy.

I3. At 0900, a Partisan reported a large warship with two funnels in a cove on the east coast of Mulat, a moderately alarming report to receive at any time, but this dwindled to an F-lighter by I000, an E-boat by II00 and a "trick of the light" by I200.

I4. At I730, a conference was held with the local authorities and it was decided to repeat the previous night's patrol, with the additional proviso that if any shipping at all was sighted near Ist, a pre-arranged pyrotechnic signal would be made from the Partisan lookout post.

Having thus secured the rear, the unit proceeded to Vir at I825.

I5. It had been decided that the big demonstration put up by the enemy the previous night (which included torpedoes fired by E-boats at Mulat breakwater) was aimed at eliminating some "tigers" and/or M.G.B.s and that it was probable he would try and run a big convoy north this night. Hence the unit closed Vir Island and was disposed along the coast to meet a northbound convoy.

I6. Some flares were seen to the southwards, and there were lights and flickerings in the sky over Nin – all appeared to be set. At 22I5 some vertical tracer was seen off Zara.

At about 2220 H.M. M.T.B.634's starboard outer engine pushed a conrod through the crank case and most of the engine-room crew were overcome by fumes.

At about 2245 all the boats started rolling, as if a lot of ships had passed by to seawards, so at 2300 the unit proceeded northwards, a guess that eventually proved correct.

I7. The visibility was now very low, due to widely scattered low cloud, but I was not prepared for the shock of suddenly seeing enemy ships on the port bow, at about four hundred yards' range.

The unit was at once stopped and the boats headed into the shore just north of Vir light. The targets were now seen to be four F-lighters, of which one was altering course towards us: he appeared to be higher out of the water than the others and was possibly an escorting flak lighter: he had probably sighted one or more of the unit and was closing to drive us off.

I8. H.M. M.T.B.634 was ordered to try and carry out a snap torpedo attack on this target, whilst H.M. M.G.B.662 ordered "single line ahead, speed 8 knots", and went ahead in order to engage the remainder by gunfire.

The flak boat opened fire on H.M. M.G.B.662 at 2306, at once killing one of the pom-pom loading numbers. Fire was returned from all guns and H.M. M.T.B.638 illuminated with starshell.

I9. It is scarcely possible to describe the next ten minutes. The visibility was such that the leading boat in the line had a completely different picture from the fourth boat, and the slight offshore breeze was blowing the smoke from H.M. M.G.B.662's gunfire across the line of sight of our ships and the enemy convoy, which was, of course, much more of an advantage to us than them as we had the inshore position and knew where to expect them, while the only ship that they could see was H.M. M.G.B.662. But it will, in fact, be easier to give the impressions of each boat during this phase of the action and try to paint the picture that each one saw, than to give a coherent account of what the unit did.

H.M. M.G.B.662's *Narrative.*

20. H.M. M.G.B.662 had drawn ahead of H.M. M.T.B.634, who had manoeuvred for a torpedo attack, and was engaging many targets on the port side, including F-lighters, Pi-L Boats‡‡ and E-boats. Very heavy 88-m.m. and 20-m.m. was coming our way, all high, from a variety of enemy vessels and this fire had a strong blinding effect on my bridge. Nevertheless, I saw a Pi-L Boat hit by the 6-pounder and blow up, starting a petrol fire on the surface of the water.

In the light of H.M. M.T.B.638's starshell ahead, I saw F-lighters being hit by my pom-pom and Oerlikon. I saw an E-boat in the light of the petrol fire hit, set alight and blow up – a victory achieved by the bridge .303-inch Vickers, and on the port quarter I witnessed an inspiring display of 6-pounder gunnery. An F-lighter, at about four hundred yards, was steering away from us, unilluminated and almost invisible, even through binoculars, yet the 6-pounder fired nearly thirty rounds that scored hits in about a minute. The 6-pounder also hit and sank a Pi-L Boat with an inert cargo.

Meanwhile, H.M. M.G.B.662 had crossed the northern end of the convoys and was lying stopped, waiting for the other boats to rejoin, and trying to ensure that no enemy got away.

It had been intended to work round to the west of the enemy immediately and engage them against the fires of their burning vessels, but this was not possible until all the boats had come round.

Everywhere on the port side there were burning ships and explosions. There were visible many more ships than the original four F-lighters. The sight was fantastic.

H.M. M.T.B.634's *Narrative.*

2I. H.M. M.T.B.634 says – "The Senior Officer signalled single line ahead speed 8 knots and opened fire on the enemy, which now appeared clearly as four F-lighters, three of which were stopped or proceeding slowly northwards in single port cruising line. One was closing. I prepared to attack the flak-lighter with torpedoes, but the range had closed to one hundred yards by the time the sight was on and I decided that it was too close, so I altered back to starboard, and opened up with all guns on the flak-lighter who was firing at H.M. M.G.B.662. As I turned, less than fifty yards from the flak-lighter, H.M. M.T.B.634 was hit in the port pom-pom ready use locker which exploded and went up in flames. The fire was promptly extinguished. All our guns continued to pour an intense fire into the flak-lighter which burst into flames from stem to stern, by the light of which every detail of her could be discerned. She appeared to have an 88-m.m. amidships, a quadruple 20-m.m. aft and many 20-m.m. in sponsons down the starboard side. Her bridge collapsed and she appeared to be breaking in two. I steered parallel to the enemy who was turning slowly to port, at less than forty yards. Then another F-lighter, followed by two more, appeared very close to seaward of the burning flak-lighter. They were well lit up by the flames and steering southwards in single line ahead. All my guns fired on the middle one and then the last one, and fires were started on both. All three were seen to be engaged by H.M. M.T.B.s 637 and 638. Astern of the south going F-lighters, what looked like an E-boat, bows on to us, appeared. This was engaged by the port .5-inch turret and was seen by me to explode and disappear.

On rejoining, the flak-lighter of the northbound group was seen to sink in a cloud of smoke and steam, half-a-mile to seaward of the engagement and all the remaining F-lighters appear to have been driven south by H.M. M.G.B.662."

*HM. M.T.B.*637's *Narrative.*

22. H.M. M.T.B.637 says – "At 2306, the enemy opened fire and H.M. M.T.B.634 altered course to port to attack with torpedoes. The Senior Officer and H.M. M.T.B.634 were engaging targets unseen by us, but fires could be seen breaking out. My pom-pom gunner was engaging a northbound F-lighter, but as H.M. M.T.B.638 was on the port beam, no other guns could fire. (This was due to the fact that I was manoeuvring to keep station on H.M. M.T.B.634's gun flashes.) However, in a few seconds I opened fire with all guns on a target which was headed northwards. It was bows on to another burning F-lighter. The range of the target was about seventy-five yards and every detail of the vessel was discerned. At this range none of our guns could miss. She immediately caught fire. The after superstructure of this vessel resembled Wembley Stadium on a dark night, except for the Nazi flag. The gunners reduced it to a blazing wreck, and another large target seen abeam of this blaze was being engaged by H.M. M.T.B.638 with accurate fire.

At 2317 two large objects were observed on the port beam and turned out to be upturned vessels."

*H.M. M.T.B.*638's *Narrative.*

23. H.M. M.T.B.638 says – "At 2305 the Senior Officer signalled enemy ahead. They were invisible to us at this moment. The boats ahead opened fire. My pom-pom illuminated with starshell as previously arranged. An F-lighter was set on fire, fine on my port bow and this illuminated two F-lighters, a Pi-L Boat and an E-boat on my port beam, steering southwards. We sank the Pi-L Boat with Oerlikon and concentrated on an F-lighter at two hundred yards. Shells could be seen ripping open her side. This target was left burning fiercely, and fire was directed on another F-lighter which was hit with all guns and set on fire. An E-boat appeared on the starboard quarter, and was bit with Oerlikon. We sustained one 20-m.m. hit in this engagement."

24. At 2314 the situation was resolving itself and a sweep was carried out round to the west and south to discourage any of the enemy from returning to Zara. An active F-lighter could be seen to seaward of the scene of the action, steering south, but he turned inshore, and I was confident that we would easily find him again: I somehow

felt that none of the enemy would try and push any further north, and was mostly concerned with the southern flank.

25. At 2346, when about one mile from Vir light, an F-lighter was seen close inshore; it turned over and submerged, and was thought to be the one that had been damaged by H.M. M.G.B.662's six-pounder. There was another possible small target here also, but I was looking for the other F-lighters and decided not to investigate. It was probably a wreck anyhow.

26. At 2353, targets were sighted at Green 20°,§ and H.M. M.T.B.637 was ordered to illuminate with starshell. This was done well, and H.M. M.G.B.662 opened fire with all guns on an F-lighter and a Pi-L Boat or E-boat lying close inshore, near Vir Point. The F-lighter was seen to sink; the smaller craft was also hit. The enemy now opened heavy fire from a position abaft the beam, almost certainly one or more F-lighters lying very close to the beach, well north of Vir light and completely invisible. All boats returned fire at the flashes, and some damage may have been inflicted, as the enemy craft ceased fire until we were going away to the northward, when they fired vigorously at nothing to the south-west.

27. It was thus decided to go away and lie off until the moon got up, and the light improved, and then come back and torpedo the remaining enemy. This entailed some risk of losing the enemy if he crept close to the coast, but I decided to place complete confidence and reliance in my radar set and its experienced operator, and to lie off, stopped at about four thousand yards. I felt certain that we should be able to pick up any F-lighters that tried to move, but had to admit that if a Pi-L Boat wanted to get away – well then it could; but I did not want to risk losing any boats by taking them into a dark coast with a belligerent group of well-armed vessels lying on the beach, when there was a big improvement of visibility due in two hours' time.

Various echoes were plotted during the next two hours but they turned out to be ghost or aircraft echoes in the centre of the channel.

28. It was now planned to approach the coast just north of Vir light in very broad single line abreast to starboard, on a north-easterly course with torpedoes ready for immediate firing. H.M. M.G.B.662 was to illuminate the coast line with starshell, and the first M.T.B. to sight an F-lighter was to fire torpedoes and say so at once on the inter-communication; no other M.T.B. was to fire torpedoes until the result of the first attack was observed. By spreading out the unit, danger from enemy fire was reduced and perfect inter-communication ensured that good control could be maintained.

It is at this point worth noting that during the waiting period there were several little explosions from two positions on the coast between Vir Point and Vir light.

29. At 0151 the moon was giving moderate light and it was decided to carry out the third attack of the night. All went according to plan until 0221 when H.M. M.G.B.662 opened fire with starshell. Then the first hitch occurred, in that under the light of the shells that did illuminate, nothing of any size could be seen. After twenty minutes searching with starshell by both H.M. M.G.B.662 and H.M. M.T.B.634, and some pom-pom fire from all boats, at the two small objects north of Vir light that had

been seen, and nothing having happened from the beach, it was decided to close very near the coast and run down to the southwards.

30. At 0251, when about fifty yards off the coast line the unit was brought round to southwest and set off down the coast in single line ahead at eight knots.

At 0254, a very large F-lighter was sighted dead ahead, at about four hundred and fifty yards, with bows into the beach, a perfect torpedo target. H.M. M.G.B.662 at once altered round to starboard, ordering H.M. M.T.B.634 to sink the target with torpedoes, and lay off ready to engage with covering gunfire. H.M. M.T.B.634 fired at 0256, scoring hits with both torpedoes, and the unit, in loose formation, was stopped to the eastwards of the smoking wreckage.

31. At 0310, H.M. M.G.B.662 decided to close the small piece of F-lighter still visible to try and identify it. Smoke was being carried away from the shore by a light breeze and H.M. M.G.B.662 went through this "screen" to the southwards at 0314. At that moment I found myself only 50 yards from a beached convoy of two F-Lighters and some small craft. Fire was at once opened with all guns and the unit called up to close me with despatch. These beached craft were heavily damaged by gunfire from all boats, and the one F-lighter that was not burning was sunk by a torpedo from H.M. M.T.B.637 at 0337.

During the whole of this third attack the enemy could not have fired more than twenty rounds in all.

32. It was now decided to withdraw. Two of these last F-lighters had been torpedoed, hit, and the third was well ablaze. Any small craft that were alongside the lighters had been sunk. There seemed no object in staying and it was desired to get out of the channel before the Royal Air Force came over: accordingly at 0355 the unit proceeded to Ist. All the way across the burning F-lighter was seen to be blowing up continuously.

33. We informed the L.R.D.G. and Partisan authorities of what had occurred and then proceeded to Komiza in two units, H.M. M.G.B.662 and H.M. M.T.B.637 at twenty-two knots, and H.M. M.T.B.s 634 (who had a defective engine) and 638 at fourteen knots.

34. As regards assessing the actual damage suffered by the enemy, great difficulty has been experienced. The natural desire to claim what one believes to have been sunk has been curbed by the almost too satisfactory nature of the best possible results. Conservative and considered estimates are:-

First attack:

I F-lighter heavily hit by M.T.B.634 and seen to sink by all boats.
I F-lighter heavily damaged by H.M. M.G.B.662 and seen to sink later by all boats.
I F-lighter heavily damaged by H.M. M.T.B.637, probably sunk.
2 F-lighters set on fire by H.M. M.T.B.s 637 and 638.
(I F-lighter seen to be undamaged and going to the beach).
2 Pi-L Boats fired and sunk by H.M. M.G.B.662 and H.M. M.T.B.638.
I Pi-L Boat sunk by H.M. M.G.B.662.

I E-boat sunk by H.M. M.G.B.662.
I E-boat damaged by H.M. M.T.B.638.
I E-boat damaged by H.M. M.T.B.634.

Second attack:

I F-lighter sunk by H.M. M.G.B.662 and H.M. M.T.B.634.
I F-lighter damaged by all boats.
I Pi-L Boat damaged by H.M. M.T.B.637.

Third attack:

2 F-lighters sunk by torpedoes.
I F-lighter beached and completely on fire.
I Pi-L Boat sunk by gunfire from H.M. M.G.B.662.
I possible E-boat sunk by gunfire from H.M. M.T.B.637.
or in brief,
6 F-lighters sunk.
I F-lighter probably sunk.
4 Pi-L Boats sunk.
I E-boat sunk.
I E-boat possibly sunk.
2 E-boats damaged by gunfire.

It is felt certain by all our boats that no F-lighters got away, although it is possible that one or more may have beached in a more or less invisible manner.

The Pi-L Boats were the larger type of small German lighter, with a silhouette like an R.C.L.§§ but the high bow and stern made it impossible to distinguish them from an F-lighter, except in fairly full side view.

Casualties and Damage to Own Force.

35. On the other hand our force suffered only superficial damage and the following casualties:-
   One A.B. killed, and two seriously and one slightly wounded.

Items of interest.

36. The enemy used no light signals, but one ship fired a three white star cartridge during the latter part of the first attack. Except for the flak-lighter the enemy displayed a lack of vigilance, courage, initiative, and resource. It is possible that the unit was

fortunate enough to contact the enemy at the crossing place of two convoys, the one coming up from Sibenik and Zara and the other coming down from the north. This would account for the fact that some of the enemy vessels never at any time opened fire, due to their not knowing which ship was which, the northbound convoy being sighted first.

37. The enemy vessels' armament was the normal one for F-lighters and other craft, except that more than one F-lighter had the 88-m.m., quadruple 20-m.m., twin 20-m.m. and single 20-m.m. that is normally associated with flaklighters. The flak-lighter had more armament than this and may have been the one bombarding Mulat the previous night.

38. Partisans on Ist reported four beached vessels the following morning. L.R.D.G. on Rivanj reported three. Royal Air Force reconnaissance on the morning of the I3th, reported three aground, two still burning. Also, Partisans reported a northbound convoy going through the Pasman Channel earlier on the evening of the IIth.

Most of the enemy vessels were laden, at least one with petrol, and one F-lighter with ammunition.

A report just received indicates that there was a southbound convoy that night going from Trieste to Split and it was probable that this was one of the convoys attacked.

Strategic or Tactical Conclusions.

39. This was the first really decisive victory of D-boats[§§§] over the old enemy, F-lighters, and was made possible due to low visibility, land background, uncertainty of identification, absurdly close ranges, excellent gunnery and admirable coolness on the part of the three following Commanding Officers. In fact D-boats are not suited to a "snap" torpedo attack and the fact that H.M. M.T.B.634 was having to manoeuvre on inner engines made her slower on the turn than usual. This kept the three M.T.B.s well behind the Senior Officer. As it turned out, no tactic could have been more successful. H.M. M.G.B.662 drew all the enemy's fire and attention away from the body of the unit, and the smoke from the guns drifted across the line of sight of the enemy so that they were able to get into within one hundred yards without ever being fired on. The first that the enemy knew of there being any ships there other than H.M. M.G.B.662 was the full broadsides of three "Ds" from under one hundred yards away. This contributed materially to the success of an action which in its results surpasses anything this flotilla has yet done, for the cost of very few casualties and very slight damage.

There is little to say about the second and third attacks, as intuition is incapable of analysis.

40. I would not, on the strength of this action, recommend that units of D-boats can take on units of F-lighters, unless the action can, as it were, be fought on a site of the D-boats' choosing. On this particular occasion the enemy was firing at us with very much heavier armament than we possess, and if the visibility had been a hundred

yards or so better I cannot but feel that we would have lost at least one boat. What is certain, though, is that once the action is joined, and both sides are firing, the enemy will be the first to become erratic.

(Signed) T.J. BLIGH,
Lieutenant-Commander, R.N.V.R.

Admiralty footnotes:-
* *F-lighter – comparable to an armed tank landing craft.*
** *Wind force 1-2 – light air to light breeze (1-6 m.p.h.).*
***L.R.D.G. *– Long Range Desert Group.*
†*Tigers – any minor partisan craft employed on reconnaissance or patrol duties.*
†† *Siebel ferry – a type of German landing craft.*
‡ *R/T – radio-telephony.*
‡‡ *Pi-L boats – Pioneer Landing Craft.*
§ *Green 20° – 20 degrees from right ahead on the starboard side.*
§§ *R.C.L. – Ramped Cargo Lighter.*
§§§ *D-boat – a "Fairmile" type of M.T.B. and M.G.B.*

9

NAVAL OPERATIONS IN THE AEGEAN

7 SEPTEMBER 1943 TO 28 NOVEMBER 1943

The following Despatch was submitted to the Lords Commissioners of the Admiralty on the 27th December, I943, by Vice-Admiral Sir ALGERNON U. WILLIS, K.C.B., D.S.O., Commander-in-Chief, Levant.

Levant.
27th December, I943.

Be pleased to lay before Their Lordships the attached report of Naval Operations in the Aegean between the 7th September, I943 and 28th November, I943.

(Signed) A.U. WILLIS,
Vice-Admiral,
Commander-in-Chief.

GENERAL REPORT ON AEGEAN OPERATIONS.
EVENTS LEADING UP TO OUR ENTRY INTO THE AEGEAN.

The possibility of capturing the island of Rhodes and subsequently opening up the Aegean (Operation "Accolade") had been under active consideration since January, 1943. Outline plans were drawn up but the requirements of the advance in North Africa and later the invasion of Sicily ("Husky"), prohibited the allocation of forces necessary to mount such an operation.

2. In April, Force Commanders and their staffs were assembled in Cairo to plan for "Accolade" to take place shortly after the landing in Sicily, when an Italian surrender was considered possible. By the middle of June, however, it became

apparent that assault shipping, craft and air forces would not be available and the Naval Force Commander and staff were sent to Algiers to plan "post-Husky" operations in the Central Mediterranean.

3. Following our successful landings in Sicily with unexpectedly small losses of assault shipping and craft, an attempt was made to plan and mount "Accolade" using such forces as were available in the Middle East or were earmarked for India. Once again, it became necessary to call on General Eisenhower to make up deficiencies, particularly in long range fighters, and, as a result, "Accolade" was cancelled by decision of the Combined Chiefs of Staff, at the Quadrant Conference.* The Commanders-in-Chief, Middle East informed the Chiefs of Staff on 31st August that the only operations which could be mounted from Middle East were:-

(*a*) Small Scale Raids.

(*b*) Sabotage and Guerilla operations by Resistance Groups.

(*c*) Unopposed "walk-in" to areas evacuated by the enemy.

Admiralty footnote:-
* *Quadrant Conference – the British-American conference held at Quebec in August, 1943.*

PHASE I.
Surrender of Italy to the opening of the German Air Offensive.
8th to 26th September, 1943.

4. When it was known that Italy had surrendered, it was decided to take advantage of this situation by encouraging the Italian garrisons to hold such Aegean islands as they could against the Germans, and to stiffen their resistance by sending in small parties of British troops. Between 8th and 16th September, Casteloriso, Kos, Leros, Samos, Kalymnos, Symi and Stampalia were all occupied by small detachments of Raiding Force troops accompanied by Civil Affairs Officers. Fairmile motor launches and caiques of the Levant Schooner Flotilla manned by Royal Naval crews provided the transport.

5. In Rhodes our emissaries were unable to prevent the Italian Governor surrendering the island to the Germans after a short resistance. (There were 30,000 Italian and 7,000 German troops in the island.) The combined service mission waiting at Casteloriso and the 234 Infantry Brigade waiting to proceed to Rhodes were therefore held available to reinforce the British forces in the other islands.

6. During this phase our naval forces, consisting of six Fleet destroyers of the 8th Destroyer Flotilla, 2 Hunt class destroyers, 1st Submarine Flotilla, 6 motor launches, 4 L.C.F.* caiques and 8 R.A.F. high speed launches and pinnaces were employed on:-

(*a*) Building up British forces and supplies in the islands.

(*b*) Intercepting enemy shipping proceeding from the Piraeus to the Dodecanese.

7. By 28th September, the following had been landed:-

2,700 men, 2I guns, 7 vehicles, 450 tons of stores and ammunition.

8. Acting on air reconnaissance, on reports from agents in the Piraeus area and from Italian reporting posts and L.R.D.G.† patrols in the Cyclades, destroyers carried out sweeps in the Aegean by night, retiring to the southward or lying up in Leros during the day. On I8th September, H.M.S. FAULKNOR (Captain A.K. Scott-Moncrieff, D.S.O., R.N.), H.M.S. ECLIPSE (Commander E. Mack, D.S.O., D.S.C., R.N.) and H.H.M.S. QUEEN OLGA (Lieutenant-Commander G. Blessas, D.S.O., R.H.N.) sank a 3,000 ton merchant vessel and a I,200 ton merchant vessel north of Stampalia and damaged the escort vessel, which put into Stampalia and was captured by one of our patrols assisted by the Italian garrison. This convoy was carrying specialist personnel and supplies to Rhodes. On 23rd September, H.M.S. ECLIPSE sank a 2,500 ton merchant vessel off the S.W. point of Rhodes which had landed reinforcements in Rhodes and was returning to the westward. An ex-Italian torpedo-boat was driven ashore and later destroyed by the R.A.F.

9. Prior to the Italian surrender, the Germans had made preparations to take over the entire military administration of Greece as from 6th September and had disposed sufficient forces on the west coast of Greece, the Peloponnesus, Melos, Crete, Scarpanto and Rhodes, to ensure the retention of their control in these key positions. In the period immediately following the surrender, the Germans were in no position to undertake seaborne operations, owing to the lack of shipping, escort vessels and landing craft, which they had to obtain from the Italians or transfer from other areas. By the middle of September, however, they had collected enough craft to despatch raiding forces to the Cyclades to evacuate the Italian garrisons and such food and war material as they could lay their hands on. With the exception of Syra they established observation posts only and did not garrison the islands in force.

I0. Apart from Rhodes, the Italians' attitude was co-operative in the islands visited by us, though their fighting value was low. It was considered that even if Leros were reinforced by such British troops as were available and Kos airfields developed and defended adequately, we should not be in a secure position to continue operations in the Aegean until Rhodes was in our possession. Accordingly on 22nd September the Chiefs' of Staff approval was obtained to mount "Accolade" before the end of October with such forces as were available in the Middle East and could be spared from the Central Mediterranean.

Admiralty footnotes:-

* L.C.F. – large landing craft converted to mount A.A. guns for air defence in combined operations.

† L.R.D.G. – Long Range Desert Group.

PHASE II.
The Start of the German Offensive.
26th September-12th October.

11. With the arrival of large enemy air reinforcements from France and the Russian front and the proved inefficiency of the A.A. defences of Leros, as shewn by the sinking of H.M.S. INTREPID (Commander C.A. de W. Kitcat, R.N.) and H.H.M.S. QUEEN OLGA in Leros harbour on 26th September, operations of our surface forces in the Aegean were restricted to sweeps during the dark hours with forces who retired to the south-eastward to obtain fighter cover from Cyprus during the day. On 1st October all available Fleet destroyers were sailed to Malta as escort to H.M. Ships HOWE and KING GEORGE V, leaving us with the Hunts whose speed and endurance made it difficult for them to operate far into the Aegean and still be clear by daylight. As a result, H.M.S. ALDENHAM (Lieutenant-Commander J.I. Jones, D.S.O., D.S.C., R.N.R.), H.H.M.S. MIAOULIS (Commander C. Nikitiades) and H.H.M.S. THEMISTOCLES (Lieutenant-Commander N. Sams, R.H.N.) who were patrolling off Kaso Strait on the night of the 2nd/3rd October, were short of fuel and in no position to take action on an aircraft report of an enemy convoy sighted off Naxos and believed on all available intelligence to be bound for Rhodes. They were ordered to withdraw to Alexandria for fuel. This convoy, in fact, carried an invasion force which was landed on Kos at 0500 on October 3rd and captured the island in spite of stubborn resistance from the British battalion, who received small assistance from the Italian garrison.

12. No surface force was available to interfere with the landing, but submarines on patrol were ordered to proceed to the Kos area to attack invasion shipping, and on 4th October the 12th Cruiser Squadron, consisting of H.M. Ships AURORA, flying the broad pendant of Commodore W.E. Agnew, C.B., D.S.O., R.N., PENELOPE (Captain G.D. Belben, D.S.C., A.M., R.N.), SIRIUS (Captain P.W.B. Brooking, D.S.C., R.N.) and DIDO (Captain J. Terry, M.V.O., R.N.), with five Fleet destroyers sailed from Malta at high speed to be available for operations in the Aegean. From the night of 5th/6th onwards a force of cruisers and destroyers patrolled close off the Kaso or Scarpanto Straits ready to act on any enemy reports which might be received, retiring to the south-eastward by day.

13. H.M. Ships SIRIUS, PENELOPE, FAULKNOR and FURY (Lieutenant-Commander T.F. Taylor, R.N.) entered the Aegean on the night of 6th/7th October when reconnaissance indicated that enemy reinforcements were arriving from the westward, and assisted by an enemy report from H.M. Submarine UNRULY (Lieutenant J.P. Fyfe, R.N.) received at 0630 on 7th, they located and sank an enemy convoy consisting of an ammunition ship, an armed trawler and six landing craft. This encounter delayed the retirement of our force, which was attacked in daylight in the Scarpanto Strait by J.U.88s and 87s, H.M.S. PENELOPE being hit by an unexploded bomb and her speed reduced to 23 knots. (The destruction of this convoy probably prevented the enemy from making an immediate assault on Leros.)

14. A force under H.M.S. CARLISLE (Captain H.F. Nalder, R.N.) carried out a

sweep on the nights of 7th/8th and 8th/9th October to intercept any further enemy forces attempting to reach the Dodecanese from the Piraeus. No sightings were made and at 1215 on 9th October, when the force was proceeding south through Scarpanto Strait, it was heavily attacked by J.U.87s and although the escorting Lightnings shot down 15 enemy aircraft and ships accounted for three more, H.M.S. PANTHER (Lieutenant-Commander Viscount Jocelyn, R.N.) was hit and sunk and H.M.S. CARLISLE, was hit aft and was towed to Alexandria by ROCKWOOD.

15. It now became apparent that our forces could not enter the Aegean to intercept enemy shipping and be clear again by daylight, and that further attempts would lead to unacceptable losses, more especially as the Lightning Squadrons were withdrawn to the Central Mediterranean. Accordingly the policy was adopted of operating destroyers only as an anti-invasion force, and using cruisers to provide A. A. and fighter direction during approach and retirement from the Aegean and for operations in such areas they could reach during the night.

16. The loss of Kos airfields, besides finally destroying our hopes of fighter cover for our surface forces, greatly increased the difficulties of supply as it prevented the passage and unloading of merchant ships and heavy lift ships which were urgently required to provide heavy A.A. defences and to improve the transport situation in Leros. The capture of Rhodes became increasingly important for the continuation of our operations.

17. On 9th October, a meeting was held at Tunis, attended by General Eisenhower, the First Sea Lord (Admiral of the Fleet Sir Andrew B. Cunningham, Bt, G.C.B., D.S.O.) and all Commanders-in-Chief in the Mediterranean and Middle East, including the Commander-in- Chief, Levant, Admiral Sir John H.D. Cunningham, K.C.B., M.V.O., to consider the situation, and it was finally decided that our resources would not allow us to mount Operation "Accolade", but that we should try to hold Leros and Samos as long as supplies could be maintained.

PHASE III.
We build up Leros and Samos whilst the Germans prepare to invade.
12th October-5th November.

18. On their return from Tunis, the Commanders-in-Chief, Middle East, at a meeting presided over by the Foreign Secretary and attended by the First Sea Lord, confirmed the decision to hold Leros and Samos, using all means in their power to do so, and at the same time decided that it would be impossible to recapture Kos with the forces at their disposal. Approval was given for the use of four Italian submarines (ZOEA, ATROPO, CORRIDONI, MENOTTI) and H.M. Submarines SEVERN (Lieutenant-Commander A.N.G. Campbell, R.N.) and RORQUAL (Lieutenant-Commander L.W. Napier, D.S.O., R.N.) to assist in running supplies. Preparations were made to run a vessel of the Turkish ferry type through to Leros with heavy vehicles during the November non-moon period. This latter venture was subsequently abandoned.

19. On 14th October, Vice-Admiral Sir Algernon U. Willis, K.C.B., D.S.O. relieved

Admiral Sir John H.D. Cunningham, K.C.B., M.V.O. as Commander-in-Chief, Levant.

20. Intelligence now suggested that the enemy would stage an invasion of Leros from Kos and Kalymnos with the 4,000 troops believed to be already there, as soon as he could transfer additional shipping and landing craft from the Piraeus. Our surface forces were therefore employed in conjunction with air reconnaissance and striking forces, to prevent the arrival of such shipping. A striking force was kept almost continuously available in the area, which was employed on anti-shipping patrols, bombardments of ports and harbours in Kos and Kalymnos islands. It was hoped by a display of activity to induce the enemy to believe we were capable of exerting greater naval strength in the area than was actually the case.

2I. Reports at noon on I5th October showed an enemy convoy of two merchant ships and two landing craft off Naxos proceeding to the eastward and H.M. Ships BELVOIR (Lieutenant J.F.D. Bush, D.S.C., R.N.) and BEAUFORT (Lieutenant-Commander Sir Standish O'G. Roche, Bt., D.S.O.) were ordered to intercept and destroy it. They were reported and heavily attacked by J.U.88s and J.U.87s though fortunately without incurring damage, and the convoy was diverted to the northward, thereby evading our force who had to withdraw to the southward due to lack of fuel. H.M. Ships PHEOBE (Captain C.P. Frend, R.N.), FAULKNOR (Captain M.S. Thomas, D.S.O., R.N.) and FURY who entered the Aegean at dark, continued to search, but made no sighting and had to withdraw from the Aegean before daylight. At I300B on I6th October, H.M. Submarine TORBAY (Lieutenant R.J. Clutterbuck, R.N.) sighted the convoy to the northward of Levitha and sank one of the merchant ships. During the night of the I6th/I7th, H.M.S. HURSLEY (Lieutenant-Commander W.J.P. Church, D.S.O., D.S.C., R.N.) and H.H.M.S. MIAOULIS (Commander E. Boudouris, R.H.N.) searched Kos roads and the east side of Kalymnos, setting a small merchant ship on fire in Port Vathi, sinking an E-boat and a landing craft and setting a sloop on fire in Port Akti. This was a very spirited close range action. On the following night H.M. Ships JERVIS (Captain J.S. Crawford, D.S.O., R.N.) and PENN (Lieutenant-Commander J.H. Swain, D.S.O., R.N.) bombarded Port Kalymnos and set a merchant ship in the harbour on fire. This was evidently the second ship of the enemy convoy.

22. The above enemy losses, with the addition of the damage of four F-lighters on the I8th and 20th by Mitchell aircraft of the U.S.A.A.F. and Beaufighter aircraft of the R.A.F. and torpedoing of a 600 ton merchant ship and a lighter by motor torpedo boats on the night I9th/20th, reduced the chances of the enemy being in a position to invade Leros for the time being and our naval forces then concentrated on the reinforcement and supply of Leros and Samos during the non-moon period.

23. The supply of the garrison at Leros had by this time (I8th October) become unsatisfactory. An organisation was being set up for supply by caique through Casteloriso and through Samos, but owing to various difficulties, only very small quantities of supplies had so far reached Leros by either of these methods, though supplies to Samos were going well. Some supplies were being put into Leros by air, but this was falling off owing to shortage of transport aircraft. Supply by submarine

could not start for a week and these would only provide a proportion of the tonnage needed to maintain the garrison, much less build up a reserve. The situation was complicated by the fact that the reinforcement of the garrison of Leros, which then consisted of one battalion and one company of infantry plus various details making about I,200 in all, was dependent to a considerable extent on the creation of a regular supply service.

24. In these circumstances – at any rate temporarily until the caique service and submarines got going – it was decided that the Navy would have to undertake the supply of Leros with destroyers by night. This proved arduous and trying work for the destroyers who were constantly shadowed and attacked by enemy aircraft during their approach and withdrawal from the island. That the destroyers avoided damage in harbour was due primarily to the careful organisation and good judgment of the Senior British Naval Officer, Aegean (Acting Captain E.H.B. Baker, R.N.) who, by varying the timing of the visits and the unloading ports and by reducing the time of discharge to a minimum, was able on most occasions to frustrate the enemy efforts to locate and bomb our ships whilst they were unloading.

25. During the period I6th to 30th October, the following reinforcements were put into Leros:-

By Surface Craft:-	*By Submarine:-*
950 men,	I7 men,
290 tons of stores,	255 tons of stores,
6 guns,	I2 guns,
II jeeps,	I jeep.
II trailers;	

26. As a result of a visit to Leros of senior Army Staff Officers from General Headquarters, Middle East, policy was reviewed by the three Commanders-in-Chief on the 30th October. It was then decided still further to reinforce the island, which the Army considered needed some I,200-I,300 more troops and additional guns and equipment to make it reasonably tactically secure and capable of beating off an attempt at invasion by the enemy. This was all the more necessary in view not only of the difficulty of intercepting an assault across the very short distances from the harbours and bays of Kos and Kalymnos islands and the quantity of minefields in the area, but also because of the approach of winter and the strain on the destroyers, for owing to losses, the distance from Alexandria, and other factors, it was becoming increasingly difficult to maintain a striking force constantly in the area.

27. Every possible means was utilised for passing in these reinforcements, destroyers, submarines, M.L.s, M.G.B.s, M.M.S.s, B.Y.M.S.,* caiques and schooners, and between 3Ist October and 7th November, the following were put into Leros:-

By Surface Craft:-	*By Submarine:-*
I,280 men,	33 tons of stores.
I80 tons of stores,	
I4 jeeps,	
I trailer;	

28. During this period of build up no contact was made with enemy forces, though our ships carried out occasional bombardments of enemy ports whilst entering and leaving the Aegean. We were unfortunate in that three destroyers were mined to the eastward of Kalymnos, H.M. Ships HURWORTH (Commander R.H. Wright, D.S.C., R.N.) and ECLIPSE were sunk and H.H.M.S. ADRIAS had her bows blown off. On board H.M.S. ECLIPSE were some 200 military reinforcements for Leros among whom casualties were heavy. Although subject to a considerable weight of air attack both by day and night no ships were sunk by this method, though H.M. Ships SIRIUS and AURORA were both hit and damaged seriously and H.M.S. BELVOIR sustained minor damage from an unexploded bomb.

29. During the last week of October there were clear indications of the mounting of a major assault force in the Piraeus. To overcome the shortage of landing craft, thirteen 60 ft. powered lighters of the I-boat class arrived by rail from the north. Simultaneously a group of three escort vessels of U-J type were sailed from Piraeus to the Cyclades. The loading of several merchant vessels with munitions, guns and supplies suggested preparations for a follow-up convoy.

30. It was not clear if the assault was intended for Samos or Leros, but a series of heavy air raids suggested the former. The sinking of a 1,200 ton eastbound merchant vessel off Anaphi by H.M. Submarine UNSPARING on 29th October made it probable that the operation would be postponed, and this impression was confirmed by the return of a 2,000 ton merchant vessel from Syra to Piraeus on Ist November.

Admiralty footnote:-
* M.L. – Motor Launch; M.G.B. – Motor Gun Boat; M.M.S. – Motor Minesweeper; B.Y.M.S. –
British Yacht Minesweeper.

PHASE IV.
Invasion of Leros – 3rd November to I6th November.

3I. On 3rd November, landing craft and escorts were in Lavrion and agents reported they were carrying out landing exercises. Photographic reconnaissance on 4th November showed nine landing craft and two escort vessels in Lavrion with a further four landing craft at Zea. They were reported moving eastward on 5th November. Between then and the evening of I0th November when they arrived in the Kos/Kalymnos area, they moved only by day under heavy fighter protection, dispersing and lying up during the night, first in the Paros/Naxos area and later in Amorgos, Levitha and Stampalia.

32. Every effort was made to intercept the force. Beaufighters and Mitchells of 20I (Naval Co-operation) Group attacked it by day, and at night our destroyers often under an attack searched the areas where the landing craft were expected to be lying up, and bombarded harbours in these areas. Our efforts met with small success, due by day to the heavy scale of fighter protection the enemy maintained over the convoy and by night to the difficulty of spotting the craft which were probably beached and

camouflaged in the many small bays available. One F-lighter, one landing craft and two caiques remained behind in Amorgos on 9th November, after the rest of the force had sailed, and these were probably damaged by Beaufighters during their attack p.m. on 8th November. H.M. Ships PENN and PATHFINDER (Lieutenant-Commander C.W. Malins, R.N.) sank a caique (probably a Naval Auxiliary) south of Paros on the night 6th/7th November.

33. With the arrival of this force at Kos and Kalymnos on IIth November, the enemy had available a total force of 4 serviceable F-boats, I3 I-boats, 5 Auxiliary Naval craft and a number of armed caiques, and into these he loaded troops and equipment already assembled in these islands.

APPRECIATION ON THE MORNING ENEMY INVASION FLOTILLA REACHED KOS/KALYMNOS (I0TH NOVEMBER).

34. Despite the efforts of our destroyers and Air Force, the enemy had, as previously described, succeeded in getting the bulk of his invasion flotilla to its destination. The delays imposed upon him by our activities had at any rate given time to the reinforced Leros garrison to re-organise and prepare for the impending invasion. It was now necessary to decide on the policy for the employment of destroyers in the event of Leros being assaulted from the neighbouring islands.

35. The following factors governed the matter:-

(*a*) The opinion of the Army Command that the reinforced garrison of Leros should be able to beat off, or at any rate destroy after landing, an initial attack provided that reinforcements in strength and heavy equipment could be prevented from reaching the enemy.

(*b*) The enemy's complete air superiority in the area, and the heavy scale of attack he could inflict on the ships by J.U. 88s and J.U. 87s with fighter escort. Experience has shown that the enemy had no intention of refraining from attacking ships under way in Turkish waters.

(*c*) The limited number of destroyers it was possible to maintain in the area over the period of waiting for the invasion to start. Due to the distance from Alexandria or Limassol ships could only remain in the area for a short period. For example, the Hunts had only enough fuel for one whole night's sortie at high speed and the return journey to Alexandria or Limassol.

(*d*) The short haul for enemy invasion craft for the actual assault, particularly if, as was expected, they assembled first in the various bays of Kalymnos Island and then moved off to attack at the selected moment.

36. Accordingly it was decided that if Leros was being invaded, destroyers could best contribute by endeavouring to intercept at night and destroy the follow-up convoys, which it was considered would be vital to the enemy. Destroyers were therefore

instructed that they should not leave their lying up positions by day in order to intercept invading forces unless specifically ordered to do so by the Commander-in-Chief.

37. Motor launches, motor torpedo boats and motor gun boats were placed under the orders of the Senior British Naval Officer, Aegean. At night the motor launches carried out anti-invasion patrols, whilst the motor torpedo boats and motor gun boats were held at immediate notice in harbour to act on enemy reports. Fuel stocks for coastal forces were established in Samos and in caiques, with small emergency stocks in Leros.

Situation on evening of 10th November.

38. The bulk of the enemy invasion flotilla having arrived at Port Kalymnos and Kos harbour, it was hoped that they would have to spend at least one night there fuelling and preparing to move up to the northern bays of Kalymnos, from which the invasion was expected to be launched.

39. Bombardments of Port Kalymnos and Kos harbour and roads were therefore carried out in bright moonlight on night 10th/11th November respectively by destroyer forces under Commanding Officer, H.M.S. PETARD (Commander R.C. Egan, R.N.) and Captain (D), 8th Destroyer Flotilla (Captain M.S. Thomas, D.S.O., R.N.) in FAULKNOR. H.M.S. PETARD's force, consisting of H.M. Ships PETARD, ROCKWOOD (Lieutenant S.R. le H. Lombard-Hobson, R.N.) and O.R.P. KRAKOWIAK, spent one and a half hours close off Port Kalymnos and pumped 1,500 rounds of 4-inch into this small harbour. A ship which had been damaged previously was set on fire and capsized, but it is not known whether damage was done to landing craft.

40. Both forces were bombed and H.M.S. ROCKWOOD in PETARD's force, damaged by an unexploded glider bomb, hit in the gearing room. By a fine feat of seamanship, ROCKWOOD was towed by H.M.S. PETARD under constant bombing attack to Losta Bay in the Gulf of Doris, where they arrived by daylight.

41. Captain (D), 8th Destroyer Flotilla who had been instructed to proceed with his force on completion of his bombardment remained in the Gulf of Kos so as to be in a position to assist H.M.S. PETARD with H.M.S. ROCKWOOD if required.

42. During 11th, air reconnaissance showed considerable movement of landing craft between Kos and Kalymnos, and it appeared that preparations to mount the assault on Leros were in train. The afternoon reconnaissance showed a concentration of landing craft in Kos harbour.

43. The enemy intentions were still not clear. As the next force of destroyers could not reach the area until late on the night 12th/13th, it was essential to conserve fuel in Captain (D), 8th Destroyer Flotilla's force. He was therefore ordered to move to an anchorage nearer to Kos Channel and to send his two Hunts to attack any landing craft in Kos roads reported by air reconnaissance.

44. Motor Torpedo Boat 307 (Lieutenant J.G.G. Muir, R.N.V.R.) on passage from

Casteloriso to Leros was in action with two unknown destroyers off Kalymnos at 0330/I2th November, and at 0445/I2th the motor torpedo boat force sailed from Alinda Bay at full speed to search for an enemy merchant ship reported 4-5 miles south-east of Leros. No sighting was made, but later when sweeping to the northward, two destroyers were sighted off Pharmaco. These were mistaken for British destroyers.

45. At approximately 0400/I2th November Motor Launch 456 (Lieutenant-Commander F.P. Monckton, R.N.R.) on patrol to the east of Alinda sighted and reported enemy forces I2 miles east of Leros proceeding north and later engaged a force of two destroyers and ten landing craft. After a short and gallant action Motor Launch 456 was damaged and forced to return to Alinda Bay where she landed wounded.

46. Between 0600 and 0830/I2th November the enemy succeeded in landing both north and south of Alinda Bay with the object of "pinching out" the bay where he would then be able to land heavy support weapons. A further landing was attempted at Blefuti Bay on the north of the island, but was repelled with the loss of two landing craft. It would appear that the Italian C.D.* guns did not open fire until too late, and this coupled with the fact that our close range weapons were sited to cover the more important bays, enabled the enemy to land forces at Palma, Pasti Di Sotto, Grifo and N. Appetici with the loss of only one more landing craft. Landings were counter-attacked and held by our forces, but at I340B/I2 the situation was made more difficult by the landing of parachute troops to the west of Alinda. When darkness fell, H.M. Ships FAULKNOR, BEAUFORT and H.H.M.S. PINDOS (Lieutenant-Commander D. Fifas, R.H.N.) together with Motor Torpedo Boats 3I5 (Lieutenant L.E. Newell, D.S.C., R.N.Z.N.V.R.), 266 (Sub-Lieutenant J.N. Broad, R.N.Z.N.V.R.), and 263 (Lieutenant A.G. Fry, R.A.N.V.R.) swept in the Leros/Kalymnos/Levitha area to prevent enemy reinforcements reaching Leros, and at 22I0, Mount Clido battery, Leros was bombarded from the eastward at the request of the Army ashore. They made no sightings. H.M. Ships DULVERTON, ECHO (Lieutenant-Commander R.H.C. Wyld, R.N.) and BELVOIR were picked up by enemy aircraft whilst entering the Aegean and shadowed, and H.M.S. DULVERTON was hit by a glider bomb at 0I45/I3th and sunk. ECHO and BELVOIR, after picking up survivors, proceeded. Minesweepers and motor launches which had been sent to Samos from Leros were loaded with reinforcements and ammunition, but since time would not permit their reaching Leros that night, they were held at Samos.

47. During the night I2th/I3th November a southerly gale blew up which restricted the operation of light craft on both sides. On I3th November fighting continued ashore, and in spite of very heavy bombing by the enemy and a further parachute landing at 0900B/I3th November, which suffered high casualties due to the strong wind blowing, our forces kept the enemy pinned down to the eastern shore in the Alinda Bay area. During the night of I3th/I4th November, H.M. Ships FAULKNOR, BEAUFORT, and H.H.M.S. PINDOS after attempting to bombard enemy positions in Leros, left the Aegean owing to shortage of fuel. H.M. Ships ECHO and BELVOIR however bombarded enemy positions on Leros at the request of the Army, and later

carried out a sweep in the area without making a sighting. Reinforcements from Samos in the motor launches and minesweepers were turned back by the weather. H.M. Ships PENN, ALDENHAM and BLENCATHRA (Lieutenant E.G. Warren, R.N.) entered the Aegean.

48. At Leros all naval signal publications were destroyed at 0700/I4th November when an enemy attack threatened to overrun the naval headquarters and this seriously interfered with communications and therefore with operations. From then on, signalling with the Senior British Naval Officer at Leros had to be done through army channels using army cyphers.

49. During the day of the I4th November, fighting in Leros continued, our forces counter-attacking with some success in the forenoon, but with the growing weariness of our garrison who had been fighting for 48 hours with no real rest under heavy scale air attack, fresh troops and more ammunition were urgently required. These were collected during the night from Samos by H.M. Ships ECHO and BELVOIR. ECHO, by proceeding at 30 knots, managed to land her 250 troops at Portolago before daylight, but BELVOIR with her slower speed was forced to lie up.

50. Enemy positions were attacked from the seaward by H.M. Ships PENN, ALDENHAM and BLENCATHRA who arrived at Alinda Bay at dusk on I4th November. Unfortunately only three enemy caiques were in the bay, but these were engaged and targets ashore, pointed out by our forces, were taken under fire. H.M.S. PENN and her force then patrolled in this area being repeatedly attacked by enemy aircraft including glider bombers. She was searching for landing craft reported by Leros, but failed to find. They had evidently turned back as a result of enemy air reports of H.M.S. PENN's force.

5I. Motor torpedo boats again patrolled the area and shortly before daylight they joined H.M.S. ECHO, who was returning from Portolago, in attacking an enemy force which was approaching Alinda Bay, sinking an F-lighter and two landing barges all laden with troops.

52. Thus, on the morning of I5th November, our forces had been reinforced; whereas the enemy, though possibly reinforced late on the I4th, had been deprived of some of the reinforcements due to arrive on the morning of the I5th. We were, however, owing to the heavy bombing, and the physical condition of our troops, unable to score decisively against the enemy during the day.

53. H.M. Ships PENN and ECHO's forces had been shadowed continuously by aircraft during the night of I4th/I5th November, and bombed from time to time, and it was evident that the enemy were making use of air reconnaissance to keep their forces clear of ours; on the night I5th/I6th, therefore, H.M.S. PENN and her force were ordered to remain at immediate readiness and to act on enemy reports, hoping thereby that enemy forces would be committed to a landing and that we would be able to intercept them. Owing to breakdown of W/T in Leros, reports of enemy landing craft, relayed through Alexandria, arrived in H.M.S. PENN too late for action to be taken on them, and the dawn sweep ordered by Commander-in-Chief, Levant produced no enemy sighting. In point of fact, had the Commanding Officer of H.M.S. PENN acted as soon as he received the report, it is possible that he might have interfered with the landing craft off the beaches in Alinda Bay.

54. Motor torpedo boats, minesweepers and motor launches landed the troops ex H.M.S. BELVOIR at Portolago during the night. H.M. Ships ECHO and BELVOIR left the Aegean short of fuel, and H.M. Ships FURY, EXMOOR (Commander J. Jefferies, R.N.) and O.R.P. KRAKOWIAK arrived to take their place.

55. On the 16th November the situation ashore in Leros became critical as reinforcements received during the night allowed the enemy to overrun our headquarters and positions in the Merviglia area, and though they were driven out again by the reinforcements we had received, the continued bombing and the incessant fighting over nearly five days had so reduced the fighting power of our forces that they were unable to continue the battle and the island surrendered at approximately 1700B.

56. During the night 16th/17th November H.M.S. EXMOOR and O.R.P. KRAKOWIAK, who had been ordered to Samos to transfer the Greek "Sacred" Squadron to Leros, rejoined H.M.S. FURY. H.M. Ships PENN and ALDENHAM's bombardment of the Alinda Bay area had to be cancelled and they bombarded Kos harbour on their way south to join H.M.S. BLENCATHRA, who was towing H.M.S. ROCKWOOD from the Gulf of Kos to Alexandria.

PHASE V.
WITHDRAWAL FROM AEGEAN.

57. Plans were made in mid-October to collect a number of caiques to be available in case it became necessary to withdraw our troops from Samos and Leros. The number of small craft under the orders of the Senior British Naval Officer, Aegean was also increased for general operational purposes and to assist in a possible withdrawal.

58. The course taken by the fighting in Leros, however, prevented any action by these caiques though in the final stages a number of army and naval personnel managed to escape in various craft.

59. After its fall on 16th November, evacuation of such troops as could be got out of Leros was conducted by Lieutenant-Commander L.F. Ramseyer, R.N.V.R., from a caique, he himself having escaped from Leros by caique 12 hours after its surrender. Naval craft and a number of R.A.F. high speed launches were used, S.B.S.† patrols being landed to round up British troops still at liberty. An R.A.F. launch and Levant Schooner No. 2 successfully evacuated the L.R.D.G. patrols from Seriphos and Mykoni respectively.

60. Following the fall of Leros it was decided to withdraw Allied forces still remaining in Samos. These consisted of 220 British troops and 380 of the Greek Sacred Squadron. This was successfully carried out by caiques on the night of 19th/20th November; in addition, 8,300 Italian troops, Greek guerillas and civilians were evacuated. This movement was covered by various naval and R.A.F. craft. The majority of these troops together with a number of Italians from the Samos garrison and Greek refugees were sent by train to Syria, having turned over their arms.

6I. The remainder of the British naval and military personnel from Samos and the escapees from Leros found their way south in a variety of craft, including two Italian F-lighters, one towing an L.C.M., two L.C.T.s‡, an Italian tug towing a M.M.S., various minesweepers and coastal craft, all of whom arrived in Levant ports by 2nd December. One of these F-lighters which left Leros on I5th November under the command of Lieutenant Stowell, R.N.R., reached Haifa via Samos with I77 German prisoners from Leros still on board on 25th November.

62. The direction of these operations was seriously hampered by the capture of B.Y.M.S. 72 at Kalymnos on the night of IIth/I2th November, which resulted in all the codes carried by these small craft being compromised.

63. Following our withdrawal from the Aegean it was decided to reduce the status of Casteloriso to that of an outpost which could be evacuated if a heavy attack developed against it; accordingly on the night of 27th/28th November surplus men, guns and equipment were withdrawn to the Levant by destroyer and L.C.T. without incident.

64. A satisfactory sequel to these disappointing operations was the successful withdrawal of the damaged H.H.M.S. ADRIAS through Kos Channel and north of Rhodes. She left on Ist December, and reached Alexandria under her own steam on 6th December. Fortune favoured this hazardous passage in that unforeseen circumstances prevented her movements being known to the enemy until she was east of Casteloriso. In the first place a German hospital ship on opposite course passed her in the Kos Channel and the enemy searchlight was extinguished during a critical period; later, when north of Rhodes, the ship escaped detection in continuous rain storms.

Admiralty footnotes:-
* *C.D. – coast defence.*
† *S.B.S. – Special Boat Squadron, an Army unit (see paragraph 7I).*
‡ *L.C.M. – Landing Craft, Mechanised vehicles; L.C.T. – Landing Craft, Tank.*

GENERAL REMARKS ON THE OPERATIONS AS A WHOLE.

Air Cover.

65. Throughout the operations our surface forces were unable to exercise that command of the Aegean to which their superiority to the enemy surface forces entitled them due to the complete enemy command of the air.

66. With the help of our submarines and air, and by accepting heavy losses from air attacks by day and latterly with increasing accuracy by night, we were able to interfere seriously with enemy merchant ship convoys to Rhodes and the Dodecanese, but we were unable to stop craft of all types moving by day only with heavy fighter cover and hiding up in out of the way bays and inlets by night. Once again the fact that surface forces cannot exercise their proper functions in restricted waters without air cover was clearly demonstrated.

Distance of Area of Operations from our Bases.

67. The fact that the centre of the area of operations was 350 miles from our bases in Alexandria and Cyprus had the following adverse effect on the operations of surface forces:-

(*a*) Operations of the destroyers were limited to two nights in the Aegean at the most, after which they had to return to refuel.

(*b*) Even when fighter cover was available, long gaps were inevitable, as our fighters usually had to return to base after the first attack owing to shortage of petrol, and it took anything up to 3 hours for reliefs to arrive.

68. It was impracticable to base small craft on Casteloriso or any of the Aegean islands owing to enemy air attack which was very accurate by day, and the policy was for all craft to lie up during daylight.

Command.

69. The question of command was not entirely satisfactory. Policy and major decisions were made by the Commanders-in-Chief Committee in Cairo, but whereas naval operations were conducted by the Commander-in-Chief, Levant from his headquarters, which was combined with that of No. 20I (Naval Co-operation) Group, R.A.F., at Alexandria, the Army appointed a Corps Commander with a Headquarters in Cairo, and the R.A.F. an Air Vice Marshal who, though himself in Cairo, had his operational headquarters in Cyprus. This did not work out well in practice, and finally General Headquarters, Middle East and Headquarters, Royal Air Force, Middle East took over the direct control of operations.

70. On the naval side, experience in the Levant has shown that the best results are obtained by using the normal station operational organisations to the maximum, and that new operational staffs should be limited to those required to enable local naval commanders to exercise operational control in the area of operations.

Operations of Raiding and Reconnaissance Forces.

7I. The activities of the Raiding and Reconnaissance Forces merit special mention. When the Axis had been expelled from North Africa the Long Range Desert Group and Special Boat Squadron of the Special Air Support Regiment returned to the Middle East. As it was now necessary for them to cross the sea to continue their activities against the enemy, they were trained on the Levant coast to operate from submarines, Fairmile motor launches and coastal force craft of all types, and a force of caiques and schooners, known as the Levant Schooner Force, was formed under Commander Coastal Forces, Eastern Mediterranean, manned by specially selected officers and men to work with them. These latter craft were fitted with Tank engines giving them a speed of 6 knots and an endurance of 2,000 miles. With the mast down they could be camouflaged so effectually that they could not be spotted when lying up close inshore.

72. These forces were acting over the Southern Aegean throughout the period of operations. They were the first to arrive and the last to leave, and carried out many daring and successful operations in enemy-occupied islands. There is no doubt that forces of this type, well-trained and led, can be of great value both for harassing the enemy and obtaining important intelligence.

Submarine Operations.

73. In common with all other forces operating in the Aegean during this period the submarines were driven hard. Their patrols, which were largely carried out in narrow waters in close proximity to known or suspected minefields, were often considerably prolonged owing to the series of local emergencies which kept developing, and which required the presence of a submarine in the area.

74. In the majority of areas the submarines were subjected to continual surface and air anti-submarine activity, and in addition our own surface forces were always liable to be encountered at night. These factors, coupled with the fact that few torpedo targets were encountered, threw a very heavy strain on all concerned, and particularly on Commanding Officers.

75. It speaks well for the aggressive and determined temper of the First Submarine Flotilla that under these difficult conditions three merchant ships, totalling 7,500 tons, and a 400 ft. floating dock were torpedoed and sunk, and twenty-one caiques and schooners destroyed, mostly by gunfire.

76. The task of the supply submarines was not easy, owing chiefly to dislocation in the working of the ports at Leros. The heavy air attacks which developed at night during moonlight periods, made unloading submarines impracticable at these times.

77. H.M. Submarine SEVERN had to be withdrawn from the supply service after one trip owing to complete failure of her main and auxiliary engines. Of the five Italians, one never left Haifa, and the mechanical condition of the other four was giving rise to considerable concern. They carried out their tasks efficiently and with considerable enthusiasm.

CONCLUSION.

78. These operations were carried out to take advantage of the Italian surrender to obtain a foothold in the Aegean with such forces as were available in the Middle East. We failed because we were unable to establish airfields in the area of operations.

79. The enemy's command of the air enabled him so to limit the operations and impair the efficiency of land, sea and air forces that by picking his time he could deploy his comparatively small forces with decisive results.

80. The naval forces engaged on these operations, cruisers, destroyers, submarines and coastal craft, and the small force of aircraft available to 20I (Naval Co-operation) Group all fought hard and did valiant work under particularly trying conditions. They achieved considerable success against the enemy and held off the attack on Leros for some time, but not without heavy casualties to our own forces.

8I. Had more aircraft been available, especially modern long range fighters, and given more luck, the operations might have been prolonged, but after the loss of Kos, if the enemy was prepared to divert the necessary effort, it is doubtful if Leros could have been held indefinitely without our embarking on a major operation for which no forces were available.

82. It may be, however, that the inroad made in the enemy's shipping resources – which process is still going on – will prove a fatal handicap to him when the time comes for us to embark on an "all in" offensive in the Aegean, with adequate forces.

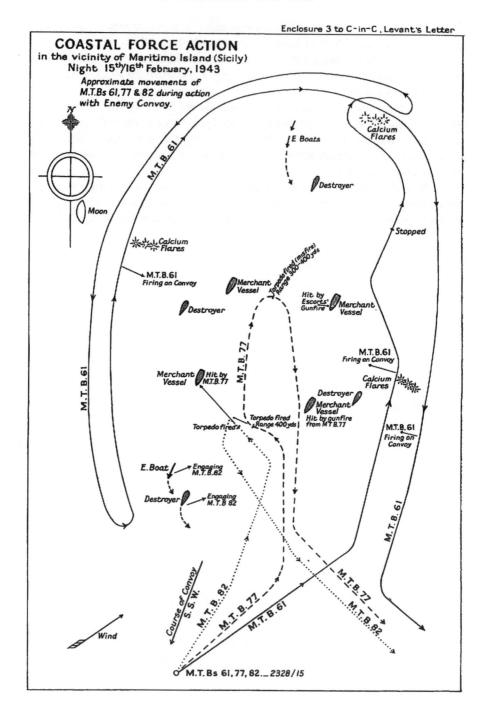

COASTAL FORCE ACTION
in the vicinity of Maritimo Island (Sicily)
Night 15th/16th February, 1943

Approximate movements of
M.T.Bs 61,77 & 82 during action
with Enemy Convoy.

N

Moon

E Boats

Calcium
Flares

Destroyer

Stopped

Calcium
Flares

M.T.B.61
Firing on Convoy

Merchant
Vessel

Torpedo fired (mis fired)
Range 300-400 yds

Hit by
Escorts'
Gunfire

Merchant
Vessel

Destroyer

M.T.B.77

M.T.B.61
Firing on Convoy

Calcium
Flares

M.T.B.61

Merchant
Vessel

Hit by
M.T.B.77

Destroyer

Merchant
Vessel

Hit by gunfire
from M.T.B.77

Torpedo fired
Range 400 yds

Torpedo fired ↗

M.T.B.61
Firing on
Convoy

E.Boat

Engaging
M.T.B.82

Destroyer

Engaging
M.T.B.82

M.T.B.61

Course of Convoy
S.S.W.

M.T.B.82

M.T.B.77

M.T.B.61

M.T.B.77

M.T.B.82

Wind

M.T.Bs 61,77, 82._ 2328/15

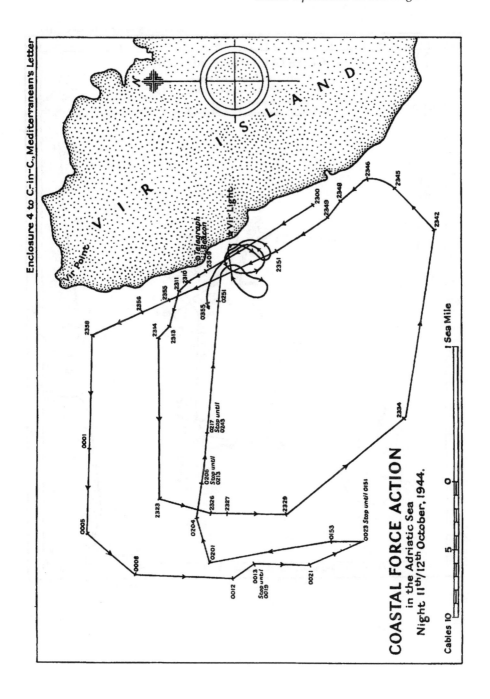

Enclosure 4 to C-in-C, Mediterranean's Letter

VIR ISLAND

Vir Point

Telegraph Beacon

Vir Light

COASTAL FORCE ACTION
in the Adriatic Sea
Night 11th/12th October, 1944.

Cables 10   5   0   1 Sea Mile

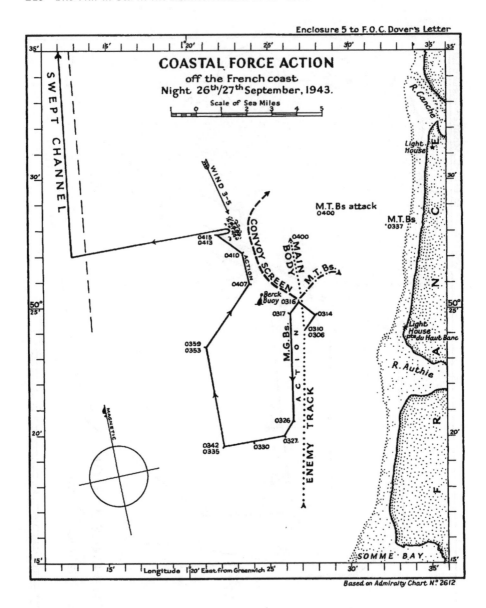

COASTAL FORCE ACTION
off the French coast
Night 26th/27th September, 1943.

Scale of Sea Miles

Based on Admiralty Chart N.° 2612

ABBREVIATIONS

AA	Anti-aircraft
AC	Admiral Commanding
ADM	Admiralty
ADP	Air Defence Position
AM	Albert Medal
A/S	Anti-Submarine
Asdic	Underwater detection device (stands for Anti-Submarine Detection Investigation Committee)
ASPS	Anti-Submarine Patrols
ASV	Air to Surface Vessel
A/T	Anti-Torpedo
Bt.	(Bart), Baronet
BYMS	British Yacht Mine Sweeper.
C. IN C.,	Commander-in-Chief
CB	Companion of The Most Honourable Order of the Bath
CBE	Commander of the Most Excellent Order of the British Empire
CD	Coast(al) Defence
CVO	Commander of the Royal Victorian Order
D-boats	Dog-boats (Fairmile D motor torpedo boat)
DCT	Director Control Tower
DSC	Distinguished Service Cross
DSO	Distinguished Service Order
E-boat	*See S-boat*
ETA	Estimated Time of Arrival
FAA	Fleet Air Arm
GAB	General Alarm Bearing
GCB	Knight Grand Cross of the Most Honourable Order of the Bath
HA	High Altitude; High Angle (armament)
HE	High Explosive
H/F	High Frequency
HHMS	His Hellenic Majesty's Ship
H/L	High Level
HLB	High Level Bombing
HM	His Majesty

HMAS	His Majesty's Australian Ship
HMCS	His Majesty's Canadian Ship
HMMTB	His Majesty's Motor Torpedo Boat
HMNZS	His Majesty's New Zealand Ship
HMS	His Majesty's Ship
HMSAS	His Majesty's South African Ship
HMT	His Majesty's Trawler; His Majesty's Troopship
HQ	Head Quarters
IFF	Identification Friend or Foe
KCB	Knight Commander of the Most Honourable Order of the Bath
LA	Low Angle (armament)
LCF	Landing Craft, Flak
LCM	Landing Craft, Mechanized
LCT	Landing Craft, Tank
LRDG	Long Range Desert Group
MGB	Motor Gun Boat
ML	Motor Launch
MLA	Mean Line of Advance
MMS	Motor Mine Sweeper
M/S	Motor Ship; Mine-Sweeping
MT	Motor Tanker
MTB	Motor Torpedo Boat
MV, M/V	Motor Vessel
NLO	Naval Liaison Officer
OBE	Officer of the Order of the British Empire
OC	Officer Commanding
ON	Official Number
ORP	*Okręt Rzeczypospolitej Polskiej* (Ship of the Republic of Poland)
para.	paragraph
R Neth N	Royal Netherlands Navy
RA	Rear Admiral
RAC	Rear Admiral Commanding
RAF	Royal Air Force
RAN	Royal Australian Navy
RANVR	Royal Australian Navy Volunteer Reserve
R-boat	*Räumboote*; a group of small naval vessels, built as minesweepers but used for a multitude of purposes
RCN	Royal Canadian Navy
RCNVR	Royal Canadian Navy Volunteer Reserve
RDF, R D/F	Radio Direction Finder; Range and Direction Finding; Radar
RFA	Royal Fleet Auxiliary
RFR	Royal Fleet Reserve
RHN	Royal Hellenic Navy
RM	Royal Marines

RML	Rescue Motor Launch
RN	Royal Navy
RNR	Royal Naval Reserve
RNVR	Royal Naval Volunteer Reserve
RNZNVR	Royal New Zealand Navy Volunteer Reserve
R/T, RT	Radio Telephony
SAP	Semi-Armour-Piercing
S-boat	*Schnellboot*, or *S-Boot*, meaning "fast boat" (E-boat in English)
SBS	Special Boat Squadron
SNO	Senior Naval Officer
SO	Senior Officer
SS	Steam Ship
T/B	Torpedo Boat; Torpedo Bombers
TOO	Time Of Origin
TS	Transmitting Station
TSDS	Two Speed Destroyer mine Sweep
TSR	Torpedo/Spotter/Reconnaissance
USAAF	United States Army Air Force
VA	Vice-Admiral
VA Dover	Vice-Admiral Dover
VALF	Vice-Admiral, Light Forces
VAM	Vice-Admiral Malta
VHF	Very High Frequency
V/S	Visual Signal
W/T	Wireless Telegraphy

INDEX OF
MILITARY AND NAVAL
UNITS

INDEX OF PERSONS